THE IMAGE
OF AMERICA IN
MONTAIGNE, SPENSER,
AND SHAKESPEARE

THE IMAGE
OF AMERICA IN
MONTAIGNE, SPENSER,
AND SHAKESPEARE

Renaissance Ethnography and Literary Reflection

William M. Hamlin

St. Martin's Press
New York

ISBN 0-312-12506-2

PR
129
.A4
H36
1995

Library of Congress Cataloging-In-Publication Data

Hamlin, William M., 1957-
   The Image of America in Montaigne, Spenser, and Shakespeare :
Renaissance ethnography and literary reflection / William M. Hamlin.
        p.   cm.
   Includes bibliographical references (p.).
   ISBN 0-312-12506-2
   1. English literature—Early modern, 1500-1700—History and
criticism. 2. Montaigne, Michel de, 1533-1592—Knowledge—America.
3. Spenser, Edmund, 1552?-1599—Knowledge—America. 4. Shakespeare,
William, 1564-1616—Knowledge—America. 5. English literature—
American influences. 6. French literature—American influences.
7. Ethnology—History—16th century. 8. Primitivism in literature.
9. Ethnology in literature. 10. America—In literature.
11. Indians in literature. 12. Renaissance—England.
13. Renaissance—France. I. Title.
PR129.A4H36   1995
820.9'3273—dc20   94-45082
                                                                  CIP

Book design by Acme Art, Inc

First Edition: September 1995
10 9 8 7 6 5 4 3 2 1

For Theresa

Cette découverte d'un pays infini
semble être de considération.

Michel de Montaigne

Contents

Acknowledgments

I am grateful, first of all, to Leeds Barroll and Marcel Tetel—the editors, respectively, of *Shakespeare Studies* and *The Journal of Medieval and Renaissance Studies*—for granting me permission to publish revised versions of essays and portions of essays that first appeared in their publications. I wish to acknowledge, in addition, that the Robert B. Heilman Prize at the University of Washington, the Saint Mary's College of California Faculty Development Fund, the Idaho Humanities Council, and the Idaho State University Faculty Research Committee have all enabled me, in varying ways, to sustain work on this project.

During the years in which this book has taken shape I have received generous assistance, support, and encouragement from many people; I want to express my thanks here to at least of few of them: To the librarians and staff members of the Suzzallo Library at the University of Washington, the Bancroft Library at the University of California, Berkeley, the John Carter Brown Library at Brown University, and the Oboler Library at Idaho State University; to Laura Heymann and Jennifer Farthing at St. Martin's Press; to DeSales Perez for inviting me to lead seminars on Columbus, Las Casas, and Montaigne in 1990 at Saint Mary's College of California; to Edward Biglin for supporting my development of an interdisciplinary Renaissance course, "The Old World's New World," also at Saint Mary's College; to Sharon Beehler, Robert Gorsch, Eric LaGuardia, Fritz Levy, Thomas Lockwood, Otto Reinert, and Douglas Rutledge for graciously reading and perceptively commenting on drafts of part or all of the manuscript; to several anonymous readers who offered thorough and constructive assessments of the entire book in various earlier forms; to my friends and colleagues Dante Cantrill, Ken Fox, John Kijinski, Dick Mertens, Frank Murray, Pierre Mvuyekure, Jack Owens, Roger Schmidt, and Wayne Schow for their unfailing willingness to inquire, listen, and respond; to Elisabeth Lapeyre and the late Paul Riesman for being remarkable, inspiring teachers; and, most especially, to Joanne Altieri, David Bevington, and Charles Frey, all of whom not only read the complete manuscript and offered invaluable suggestions but, in addition, extended to me their interest and shared their good judgment in ways to which an acknowledgment such as this can never do justice.

A Note on Abbreviations and Citations

For concision's sake I have used an abbreviated citation format in my endnotes, truncating many of the longer titles; complete citations may be found in the bibliography. I have also employed the following abbreviations for journals, reference works, collections of primary texts, and Shakespearean plays:

Journals and Reference Works:

AA	*American Anthropologist*
CI	*Critical Inquiry*
CSSH	*Comparative Studies in Society and History*
ELH	*Journal of English Literary History*
ELR	*English Literary Renaissance*
HI	*Hispanic Issues*
HLQ	*Huntington Library Quarterly*
JEGP	*Journal of English and Germanic Philology*
JMRS	*Journal of Medieval and Renaissance Studies*
KASP	*The Kroeber Anthropological Society Papers*
MLQ	*Modern Language Quarterly*
MLR	*Modern Language Review*
MP	*Modern Philology*
NYRB	*The New York Review of Books*
OED	*The Oxford English Dictionary* (2d ed.)
PAAS	*Proceedings of the American Antiquarian Society*
PAPS	*Proceedings of the American Philosophical Society*
PBA	*Proceedings of the British Academy*
PMLA	*Publication of the Modern Language Association*
Rep	*Representations*
SQ	*Shakespeare Quarterly*
ShakS	*Shakespeare Studies*
SbS	*Shakespeare Survey*
SEL	*Studies in English Literature, 1500–1900*
TDR	*Tulane Drama Review*
YFS	*Yale French Studies*

Collections of Primary Documents:

De Orbe Novo: Martyr, Peter. *De Orbe Novo: The Eight Decades of Peter Martyr D'Anghera.* Trans. Francis Augustus MacNutt of Martyr's *De orbe novo,* decades 1-8. [Ca. 1511-30; Alcalá, 1516; Basel, 1533.] 2 vols. New York: Putnam's, 1912. Rpt. New York: Burt Franklin, 1970. (My citations identify decade and book as well as page numbers; thus, for example, 3.8.134 refers to Decade 3, Book 8, page 134.)

Decades: Eden, Richard. *The Decades of the newe worlde or west India* [London, 1555]. Trans. Richard Eden of Peter Martyr's *De orbe novo,* decades 1-3. March of America Facsimile Series, 4. Ann Arbor, MI: University Microfilms, 1966. (As with *De Orbe Novo,* my citations refer to decade, book, and page.)

Diario: The Diario of *Christopher Columbus's First Voyage to America, 1492-1493.* Abstracted by Fray Bartolomé de Las Casas. Transcribed and translated by Oliver Dunn and James E. Kelley, Jr. Norman, OK: University of Oklahoma Press, 1989.

Elizabethans: The Elizabethans' America: *A Collection of Early Reports by Englishmen on the New World.* Ed. Louis B. Wright. Cambridge, MA: Harvard University Press, 1965.

First Three Books: The first Three English books on America. Ed. Edward Arber. Birmingham, 1885. (Includes Eden's *Decades* [pages 43-398] as well as two earlier books: "Of the newe landes and of ye people founde by the messengers of the kynge of portyngale named Emanuel" [Antwerp, ca. 1511]; and Eden's *A Treatyse of the Newe India* [London, 1553], a redaction of Sebastian Munster's *Cosmographiae* [1544]).

Four Voyages: Columbus, Christopher, et al. *Four Voyages to the New World: Letters and Selected Documents.* Bilingual edition. Ed. and trans. R. H. Major. Gloucester, MA: Peter Smith, 1978.

Hakluytus Posthumous: Purchas, Samuel. *Hakluytus Posthumous, or Purchas His Pilgrimes.* [London, 1625]. 20 vols. Glasgow: J. MacLehose and Sons, 1905-07.

New Iberian World: New Iberian World: A Documentary History of the Discovery and Settlement of Latin America to the Early 17th Century. Ed. John H. Parry and Robert G. Keith. 5 vols. New York: Times Books, 1984.

Principal Navigations: Hakluyt, Richard (the younger). *The Principal Navigations Voyages Traffiques and Discoveries of the English Nation.* [London, 1589-90, 1598-1600]. 12 vols. Glasgow: J. MacLehose and Sons, 1903-04. Rpt. New York: AMS Press, 1965.

Tracts: Tracts and Other Papers, Relating Principally to the Origin, Settlement, and Progress of the Colonies in North America. Ed. Peter Force. 4 vols. New York: Peter Smith, 1947.

Virginia Voyages: Virginia Voyages from Hakluyt. Ed. David B. Quinn and Alison M. Quinn. London: Oxford University Press, 1973.

Plays by Shakespeare:

AWW	*All's Well That Ends Well*
AYL	*As You Like It*
Err.	*The Comedy of Errors*
1H4	*Henry the Fourth, Part One*
Lr.	*King Lear*
LLL	*Love's Labor's Lost*
Mac.	*Macbeth*
MV	*The Merchant of Venice*
Oth.	*Othello*
Tmp.	*The Tempest*
TN	*Twelfth Night*
Tro.	*Troilus and Cressida*
Wiv.	*The Merry Wives of Windsor*
WT	*The Winter's Tale*

Quotations from Montaigne:

Quotations from Montaigne's *Essays* (including essay titles) are generally drawn from Donald M. Frame's fine English translation (*The Complete Essays of Montaigne* [Stanford: Stanford University Press, 1958]); my in-text citations refer to this translation. But because I am also interested in preserving the character of Montaigne's essays as encountered by Tudor and Stuart audiences, I occasionally quote from the 1603 English rendering by John Florio (*The Essayes of Michael Lord of Montaigne* [New York: Modern Library, 1933]). Florio's translation is not always entirely reliable, however, so when I cite it I also include corresponding page references to Frame's version. Quotations in the original French are drawn from Michel de Montaigne, *Les Essais*, ed. Pierre Villey and reissued under the direction of V. L. Saulnier, 2d ed., 3 vols. (Paris: Presses Universitaires de France, 1992). Although both Villey and Frame follow the usual practice of indicating the edition of the *Essays* in which a given passage first appeared (by using the superscripted or bracketed letters A, B, and C to refer respectively to the editions of 1580, 1588, and 1595), I have departed from their precedent, preferring instead to mention dates of composition and publication only when they are directly relevant to my argument.

Quotations from the Holy Bible are drawn from the Authorized Version of 1611.

Chronology

1558:	Accession of Queen Elizabeth I
1564:	Shakespeare born
1572:	Saint Bartholomew's Day Massacre
1576:	Las Casas dies
1577-80:	Drake's circumnavigation
1578:	Léry's *Histoire d'un voyage*
1580:	Montaigne's *Essais* (Books 1 and 2)
1584-87:	English colonizing venture on Roanoke Island
1588:	Harriot's *Briefe and true report*
	Montaigne's *Essais* (including Book 3)
	Defeat of Spanish Armada
1589:	Hakluyt's *Principal Navigations*
1590:	Spenser's *The Faerie Queene* (Books 1-3)
1592:	Montaigne dies
1595:	Ralegh's first voyage to Guiana
1596:	Spenser's *The Faerie Queene* (Books 1-6)
	Ralegh's *Discoverie of Guiana*
	Spenser's *View of Ireland* composed
1598-1600:	Hakluyt's *Principal Navigations* (expanded edition)
1599:	Spenser dies
1603:	Queen Elizabeth I dies
	Accession of King James I
	Florio's translation of Montaigne's *Essais*
1605-06:	Shakespeare's *King Lear*
1607:	Jamestown founded
1609-10:	Voyage and shipwreck of the *Sea-Venture*
1611-12:	Shakespeare's *The Tempest*
1616:	Shakespeare dies
1623:	Shakespeare's First Folio
1624:	Smith's *General Historie of Virginia*
1625:	Purchas's *Hakluytus Posthumous*

Prologue

Lizards, Toads, and Spiders

At the heart of one of Shakespeare's supreme fictions—the sequence of wild, phantasmagoric storm scenes in *King Lear*—the Earl of Gloucester walks onstage with a torch, searching for the King and his companions. In the faint light and cacophonous din he hears voices and perhaps discerns the vague shapes of several men, but when he calls out to them he is answered not by Lear or Kent or the Fool but by his own son, Edgar, who has discarded his clothes, abandoned all show of reason, and effaced his aristocratic identity in order to seem a Bedlam beggar. The father's questions are short and direct: "What are you there? Your names?" The son's reply is as strange as it is unrecognized:

> Poor Tom, that eats the swimming frog, the toad, the todpole, the wall-newt, and the water; that in the fury of his heart, when the foul fiend rages, eats cow-dung for sallets, swallows the old rat and the ditch-dog; drinks the green mantle of the standing pool; who is whipt from tithing to tithing, and [stock-]punish'd and imprison'd; who hath [had] three suits to his back, six shirts to his body—
> Horse to ride, and weapon to wear;
> But mice and rats, and such small deer,
> Have been Tom's food for seven long year.[1]

The image here is that of a man reduced from affluence and self-respect to the most wretched degree of poverty. And the chief vehicle for the evocation of this poverty is the description of diet—one of the most intimate facets of human existence. Poor Tom, already "unaccommodated" (3.4.106) in that he owes the worm no silk and the beast no hide, is further diminished to the extent that he eats whatever he finds that is edible, even that which is not conventionally considered human food. His transformation echoes that of Nebuchadnezzar, who during his punishment "was driven from men, and did eat grass as oxen" (Daniel 4:33), and it perhaps obliquely foreshadows the fantasy of the usurer's wife from Autolycus's ballad in *The Winter's Tale*: "she long'd to eat adders' heads and toads carbonado'd" (4.4.264-65).[2] It makes no difference here whether Edgar is telling the truth or simply fabricating a list of dubious comestibles; the effect of his speech is to corroborate Lear's earlier assertion that he is no more than "a poor, bare, fork'd animal" (3.4.106-08).

Yet even as Poor Tom is imaged as a man reduced to the status of a beast, he is simultaneously portrayed as a being capable of using language concretely and evocatively, someone Lear can desire to speak with and refer to as a "Noble philosopher," a "learned Theban" (3.4.172, 157-58). By his own admission, he was once a "hog in sloth, fox in stealth, wolf in greediness, dog in madness, lion in prey" (3.4.93-95); but now, vexed by the "foul fiend," he is fearful and penitent, his abject condition suggesting to Lear that both of them are "discarded fathers" (3.4.60, 72). In Poor Tom's depiction, then, we see the conflation of two ideas: that humans share an existential continuum with nonhuman animals, and that they simultaneously retain traits that distinguish them from these animals and make them, as members of a collective body, both recognizable and necessary to one another. That the unfolding of these ideas depends in part upon a king whose "wits begin t' unsettle" (3.4.162) does not affect their validity; on the contrary, a great deal of evidence in the play may be adduced to suggest that Lear's moral perceptions are sharpened during his derangement and that, as Edgar later remarks, his words reveal "matter and impertinency mix'd, / Reason in madness!" (4.6.174-75). Poor Tom may be an "unaccommodated man," but he is a *man* nonetheless—and in so being, he is accommodated in certain ways beyond the threat of deprivation.

Slightly more than a century before Shakespeare wrote *King Lear*, a Spanish surgeon named Diego Alvarez Chanca accompanied Columbus on his second voyage to the West Indies and took careful—if opinionated—ethnographic notes on the native inhabitants of Española, Cuba, and other Caribbean islands. In striking opposition to Columbus, who frequently commented on the gentleness and intelligence of these islanders, Chanca was for the most part appalled by their habits. In particular, their diet revolted him. He described them, among other things, as consuming "all the snakes, and lizards, and spiders, and worms, that they find upon the ground; so that, to my fancy, their bestiality is greater than that of any beast upon the face of the earth."[3] Chanca's narrative remained long in manuscript in Madrid, not finding its way into print until 1825, but its antipathetic attitude toward autochthonous Americans and their customs is entirely characteristic of many documents of its time—documents of the late fifteenth and entire sixteenth centuries detailing encounters between Europeans and inhabitants of the New World.[4] Proceeding on the grounds of observed physical and cultural difference, writers in this antipathetic vein frequently conclude that American natives partake of a degree of humanity somehow inferior to that of European Christians, or else that they lack humanity altogether. One need only recall the celebrated 1550-51 debate between Juan Ginés de Sepúlveda and Bartolomé de Las Casas to find a revealing example of this. Using empirical observations culled from the histories of Gonzalo Fernández de Oviedo and philosophical arguments derived from Aristotle and St. Thomas Aquinas, Sepúlveda claimed that American Indians were inferior to Spaniards as rational beings, and thus fit to be their natural servants.[5] Las Casas, in contrast, defended the Indians, claiming as Columbus had before him that they were peaceable and open to Christian conversion. And in the end, Las Casas won the debate—or, at any rate, persuaded the Council of the Indies that Sepúlveda's arguments were doctrinally unsound.[6] But Castilian policies toward New World natives changed little as a consequence of this academic, if passionate, dispute: Despite the idealization of the Indian typical of Las Casas and certain other writers, the enslavement, exploitation, and general disenfranchisement of American natives continued more or less unabated throughout the sixteenth century. The attitude of Chanca—that the Indian is radically different, and therefore barbaric or even subhuman—reigned supreme as an assumption upon which acts of political and religious hegemony could be grounded and justified. Native Americans, generally speaking, were perceived as "unaccommodated" humans—unacquainted with Christianity and European civility—and thus next of kin to the beasts; their lives were stereotyped as solitary and poor, nasty and brutish. Few Europeans were willing to accept them on equal terms and engage either literally or figuratively in conversation with them, as Lear does with his "good Athenian" (3.4.180).

Michel de Montaigne was one of these few. We know this first of all because he tells us so himself, at the end of his essay "Of cannibals."[7] Three Tupinamba natives from coastal Brazil were displayed in Rouen for part of the year 1562, and Montaigne claims to have spoken at length with one of them. From what he chooses to record, he seems to have been quite impressed with the man. But more generally, and irrespective of his never having visited the New World himself, Montaigne was fascinated with the customs and mores of the peoples from "that other world" (150). It appears, for example, that he avidly read the conquest chronicles of Francisco López de Gómara, and he clearly was intrigued by the mid-century colonial ventures of Gaspard de Coligny and Nicolas Durand de Villegagnon in Brazil.[8] Undoubtedly, much of what Montaigne accepted as truthful information was in fact greatly distorted (if not wholly false); but more important than the truth value of

Montaigne's claims is the manner in which he incorporates them into his understanding of humanity. In his essay "Of custom," for instance, after alluding to a young woman who had accustomed herself to eating nothing but spiders, he avers that "in that world of the new Indies there were found great nations, and in very varied climates, who lived upon spiders, made provision of them, and raised and fattened them, as they did also with grasshoppers, ants, lizards, and bats; and a toad was sold for six crowns during a food shortage. They cook them and prepare them with various sauces" (77-78). It is characteristic of Montaigne that he reports this alimentary information wholly without disparagement.[9] Unlike Chanca, who also touches on this standard element of New World iconography when he writes that American natives subsist at least partly upon spiders and lizards, Montaigne evidences no disgust and no readiness to qualify or deny the human status of these beings. Whereas Chanca relies upon a facile equation of human custom with fundamental human nature, Montaigne considers the dietary behavior of these Indians proof of one of his oft-repeated observations: that custom or habit is *second* nature. It is true that these people are different from Europeans, but this difference cannot be hermeneutically channelled into categories of subhumanity or cultural unaccommodation. In Montaigne's view, there is no such thing as a pre-cultural or wholly unaccommodated human.

Which brings us back to *King Lear*. For Gloucester, who is unable to recognize his naked son, Poor Tom's speech can only evoke a predictably conventional response: "What, hath your Grace no better company?" (3.4.142). For Lear, though, Poor Tom is both "the thing itself" and "my philosopher" (3.4.106, 176): both natural man without a cultural overlay and cultural man with wisdom to impart. He is, at one extreme, Chanca's bestial savage momentarily redeemed from subhumanity, and at the other, Montaigne's New World exemplar. It is as if Shakespeare is testing the capacity of these two notions to coexist. Perhaps, he may be saying, they can do so only in the mind of a man going mad. In any event, it is my contention that representations of savagery and civility derived from early attempts at New World ethnographic description played a substantial role in the thinking of early modern Europeans as they meditated upon the meanings of humanity and civilization. *King Lear*, the narrative of Chanca, and the American essays of Montaigne are only a few of the many Renaissance texts animated by a consideration of the complex group of ideas, images, and associations suggested by the theme of "unaccommodated" humanity.

THE IMAGE
OF AMERICA IN
MONTAIGNE, SPENSER,
AND SHAKESPEARE

1

Unaccommodated Man:
Representation and Theory

COLUMBUS AND ETHNOGRAPHIC ASSIMILATIONISM

To speak of Renaissance ethnography is to risk the charge of anachronism. European writers of the fifteenth, sixteenth, and seventeenth centuries who attempt to describe the customs and beliefs of non-European peoples do not ground their accounts upon explicit theoretical and methodological principles. Like their classical forebears—among them Herodotus, Xenophon, Pliny the Elder, Josephus, Tacitus, and Diodorus Siculus—these writers most often proceed on the evaluative assumption that they are characterizing societies inferior to their own; they do not operate, as do twentieth-century anthropologists following the tradition of Bronislaw Malinowski, Margaret Mead, and E. E. Evans-Pritchard, in a spirit of disinterested inquiry as participant-observers and with a firmly-established conviction of cultural relativism. Moreover, since their accounts are frequently embedded in letters, polemics, governmental reports, clerical documents, and narratives of exploration, conquest, and colonization, these writers' motives seldom appear free from personal or ideological bias, and there is a pronounced tendency—even when their writings are not clearly self-serving—for their cultural description to lack focus and organization, to betray various racial, ethnocentric, and xenophobic prejudices, to be unbalanced and haphazard in presentation, and, in short, to confuse in the very attempt to clarify. Anthony Pagden has written that the early chroniclers of the Americas "were not committed to an accurate description of the world 'out there'," and this claim no doubt holds true for the great majority of Renaissance Europeans who engaged in cultural description, American and otherwise.[1] It has even been argued that ethnography did not exist at all in the Renaissance, and, if one subscribes to a sufficiently narrow definition of the enterprise—laying particular emphasis on the need for systematic rigor, theoretical self-consciousness, and absolute dissociation from any form of exploitive motivation—one can certainly maintain such a position.[2]

But if ethnography is understood in the broader and more basic sense of "written cultural description" and is taken to be a reflection—however naively or obtusely expressed, however contingent upon power relations—of genuine interest in the diversity of human societies and implicit grappling with the epistemological problems attendant upon cultural encounters, then ethnographic practices unquestionably took place in the European Renaissance. Perhaps it would be more accurate to speak of "incidental" or "inchoate" ethnography; Mircea Eliade, for example, once characterized the writings of Christopher Columbus and other Renaissance travelers "a dossier for an ethnography yet to be born."[3] In any case, there is no dearth of European documents composed between, say, 1492 and 1625 that attempt, in varying ways and with varying degrees of expertise and thoroughness, to represent the appearance, social structures, traditions, beliefs, and lifeways of non-European peoples. It is true that these documents almost always register some form of subjective or evaluative reaction, and frequently a combination of reactions: One becomes accustomed, for instance, to encountering expressions of distaste, repulsion, horror, curiosity, admiration, wonder, ambivalence, thoroughgoing confusion, and even voyeuristic fascination. "Objectivity" seldom enters one's mind as a possible characterization of these writings. Moreover, the documents can hardly be said to divorce themselves effectively from ideological contingency, and they often contain highly improbable "facts" naively presented as accurate information. In short, one is skeptical of amassing these documents indiscriminately together as contributions to a Renaissance version of comparative ethnology. But inasmuch as absolute objectivity is unattainable in the first place, and to the extent that ideological contingencies always obtain, I would submit that early modern texts that attempt cultural description are—for all their expression of personal bias and evaluative judgment—fundamentally ethnographic in character, and in many instances as important for what they tell us about the cultural other as for what they tell us about their writers.[4] Bernardino de Sahagún's *Florentine Codex*, for example—a mid-sixteenth-century encyclopedia of Mexican culture—has been described by Octavio Paz as "one of the founding works of the science of anthropology" and by J. H. Elliott as "a highly sophisticated piece of ethnographical field-work"; Anthony Pagden has characterized the massive *Apologética historia sumaria [Apologetic history of the Indies]* of Bartolomé de Las Casas as "an expansive piece of comparative ethnology"; and David B. Quinn has argued that the Renaissance "tendency to observe alien cultures for their own sake"—and in particular the English tendency to observe the Irish—led to "an elementary ethnology, if not precisely to a social anthropology."[5] The opinions of scholars such as these—scholars content to speak of the anthropological character of various Renaissance texts—can only serve to buttress the view that the early modern period possessed an inchoate ethnography.

In addition to the works just mentioned, one might add, in a preliminary list of Renaissance ethnographic accounts, Giorgio Iteriano's *La vita & sito di Zichi, chiamiti Ciarcassi [The life and locale of Zichi, known as Circassia]* (1502), Alvise da Ca'da Mosto's *Le navigazioni atlantiche [Atlantic navigations]* (1507), Damiao de Góis's *Fides, Religio, Moresque Aethiopum [The faith, religion, and customs of the Ethiopians]* (1540), and two books on China: a collection of letters from Jesuit missionaries entitled *L'Institution des loix, coustumes et autres choses merveilleuses & memorables tant du royaume de la Chine [The establishment of laws, customs, and many other marvelous and memorable things in the kingdom of China]* (1556), and Juan González de Mendoza's *Historia de las cosas mas notables, ritos, y costumbres, del gran reyno de la China [History of the most notable things, rites, and customs of the great kingdom of China]* (1585).[6] Joannes Boemus, of course, had published in 1520 his general survey *Omniun Gentium Mores Leges et Ritus* [translated into English in 1611 as *The manners lawes and customs of all nations*], and in later editions of this popular book, various supplements were added: Francisco Tamara's 1556 Spanish translation included a large section on America; and E. Aston's 1611 English rendering contained excerpts from Jean de Léry's account of his year-long sojourn in Brazil. But while books on the Levant and Asia proliferated, perhaps because they could offer descriptions of foreign courts and relatively sophisticated societies, one of the largest groups of Renaissance ethnographies was that which dealt primarily or exclusively with peoples of the New World. Jean de Léry's book is a good example; entitled *Histoire d'un voyage fait en la terre du Brésil [History of a Voyage to the Land of Brazil]* and published at Geneva in 1578, his work indicates through a subtitle one of its principal concerns: "les meurs & façons de vivre estranges des sauvages ameriquains, avec un colloque de leur langage" [the customs and strange ways of life of the American savages, along with a colloquy in their language].[7] Léry's "Preface," moreover, contains the following remarkable passage, at once an Herodotean claim to eyewitness authenticity and a calmly confident disclaimer:

> If someone finds it ill that hereafter, when I speak of savage customs, I often use this kind of expression—"I saw," "I found," "this happened to me," and so on (as if I wanted to show myself off)—I reply that not only are these things within my

own subject but also I am speaking out of my own knowledge, that is, from my own seeing and experience; indeed, I will speak of things that very likely no one before me has ever seen, much less written about. I mean this, however, not about all of America in general, but only about the place where I lived for about a year: that is, under the tropic of Capricorn among the savages called the *Tupinamba*.[8]

We are reminded of Michel de Montaigne's contemporaneous wish (as rendered by his Elizabethan translator): "I would have everie man write what he knowes, and no more."[9]

Other Renaissance Europeans—or, in some cases, mestizo descendants of Europeans—whose written accounts demonstrate sustained interest in the history, customs and mores of native Americans include Ramon Pané, Peter Martyr, Andrés de Olmos, Toribio Motolinía, Diego Durán, Manoel da Nóbrega, Hans Staden, Alvar Núñez Cabeza de Vaca, Juan Bautista Pomar, Pedro Cieza de León, Olfert Dapper, André Thevet, Alonso de Zorita, Thomas Harriot, José de Acosta, Samuel de Champlain, Garcilaso de la Vega, John Smith, and of course Sahagún and Las Casas; I will have occasion elsewhere to refer to the writings of many of these authors. And, to dwell for a moment on just one feature of ethnographic description, I will add that Léry's interest in providing his readers with a sampling of Amerindian language was by no means exceptional; similar word lists and colloquies were appended to accounts by Pané, Martyr, Smith, Antonio Pigafetta, and Jacques Cartier, and three published linguistic tracts deserve special mention: the Dominican friar Domingo de Santo Tomás's 1560 grammar of Quechua, Alonso de Molina's 1571 Spanish/Nahuatl dictionary, and Gabriel Sagard's 1632 study of the Huron language.[10] Indeed, as John Howland Rowe has written, it seems beyond dispute that the sixteenth century saw "a great expansion of anthropological observation"—particularly New World observation—and thus it is wholly legitimate to speak of an inchoate ethnography of the Renaissance, an ethnographic discourse within which it is possible to locate many exemplary texts and against which many other contemporary writings—writings conventionally termed "literary"—may be placed for illumination.[11] There are perhaps no absolute correspondences between these two textual realms, no inevitable and fully demonstrable homologies, but at the same time completely separating the two seems arbitrary and, worse, counterintuitive. Doing so would almost certainly not have occurred to a Renaissance European. Juxtaposing them, on the other hand, creates a new and hybrid discursive space within which intuition has room to work; one notes echoes, resonances, elliptical progressions, and shared assumptions that one might otherwise overlook. There is room here, precisely due to the absence of strict connectedness, for the exercise of a modest form of negative capability. The amalgam of early modern ethnography and Renaissance literature holds enormous potential as a discursive field in which European attitudes toward ethnic, cultural, and gender difference may be discerned and analyzed, and in which, ultimately, central concerns of the Renaissance—concerns such as those bound up in the attributions of savagery, civility, divinity, bestiality, and demonism—may be clarified due to the reciprocal illumination attendant upon the textual fusion.

There is perhaps no better place to begin discussing Renaissance ethnography and European perceptions of the New World's autochthonous peoples than with the journal and letters of Christopher Columbus. It is true, of course, that Columbus died in the belief that the lands he had explored were part of the easternmost reaches of Asia; for him there was never such a thing as the "New World." It was Amerigo Vespucci rather than Columbus who first recognized the lands across the Atlantic as a *Mundus Novus* unconnected to the traditional and tripartite *orbis terrarum* of Europe, Africa, and Asia—a fact commemorated in 1507 by Martin Waldseemüller's famous map of the world.[12] Nonetheless, the Taino, Ciguayo, Carib, and Arawakan peoples Columbus encountered in the Caribbean archipelago were "new" insofar as they were people with whom Europeans—to the best of their contemporary knowledge—had never had prior contact. In all likelihood, Columbus was the first transoceanic outsider to write about these people, seize them for display in Europe, and contemplate their conversion to Christianity. It is no doubt true, as Stephen Greenblatt has written, that for Columbus "the idea of discovery as entailing an act of sustained, highly particularized narrative representation of differences was quite alien," but it is true as well that Columbus's records, for all their ethnographic inadequacy, offer invaluable observations about an initial, virtually unreenactable encounter: that between European Christians and non-Indo-European, non-Judeo-Christian women and men.[13]

In his *Diario*, or logbook, for instance, it is remarkable to what an extent Columbus's very first entry regarding American natives—the people he referred to as *los Indios*—anticipates the centuries-long debate between what Lewis Hanke has referred to as "the 'dirty dog' and the 'noble savage' schools of thought" about the indigenous inhabitants of the New World.[14] Immediately upon landing at the small island later found to be called "Guanahaní," the European mariners were confronted with the sight of many naked people, some of whom later swam out through the surf to the ships and offered gifts of parrots, spears, and balls of cotton thread. In return, Columbus and his men gave the Indians glass beads and hawks' bells. It was the morning of October 12, 1492; the first European-American exchange had occurred. Here is how Columbus reports it:

> In sum, they took everything and gave of what they had very willingly. But it seemed to me that they were a people very poor in everything. All of them go around as naked as their mothers bore them; and the women also, although I did not see more than one quite young girl. And all those that I saw were young people, for none did I see of more than 30 years of age. They are very well formed, with handsome bodies and good faces. Their hair [is] coarse—almost like the tail of a horse—and short. They wear their hair down over their eyebrows except for a little in the back which they wear long and never cut. Some of them paint themselves with black, and they are of the color of the Canarians, neither black nor white; and some of them paint themselves with white, and some of them with red, and some of them with whatever they find. And some of them paint their faces, and some of them the whole body, and some of them only the eyes, and some of them only the nose. They do not carry arms nor are they acquainted with them, because I showed them swords and they took them by the edge and through ignorance cut themselves. They have no iron. Their javelins are shafts without iron and some of them have at the end a fish tooth and others of other things. All of them alike are of good-sized stature and carry themselves well. I saw some who had marks of wounds on their bodies and I made signs to them asking what they were; and they showed me how people from other islands nearby came there and tried to take them, and how they defended themselves; and I believed and believe that they come here from the *tierra firme* to take them captive. They should be good and intelligent servants, for I see that they say very quickly everything that is said to them; and I believe that they would become Christians very easily, for it seemed to me that they had no religion. Our Lord pleasing, at the time of my departure I will take six of them from here to Your Highnesses in order that they may learn to speak. No animal of any kind did I see on this island except parrots.[15]

On the one hand, we see here the depiction of a generous, friendly, goodwilled people, a people quick in intelligence and handsome in body. Their nudity is accompanied by no explicit moral judgment; we can imagine the ease with which it might be linked to their clearly positive traits so as to amplify the suggestion of primal innocence and goodness, of innate gentility in uncivilized, "unaccommodated" humanity. And so it was—both by Columbus elsewhere in his *Diario* and by numerous other early raconteurs and chroniclers of the New World. Indeed, not only was nakedness accorded a positive sign, but also such other elements of the standard iconography of

America as free love, lack of private property, egalitarianism, and the absence of laws and writing. As Tzvetan Todorov aptly notes, Columbus's observations about indigenous Americans made "an important contribution to the myth of the noble savage."[16]

On the other hand, we also see in this entry a readiness to make quick generalizations about the cultural traits—or lack thereof—of these people. Among other things, they do not bear arms (even though they carry pointed spears), they need to "learn to speak" (even though "they say very quickly everything that is said to them"), and they have "no religion"—this last an oft-repeated allegation throughout Columbus's writings. Moreover, we see heavy emphasis placed upon these people's non-European fashions of bodily decoration. But most significant, Columbus stresses the ignorance of these Indians through the vivid example of their cutting themselves upon the sharp iron of the Spaniards' swords; perhaps this image contributes in his own mind to his vague and apparently unsupported generalization that "they were a people very poor in everything." In any case, he quickly moves to the wholly unabashed conclusion that these men and women will make good servants and Christians, and he follows by casually proposing the first of what turned out to be a long and brutal series of kidnappings of American natives—many of whom never made it to Europe alive.[17]

In short, through an uncritical scrutiny typical of many early writers on the New World, Columbus reveals here a deep confusion about what he believes these new people to be. Because they are gentle they will easily become Christians; and—in theory at least—because they will become Christians they obviously have the capacity to receive God's grace and are thus fully human and fundamentally equal to Europeans. However, the very fact that they lack Christianity seems to indicate to Columbus that they suffer from a broad cultural deficiency. They are blank pages, *tabulae rasae;* their physical nakedness serves as a sign, an unmistakable outward manifestation, of their cultural and religious nakedness. And their apparent ignorance of certain well-established European traditions—the fine art of war, for example—quickly modulates in Columbus's mind into a sign of human inferiority. Just two months after the landing at Guanahaní, Columbus records the following observation in his *Diario* about the inhabitants of the island now known as Española: "They do not have arms and they are all naked, and of no skill in arms, and so very cowardly that a thousand would not stand against three. And so they are fit to be ordered about and made to work, plant, and do everything else that may be needed, and build towns and be taught our customs, and to go about clothed."[18] Ignorance has become cowardice, and we sense a contempt in Columbus's voice, apparently arising from the fact that the people he speaks of show no signs of aggression and warlike behavior. How ironic this is, when he has earlier praised them for this very gentleness—and when he will again, shortly, after his flagship founders and sinks off the northeast coast of Española on Christmas Day. On that occasion, natives from a nearby village will work side by side with Columbus's men to salvage everything possible from the *Santa Maria*, and Columbus will write that "in the world there are no better people or a better land. They love their neighbors as themselves, and they have the sweetest speech in the world; and [they are] gentle and are always laughing."[19] Here, once again, the natives are proto-Christians, their gentleness and helpfulness proving their aptness for conversion. It was undoubtedly passages such as this that led Bartolomé de Las Casas to revere Columbus as one of the few conquistadors who held the Indians at their proper estimation. Apparently Las Casas was able to ignore the fact that Columbus also frequently thought of them as deficient and "unaccommodated" men and women.

Todorov has noticed this seeming schizophrenia in Columbus's attitude toward American natives and schematized it in the following fashion:

Either he [Columbus] conceives the Indians (though without using these words) as human beings altogether, having the same rights as himself; but then he sees them not only as equals but also as identical, and this behavior leads to assimilationism, the projection of his own values on the others. Or else he starts from the difference, but the latter is immediately translated into terms of superiority and inferiority (in his case, obviously it is the Indians who are inferior).[20]

In short, Todorov implies that one can either acknowledge *equality* and conclude *identity* or acknowledge *difference* and conclude *inferiority*. (Or, Columbus-like, one can do both at different moments.) The second maneuver, which might be characterized as typical of a dialectical imagination, is exemplified by the earlier-quoted remarks of Diego Alvarez Chanca, Antonio Pigafetta, and Tomaso Ortiz, and implicit in many of the writings of other authors such as Domingo de Betanzos, Gonzalo Fernández de Oviedo, and Juan Ginés de Sepúlveda. The first maneuver, in contrast, suggests an analogical or appropriative imagination, and is typical of Las Casas and sporadically apparent in a number of other early writers such as Hernán Cortés, Vasco de Quiroga, and Alonso de Zorita. In fact, both basic maneuvers must of necessity begin with an implicit acknowledgment of difference, but the former quickly relegates this difference to the superficial level of local custom and is thus enabled to work from the premise of fundamental equality.

The latter, however, equates difference of custom with difference of fundamental nature.

Although Todorov's binary formula provides an illuminating rubric within which to initiate discussions of European ethnographic perception, it obscures several important distinctions and may be usefully refined to comprehend other and perhaps equally common perceptual and categorizing maneuvers characteristic of early modern Europeans in their confrontation with cultural aliens such as New World natives.[21] For instance, Todorov's formula blurs the difference between regarding American natives as proto-Christians and regarding them as noble savages—both of which views seem implicit at different points in Columbus's *Diario*. One might argue, in the interest of clarity, that an acknowledgment of fundamental equality followed by a conclusion of circumstantial superiority (due to lack of societal corruption) forms the standard progression to primitivism and the noble savage claim. Furthermore, an acknowledgment of complete equality followed by a refusal to conclude identity—an admission, therefore, of a neutral difference-in-equality, and of the full subjectivity of the other—would be an invitation to thoroughgoing cultural relativism in which subjects perceive themselves as engaged in dialogical relations (thereby implicitly conceding the demise of notions of absolute and transcultural value). Views such as these, of course, could be dangerously heterodox in the sixteenth century, and accordingly are seldom implied or articulated; nonetheless, in their separate ways, they are closely related to aspects of the stances taken later by Montaigne in such essays as "Of cannibals" and "Of coaches."

Todorov clearly connects assimilationism with the first of the two perceptual maneuvers he attributes to Columbus—acknowledging *equality* and concluding *identity*. And he defines assimilationism as projecting one's own values upon others. I submit, however, that *all* attempts to represent and account for the autochthonous inhabitants of America are forms of assimilationism; all contain an epistemologically appropriative dimension, regardless whether they posit superiority, inferiority, identity, or difference-in-equality. All inevitably project, to a greater or lesser degree, the values and cultural preconceptions of the perceiving subjects (the Europeans, in this case), and all try to locate the indigenous Americans within a preestablished and reasonably stable world view. Roy Wagner has claimed, speaking of the anthropological project generally, that "an anthropologist 'invents' the culture he believes himself to be studying";[22] and while this may seem, on the face of it, an exaggeration, its apparent hyperbole conceals a valuable truth. In the case of early modern ethnography, Wagner's assertion remains pertinent regardless of whether the descriptive strategy is to liken the Indians to people of the Golden Age or to compare them, as Sepúlveda does, to monkeys; either way, they are being assimilated to European conceptions of the world. As Edward Said has written, in reference to the Western understanding of Islam, "the real issue is whether indeed there can be a true representation of anything, or whether any and all representations, because they *are* representations, are embedded first in the language and then in the culture, institutions, and political ambience of the representer."[23] One might well ask whether it is even possible—as Todorov seems to suggest—that European explorers could have thought and written otherwise than they did about the inhabitants of the New World. Todorov claims that what Columbus denies the Americans is "the existence of a human substance truly other, something capable of being not merely an imperfect state of oneself";[24] but this assertion might be countered by the question of whether it is humanly possible to grant such an existence. Perhaps, on the contrary, humans are incapable of engaging in an act of knowing an ethnic or cultural other without employing the very terms and conceptions by which they know and define themselves. Todorov mentions, apropos of this discussion, that Albrecht Dürer, around 1520, "admires the works of Indian craftsmanship Cortés sends to the royal court, but it does not occur to him to try making anything of the kind; the Indian images themselves as drawn by Dürer remain entirely faithful to the European style."[25] True enough; but even *had* Dürer attempted to draw in the "Indian style," his mimetic practice would inevitably have revealed its own distinctly European grounding, much in the same way that twentieth-century *Art Nègre* was an imitation rather than a reproduction of African art. Perhaps this seems a point too obvious to mention, but I want to stress the basic and inevitable epistemic assimilationism that accompanies any attempt, however generous or even self-negating, to comprehend that which is different or alien.

In any event, it is unquestionably the case that Europeans resorted to all kinds of strategies, conscious and unconscious, to describe, account for, and evaluate the peoples of the New World. Among the most common of these, particularly during the early years of exploration, was the habit of characterizing native Americans as though they were inhabitants of the Earthly Paradise or the Golden World.[26] The Italian humanist Peter Martyr (Pietro Martire d'Anghiera)—who never actually visited America—was notably fond of doing this; his *De orbe novo [The Decades of the New World]* (1516, 1533) is filled with euphoric descriptions, such as the following, that seem almost to expose an atavistic longing in the European psyche:

> For it is certeyne, that amonge them, the lande is as common as the sonne and the water: And that Myne and Thyne (the seedes of all myscheefe) have no place

with them. They are contente with soo lyttle, that in soo large a countrey, they have rather superfluitie then scarsenes. Soo that (as wee have sayde before) they seeme to lyve in the goulden worlde, without toyle, lyvinge in open gardens, not intrenched with dykes, dyvyded with hedges, or defended with waules. They deale trewely one with another, without lawes, without bookes, and without Iudges.[27]

Likening the inhabitants of America to the mythic, pagan, or proto-Christian ancestors of contemporary Europeans had the simultaneous effects of decreasing or taming their novelty—domesticating them, to a degree—yet still keeping them sufficiently distant that their otherness remained readily apparent.[28] However, as schemes of conquest, conversion, colonization, and material exploitation began to dominate the minds of European adventurers, such fanciful and remote comparisons often gave way to more plausible—if not more accurate and realistic—parallels. Once again, Peter Martyr provides a revealing example. Summarizing the ethnographic account of Española's Taino natives composed by the Jeronymite friar Ramon Pané at Columbus's request during the latter's second New World voyage (1493-96), Martyr writes:

But nowe (most noble prince) you shall heare a more pleasaunt fable. There is a certeyne caue called Iouanaboina, in the territorye of a certeyne kynge whose name is Machinnech. This caue they [the Tainos] honour more religiously then dyd the Grekes in tyme paste, Corinth, Cyrrha, or Nysa: And haue adourned it with pictures of a thousand fasshions. In the entrance of this caue they haue twoo grauen Zemes [idols], whereof the one is cauled Binthaitel, and the other Marohu. Beinge demaunded why they had this caue in so great reuerence, they answered ernestly, bycause the Soonne and the Moone came fyrst owt of the same to gyue lyght to the world. They haue religious concourse to these caues, as wee are accustomed to goo on Pylgramage to Rome or Vaticane, Compostele, or Hierusalem, and most holye and heade places of owre Religion.[29]

Here, in the midst of a partial relation of Taino cosmogony—and Pané is remarkable for his careful reporting of Taino myth, custom, and vocabulary—Martyr familiarizes the strange in a sadly predictable way. Similarly, though less spectacularly, Hernán Cortés writes in 1522 that the natives of Mexico "live almost like those in Spain, and in as much harmony and order as there, and considering that they are barbarous and so far from the knowledge of God and cut off from all civilized nations, it is truly remarkable to see what they have achieved in all things."[30] At the turn of the century

Amerigo Vespucci christens a region of South America "Venezuela" because its villages, built on piles in the water, remind him of Venice; in 1535, Gonzalo Fernández de Oviedo likens the native peoples of America to "Ethiopians" and "Thracians"; and fifty years later the Englishman Thomas Harriot translates the Algonquian word "wiroans" as "chiefe Lorde."[31] The effect of these kinds of appropriative analogizing is obvious: The strange or alien is rendered far more recognizable than it could possibly be by far-flung allusions to Eden or Arcadia or the Hesperides. The unfamiliar is made comfortably familiar—assimilated to contemporary rather than historical categories—and, as the saying goes, familiarity breeds contempt. Such descriptive tactics as those commonly employed by Cortés or Oviedo had the insidious effect of indirectly justifying the conquest of American peoples on the grounds that they were fundamentally akin to Europeans, though lagging behind in civilization, and thus in need of—or even passively awaiting—the direction and guidance of their superiors. The Americans, in effect, are infantilized, and their inferior status, by definition, demands subordination and the assumption of an appropriately protectionist attitude on the part of their "masters."

Of course, conquest and colonization could also be justified on the grounds that aboriginal Americans were not people at all; as Pagden has written, "De-humanisation is, perhaps, the simplest method of dealing with all that is culturally unfamiliar."[32] If, as Chanca and Ortiz seemed to believe, these natives were savage and subhuman, European domination was not only easily vindicated but proper and inevitable. In a letter to Spain's Philip II in 1558, for example, Friar Pedro de Gante complained that the Indians of the New World were "like unruly animals without reason; we cannot bring them either to the lap of the church nor to its doctrine . . . they run like savages from the friars."[33] Similarly, Richard Hakluyt wrote that the natives encountered by Martin Frobisher in his three voyages to "Meta Incognita" (1576-78) "live in Caves of the earth, and hunt for their dinners or praye, even as the beare or other wild beastes do. They eat raw flesh and fish, and refuse no meat howsoever it be stinking."[34] And no citizens of Castile, Portugal, France, or England would likely object to their countries' imperialist ambitions if they took to heart such descriptions of New World inhabitants as the following:

> These folk lyven like bestes without any resonablenes and the wymen be also as comon. And the men hath conversacyon with the wymen / who that they ben or who they fyrst mete / is she his syster / his mother / his daughter / or any other kyndred. And the wymen be very hoote and dyposed to lecherdnes. And they ete also on a nother. The man eteth his wyfe his chylderne / as we also haue seen

and they hange also the bodyes or persons fleeshe in the smoke / as men do with
vs swynes fleshe. And that lande is ryght full of folke / for they lyue commonly.
iii. C. [300] yere and more as with sykenesse they dye nat / . . . And they werre
also on vpon a nother / . . . they take the other prysoners And they brynge them
to deth and ete them / and as the dede is eten then sley they the rest.

For these wylye hunters of men [the "Canibales"], gyue them selues to none other
kynde of exercyse but onely to manhuntynge and tyllage after theyr manner. At the
commynge therfore of owre men into theyr regions, they loke as surely to haue them
faule into their snares as if they were hartes or wylde bores: and with no lesse
confydence licke their lippes secreately in hope of their praye. If they gette the vpper
hande, they eate them greedely: If they mystruste them selues to bee the weaker
parte, they truste to theyr feete, and flye swyfter then the wynde.[35]

Indeed, allegations of American cannibalism began with Columbus, and per-
sisted—perhaps with good reason—through the sixteenth century and beyond; they contribute substantially to what Howard Mumford Jones has called
the "anti-image" of the New World.[36] But even leaving aside the charge that
American natives sometimes ate one another, Europeans also had to contend
with the popular and quickly-entrenched stereotypes that these Indians were
stupid, promiscuous, filthy, idle, thievish, pox-infested, sodomous, ungrateful,
gluttonous, disobedient, and unteachable. Small wonder, then, that few Old
World citizens ever spoke up strongly in favor of the full human status of these
peoples. The project of Christian conversion rested on the assumption that
they were in fact fully human; but as Gante's remarks suggest, it may have been
the exception rather than the rule even for the clergy—let alone the conquistadors—to acknowledge this. We may perhaps marvel nowadays that such
blatantly self-contradictory attitudes could so readily coexist. But even in the
twentieth century we have been offered eloquent testimony to the fact that
denying complete human status to human beings different from ourselves is
surprisingly easy. As George Orwell writes, in his essay "Marrakech,"

When you walk through a town like this—two hundred thousand inhabitants,
of whom at least twenty thousand own literally nothing except the rags they
stand up in—when you see how the people live, and still more how easily they
die, it is always difficult to believe that you are walking among human beings.
All colonial empires are in reality founded upon that fact. The people have brown
faces—besides, there are so many of them! Are they really the same flesh as
yourself? Do they even have names? Or are they merely a kind of undifferentiated
brown stuff, about as individual as bees or coral insects?[37]

The attitude that indigenous Americans are subhuman or bestial clearly relies on Todorov's second perceptual maneuver—the acknowledgment of *difference* followed by the conclusion of *inferiority*. But in spite of Todorov's implications to the contrary, this attitude too is assimilationist insofar as it represents a grasping of the unknown by means of the known; in this case, however, the autochthonous peoples of the New World are equated with nonhuman animals rather than with European men and women, and the human/animal binarism—with all its religious and moral trappings—is employed without scrutiny as a valid interpretive schema. I think it is self-evident, then, that both euphoric and antipathetic views of American Indians—both the "noble savage" and "dirty dog" schools of thought—are and cannot avoid being attempts at comprehension based on a projection of the perceiving subject's ordinary (and sometimes extraordinary) knowledge. They are both assimilative, in other words; indeed, not only this "stereotypical dualism" of European response but the whole complex web of American colonial and ethnographic discourse is enormously one-sided and epistemologically centered in conventional European perception.[38] But it is fruitless to take this discursive realm to task because of its inherent biases. Far more productive is the strategy suggested by J. H. Elliott—that of searching for evidence that Europe and Europeans underwent fundamental changes as a consequence of the discovery, conquest, and colonization of the New World. As Elliott writes, "the attempt of one society to comprehend another inevitably forces it to reappraise itself. . . . This process is bound to be an agonizing one, involving the jettisoning of many traditional preconceptions and inherited ideas."[39] Perhaps without realizing it, writers as early as Columbus, Chanca, and Pané are interrogating their own cultural norms and values even as they employ them to think about and describe the strange peoples they have encountered. They are searching for a way to encompass both the old and the new in a coherent whole. Thus, while their expressed views, to our late twentieth-century tastes, are frequently reprehensible, they nonetheless constitute, in their small way, part of an evolution away from various inadequate or outdated European conceptions about the nature of humanity. If the Old World's discovery of the New led to the razing of many features of New World culture, it also led to a partial erasure and reconstitution of certain Old World habits of thought.

This is not to imply, of course, that all ethnographic accounts—or, by extension, all varieties of assimilative comprehension—are equally valuable or productive as strategies of interrogation. On the contrary, those that minimize the differences between New and Old World peoples—those that rely overmuch on simile, analogies to contemporary European society, and appropriative projections of value—are epistemologically the least interesting because they are least likely to prompt productive self-scrutiny on the part of Europeans. However, in contrast to Todorov, I do not believe that views such as those of Chanca, Pigafetta, Ortiz, Oviedo, and Sepúlveda—views that stress the extreme difference of American natives, often leading to a conclusion of their essential inferiority—are the most epistemologically satisfying, even if morally offensive.[40] Rather, the approach typified by Las Casas is, in the long run, more likely than these other views to provoke a valuable interrogation of European values and habits of perception. It is true, as Todorov points out, that Las Casas's Christianity equipped him with an ethnocentric screen through which he looked when describing the Indians; but as I have demonstrated, *all* European writers are equipped with similar screens of one sort or another. Las Casas does indeed acknowledge *equality* and ultimately conclude *identity*; but is not this acknowledgment of equality in the face of clear physical and cultural difference superior to adopting a conventional hierarchic perspective and collapsing otherness into inferiority? Las Casas's attitudes are certainly open to modern critique, but I believe they merit admiration in their implicit suggestion of the finite limits of human reason and the need for acts of faith when confronting the new and strange.

LAS CASAS AND SEPÚLVEDA

Bartolomé de Las Casas sailed from Spain to Española in 1502 and spent roughly forty years in the New World. He was an acquaintance of Columbus and Cortés, a participant in the conquest of Cuba, an *encomendero* and slave-holder for a short time, and, in 1512, the first priest ordained in the Americas. Later he joined the Dominican order, becoming in 1543 the Bishop of Chiapas in southern Mexico. Like Fray Antonio de Montesinos before him, Las Casas grew to be appalled at the Spanish exploitation of native Americans, and from 1514 until his death in 1576 he waged an unceasing campaign to improve the treatment of these peoples by their European conquerors;[41] as a result of these efforts he has come to be known variously as the "Defender of the Indians" and, in Simón Bolívar's phrase, the "Apostle of America." He wrote prodigiously—everything from propagandistic tracts to carefully researched chronicles—and his major works have been accorded high praise by historical scholars: Anthony Pagden has called the *Apologética historia sumaria* "a truly 'original' work. . . . an expansive piece of comparative ethnology"; and the *Historia de las Indias [History of the Indies]* has been characterized by Samuel Eliot Morison as "the one book on the discovery of America that I should wish to preserve if all others were destroyed."[42]

Las Casas is often grouped with Columbus, Vespucci, and Martyr as one of the early idealizers of American natives. However, if we take seriously J. H. Elliott's claim that "the image of the innocent Indian was most easily maintained by those Europeans who had never seen one",[43] we must draw a distinction between a man such as Las Casas—who not only saw Indians but spent half his long life among them—and men like Martyr and the early explorers, who, despite brief encounters with New World natives, had little or no opportunity to learn about their material or spiritual cultures. "No one knew the country and its natives so well and so long," writes Carl Ortwin Sauer of Las Casas's acquaintance with the land and people of the Greater Antilles.[44] In light of this, it seems all the more striking that Las Casas can speak about native Americans in such a manner as the following:

> And of all the infinite universe of humanity, these people are the most guileless, the most devoid of wickedness and duplicity, the most obedient and faithful to their native masters and to the Spanish Christians whom they serve. They are by nature the most humble, patient, and peaceable, holding no grudges, free from embroilments, neither excitable nor quarrelsome. These people are the most devoid of rancors, hatreds, or desire for vengeance of any people in the world. . . . They are also poor people, for they not only possess little but have no desire to possess worldly goods. For this reason they are not arrogant, embittered, or greedy. . . . They are very clean in their persons, with alert, intelligent minds, docile and open to doctrine, very apt to receive our holy Catholic faith, to be endowed with virtuous customs, and to behave in a godly fashion. And once they begin to hear the tidings of the Faith, they are so insistent on knowing more and on taking the sacraments of the Church and on observing the divine cult that, truly, the missionaries who are here need to be endowed by God with great patience in order to cope with such eagerness. Some of the secular Spaniards who have been here for many years say that the goodness of the Indians is undeniable and that if this gifted people could be brought to know the one true God they would be the most fortunate people in the world.[45]

It is true that the general tenor of these claims is hyperbolic; it is also true that Las Casas, as a Christian missionary, leaves no room for the possibility that Christian conversion might not be the best alternative for these people. Still, we must remember that Las Casas was writing at a time when many of his contemporaries were unwilling to grant even basic humanity to the

Indians. It was only in 1537, after all, that Pope Paul III, in his bull *Sublimis Deus*, condemned the idea that American natives are "dumb brutes created for our service . . . incapable of receiving the Catholic faith" and declared that "they are real men and that, not only are they capable of understanding the Catholic faith, but that, according to our informations, they are anxious to receive it."[46] Perhaps the zealousness of Las Casas's tone may be excused on the grounds that the very nature of the debate in which he was engaged encouraged extreme positions—as such debates generally do. In any case, we cannot take lightly these opinions of a man who devoted his life to living among and defending the inhabitants of the New World.

A more serious criticism of Las Casas's attitude is that it denies a cultural inheritance to the Indians, that it rests on the assumption that their minds are, collectively, *tabulae rasae*.[47] This assumption is characteristic of the writings of Columbus—who never tires of pointing out that New World natives seem to have "no religion"[48]—and it is perhaps best expressed in this passage from Martyr's *De orbe novo*: "For lyke as rased or vnpaynted tables, are apte to receaue what formes soo euer are fyrst drawen theron by the hande of the paynter, euen soo these naked and simple people, doo soone receaue the customes of owre Religion, and by conuersation with owre men, shake of theyr fierce and natiue barbarousnes."[49] But in Las Casas such a view seems surprising, even disturbing, since we know that his acquaintance with the Indians was vastly greater than that of either of the former writers. Still, it is undeniable—as the curious repetition of the phrase "apt to receive" almost emblematically demonstrates—that a passive readiness to be inscribed with Christian faith and European civility is a motif common to Las Casas's and Martyr's portrayals of the Indians. Probably the best that can be said about this belief is that it is certainly preferable—on either Christian or other conventional moral grounds—to supposing that the Indians are ineducable and unregenerate. Las Casas finds in these natives' alleged aptness to learn and eagerness to be converted a sort of proof that they are no different from Europeans in their fundamental human potential. Perhaps, like at least a few of his contemporaries, he was deeply enough imbued with the spirit of Renaissance humanism to be capable of imagining the fundamental equality of Europeans and native Americans while simultaneously incapable of perceiving the latters' separation from Greco-Roman and Judeo-Christian traditions as anything other than a crippling disadvantage.

But this is to skirt the central issue. To the extent that Las Casas acknowledges *equality* and concludes *identity*, to that same extent he robs native Americans of their *difference*. As the Mexican scholar Edmundo O'Gorman has written, the consequence of situating the New World within the context of Christian history was that "the native cultures of the newly-found lands could not be recognized and respected in their own right, as an original way of realizing human ideals and values, but only for the meaning they might have in relation to Christian European culture, the self-appointed judge and model of human behavior."[50] O'Gorman's words, though not specifically directed toward Las Casas, nonetheless serve admirably as a proto-critique of the Spanish priest's views, and have clearly influenced the direction of the historical debate in recent years. José Rabasa, for instance, in contesting the claims of Pagden and others that Las Casas's work antici-pates the comparative ethnology of later centuries, argues that Las Casas defends native Americans by assimilating them to the vexed category of noble savagery, and in so doing exposes his own ethnographic inadequacy: "If 'noble' encompasses Christian and civilized ideals, which is certainly the meaning Las Casas gives to the term when he attributes it to the Amerindians, who in turn are reduced to 'savages' or 'barbarians' in apologetics of conquest, the *noble savage* figure cancels the opposition while prompting a fetishistic reification. . . . At its face value, the *noble savage* figure is a contradiction of terms and works against itself."[51] And Todorov writes, apropos of the perceptive strategies expressed above, that "precisely because he [Las Casas] was a Christian, his perception of the Indians was poor. Can we really love someone if we know little or nothing of his identity; if we see, in place of that identity, a projection of ourselves or of our ideals?"[52] This articulation gets at the core of what Todorov considers the problem with *tabula rasa* views: their epistemological invalidity due to their appropriative tactics and their superimposition of the self upon the other. However, Todorov offers no theoretical alternative to such views; and though he does suggest that Spanish mendicants like Sahagún and Durán penetrated New World cultures in a way that Las Casas never did, he is not able to argue that they did so because they were in some way capable of abandoning their subjectivity. Indeed, the problem with the theoretical justification of Todorov's critique of Las Casas is not that it is incorrect but that it applies equally well to *all* cultural observers. Las Casas's zealous Christianity certainly impaired his perception of the Indians, but who is to say that a non-Christian observer might not be equally impaired by some other set of less conspicuous but still operative preconceptions? Can any observer wholly escape ethnocentric subjectivity?[53]

This is not to say that a critique of Las Casas is unwarranted, but only that it must take into account the character of the momentous debate in which the priest was engaged. The famous Valladolid Disputation of 1550-51 serves admirably as an emblem of this debate. Since a number of scholars—among them Lewis Hanke, Stafford Poole, and Anthony Pagden—have written extensively about the Disputation and the nature and derivation of its arguments, I will merely provide a brief summary here.[54] The question at issue was whether Castile was justified in making war on American Indians, and the central point of controversy involved the problem of ascertaining the Indians' degree of rationality. Cortés's friend Juan Ginés de Sepúlveda, a renowned Spanish scholar and lawyer who had never travelled to the New World, claimed that the Indians were clearly deficient in reason and thus fit—on the Aristotelian ground of natural subordination—to be the Spaniards' slaves.[55] His arguments drew heavily on observations made by Gonzalo Fernández de Oviedo in his *Historia general y natural de las Indias [Natural History of the West Indies]* (1535), a book noted for its encyclopedic detail about the natural phenomena of the New World as well as its native inhabitants. Unfortunately, Oviedo was not always a reliable authority. Among other things, he concluded—somewhat in the fashion of nineteenth-century craniology, but with his own ludicrous twist—that "the bones of the sculles of theyr heades [the "Coronati" Indians of the "firme lande"] are foure tymes thycker and much stronger then owres. So that in commyng to hand strokes with them, it shalbe requisite not to strike them on the heades with swoordes, for so have many swoordes bynne broken on theyr heades with lyttle hurt doone."[56] Such claims as this could only reinforce Sepúlveda's already low opinion of American natives. Hence it is no surprise that among his principal conclusions were that they are "little men *(homunculos)* in whom you will scarcely find traces of humanity": They "lack culture," "keep no records of their history except certain obscure and vague reminiscences of some things put down in certain pictures," possess "only barbarous institutions and customs," and are "in prudence, talent, virtue, and humanity . . . as inferior to the Spaniards as children to adults, women to men, as the wild and cruel to the most meek, as the prodigiously intemperate to the continent and the temperate, that I have almost said, as monkeys to men."[57] Sepúlveda's restraint here in not actually making the bestial equation is all the more damning; one can imagine the admiration he may have inspired among sympathetic contemporaries by such gallant gestures of giving the benefit of the doubt in a doubtful cause.

Small wonder, then, that Las Casas "loosed all his wrath upon both Oviedo and Sepúlveda."[58] Critics of the priest's assimilative habit of thought seldom point out that the great bulk of his writings come from the years just before and after the Valladolid controversy. The *Historia*, for instance, was composed between 1527 and 1559; the *Apologia (In Defense of the Indians)* was completed in 1550; the *Apologética historia sumaria* was begun sometime in or after 1551;

and the inflammatory *Brevisima relación de la destruccion de las Indias [A Short Account of the Destruction of the Indies]*, while written in 1542, was published along with several other tracts in 1552—presumably at least in part as a follow-up to Las Casas's public defense of the Indians two years earlier.[59] In that defense, Las Casas maintained against Sepúlveda that New World natives were fully human and fully rational; their apparent "barbarities," such as illiteracy and paganism, were merely circumstantial accidents, not reflections of innate inferiority. As always, Las Casas wrote from the perspective of a Christian missionary, with the result that religious conversion of the Indians was invariably perceived as a desirable end. But we cannot fault Las Casas too greatly—given the nature of his opponent's argument—when we see him make the following counter-claims:

> The Creator of every being has not so despised these peoples of the New World that he willed them to lack reason and made them like brute animals, so that they should be called barbarians, savages, wild men, and brutes, as they [Sepúlveda and his supporters] think or imagine. On the contrary, they are of such gentleness and decency that they are, more than the other nations of the entire world, supremely fitted and prepared to abandon the worship of idols and to accept, province by province and people by people, the word of God and the preaching of the truth.[60]

This might be called a deductive rather than an inductive argument, a defense grounded primarily on doctrine rather than on empirical evidence, but such a grounding is hardly surprising in light of the presumed convictions of Las Casas's audience—a council of sixteenth-century Castilian Christians.

Elsewhere, as Elliott and Pagden have pointed out, Las Casas was fully capable of drawing attention to the Indians' civil accomplishments, such as "the very ancient vaulted and pyramid-like buildings" of central Mexico, which provided "no small index of their prudence and good polity."[61] For early modern Europeans, architectural capacity—and in particular, the building of cities—was certainly an indication of rationality and thus of non-bestiality; it pointed to the facts of careful planning, a settled existence, and large-scale social cooperation. Las Casas was also deeply impressed by the Indians' craftsmanship, particularly as manifested in featherwork and orna-mental silversmithing. He writes in the *Apologética historia*, for instance, that "what appears without doubt to exceed all human genius . . . is the art which those Mexican peoples have so perfectly mastered, of making from natural feathers, fixed in position with their own natural colors, anything that they or any other first-class painters can paint with brushes," and he goes on to describe the craft in detail and with obvious admiration for its practitioners.[62] Today, we may wonder why Las Casas did not privilege such observations, with their empirical ethnographic specificity, over deductive arguments from Christian authority. The reason almost certainly lies in the fact that Las Casas felt he must employ the most potent defense available to him: the assertion of the essential non-difference of native Americans on the grounds of Christian universalism. Only in this way could he adequately counter the extreme claims of his adversaries.

If we grant, then, the importance of rhetorical contexts—and in particular the debate with Sepúlveda—in determining the nature of many of Las Casas's pronouncements about American natives, we are in a better position to evaluate the undeniable traces of cultural relativism that also appear in Las Casas's writings. Even Todorov admits that these exist, though he labels them as instances of "perspectivism" and seems unwilling to separate them from what he sees as Las Casas's ideology of colonialism.[63] To me, however, at least a few of these passages appear strangely free from the concerns of both religious and cultural conversion; they are detached, reflective, and indeed quite suggestive of some of the thoughts Montaigne was to record in his *Essays* thirty years later. Here, for example, is Las Casas speculating on the meaning of "barbarity" in the conclusion to his *Apologética historia*:

> A man is apt to be called barbarous, in comparison with another, because he is strange in his manner of speech and mispronounces the language of the other. . . . According to Strabo, Book XIV, this was the chief reason the Greeks called other peoples barbarous, that is, because they were mispronouncing the Greek language. But from this point of view, there is no man or race which is not barbarous with respect to some other man or race. . . . Thus, just as we esteemed these peoples of the Indies barbarous, so they considered us, because of not understanding us.[64]

The notion of heathenism does not enter into this reflection, in spite of the fact that it would seem the most readily available illustration of barbarity for someone in Las Casas's position. Rather, Las Casas moves to a higher level of abstraction—momentarily detaching himself both from the Indians and from the Christian culture to which he belongs—and observes that barbarity is an ethnocentric allegation, a claim that can understandably and simultaneously proceed in both directions upon the axis of alterity. To make such an observation, of course, is by no means wholly to escape one's own cultural conditioning or ethnocentrism, but it *is* to attain an angle of perception that allows for a more nuanced understanding of other peoples and cultures—an angle of perception that, if persistently maintained, can ultimately lead to the abandonment of ideas about absolute and transcultural values. This implicit comparativism is sounded elsewhere as well: "Let us now leave behind all these kingdoms, within which if we were perceptive enough we would see more things in their polity and such order that we would be better off learning from them how to perfect our own than insulting theirs."[65] Las Casas does *not* consistently maintain these levels of perception, but the fact that he is capable of achieving them belies the frequent criticism that he is unable to move beyond a Christian/heathen polarity.

Todorov has written that "in the best of cases, the Spanish authors speak well *of* the Indians, but with very few exceptions they do not speak *to* the Indians. Now, it is only by speaking to the other (not giving orders but engaging in dialogue) that *I* can acknowledge *him* as subject, comparable to what I am myself".[66] Todorov recognizes Las Casas, obviously, as an author who speaks well *of* the Indians, but he does not grant that the priest speaks *to* them. However, such passages as those quoted above clearly indicate that Las Casas—at least some of the time—conceptualized native Americans and Europeans in a dialogical relationship. To acknowledge that Europeans might learn from Indians or that Indians might regard a European custom or language as barbaric is to acknowledge Indians as perceiving and reasoning subjects. To reach such a conclusion is not, of course, to attain an "objective" vantage point, nor is it to move beyond assimilationism in the act of knowing. But it *is* to move beyond the appropriative narcissism of, say, Cortés—who appears to have seen a great deal of Spain in Mexico—or the naive and uncritical *tabula rasa* view typified by Columbus. In short, Las Casas's acknowledgment of *equality* is not followed by a conclusion of *identity* as unquestioningly and unhesitantly as Todorov maintains. Rather, it is followed by some recognition of difference and separateness, however brief or constricted. But for Las Casas, who was engaged in a fight against the brutal exploitation, *de facto* enslavement, and possible genocidal annihilation of native American peoples, stressing an unqualified identity seemed more likely to save lives than pointing to aspects of cultural difference.[67] We must set Las Casas's writings in this context; otherwise we risk the myopic mistake of attacking his words while ignoring his actions.

Far more significant than Las Casas's conclusion of identity is his prior acknowledgment of equality. And perhaps no better brief statement of this acknowledgment may be found than in the *Apologética historia*:

> Thus the entire human race is one; all men are alike with respect to their creation and the things of nature, and none is born already taught. . . . All the races of the world have understanding and will and that which results from these two faculties

in man—that is, free choice. And consequently, all have the power and ability or capacity . . . to be instructed, persuaded, and attracted to order and reason and laws and virtue and all goodness.[68]

By quoting such a passage I do not mean to deny that the perception of genuine cultural differences led Las Casas to subscribe to a theory of cultural evolution; Pagden has admirably discussed this subscription, and there is no question that it qualifies, on circumstantial grounds, Las Casas's assertion of European-Amerindian equality.[69] In effect, the positioning of native Americans in an evolutionary model amounts to an infantilization, and this is a form of subjection.[70] But in contrast to the infantilization implied by, say, Cortés's writings, Las Casas's version insists that the ultimate equality of American natives must serve as a guarantee for their freedom from slavery and exploitation. If it is true, as Margaret T. Hodgen has asserted, that "an unfavorable verdict upon the newly discovered peoples [of America and Africa] was far more often employed than a favorable one" by Renaissance Europeans, then Las Casas's position, as represented by the preceding quotation, is all the more admirable for its rarity.[71] Rationalist critiques such as Todorov's, while intriguing, are in my estimation somewhat misleading in that they suggest: (1) that writers can divorce their thoughts from the exigencies of the political and rhetorical situations in which they are enmeshed, and (2) that humans can escape assimilationism in their attempts at comprehension. Las Casas granted American natives equality with Europeans on the grounds of Christian doctrine, which is to say that he ultimately relied on faith in a particular moral and metaphysical system rather than on acts of empirical reasoning assumed to yield objectivity of judgment. For all his Scholastic training, he undoubtedly had a deep conviction regarding the finite limits of reason. But in contrast to Sepúlveda, who relied on a source of authority promoting separation and subordination, Las Casas chose to rely on an authority promoting—however idealistically—integration and basic equality.

THE SAVAGE, THE CIVIL, AND THE NEW-HISTORICAL-CULTURAL-POETICAL

Las Casas would undoubtedly be regarded as an "essentialist" by the majority of critics aligned with the varied interpretive practices of new historicism, cultural poetics, or Marxian cultural materialism.[72] He would be seen, that is, as a writer who insists on the existence of an intrinsic and transcultural human nature, a spiritual and behavioral core that up to some unknown point resists social manipulation and is, additionally, self-aware. Michel Foucault, who has claimed that "man is an invention of recent date," is one of the principal twentieth-century challengers of this essentialist view.[73] By "man" Foucault means the concept of a fundamentally unified humanity, a human race whose every member is endowed with "primary reality," "density," and a transhistorical, self-generative core of being. Foucault disputes that such a conception existed until after the demise of what he calls the "Classical episteme."[74] Jonathan Dollimore, who relies heavily on Foucault in his theoretical formulation of cultural materialism, draws on this essentialist definition of "man" and insists on a further distinction between Christian essentialism and essentialist humanism—the latter being primarily a product of the Enlightenment, the former a much earlier notion inseparable from the Christian etiology of the Incarnation and the salvageability of all human souls.[75] Christian essentialism, in Dollimore's view, stems from a belief that the human soul is "metaphysically derivative," and thus incompatible with the "autonomous, unified self-generating subject postulated by essentialist humanism."[76] But the two essentialisms are alike inasmuch as both posit a fixed and interior human substance; neither admits that human identity is principally constructed by exterior social, economic, and historical forces. Dollimore's "anti-essentialism," then, involves a critique of the non-contingency or ahistoricism of essentialist views combined with a reliance upon the Foucaultian notion of discontinuous history, of the radical difference of earlier historical epistemes. Yet he concludes, among other things, that certain Renaissance writers bear a great resemblance to certain nineteenth- and twentieth-century theorists: Montaigne prefiguring Louis Althusser, for instance (in their versions of the "decentring of man"), and Niccolò Machiavelli prefiguring Karl Marx (in their concern with the philosophy of praxis).[77]

The project of stressing the strangeness of the past—a project which has engaged the energies of such cultural critics as Hayden White and Stephen Greenblatt in addition to Foucault—is admirable in its determined refusal to construct what Jean Howard has aptly termed "narratives of continuity." And, as Howard has pointed out, this project has produced remarkable results.[78] For instance, in Foucault's search for "discontinuities, ruptures, gaps," his rejection of such explanatory models as dialectical progression, and his contribution to the notion of "discourse" as a network of thought, writing, and lived practices permeated by ideology, he has shaken up traditional historical methodology and valuably refocused the interests and concerns of historiographical theorists and practitioners.[79] Still, as Foucault himself has acknowledged, any writer is historically situated and thus conditioned by cultural norms and presuppositions; no one is capable of wholly avoiding a projection of the present into the past. Just as all Renaissance ethnographic accounts involve a degree of assimilationism, all historical constructs are likewise assimilative: They necessarily rely upon attempts to describe and understand the past that are grounded in ways of knowing derived from attempts to describe and understand the present.[80] It is self-evident that "objectivity" in such projects is an illusory goal; as James Clifford has written, there is "no Archimedian point from which to represent the world."[81] This is not to suggest, however, that we are immediately reduced thereby to a banal relativism, nor to claim that there are not comparative degrees both of ethnographic accuracy and cultural narcissism; Las Casas's representation of American natives, for instance, is preferable to either Cortés's or Sepúlveda's. But inasmuch as particularized human subjectivity is an inescapable condition of the act of knowing, on a priori grounds any attempt to avoid perceptions of continuity in ethnographic or historical representation has intrinsic limitations.[82] As Greenblatt has put it—in a somewhat different context—"if I wanted to hear the voice of the other, I had to hear my own voice."[83]

I suggest, then, that any perception of the early modern era as a period similar to our own in its tendency to question and subvert dominant ideologies is inevitably a domestication of the past, an appropriative perception of continuity.[84] This is not to say that it is an incorrect or unhelpful perception; to argue that we cannot fully detach ourselves from our historical situation is by no means to argue that our observations about the past—or about the cultural other—are without value. But it *is* to stress the very contingency of perception that seems central to cultural materialist and new historicist projects and yet sometimes appears to be ignored in practice. If Montaigne is to be read as a precursor of Althusser, for example, and thereby understood as a Renaissance writer in whom an implicit anti-essentialism finds articulation, it is crucial to point out that such a reading clearly relies upon an appropriative projection of the present into the past and is thus a practice explicitly discouraged by Foucault and other advocates of historical discontinuity.[85]

More generally, the frequent readiness among politically-oriented Renaissance critics to abandon all idealist philosophy in favor of materialism leads to a premature jettisoning of certain notions that might contribute to a more careful and nuanced theoretical position. As a case in point I want to briefly discuss Immanuel Kant.[86] Materialist critics ordinarily reject Kantian idealism on the grounds that it is based upon and legitimates a form of essentialism; Kant argues that the perception of phenomenal reality is structured by categories of consciousness inherent to the human mind. But such a rejection conveniently ignores the fact that Kant also places great emphasis on the ultimate unknowability of noumenal reality, "things in themselves." This fundamental skepticism regarding the human capacity to know truly the underlying nature of things—as opposed to their appearances, their immanence—is a central thesis in his *Critique of Pure Reason* and, moreover, a conceptual position bearing remarkable similarities to Montaigne's earlier justification of epistemological skepticism in the "Apology for Raymond Sebond." Montaigne argues, for example (in a passage that in some ways anticipates the much later claims of phenomenology and uncertainty theory in physics), that most human knowledge is radically qualified due to its reliance upon the imperfect faculties of perception:

> Now, since our condition [*nostre estat*] accommodates things to itself and transforms them according to itself, we no longer know what things are in truth; for nothing comes to us except falsified and altered by our senses. When the compass, the square, and the ruler are off, all the proportions drawn from them, all the buildings erected by their measure, are also necessarily imperfect and defective. The uncertainty of our senses makes everything they produce uncertain . . . Our conception [*Nostre fantasie*] is not itself applied to foreign objects, but is conceived through the mediation of the senses; and the senses do not comprehend the foreign object, but only their own impressions [*leur propres passions*]. And thus the conception and semblance we form is not of the object, but only of the impression and effect made on the sense; which impression and the object are different things. Wherefore whoever judges by appearances judges by something other than the object.[87]

It is true that Montaigne's skepticism differs from Kant's in that it never advances beyond the stage of attributing fallibility to the perceiving subject, but in its basic questioning of our ability to know things *en verité* it certainly shares a fundamental assumption with Kantian epistemology. I do not quarrel, of course, with either the standard characterization of Kant as an essentialist or with the predominant emphasis in literary criticism on Kant's aesthetics rather than his epistemology and metaphysics. But Kant's distinction between phenomenal and noumenal reality and his skepticism regarding our ability to know the latter are concepts valuable to a criticism hoping to move beyond positivist assumptions about history. Moreover, to the extent that these concepts exist prior to Kant's postulation of a structuring and shaping consciousness (as opposed to a merely receptive consciousness), they are separable from his transcendental idealism. Perhaps a reluctance to be charged with critical eclecticism plays some role in any wholesale rejection of Kant, but at the same time Kant's own famous admission that Hume awakened him from his "dogmatic slumber" hints strongly at the inevitable eclecticism in all philosophical systems.[88]

One of the principal consequences of a deep skepticism about the human ability to know Kantian noumena is a need to justify knowing on the grounds of belief. In a religious context this is fideism, but the fideistic impulse exists on the epistemological level as well: It amounts to a recognition that while doubt always obtains about the reliability of human reason and perception, and thus about the nature and extent of what can be known, we can nonetheless believe through the agency of discrete—and frequently unconscious—acts of faith. It is true that Kant argues that the very existence of a stratum of noumenal reality is a "critical deduction" rather than a fideistic inference, but it is also true that he explicitly acknowledges the dimension of the non-rational: "I have therefore found it necessary to deny knowledge, in order to make room for faith."[89] Transferred analogically to the realm of discursive formations, these Kantian qualifications suggest both that linguistic referentiality is assumptive rather than demonstrative and that knowledge claims about specific sociohistorical events, conditions, customs, or relations are first and foremost belief claims: human constructs based upon inferences from a finite range of phenomenal perceptions—perceptions, so to speak, of the "raw data" of history. And when these belief claims, in turn, are viewed as constituent parts of an encounter in which further possibilities for meaning and thus further belief claims are created—the encounter of the historically-situated reader with the historical narrative or text—it becomes abundantly clear that any pretense to objective knowledge has grown tenuous to the point of nonexistence.

To a certain extent this argument is simply a restatement of the fundamental principle upon which reader-response and reception theories are constructed: No reading of a text can have "objective" status, since each reader—or community of readers—brings different ideas and preconceptions to the text, and the text itself is a linguistic artifact with an inherently complex texture that may present all sorts of ambiguities, indeterminacies, and subtle resistances.[90] Indeed, as Stanley Fish has argued, the very terms "objective" and "subjective" quickly lapse into questionable worth when closely scrutinized, since they assume, without challenging the assumption, that "interpreters and their objects are two different kinds of acontextual entities."[91] But my point is that Kantian skepticism regarding our ability to know "things in themselves" is relevant to cultural materialist and new historicist critical practices; it supports their own assumptions about the constructed nature of historical narratives and contexts. Moreover, it contributes to the problematization of "background" and "foreground" as concepts in discourse analysis. As Greenblatt writes, referring to his tendency to adduce cultural practices in order to illuminate works of art, "It is difficult to keep those practices in the background if the very concept of historical background has been called into question."[92] The dimension of Kantian skepticism that I have isolated need not be accompanied by all the trappings of transcendental idealism; on the contrary, like René Descartes's *cogito*— whose validity is by no means compromised by the subsequent rationalist structure that he builds around and upon it—Kant's principle that our knowledge has radical limitations may be usefully separated from the remainder of his architectonic. This principle is in fact congruent with the aims and assumptions of contemporary historicist criticism, and thus I find a positioning such as the complete rejection of Kant a needless overreaction. Edward Pechter has written that "It is impossible to serve Kant and Marx, say the new historicists, but the young [William] Empson did just that."[93] I would add that many critics aligned with new historicist and cultural materialist practices are doing it too.

Kant's combination of epistemological skepticism and affirmation of the non-rational is hardly unique in Western thought; Saint Augustine, Blaise Pascal, and Sören Kierkegaard are all well known exemplars of similar conceptual moves, and Montaigne—one of the thinkers Dollimore aligns himself with—epitomizes this balancing and anti-totalizing tendency in the early modern period.[94] But I single out Kant because he is characterized by Dollimore and others as being wholly antithetical to the assumptions of cultural materialism. In fact, as I have shown, one of Kant's fundamental epistemological principles is quite congenial to these assumptions. For if "history" is taken to be not only a realm of retrievable facts but also a set of interpretive constructions—if, as White claims, historical narratives are in some sense "verbal fictions, the contents of which are as much *invented* as *found*"—then a profound dubiety regarding the capacity of human reason to know objective reality is entirely fitting and appropriate as an epistemological stance.[95] Indeed, it is inescapable; any stance more positivistic in outlook is unacceptable. Kant's skepticism is fundamentally incompatible with the naive and antiquarian strategies of older forms of historicist criticism.

Just as one's historical present plays an inevitable role in determining one's perception and representation of the past, then, one's cultural identity plays an equally crucial role in determining one's perception and representation of the cultural other. As a corollary of the first point, I would stress that even when we encounter, say, a Renaissance writer discussing topics in contemporary Renaissance history, we can never naively assume that an "objective" historical representation inevitably results. On the contrary, we must suppose that textual opacities arising from historical and cultural contingency will always manifest themselves—just as they do in historical accounts written four hundred years later. And, to further complicate matters, though we may readily accept the Althusserian notion that all representations of reality are inscribed by ideology, and thus stamped with the mark of their historical moment, it does not necessarily follow that: (1) this ideological inscription is clearly separable from other accretions in the text (including structures and representations freely chosen by the writer), or that (2) as readers of the text we will be able to sharply distinguish this ideological inscription from our own imported ideas and presuppositions.[96] When we read Las Casas or Montaigne on the conquest of Mexico, for instance, can we clearly separate our own postcolonial repugnance at the cruelty of European invaders from the sentiments these authors express? Or can we separate these authors' respect for the indigenous civilizations of America from a small but undeniable tradition of respect for and curiosity about the cultural other that stretches back in European writing to Homer, Herodotus, and Tacitus?[97] I am not convinced that we can, and thus I think that we are constrained to speak not of "history" but of "histories"—the ones that we ourselves participate in when we read such texts as Las Casas's chronicles or Montaigne's meditations. And when we speak of histories, are we not in some sense speaking of fictions?[98] We see here a clear instance of the breakdown of the ultimately artificial set of distinctions between history and literature, between context and text. As poststructuralist theory has suggested through its insistent problematization of the notion of discourse, these pairs of terms merge in their status as mutually-influential forms of representation, forms inevitably engaged in a relation of reciprocity.

With respect to the second point just posed—that one inevitably sees aspects of one's culture or oneself in the cultural other—the notion of the interpenetration of text and context yields a valuable starting place from which to proceed. If it is true, as I have argued, that one can no more avoid perceptions of continuity in ethnographic writing than one can avoid narratives of continuity in historical writing, then even in cases where the other is perceived as radically different—lacking human subjectivity, for example—this very difference is structured by the perceiving subject's habitual notions of margin and boundary. Chanca or Sepúlveda can deny full human status to American natives precisely because these natives are seen to exist in a realm beyond the conventional limits attributed to humanity. Las Casas, in contrast, can grant them full human status because he construes these limits differently. In both cases—and I rely in part upon Clifford Geertz here—

interpretive acts are clearly of central importance;[99] and interpretation, however much influenced by internalized ideology and social norms, is still at some level a deeply subjective intellectual motion—a motion frequently accompanied, moreover, by choices that are, strictly speaking, non-rational: in short, acts of faith.[100] If this were not the case, how would we account, at the most fundamental level, for the differences between the choices of Sepúlveda and Las Casas? I think, then, that perceptions of continuity in accounts of the other are not only inescapable but in many respects epistemologically fideistic as well. They may not always be recognized as such by their representers, but we, as interpreters of these representations, can only stand to gain by acknowledging their assimilative nature and their implicit reliance upon beliefs beyond the ken of reason.

When early modern writers, then, speak of the savagery or civility of an ethnic or cultural other, they may be said to be engaged in a discourse conditioned by two fundamental principles: first, that their conception of the savage or the civil is, whether they recognize it or not, culturally determined, though subject to significant variations due to the influence of subcultural interpretive communities; and second, that their attribution of savagery or civility is at some level non-rational, since the other, like the historical past or Kantian noumenal reality, is ultimately unknowable through positivist or empirical strategies. Just as Las Casas's acknowledgment of native Americans' complete equality with Europeans implies an abandonment of strict reason in favor of the adoption of a view based in part on faith, any claim regarding the savagery or civility of native Americans likewise involves a non-rational element. Such a judgment, after all, is in the end just as much an estimation of the cultural and ontological status of the other as is a judgment of equality or difference. I do not mean to overemphasize the non-rationality of these judgments—as though human reason were wholly useless in their formation—but I do want to insist that if we accept the skepticism of new historicist attitudes toward unbiased, comprehensive, "objective" knowledge of history and the other, we must grant that the attribution of terms like savagery and civility involves epistemological fideism.

Both "savagery" and "civility" are nouns employed to characterize modes of human existence and behavior. Both are understood relationally: They derive meaning from their contrast with other characterizations of existence. Frequently the two words are understood in relation to each other, especially in a relation of mutual exclusion: Civility precludes savagery, and vice versa. The Puritan celebrant of English colonization, Samuel Purchas, perfectly exemplifies this Manichean opposition when he asks, early in the seventeenth century, "Can a Leopard change his spots? Can a Savage remayning a Savage be civill? Were not wee our selves made and not borne civill in our Progenitors dayes? and were not Caesars Britaines as brutish as Virginians?"[101] But a relation of mutual exclusivity does not always obtain. What is important is that the ideas conveyed by these words are capable of evolution. Indeed, part of my argument is that the ideas *did* evolve—and evolve substantially—as a result of early modern discourse about the New World and its inhabitants. For the remainder of this chapter I would like to discuss these ideas in somewhat greater detail, always keeping in mind that the contingencies I have described impinge both upon their application and upon our understanding of their meaning.

"Savagery," even more than "barbarity," suggests a rude and uncultivated condition of life.[102] The word has connotations of cruelty and violence, thus facilitating its application to people presumed to be cannibalistic, but its principal meaning in our context is that of pre-civil life, life before the formation of the *civis* and a stable social order.[103] As such, it comprehends both "noble" and "ignoble" forms. In either form, however, savage peoples are by Renaissance standards peoples without government, laws, commerce, or enduring social institutions providing guarantees against or restraints upon instinctual behavior. They are nomadic peoples, commonly supposed to be living close to the state of nature and either unable or unwilling to choose an existence founded upon self-discipline, large-scale social cooperation, and settled habits of life.[104] It depends almost wholly upon one's point of view and rhetorical intentions whether this condition is perceived as a blessing or a curse.

Ignoble savagery, which according to Hodgen and other writers is the most common Renaissance pronouncement upon American natives, is consubstantial with views alleging these natives' fierceness, instability, promiscuity, idleness, and unregeneracy.[105] Moreover, it is frequently aligned with the conventional equation that as the child is to the adult so is the savage human to the civil.[106] Such a notion, while in one respect sanctioning the infantilization of the cultural other, also suggests a natural and inevitable progression from savagery to civility—in short, a theory of cultural evolution or human social development. Hence the commonly held Renaissance view that the adult natives of the New World, perceived as incapable of civil behavior, are in fact childlike and permanently stunted in their growth. Ignoble savagery is also linked by tradition to views maintaining that remote parts of the world are hostile wildernesses, places where the forces of nature reign unchecked and the wild growth of plants and animals is matched by that of humans.[107] These views, in turn, reinforce stereotypes of the savage as bestial and even demonic. Dionyse Settle, for instance, writes in 1577 of the seizure of an elderly native woman along the coast of Baffin Island: "The olde wretch, whome diuers of oure Saylers supposed to be eyther a Diuell, or a Witch, had her buskins plucked off, to see if she were clouen footed." And James VI of Scotland—soon to be England's James I—offers contemporary grounding for such suppositions when he claims in his *Daemonologie* (1597) that the "wild partes of the worlde" provide Satan with his best opportunity to further the cause of evil, since "where the Deuill findes greatest ignorance and barbaritie, there assayles he grosseliest."[108] As for bestiality, we have seen in the cases of Chanca, Pigafetta, Ortiz, Gante, Oviedo, and Sepúlveda that perceptions of the savage as closer to nature than the European quickly modulate into perceptions of the savage as subhuman. The dividing lines between the attributive zones of ignoble savagery, bestiality, and demonism are, at best, ill-defined.

Given this, it should come as no surprise that savagery is sometimes equated with pre-cultural—as opposed to merely pre-civil—existence, as it frequently is, for example, in the writings of Columbus and Martyr. Not that early modern writers use the words "culture" and "cultural" in the ways that we do now, but one may infer from their interest in and frequent discussions of "custom," "creed," and "tongue" that they have ideas in mind that parallel our ideas of culture.[109] Savages, seen as beings destitute of culture, become *tabulae rasae*, truly "unaccommodated" humans. They may or may not be capable of inscription with European religion and manners; and even when they are, their transformation to civility will always be marred by the presence of vestigial remnants of savagery—or, at the very least, by the fact that, unlike Europeans, they have had to undergo a radical transformation in the first place rather than a simple process of maturation and societal adjustment. As Mary Rowlandson so clearly demonstrates in her famous seventeenth-century captivity narrative, "praying Indians" were "Indians" first—with all their Satanic attributes—and only accidentally and adjectivally Christian.[110] According to this strategy of characterization, full equality with "civilized" individuals is never a real possibility. In the late eighteenth century, enshrined within a document claiming that "all Men are created equal," Thomas Jefferson's words regarding native Americans rely upon a closely-related assumption: King George III has "endeavoured to bring on the Inhabitants of our Frontiers, the merciless Indian Savages, whose known Rule of Warfare, is an undistinguished Destruction, of all Ages, Sexes, and Conditions."[111]

Noble savagery is an alternative conclusion for Renaissance thinkers; it reverses the conventional value structure, placing a higher premium on civil or societal "unaccommodation" than on civil inheritance. Moreover, in its later maturation into a literary trope—as evidenced, for example, in Aphra Behn's *Oroonoko*, Voltaire's *L'Ingénu*, and Denis Diderot's *Supplément au Voyage de Bougainville*—it involves an implicit critique of the civil barbarity or corruption of European religion and society. Often, in fact, this critique serves as the work's raison d'être, and cultural others appear in the text less because of the author's genuine interest in them than because their very presence becomes a device employed by the author: the savage-as-critic motif. In spite of the euphoric accounts of American natives common in the early years of New World exploration, however, the noble savage view is always a minority opinion. In the first place—and probably most important—it subverts standard Judeo-Christian doctrine inasmuch as it denies the myth of the Fall and insists that, far from exacerbating human depravity, life in a state of nature preserves the innate goodness and innocence of humans. Civil society, rather than nature, becomes the source of corruption on earth, and any progressive or providential conceptions of history are immediately nullified. In addition, the noble savage view has further subversive implications in that it hints at what often seems an embarrassing atavistic yearning in its very adherents; it suggests that they are somehow deficient in their appreciation of their own society—less thoroughly inscribed by its dominant ideologies, perhaps— and thus, as malcontents, less reliable in their judgments than, for instance, adherents of ignoble savage views.

Nonetheless, the idea of noble savagery, with its emphasis on positive human attributes such as courage, generosity, honesty, and fidelity, approaches more closely than any other form of savagery to the idea of civility. But it is still fundamentally different insofar as it stresses the unlearned and innate character of these traits. Civility, in contrast, stresses education and breeding, refinement and discipline.[112] In short, as exemplified in Orlando's admission of his breach of "smooth civility" in *As You Like It* (2.7.96), it stresses art. Peoples perceived as civil are assumed not only to possess the capacities for rational thought and written verbal expression, but an ability and desire to live together with others in complex social formations.[113] They create laws, systems of exchange, forms of political authority, and societal institutions such as marriage and the division of labor; they build towns, practice animal husbandry, and harvest planted crops. They are, in a word, citizens.[114] Moreover, they are inheritors of an exportable commodity: As Sir Walter Ralegh writes in his *History of the World*, "From them [the Egyptians], the Greekes, then barbarous, received Civilitie."[115] Such a view of civility, in theory at least, has the potential to coexist readily with an underlying conviction of cultural relativism. In fact, this view is usually understood as being in implicit opposition to a *tabula rasa* notion of savagery, thereby reinforcing the commonplace supposition of inevitable human development toward a preordained social and religious end. Still, it is important to point out that an understanding of "civility" not solely as the social condition aligned with Christian culture but as something akin to the twentieth-century understanding of "civilization" is inchoate in the Renaissance.[116] And it is worth noting that the attribution of such civility to American natives finds expression not only in New World sojourners such as Las Casas and Old World meditatives such as Montaigne, but also in practical men of affairs such as the Spanish jurist Francisco de Vitoria, who writes in his *De Indiis recenter inventis, relectio prior [On the Indians Lately Discovered]* (1539) that among the natives of America "there is a certain method in their affairs, for they have polities which are orderly arranged and they have definite marriage and magistrates, overlords, laws, and workshops, and a system of exchange, all of which call for the use of reason; they also have a kind of religion."[117]

Later, "civility" weakens considerably. Toward the end of the seventeenth century, for instance, Behn appears to intend something like "humane consideration" or "gallantry" when she narrates Trefry's declaration of love to Imoinda and then informs us that "The Company laugh'd at his Civility to a Slave."[118] And by the latter part of the eighteenth century, James Boswell could be frustrated that Samuel Johnson was unwilling to let the word mean simply "Politeness; complaisance; elegance of behavior"; Johnson insisted on retaining the older and stronger sense of "Freedom from barbarity; the state of being civilized," and moreover refused to admit the word "civilization" in any other than a highly technical legal sense.[119] But Johnson was conservative in his linguistic opinions, consciously committed to preserving traditional usages and to restraining rapid denotative shifts. Boswell, we may assume, offered his advice to Johnson on the basis of actual contemporary use of "civility." What I find interesting, however, is that even had Johnson agreed with Boswell, he would still have been committing himself to a strongly ethnocentric view of civilization; and this demonstrates, I think, the enduring power of the concept of civility as almost indissolubly (though often covertly) linked to Christianity. To cite just one Renaissance example in support of this, I quote from Thomas Hacket's 1568 English translation of André Thevet's description of the Tupinamba inhabitants of coastal Brazil:

> [They are] a maruelous strange wild and brutish people, without Fayth, without Lawe, without Religion, and without any ciuilitie: but liuing like brute beasts, as nature hath brought them out, eating herbes and rootes, being alwayes naked as

well women as men, untill such time as being more visited and frequented of Christians, they may peraduenture leaue this brutish liuing, and lerne to liue after a more ciuill and humayne manner.[120]

Here we find civility explicitly distinguished from religion, but the fact that religion is similarly distinguished from faith suggests a porousness and interdependence to these categories. Generally speaking, the concept of civility is seldom employed in the Renaissance without being contextualized by religion, and particularly Christianity.[121] In other words, "civility" usually means "civil behavior allied with Christian practice," just as Thevet's "without Religion" means "without true religion"—which is of course to say, "without Christianity" (or, in Thevet's case, Counter-Reformation Roman Catholicism). Thus, in spite of the fact that "civility" has the potential in the Renaissance to suggest the idea now expressed by "civilization," it normally conveys the more limited idea of a sociocultural formation structured by Christianity and consequently superior to any alternative formation. Civil humans, according to conventional opinion, have not only the choice but the obligation to pass on their civility to those who are savage; their civility, after all, is perceived not as a relative but an absolute inheritance.

Among the early writers on America I have discussed thus far, only a few—and in particular, Las Casas—show signs of penetrating these rather schematic distinctions among kinds of savagery and civility; only a few seem capable of allowing that cultural difference, religious "unaccommodation," and human equality can all coexist. Such an outlook thoroughly complicates conventional understandings of savage and civil forms of existence. But even Las Casas, insofar as he ultimately concludes *identity* after acknowledging *equality*, simplifies the record of his perceptions in such a manner as to accord more effectively with his immediate purpose and to communicate more comprehensibly with his audience. It remains for later writers—writers less immediately engaged in altering the material conditions of human existence than was Las Casas—to scrutinize, refashion, and refine the ideas of savagery and civility embedded within the discourse of European encounters with the New World. Montaigne, Spenser, and Shakespeare are among the early modern writers who do this in the most thoughtful, illuminating, and provocative ways.

In summary, then: Savagery and civility, like equality and difference, are evaluative attributions tightly linked to cultural identity and epistemologically grounded in perceptions of continuity. These perceptions rely on culturally determined margins and boundaries and are thus inescapably ethnocentric; to deny their ultimately assimilative nature is to deny that thoughts ultimately emanate from a culturally contingent human subjectivity. Moreover, these perceptions—in their subtle linguistic transformation into allegations and verbal representations—partake of a non-rational motion of thought, a fideistic impulse. This is because they are almost always set forth as knowledge claims about the other when in fact, on a priori grounds, they may be shown to be belief claims. Indeed, as Montaigne implies, humans seldom know themselves, let alone other people: "there is as much difference between us and ourselves as between us and others."[122]

An "unaccommodated" man may be, like *King Lear*'s Poor Tom, a man deprived of shelter, clothing, conventional sustenance, linguistic normality, and the company of humans. But unaccommodation may take other forms as well. It may be, for instance, civil unaccommodation, as in standard Renaissance conceptions of savagery. It may be cultural unaccommodation, as in the more naive accounts of American natives typified by the writings of Columbus and Martyr. It may even be human unaccommodation, as in the analyses of Chanca, Pigafetta, and Sepúlveda. Or—following Marx, Foucault, and Dollimore—it may be essential unaccommodation: the view that humans lack an innate and transhistorical core of being. In all cases, the emphasis is on deprivation, and on how deprivation works to structure and define identity. My goal in the following chapters is to allow this metaphor of unaccommodation to assist me in a study of the ways in which the concepts of savagery and civility—and, indeed, many related concepts which find employment in the perception and characterization of human beings—evolved through specific historical and literary examinations in the Renaissance.

2

Montaigne's New World

MONTAIGNE, LÉRY, LAS CASAS

Michel de Montaigne was seventeen years old at the time of the momentous Valladolid Disputation between Bartolomé de Las Casas and Juan Ginés de Sepúlveda. He was twenty-nine when he engaged in his famous conversation at Rouen with a Tupinamba native from the coast of what is now Brazil—the conversation from which he drew a significant part of his information for "Of cannibals." He was sufficiently curious about New World comestibles to sample "a certain white substance like preserved coriander" which was eaten there instead of bread (he found the taste of cassava "sweet and a little flat"), and his chateau at Montaigne was ornamented with specimens of American hammocks, ropes, wrist guards, and wooden swords, as well as with large canes "open at one end" by means of which New World natives were able to "keep time in their dances."[1] In short, Montaigne was surrounded by American presences. Both because of the accident of his historical existence in mid-sixteenth-century Europe, and—more important—because he often chose to train his attention upon transatlantic subjects, his life and writings are inseparably associated with the New World. His essays contain dozens of references to America, and some of them, including "Of cannibals," "Of coaches," and the "Apology for Raymond Sebond," involve extended meditations upon American themes. Indeed, even Montaigne's brief note "To the Reader" at the beginning of the *Essays* shows how prominent a place thoughts about the New World held in its author's mind: "Had I been placed among those nations which are said to live still in the sweet freedom of nature's first laws, I assure you I should very gladly have portrayed myself here entire and wholly naked. Thus, reader, I am myself the matter of my book; you would be unreasonable to spend your leisure on so frivolous and vain a subject. So farewell. Montaigne, this first day of March, fifteen hundred and eighty" (2). In the more than four centuries since these lines were written, many readers have undoubtedly felt that notwithstanding his disclaimer, Montaigne *did* portray himself "entire and wholly naked" in the *Essays*—and this in turn suggests that in the peace and solitude of his study, Montaigne was able to imaginatively project himself and his prospective audience into the atmosphere of those same *pays lointains* where people lived under Nature's "sweet freedom."

Montaigne's sources on the New World have been a matter of some uncertainty.[2] The allusion in "Of cannibals" to the French colonizing ventures in Brazil organized by Admiral Gaspard de Coligny and headed by Nicolas Durand de Villegagnon suggests that Montaigne was familiar with the well-known accounts of these ventures composed by André Thevet, Nicolas Barré, and, in particular, Jean de Léry; indeed, other details in the *Essays* confirm this suggestion.[3] The account, for instance, by the Franciscan friar Thevet, *Les singularitéz de la France antarctique [The New Found Worlde, or Antarctike, 1568]* (Paris, 1558), enjoyed immense popularity during the late sixteenth century and— though now recognized to be the work of "a great liar"—garnered in its day the recommendations of such notables as Pierre de Ronsard and Charles de Guise.[4] It offers a generally unfavorable portrayal of the Tupinamba natives of coastal Brazil, calling them "the moste cruelleste, and inhumayne people that are in America," but admits elsewhere that these people are capable of keeping promises and performing "other charitable and honest deedes (more than among Christians)."[5] Léry's book, in contrast, depicts the Brazilians in a far more positive light. The *Histoire d'un voyage fait en la terre du Bresil, autrement dite Amerique [History of a Voyage to the Land of Brazil]* was published in Geneva in 1578, twenty years after Thevet's account, and may well have been fresh in Montaigne's mind as he composed "Of cannibals."[6] A Huguenot parson, Léry moves strongly in the direction of a critique of contemporary European society, famously reminiscing, for instance, that "although I have always loved my country and do even now, . . . I often regret that I am not among the savages, in whom (as I have amply shown in this narrative) I have known more frankness than in many over here, who, for their condemnation, bear the title of 'Christian.'"[7] However, just as Thevet includes moments of praise for the Indians within his overall condemnation, Léry occasionally reveals a deep and thoroughly Calvinistic skepticism in spite of his generally positive estimation; he concludes his description of Tupi religion, for example, with the following judgment: "And there you have the inconstancy of this poor people, a fine example of the corrupt nature of man. . . . this is a people accursed and abandoned by God, if there be any such under the heavens."[8] As Frank

Lestringant writes, a judgment such as this "should prevent us from simply seeing in [Léry's] work a first example of the myth of the Noble Savage, even if it does first announce and form a point of departure for this myth."[9] But perhaps Léry's most characteristic critical trajectory may be illustrated by the following passages from his discussions, respectively, of female nudity, cannibalism, and hospitality among the Tupinamba:

> While there is ample cause to judge that, beyond the immodesty of it, seeing these women naked would serve as a predictable enticement to concupiscence; yet, to report what was commonly perceived at the time, this crude nakedness in such a woman is much less alluring than one might expect. And I maintain that the elaborate attire, paint, wigs, curled hair, great ruffs, farthingales, robes upon robes, and all the infinity of trifles with which the women and girls over here disguise themselves and of which they never have enough, are beyond comparison the cause of more ills than the ordinary nakedness of the savage women—whose natural beauty is by no means inferior to that of the others. . . . I do not mean, however, to contradict what the Holy Scripture says about Adam and Eve, who, after their sin, were ashamed when they recognized that they were naked, nor do I wish in any way that this nakedness be approved; . . . But what I have said about these savages is to show that, while we condemn them so austerely for going about shamelessly with their bodies entirely uncovered, we ourselves, in sumptuous display, superfluity, and excess of our own costume, are hardly more laudable.

> I could add similar examples of the cruelty of the savages toward their enemies, but it seems to me that what I have said is enough to horrify you, indeed, to make your hair stand on end. Nevertheless, so that those who read these horrible things, practiced daily among these barbarous nations of the land of Brazil, may also think more carefully about the things that go on every day over here, among us: In the first place, if you consider in all candor what our big usurers do, sucking blood and marrow, and eating everyone alive—widows, orphans, and other poor people, whose throats it would be better to cut once and for all, than to make them linger in misery—you will say that they are even more cruel than the savages I speak of.

> When we finally found ourselves in a village called *Pauo*, where we had been on other occasions, we could not have received a better welcome than we had from the savages of that place. To begin with, when they heard us recount the troubles we had endured, and the danger we had been in . . . and when they saw the state we were in, all scratched up by the thorns that we had gone through in the

> wilderness, they took such pity on us that I can't help saying that the hypocritical
> welcomes of those over here who use only slippery speech for consolation of the
> afflicted is a far cry from the humanity of these people, who nonetheless we call
> "barbarians."[10]

In each case, Léry moves explicitly and insistently from "over there" to "over here," and in each case he merges ethnography with cultural critique, employing the savage-as-critic device without either idealizing the "savages" or neglecting their cultural specificity. Montaigne, in reading passages such as these, could not have helped but encounter a set of complex, ambivalent, ideologically-conditioned, and at times internally contradictory attitudes toward New World natives. And, as I will argue later in this chapter, these attitudes help to illuminate the complexity of Montaigne's own opinions—opinions that all too often have been radically simplified in the interests of representing Montaigne as an arch-primitivist and the founder of noble savagery.

Other New World accounts available to Montaigne included, most notably, Martin Fumée's 1568 rendering of López de Gómara's *Historia de las Indias* [*Pleasant Historie of the Conquest of Weast India*, 1578], and Urbain Chauveton's 1579 French translation of Girolamo Benzoni's *Historia del Mondo Nuovo* [*History of the New World*].[11] Less well-known books such as the Italian translation of Jacques Cartier's two narratives of Canadian exploration (1556) and Nicolas Le Challeux's history of French colonization in Florida were also available, as were Hans Staden's popular *True History of His Captivity* (1557) and French translations of such standard works as Christopher Columbus's "Letter to Santangel" (1493), Amerigo Vespucci's *Lettera [Letters]* (1503-05), and Peter Martyr's *De orbe novo [Decades of the New World]* (1530).[12] It seems quite likely, in addition, that Montaigne was familiar with the Spanish "Requerimiento" (1513); he alludes in "Of coaches" to the Spaniards' "usual declarations" (695) upon first encountering New World natives, and continues by offering what appears to be an ironic précis of the document.[13] Since Montaigne read Latin, he was by no means limited to geographical literature published in French—though it seems nonetheless that it was upon French editions that he primarily relied. To cite just one example of this apparent reliance, I quote from the previously-mentioned translation of Gómara by Fumée; the author is characterizing a tribe in the West Indies: "ces Indiens n'avoient aucuns vestemens, ni lettres, ni monoies, ni fer, ni grain, ni vin" [these Indians had neither clothes, nor letters, nor money, nor iron, nor grain, nor wine].[14] Montaigne, in turn, writes that the Tupinamba possess "nulle cognoissance de lettres; nulle science de nombres; . . . nuls vestemens; nulle agriculture; nul métal; nul usage de vin ou de bled" [no knowledge of letters, no science of numbers, . . . no clothes, no agriculture, no metal, no use of wine or wheat].[15] The verbal correspondences here are extremely close, and though I do not intend to suggest either that Montaigne relied upon Gómara as an authority about the Tupinamba (which he certainly was not), or that other non-French accounts of New World peoples may not have served with equal prominence as descriptive models, it is quite possible that the anaphoric trope of negative characterization employed by Gómara—and, in particular, the choice of negated customs and commodities—may have left an impression on Montaigne sufficiently strong that it found its way into the *Essays*.[16] Besides suggestive verbal parallels, however, numerous New World details and anecdotes provide nearly indisputable evidence that Montaigne carefully read both Benzoni and Gómara. His descriptions of the Inca postal system, of the altiplano road from Quito to Cuzco, of New World virgins not concealing their pudenda, of Mexican natives bearing presents to Cortés—these and other examples testify to Montaigne's reliance upon the Italian and Spanish authors in their recent French translations.[17]

One author normally left unmentioned in discussions of Montaigne's sources is Las Casas. Pierre Villey, for instance, does not include him in his "Table des Lectures de Montaigne" [Table of Montaigne's Readings]; Benjamin Keen and Bernard Weinberg stress Montaigne's reliance upon Léry, Thevet, and Gómara but say nothing of Las Casas; Marcel Bataillon writes that Montaigne knew Gómara and Benzoni but ignored Las Casas; Germán Arciniegas goes so far as to assert that "Apparently, Montaigne never read Bartholomew de Las Casas."[18] Yet a French translation of the Spanish priest's *Brevisima relación de la destruccion de las Indias [A Short Account of the Destruction of the Indies]* was published at Antwerp in 1579, and a sufficient number of anecdotal parallels exists between this notorious tract and various chapters in the *Essays* that it seems difficult to believe Montaigne was ignorant of its existence and contents.[19] Las Casas speaks frequently, for example, of the large dogs that the Spaniards brought to America for the purpose of terrorizing and sometimes killing the Indians; here we read him in the words of his Elizabethan translator: "they [the Spanish captains] taught their houndes, fierce dogs, to teare them in peeces at the first viewe, and in the space that one might say a Credo, assayled and deuoured an Indian as if it had been a swine. These dogges wrought great destructions and slaughters."[20] He also dwells extensively on the Spanish habit of burning alive intransigent natives—in one case relating the following hideous story:

> I once saw . . . four or five nobles lashed on grids and burning; I seem even to recall that there were two or three pairs of grids where others were burning, and

because they uttered such loud screams that they disturbed the captain's sleep, he ordered them to be strangled. And the constable, who was worse than an executioner, did not want to obey that order (and I know the name of that constable and know his relatives in Seville), but instead put a stick over the victims' tongues, so they could not make a sound, and he stirred up the fire, but not too much, so that they roasted slowly, as he liked.[21]

Montaigne, in turn, perhaps appropriates these examples and inflects them with his own ironic twist when he writes in "Of cannibals" that "there is more barbarity in eating a man alive than in eating him dead; and in tearing by tortures and the rack a body still full of feeling, in roasting a man bit by bit, in having him bitten and mangled by dogs and swine . . . than in roasting and eating him after he is dead" (155). Elsewhere, again quite possibly following the lead of Las Casas, he cites an instance of the immolation "all at once and in the same fire" of four hundred sixty Mexican men (697). And finally, against his cautionary observation that many of the Spaniards' ill-gotten gains were deservedly allowed by God "to be swallowed up by the sea in transit" (697), we may counterpoise Las Casas's conveniently moralized story of a Spanish vessel carrying a native king and his treasures back to Europe: "the vessel was lost at sea and with it were drowned many Christians along with the captive King, and in this shipwreck was lost a quantity of gold dust and gold nuggets weighing the equivalent of 3,600 castellanos. Such was God's vengeance for so many terrible injustices."[22]

But it is not only Las Casas's revulsion at the cruelty and greed of his fellow Europeans in America that finds a parallel in Montaigne's *Essays*;[23] it is also his dawning realization that barbarity lies in the eye of the beholder. He writes, for instance, in his *Apologética historia* that "A man is apt to be called barbarous, in comparison with another, because he is strange in his manner of speech and mispronounces the language of the other. . . . But from this point of view, there is no man or race which is not barbarous with respect to some other man or race. . . . Thus, just as we esteemed these peoples of the Indies barbarous, so they considered us, because of not understanding us."[24] As I pointed out in chapter 1, this quotation reveals Las Casas's understanding that barbarity is an ethnocentric allegation rather than an absolute attribute; in this passage we see clear evidence that Las Casas is capable of thinking in terms other than those of a Christian/heathen binarism. Still, it must be admitted that in spite of his constant vituperation and frequent emotionalism, the priest never formulates his ideas with quite the forcefulness and particularity characteristic of Montaigne: "Now, to return to my subject, I think there is nothing barbarous and savage in that nation [the homeland of the

Tupinamba], from what I have been told, except that each man calls barbarism whatever is not his own practice; for indeed it seems we have no other test of truth and reason than the example and pattern of the opinions and customs of the country we live in. *There* is always the perfect religion, the perfect government, the perfect and accomplished manners in all things" (152). The pointedness of this passage derives partly from its irony, partly from its implicit insistence that claims of "barbarity" often amount to nothing more than acknowledgments of *difference* followed by conclusions of *inferiority*, and partly from its move away from the level of rather calm abstraction that we see in the Las Casas quotation. Indeed, Montaigne differs from Las Casas precisely in his greater willingness to employ accounts of the New World as leverage in his emerging and more nuanced critique of the Old. We take away little of Montaigne's significance or originality by pointing to possible sources of his ideas.

"Sources," in fact, may be too strong a word. The *Apologética historia*, after all, was unavailable to Montaigne (unlike the *Brevísima relación*) during the time he composed his *Essays*, and we can only conjecture that he might have been familiar with the ideas of an as-yet-unpublished writer such as the Spanish lawyer and judge Alonso de Zorita, who made the following remarks: "Nor is there any reason for calling them [the Indians] barbarians, for there is no doubt that they are a very able people who have learned very easily and quickly all the mechanical arts known to the Spaniards who live in New Spain. . . . Let those who call them barbarians consider that by the same token they could call 'barbarians' the Spaniards and other peoples famed for great ability and intelligence."[25] We must also remember that the genesis of Montaigne's relativism might possibly have received impetus from such a non-contemporary authority as the Holy Bible; witness the Apostle Paul's claim in 1 Corinthians that there are "many kinds of voices in the world, and none of them is without significance. Therefore if I know not the meaning of the voice, I shall be unto him that speaketh a barbarian, and he that speaketh shall be a barbarian unto me" (14:10-11).[26] An ultimate suspension of judgment—an exercise, in effect, of the Pyrrhonian *epoche*—is perhaps the wisest policy in speculating upon Montaigne's sources, though this need not absolutely preclude incidental surmising. More important than positive source identification is a recognition that conceptual backgrounds existed in the Renaissance for most, if not all, of Montaigne's thoughts. In other words, knowing whether or not he read a particular author is not so crucial as understanding that he and his audience were more or less prepared (by their very existence in a time when certainties inherited from the past were being subjected to ever-increasing scrutiny) seriously to consider the propositions he advanced. As Charles Frey has written in connection with *The Tempest*, we read early modern travel narratives and New World histories "not necessarily to find out what Shakespeare read, but to ascertain what Shakespeare and his audience together would have been likely to know—what they would have gathered from a variety of sources."[27] We do the same with respect to Montaigne.

If Las Casas may be characterized as a writer who occasionally concludes that barbarity and savagery are Eurocentric claims, Montaigne must be seen as someone who habitually acknowledges this. While Las Casas demonstrates, from time to time, a recognition that social sophistication as well as human equality can be attributed to peoples lacking Christianity, Montaigne *assumes* this, and in so doing implicitly rejects the narrow conception of civility that equates freedom from savagery with the acquisition of "true" religion. Instead, he embraces a broader conception of civility, a conception much closer to the twentieth-century idea of civilization. As I have argued in chapter 1, this was a view inchoate in the Renaissance, though seldom articulated. It is hardly surprising, however, that Montaigne *does* articulate it, given that he launches, in his inimitable manner, one of the major critiques of contemporary European culture produced in the sixteenth century.

With this in mind, then, we can counter any claims that Montaigne robs New World natives of their *difference*. Bernard Sheehan, for instance, writes that Montaigne reveals a "proclivity to make Indians into white men," and Tzvetan Todorov argues that in Montaigne "The other is in fact never apprehended, never known."[28] Sheehan's view is remarkably similar to Todorov's contention—discussed earlier—that Las Casas sees the Indians as equal and therefore identical, or, as Jean Howard characterizes it, as "embryonic Europeans needing only the help of a Spanish education and a Spanish religion to make them mirrors of their white 'brothers'."[29] Yet Sheehan offers as evidence for this claim the passage at the end of "Of cannibals" where Montaigne records two observations about European life made by the Tupi natives with whom he spoke in Rouen:

> They said that in the first place they thought it very strange that so many grown men, bearded, strong, and armed, who were around the king (it is likely that they were talking about the Swiss of his guard) should submit to obey a child, and that one of them was not chosen to command instead. Second (they have a way in their language of speaking of men as halves of one another), they had noticed that there were among us men full and gorged with all sorts of good things, and that their other halves were beggars at their doors, emaciated with hunger and poverty; and they thought it strange that these needy halves could endure such an injustice, and did not take the others by the throat, or set fire to their houses. (159)

If anything, the central impression conveyed by this passage is not that the speakers are culturally undeveloped white men, but that they are culturally developed foreigners, people with conventions of their own that allow them to question the conventions of others. Montaigne seems far from concluding that native Americans are potential Europeans; on the contrary, the fact that he allows their observations to interrogate and implicitly criticize the system of European social subordination indicates the extent to which he grants them their own identity, their own inquisitive subjectivity. Elsewhere, for example in the later essay "Of coaches," Montaigne extends this attribution of acute observation and discerning judgment when he describes, with a remarkably sympathetic imagination, the arrival of the Spaniards from the natives' point of view (and I quote here from Florio's vivid rendering of the French): Mounted upon "great and unknowen monsters," covered with "a shining and hard skinne," armed with "slicing-keene weapons," and equipped with the "flashing-fire and thundring roare" of cannon, the Spaniards certainly merited the "astonishment which those nations might justly conceive."[30] There is no hesitation here in pointing to the (understandable) ignorance of the Indians, but Montaigne never for a moment implies that such ignorance suggests the lack of a cultural inheritance.

Similar to Las Casas, Montaigne begins his treatment of New World natives with an implicit acknowledgment of *equality*, though this acknowledgment is quite apparently based less on the assumption of Christian universalism than it is on a refreshingly confident belief in the very self-evidence of the proposition, combined with a broad tolerance derived, presumably, from familiarity with classical authors. But unlike his Spanish predecessor, Montaigne does not—except in a very limited sense—conclude *identity*. (This limited sense and its relation to Montaigne's form of essentialism will be the subject of the final section of this chapter.) Rather, he stresses cultural difference—language, religion, diet, government, arts, business, family life—and thus demonstrates an appreciation of non-European ways of realizing human potential. In this respect he works very much in the manner of Léry, who concludes, after a vivid description of the bodily appearance and ornamentation of the Tupinamba, that "their gestures and expressions are so completely different from ours, that it is difficult, I guess, to represent them well by writing or by pictures. To have the pleasure of it, then, you will have to go see and visit them in their own country."[31] Even when, as in certain passages from the "Apology for Raymond Sebond," Montaigne is concerned to show "the coincidences between a great number of fabulous popular opinions and savage customs and beliefs," he speaks, for example, of "states and great governments maintained by women, without men" and of Indian outrage at the Spanish habit of "scattering the bones of the dead while searching the tombs for riches," thereby preventing the bones from easily reuniting at the day of judgment (431-32). But perhaps no better passage exists in the *Essays* to illustrate Montaigne's emphasis upon cultural difference than the one in which he approvingly quotes what Florio terms an "amorous canzonet"—a Tupi love poem: "Adder, stay; stay, adder, that from the pattern of your coloring my sister may draw the fashion and the workmanship of a rich girdle that I may give to my love; so may your beauty and your pattern be forever preferred to all other serpents" (158). As an example of the "sufficiencie" and sophistication of New World natives this song speaks for itself, and Montaigne implicitly recognizes this.[32] But what I find most interesting is Montaigne's afterthought about the poem: "Now I am familiar enough with poetry to be a judge of this: not only is there nothing barbarous in this fancy, but it is altogether Anacreontic. Their language, moreover, is a soft language, with an agreeable sound, somewhat like Greek in its endings" (158). Here we see—even in the writing of the relativist *par excellence* of the sixteenth century—an overt example of the inevitable assimilationism that accompanies any effort to comprehend and appreciate the unfamiliar. Todorov takes this as proof of Montaigne's inability to apprehend the cultural other. But it is a mistake to let this assimilative maneuver prevent us from seeing, at the same time, a willingness to represent the unfamiliar, to let it stand on its own before the reader in as much of its original strangeness as possible, given the circumstances of its inclusion.[33] Montaigne knows too well that objectivity is a will-o'-the-wisp, so he does not hesitate to offer his opinion—but he also knows that it is only an opinion. What is important and readily apparent is that he is curious about and respects that which is different; moreover, he is willing to put this before us and let it extend our mental boundaries just as it has extended his. And—in spite of sophisticated theoretical formulations and ex post facto criticisms—I am not sure that we can ask for much more.

PRIMITIVISM AND ITS DISCONTENTS

Many years ago Arthur O. Lovejoy wrote that Montaigne's passage in "Of cannibals" on the superiority of savage humans over those "bastardized" by art is "the *locus classicus* of primitivism in modern literature."[34] Since then, especially in Anglo-American letters, this opinion has become a prevailing view, and through gradual extension it has come to comprehend not only the remainder of "Of cannibals" but, indeed, a great part of Montaigne's *oeuvre*. Writers as diverse as Frank Kermode, Edward William Tayler, Leo Marx, Jan Kott, Henri Baudet, Leslie Fiedler, Philip Edwards, and Bernard Sheehan have all intimated as much.[35] Yet to believe that Montaigne is an advocate of sentimental primitivism and an univocal champion of nature and *le bon sauvage* is to ignore the numerous points of resistance against primitivism in his *Essays*—points of resistance to which we can become sensitized through contextual study. Montaigne is not the arch-primitivist or "naturalist" that he has often been made out to be. Though certain passages in his essays tend to suggest the contrary, I argue that his overall treatment of the relation between art and nature is not so much characterized by the assumption of antithesis as it is by the suggestion of nuance and complexity—and by the fact that ultimately, the precise constitution of this relation is mysterious, perhaps beyond human resolution.[36]

First, though, it is only fair to present the opposing case. Here is the famous passage on which Lovejoy focused:

> Those people [the Tupinamba] are wild *[sauvages]*, just as we call wild the fruits that Nature has produced by herself and in her normal course; whereas really it is those which we have changed artificially and led astray from the common order, that we should rather call wild. . . . These nations, then, seem to me barbarous *[barbares]*, in this sense, that they have been fashioned very little by the human mind *[l'esprit humain]*, and are still very close to their original naturalness *[leur naifveté originelle]*. The laws of nature do yet command them, very little corrupted by ours; and they are in such a state of purity that I am sometimes vexed that they were unknown earlier, in the days when there were men able to judge them better than we. I am sorry that Lycurgus and Plato did not know of them; for it seems to me that what we actually see in these nations surpasses not only all the pictures in which poets have idealized the golden age and all their inventions in imagining a happy state of man, but also the conceptions and the very desire of philosophy. They could not imagine a naturalness so pure and simple as we see by experience; nor could they believe that our society could be maintained with so little artifice and human solder. This is a nation, I should say to Plato, in which there is no sort of traffic, no knowledge of letters, no science of numbers, no name for a magistrate or for political superiority, no custom of servitude, no riches or poverty, no contracts, no successions, no partitions, no occupations but leisure ones, no care for any but common kinship, no clothes, no agriculture, no metal, no use of wine or wheat. The very words that signify lying, treachery, dissimulation, avarice, envy, belittling, pardon—unheard of. How far from this perfection would he find the republic that he imagined. (152-53)

If this were all that Montaigne had written about New World natives, we would indeed be justified in regarding him as an exponent of an extreme and romantic primitivism. We see here, for instance, an assertion of the sufficiency of nature and an equation of original naturalness with purity and goodness—one of the prime tenets of noble savagery. We see as well the conviction that New World virtue surpasses that which poets imagined to have existed in the Golden Age. And we see, finally, the implication that continuance in a state of nature (or, at any rate, in a state fashioned only minimally by *l'esprit humain*) is a guarantee of continued innocence. Baudet very likely had this passage in mind when he wrote that "The theory of the natural goodness of man, a condition to which primitive man corresponded more closely than others, was advanced by Montaigne with the Indians of South America in mind before its later revival by Rousseau."[37]

Furthermore, it is not only in the relatively early "Of cannibals" (1578-80) that Montaigne writes as he does in the previous extract. In a late addition (post-1588) to the "Apology for Raymond Sebond" we see him returning to this sort of idealistic portrayal: "What they tell us of the Brazilians, that they die only of old age, which is attributed to the serenity and tranquillity of their air, I attribute rather to the tranquillity and serenity of their souls *[leur ame]*, unburdened with any tense or unpleasant passion or thought or occupation, as people who spent their life in admirable simplicity and ignorance, without letters, without law, without king, without religion of any kind" (362). And in his essay "Of coaches" (1585-88) we see him elaborating slightly on the concept of living in a state of nature:

> Our world has just discovered another world (and who will guarantee us that it is the last of its brothers, since the daemons, the Sibyls, and we ourselves have up to now been ignorant of this one?) no less great, full, and well-limbed than itself, yet so new and so infantile that it is still being taught its A B C; not fifty years ago it knew neither letters, nor weights and measures, nor clothes, nor wheat, nor vines. It was still quite naked at the breast, and lived only on what its nursing mother provided. (693)

Particularly of interest is that in all three of these passages—and nothing else in the *Essays* rivals them as euphoric depictions of American natives—Montaigne resorts to the traditional anaphoric trope of negative characterization that we have seen employed elsewhere by writers such as Thevet and Gómara. It is as if he is sounding a leitmotif so as to reintroduce a dominant theme of his book. However, the theme itself is left largely undeveloped.

First, we must remember that when Thevet, Gómara, and other writers utilize the device of negative characterization, they are typically engaged in a demonstration of the inferiority of New World inhabitants. We have seen, for instance, that Thevet describes the native Brazilians as "a marvelous strange wild and brutish people, without Fayth, without Lawe, without Religion, and without any ciuilitie: but liuing like brute beasts, as nature hath brought them out, eating herbes and rootes, beings alwayes naked as well women as men."[38] Similarly, Louis le Roy claims that New World natives are "without letters, without Lawes, without Kings, without common wealthes, without arts; but yet not without religion."[39] As a consequence, when Montaigne employs the same descriptive formula, he deliberately evokes in his readers' minds the antipathetic attitudes typical of these writers. He does not subscribe to their *sans roi, sans loi, sans foi* views of savagery, but his ironic turning of the tables would come perilously close to being imperceptible or misleading were it not that in each instance it is contextualized by an uncharacteristic earnestness of voice. As unexpected twists of thought, these remarks are certainly a far cry, for instance, from the broad stroke with which he ends "Of cannibals"—a line that in its English translations seldom conveys the mordancy of the original French: "Tout cela ne va pas trop mal: mais quoi, ils ne portent point de haut de chausses" ["All this is not too bad—but what's the use? They don't wear breeches."][40] I do not mean to suggest that Montaigne employs the conventional strategy of negative characterization because he is unable to provide positive portrayals; on the contrary, many examples in the *Essays* (albeit some of dubious credibility) demonstrate that he made use of the latter method. Rather, his occasional subscription to the pattern set by "anti-Indian" writers like Gómara, Thevet, and Le Roy suggests, at the very least, that he is unwilling to allow his readers to forget that less enthusiastic opinions of American natives than his own have been and will continue to be formed and advanced.

A second consideration is that Montaigne, unlike later advocates of noble savagery, is at no pains to attack Christianity.[41] This is not to deny Aldo Scaglione's point that "The image of savages being good, without being compelled to be so by force of law, and living in orderly conditions was insulting to the Christian conscience of Western man unless he was espousing that image out of a conscious need for escape and revolt."[42] Seeing the natives of the New World as innately gentle and virtuous is dangerously heterodox insofar as it denies the theory of human depravity as a consequence of the Fall. But Montaigne consistently avoids reference to the Fall, and, indeed, to most other facets of Judeo-Christian doctrine—so much so, in fact, that critical claims about his representation of the Tupinamba as "prelapsarian savages" seem strangely inappropriate.[43] If anything, Montaigne's savages are *extra*lapsarian, people spoken of almost wholly outside a conventional Judeo-Christian context. And in this respect, Montaigne bears a far closer resemblance to classical writers who attempt ethnography—and in particular,

Tacitus—than he does to later Europeans who, in advocating a doctrinaire primitivism, launch the standard double-edged attack on Christianity and European civilization.

As the *Essays* abundantly demonstrate, Montaigne was intimately familiar with the writings of Tacitus, as well as with such other classical figures as Seneca, Plutarch, Virgil, Ovid, Cicero, Horace, Catullus, Lucretius, Plato, Sextus Empiricus, and Diogenes Laertius. And though he does not quote Tacitus in either "Of cannibals" or "Of coaches," his frequent references to him elsewhere—particularly in "Of the art of discussion"—strongly suggest that he was conversant with the Roman historian's *oeuvre*, including, no doubt, his *Germania*. In that book, Tacitus praises the Germans for their courage in battle, their hospitality and family solidarity, their lack of greed and ambition, and their chastity and strict marriage codes. He claims, moreover, that "The natives take less pleasure than most people do in possessing these metals [gold and silver]"—a remark that reverberates fourteen centuries later in the idealistic portrayals of native Americans we see in Columbus and Martyr.[44] But Tacitus is far from painting a wholly unblemished portrait of the Germans. He criticizes their idleness, unpunctuality, gambling, and drunkenness, for example, and he elsewhere alleges that "the Germans have no taste for peace." Above all, he takes exception to their custom of periodic human sacrifice; speaking of an observance practiced by a tribe called the "Semnones," he writes: "The sacrifice of a human victim in the name of all marks the grisly opening of their savage ritual."[45] We need only listen to the following passage in Montaigne's "Of moderation" to hear an echo—enormously amplified—of the disapproval implied by Tacitus's reference to this custom: "And in these new lands discovered in our time, still pure and virgin compared with ours, this practice is to some extent accepted everywhere: all their idols are drenched with human blood, often with horrible cruelty. They burn the victims alive, and take them out of the brazier half roasted to tear their heart and entrails out. Others, even women, are flayed alive, and with their bloody skins they dress and disguise others" (149). Clearly, Montaigne holds no illusion that the natives of America are entirely gentle and peace-loving; like Tacitus—and, for that matter, Léry as well—he offers a mixed portrayal.[46] Accordingly, such an estimation as the following of Tacitus's *Germania* possesses an aptness equally pertinent to Montaigne's generalized portrait of native Americans: "[Tacitus's account] would appear to be based upon observation rather than upon preconceived ideas, and the usual extravagant accounts of the noble savage do not seem to have colored it. The Germans as a whole have both admirable and regrettable traits, and Tacitus, like Caesar, includes both."[47] By Boasian, "scientific," or contemporary self-conscious ethnographic standards, of course, neither Tacitus's nor Montaigne's accounts can be regarded as "based upon observation," but it certainly seems true that both work against the grain of reliance upon preconceived ideas. In particular, Montaigne appears to reject the use of euphoric description as a means to undermine confidence in the truth or value of Christianity. His complex combination of praise and censure of New World natives is much less imbricated in an invective against European religion than it is in an inquisitive consideration of ethnocentrism and the infinite variety of human more and custom.[48]

This leads to my third point. Unlike the Christian providentialist interpretation of history, which is teleological and progressive insofar as it suggests that all humankind will eventually be evangelized, primitivism is inextricably tied to a pessimistic or degenerative view of history.[49] There are, of course, deeply skeptical Christian appraisals of historical conditions and trends in the Renaissance—John Donne's "An Anatomy of the World," for instance, comes readily to mind—but even these are contained within a larger providentialism. In contrast, as Leo Marx writes, the doctrine of primitivism "denies the value of history. It says that man was happiest in the beginning— in the golden age—and that the record of human activity is a record of decline."[50] There is little evidence in the *Essays*, however, to suggest that Montaigne found such a view either attractive or persuasive. One of the strongest indications that he considered it at all may be found in a passage from the essay "Of coaches," where he makes the following observation: "I am much afraid that we shall have very greatly hastened the decline and ruin of this new world by our contagion, and that we will have sold it our opinions and our arts very dear" (693). Here we see, by implication, the idea that the decline of the New World was somehow inevitable, that it was only accelerated by the advent of Europeans. Such an idea, if seriously held, substantially mitigates the responsibility normally placed on Castile and Portugal for the catastrophic demise of native populations and even for the Black Legend—a fatalistic notion that to many writers on America, Las Casas among them, would have been wholly unacceptable.

But Montaigne, as he so often does, veers away quickly from this thought, leaving the impression not so much that he was committed to its import as that he simply glanced at it in passing but effectively abandoned the idea in his failure to retrace his steps. The next time he broaches the question of history, a few pages later, his ruminations are distinctly different:

> Why did not such a noble conquest [*une si noble conqueste*] fall to Alexander or to those ancient Greeks and Romans? Why did not such a great change and

alteration of so many empires and peoples fall into hands that would have gently polished and cleared away whatever was barbarous in them, and would have strengthened and fostered the good seeds [les bonnes semences] that nature had produced in them, not only adding to the cultivation of the earth and the adornment of cities the arts of our side of the ocean, in so far as they would have been necessary, but also adding the Greek and Roman virtues to those originally in that region? What an improvement that would have been, and what an amelioration for the entire globe, if the first examples of our conduct that were offered over there had called those peoples to the admiration and imitation of virtue and had set up between them and us a brotherly fellowship and understanding [une fraternele societé et intelligence] ! How easy it would have been to make good use of souls so fresh, so famished to learn, and having, for the most part, such fine natural beginnings! On the contrary, we took advantage of their ignorance and inexperience to incline them the more easily toward treachery, lewdness, avarice, and every sort of inhumanity and cruelty, after the example and pattern of our ways [à l'exemple et patron de nos meurs]. (694-95)

Admittedly, the train of thought here is circuitous. In the first place, Montaigne suggests that the ancient Greeks and Romans would have been better suited than sixteenth-century Europeans to discover, conquer, and colonize the New World—an idea that meshes well with Scaglione's notion of the humanist myth of modern man as "a moral and psychological pigmy" compared to his classical predecessors.[51] Montaigne, after all, had lived through the Saint Bartholomew's Day Massacre in 1572; he was well acquainted with the civil *barbarie* of his contemporaries. Nonetheless, Montaigne quickly moves to a broader alternative, implying, in Florio's words, that at least some of his contemporaries might be qualified to "incivilize" and "christianly instruct" the natives of America, as long as they respect these natives' own inherent virtues and supply only those European arts necessary to them.[52] This clearly points to the idea that a certain measure of advanced education and civilization is good: American natives have something to learn from Europeans—the *right* Europeans, at any rate. And, though Montaigne does not say it in so many words, Europeans also have something to learn from American natives; otherwise, the phrase "brotherly fellowship and understanding" would seem gratuitous in context. The peoples of the New World, in Montaigne's view, have the potential to be as civilized and virtuous—or as cruel and immoral—as any Europeans. This is why their conquest might have been "noble," though in fact, as Montaigne implies, it was tragic. Their closeness to a state of nature explains their status as "good seeds," but it provides no guarantee against ignorance and the need for further refinement.

Consequently, history can by no means be perceived as nothing more than an inevitable record of human decline.

No one reading the previous passage carefully can accept a view of Montaigne as a sentimental primitivist or credit such an apparently reductive conclusion as that "In the opposition of art and nature Montaigne placed himself squarely on the side of nature."[53] The qualifications Montaigne brings forward as he weaves his way in and out of the issue of primitivism thoroughly complicate the art/nature antithesis, making it much less a black and white matter than many commentators have been willing to admit. In "Of idleness," for instance, Montaigne opens with the construction of a tripartite analogy in which a potentially generative body (wild land/unimpregnated woman/un-disciplined mind) is granted "good and natural offspring" only through the deliberate imposition of external force and activity (cultivation/fertiliza-tion/direction) (20-21); in "Of the affection of fathers for their children" he claims that "we must indeed yield a little to the simple authority of Nature, but not let ourselves be carried away tyrannically by her: reason alone must guide our inclinations" (279). And in "Of cannibals," though Lovejoy does not acknowledge it, Montaigne presents as "natural" a society that is, at the very least, one remove from nature through its pervasive fashioning by human art: It has customs, religion, architecture, poetry. Montaigne seems to inti-mate that art (including the judicious employment of reason) and nature are mutually dependent; that nature, while originally uncorrupt, is easily cor-ruptible and thus in need of the discipline and positive reinforcement that human art can provide. But art—that is, human custom, language, reasoning, technology, moral education, and so forth—is equally dependent upon nature, both for generation and for standards of necessity, sufficiency, order, and proportion.[54] As Ben Jonson wrote half a century later, "without Art, Nature can ne'er bee perfect; &, without Nature, Art can clayme no being."[55] It follows, then, that for Montaigne both nature and art in the New World can be subject to critique, just as they can in the Old. And this leads to my final argument against the view of Montaigne as a primitivist: His constant readiness to point to the limitations and follies not only of human customs but of the human traits that give rise to these customs thoroughly undermines any illusion that he is convinced of the innate nobility of human beings.

I have previously quoted the passage from "Of moderation" in which Montaigne registers his repulsion at the practice of human sacrifice in America; I add here his understated conviction of the absurdity of a Mexican custom regarding the treatment of a new king: "Those of Mexico, after the ceremonies of his coronation are completed, no longer dare look him in the face; but as if they had deified him by his royalty, they have him swear not only to maintain their religion, their laws, their liberties, and to be valiant, just, and kind, but also to make the sun move with its customary light, the clouds shed rain in due season, the rivers run their courses, and the earth bear all things necessary for his people" ("Of the art of discussion," 714). Clearly, Montaigne hints, Europeans have no monopoly on foolishness. Indeed, it can be found everywhere—as Montaigne further substantiates by his brief treatment of New World warfare. In spite of the fact that he calls these wars "wholly noble and generous" and claims that their sole basis is "rivalry in valor," Montaigne does not hesitate to add that war, in general, is a "human disease," a practice that even in the best of cases reveals the puniness and unreasonableness of humanity ("Of cannibals," 156).[56] Likewise, in the midst of a detailed description in "Of coaches" of the Mexican cosmological myth of the Five Suns, Montaigne does not refrain from apostrophizing on human gullibility after explaining the dogma that with the demise of the Fourth Sun all humans were transformed into monkeys: "to what notions will the laxness of human credulity not submit!" (698). As these examples indicate, Montaigne never hesitates to return to his central theme of human presumption and ridiculousness; it makes no difference to him whether the humans in question live in the Old World or the New.

Perhaps the most succinct proof of this allegation of ubiquitous human folly, however, may be found in the very essay that Lovejoy considered the fountainhead of modern primitivism. As is well known, Montaigne excuses American anthropophagy on the grounds that, unlike "treachery, disloyalty, tyranny, and cruelty, which are our ordinary vices," it is a practice that can, in terms of its practitioners' notions of glory and vengeance, be readily understood. Moreover, it has its classical precedents. But critics seldom point out that Montaigne follows this quasi-defense with the remark that "we may well call these people barbarians [barbares], in respect to the rules of reason [regles de la raison], but not in respect to ourselves, who surpass them in every kind of barbarity" ("Of cannibals," 156).[57] This is a classic Montaignian stance: On the one hand, we see the implicit relativism that allows for a favorable view of New World natives; on the other, we see a deep reluctance to acknowledge that any people, American or otherwise, can live up to the absolute standards of good sense and decency discoverable by means of "reason's way" (150). It is true that in the "Apology for Raymond Sebond" Montaigne subjects this same reason to extensive attack, but we must not forget that the celebrated essay also lives up to its title as a defense of Sebond's rationalism inasmuch as it stresses that it is "a very fine and very laudable enterprise to accommodate also to the service of our faith the natural and human tools [les utils naturels et humains] that God has given us" (321). Moreover, as Donald M. Frame, Richard L. Regosin, and others have pointed out, Montaigne's Pyrrhonism is not consistently held throughout the *Essays*—or even throughout the "Apology"; rather, it represents a transitional phase before the affirmations of Book Three and the later additions to Books One and Two.[58] When Montaigne wrote "Of cannibals," three or four years after composing the bulk of the "Apology," he had very likely read Léry's *Histoire* and the new translation of Las Casas's *Brevisima relación,* and appears to have been diverted away from the speculative epistemological concerns of the earlier essay. In any event, he provides clear evidence in his meditations upon New World natives that he does not subscribe to an unqualified primitivism.

Thus we have a paradox. The "Apology," with its epistemological skepticism, offers a conceptual grounding for the less-than-euphoric estimation of human capacity that sounds as a dominant motif throughout the *Essays* and figures as a major component of the anti-primitivism in "Of cannibals" and "Of coaches." At the same time, however, we see in many of the essays that postdate the "Apology"—as well as in the "Apology"'s own affirmation of the value of judicious reasoning—a reaction against its more extreme claims and its abstraction from experience. I would like now to turn to the "Apology" and to a number of other essays in which Montaigne wrestles with questions of human capacity, reasoning, and knowledge. Even in his deepest skepticism Montaigne offers us grounds for thinking that in spite of considerable surface differences, human beings share a core of sameness and potential for productive cognition and culture acquisition that radically diminishes the otherness of others. To put it another way, while Montaigne argues both (1) that New World natives are less barbaric than Europeans, and (2) that Europeans and New World natives alike are barbaric with respect to certain imagined absolutes, it is the second of these arguments that compels his more ardent attention and commitment. Pointing to Montaigne's anti-primitivism is simply another way of stressing that his "primitivism" is ultimately subordinate to his subtle and idiosyncratic essentialism.[59]

LE NOUVEAU PYRRHONISME AND THE STAMP OF NATURE

While mid-century scholars such as Theodore Spencer, Hiram Haydn, and Rosalie L. Colie tended to discuss Montaigne in terms of his "counter-Renaissance" views and his complex relation to Continental humanism, a number of more recent critics have vastly sophisticated the ongoing discussion of the *Essays* and challenged, in varying ways, the earlier reading of Montaigne as an implicit essentialist in his attitudes toward the soul and a constitutive human nature.[60] Regosin, for instance, has exposed the vacuity of synoptic analysis and naive biographicalism in Montaigne criticism, arguing that "The question of [Montaigne's] belief is fundamentally a moot one," and stressing that linguistic mediation inevitably deforms any attempt to articulate external truth.[61] In much the same vein, Gérard Defaux has aligned himself with Jacques Derrida in rejecting the *signified* in favor of the *signifier* and affirming that "il n'y a pas de hors-texte" [there is nothing outside of the text]: for Defaux, referential readings of Montaigne have led only to the "sterile" thematism and biographical preoccupation of such writers as Hugo Friedrich, Donald M. Frame, and Richard A. Sayce.[62] Terence Cave, Antoine Compagnon, Jules Brody, and André Tournon have concerned themselves with the rhetorical, philological, and stylistic contexts of Montaigne's writings, valuably addressing the issue of disruptions, gaps, and incoherencies in texts that nonetheless present themselves—often in spite of explicit disclaimers—as unified and whole.[63] Cave concludes, for example, that "All that the *Essais* can do, with their ineradicable self-consciousness, is to posit paradigms of wholeness as features of a discourse which, as it pours itself out, celebrates its own inanity"; and Compagnon, in a book that takes Montaigne seriously as a philosopher in the nominalist tradition of William of Ockham, finds (after scrupulous study of the essay "Of names") that Montaigne extends nominalism even to proper names, ultimately managing to surmount the problem posed by his lack of a male heir by positing the consubstantiality of his *Essays* not precisely with himself but with "Michel de Montaigne," the *nom d'auteur* [author's name].[64] Todorov has provided a highly nuanced reading of the *Essays* with respect to the question of essentialism; he observes that Montaigne is "a universalist but without knowing it," and concludes, apropos of the art/nature binarism, that Montaigne assumes the taxonomy of essence and accident only to abandon it in practice: "Instead of the opposition between essence and accident can be found its simulacrum: an opposition between ancient and recent accidents. History has assumed the role of nature."[65]

Somewhat more thematic readings of Montaigne have been offered in recent years by Jean Starobinski and Jonathan Dollimore: Starobinski beginning with Montaigne's "phenomenalism" and moving toward his acceptance of custom, convention, and individualism as conferred by self-reflection and action; Dollimore aligning Montaigne with Sir Thomas More, Niccolò Machiavelli, and Thomas Hobbes as an early modern proponent of the view that human identity is radically contingent, entirely dependent upon informing sociocultural contexts.[66] In particular, Dollimore claims that Montaigne rejects "the belief that we possess some given, unalterable essence or nature in virtue of which we are human." He then proceeds to argue that Jacobean dramatists such as William Shakespeare, John Marston, Cyril Tourneur, and John Webster are not only aware of but share Montaigne's convictions and are thus engaged in a project of "decentring 'man'" and undermining "Christian essentialist" assumptions about the human soul and a transhistorical human nature.[67] Finally, Steven Rendall has cogently argued that Montaigne's *Essays* resist "totalization," and that acknowledgment of this resistance should be the starting place for any reading: "Although critics can and often do redistribute the text in accordance with explanatory narratives of their own, Montaigne does what he can to make their work harder."[68]

In light of such a body of criticism, it is clearly impossible to formulate thematic claims about the *Essays* without first confronting the fact of their imbrication within multiple discursive networks, all of which problematize the relation between text and external, non-linguistic reality. At the same time, however, we must resist the temptation to wrest the *Essays* from their historical context simply because we recognize that this context, in itself, is textual and opaque. As Timothy J. Reiss states, the dehistoricized Montaigne of many deconstructive readings is founded on a summary rejection of the attempt to situate the *Essays* in their sociocultural environment.[69] But to acknowledge the epistemological problems attendant upon naive historicism is not, of necessity, to renounce the project of historical contextualization. It may perhaps be the case that discursive formations are entirely self-referential: labyrinthine linguistic constructs which endlessly loop back upon themselves and have no truck with empirical reality—if empirical reality indeed exists. But such a supposition is surely counterintuitive. Montaigne, for one, insists that his book is consubstantial with himself: "Thus, reader, I am myself the matter of my book" ("To the Reader," 2); "I have no more made my book than my book has made me" ("Of giving the lie," 504); "In this case we go hand in hand and at the same pace, my book and I. In other cases one may commend or blame the work apart from the workman; not so here; he who touches the one, touches the other" ("Of repentance," 611-12). And I certainly proceed in my discussion on the assumption that discursive networks, such as that of Renaissance ethnography, are indeed referential. This is not to deny their dimension of textual self-reflexivity, but rather to affirm their ultimate grounding in a dialogic world where representations are assumed to be mimetic and interlocutors to be capable of sharing effective practices of communication. Neither Montaigne nor the various discourses engaged by his *Essays* are solipsistic; scrutiny of the self is always presumed to be of consequence to the other. Indeed, the very skepticism that grants plausibility to the counterintuitive assumption of disengaged discourse simultaneously affirms its imbrication in contexts beyond the demonstrable construction of human reason. Montaigne's epistemological skepticism—especially that expressed in the "Apology for Raymond Sebond," but also including that embedded within such essays as "It is folly to measure the true and false by our own capacity" and "Of Democritus and Heraclitus"—becomes for many critics an ontological skepticism as well; not only knowledge of the essential self, but the very existence of that self is subjected to an all-encompassing doubt—or, worse, a dogmatic rejection. Not surprisingly, however, such critics pay scant attention to the fideistic affirmation that accompanies Montaigne's skepticism.[70] Yet it is in this fideism—as well as more generally in Montaigne's speculations and intimations about the constitution of human identity—that we can find strong evidence to counter such arguments. This in turn will allow us to better understand how Montaigne can simultaneously acknowledge a fundamental sameness between Europeans and such non-European peoples as Brazilian natives while forcefully demonstrating that cultural differences between the two groups are capable of provoking and yielding valuable social criticism.

Moving through the *Essays*, one may easily amass a group of quotations serving to bolster the thesis that Montaigne rejects conceptions of the self that may be presumed to derive from or be aligned with Christian essentialism as manifested in early modern Europe. To begin with, there is the famous sentence with which Montaigne ends Book Two—"Their [human opinions'] most universal quality is diversity" ("Of the resemblance of children to fathers," 598)—and there is in addition the rich essay "Of the inconsistency of our actions," in which Montaigne claims that "I have nothing to say about myself absolutely, simply, and solidly, without confusion and without mixture, or in one word. *Distinguo* is the most universal member of my logic" (242). To this initial list one might well add the opening of "Of Cato the Younger"—"I do not share that common error of judging another by myself. . . . I believe in and conceive a thousand contrary ways of life; and in contrast with the common run of men, I more easily admit difference than resemblance between us" (169)—or the sentence from "Of coaches" in which Montaigne prefaces his discussion of America: "If we saw as much of the world as we do not see, we would perceive, it is likely, a perpetual multiplication and vicissitude of forms *[formes]*" (693). Indeed, these and many other passing comments in the *Essays* testify to Montaigne's continual wonder at the astonishing variations among types of human existence and behavior on earth.

But such attention to Montaigne's focus on difference tends to preempt any recognition of his habit of emphasizing custom's mutability almost as a means of underlining his relative reluctance positively to consider and characterize the essential attributes of humanity—a habit we should perhaps not be surprised to discover, given the difficulty of the task. Moreover, sustained emphasis on difference has the paradoxical potential to conjure the image of a Montaigne who never changes his mind, when, in actuality, the essayist is among the most protean, unsystematic, and consciously self-contradictory writers of the Renaissance: "My ideas follow one another, but sometimes it is from a distance, and look at each other, but with a sidelong glance" ("Of vanity," 761). As Colie has written, Montaigne's "opinions were, frankly, as unstable as his moods."[71] The conflation of various aspects of Montaigne's thought in the interest of presenting him as an explicit and systematic anti-essentialist stems in part from a desire to make the body of his writings more consistent and comprehensible than in fact it is—a desire that, though laudable in certain respects, does an injustice to the reader who has not carefully studied the *Essays*. Moreover, it fails to come to terms with the principle of uncertainty which rests at the heart of Montaigne's project and finds paramount expression in his rejection of dogmatism. Making Montaigne an intellectual precursor of materialist and Marxist philosophy, as Dollimore in particular tends to do, has the unfortunate effect of distorting and overdetermining his subtle and suggestive ideas.

To conflate Montaigne's cultural relativism with his tentative, even diffident, remarks about human nature is to allow the latter to be eclipsed by the former; any suggestion of underlying human unity is lost in the heavy emphasis on diversity. And, to the extent that Montaigne stresses custom as *second* nature in human behavior, this has a certain appropriateness.[72] Nonetheless, as a critical positioning this maneuver fails to acknowledge the complex ways in which Montaigne hints at the relationship between cultural diversity and human universality. In the "Apology," for instance, Montaigne writes:

> We admire more, and value more, foreign things than ordinary ones; and but for that I should not have spent my time on this long list. For in my opinion, if anyone studies closely what we see ordinarily of the animals that live among us, there is material there for him to find facts just as wonderful as those that we go collecting in remote countries and centuries. It is one and the same nature that rolls its course [*une mesme nature qui roule son cours*]. Anyone who had formed a competent judgment of its present state could infer from this with certainty both all the future and all the past. I once saw among us some men brought by sea from a far country. Because we did not understand their language at all, and because their ways [*leur façon*], moreover, and their bearing and their clothes were totally remote from ours, which of us did not consider them savages and brutes? Who

did not attribute it to stupidity and brutishness to see them mute, ignorant of our hand kissings and our serpentine bows, our deportment and our bearing, which human nature [la nature humaine] must take as its pattern [son patron] without fail? Everything that seems strange to us we condemn, and everything that we do not understand; as happens in our judgment of the animals. (343)

And in "Of vanity," some years later, he continues:

Besides these reasons, travel seems to me a profitable exercise. The mind is continually exercised in observing new and unknown things; and I know no better school, as I have often said, for forming one's life, than to set before it constantly the diversity of so many other lives, ideas, and customs, and to make it taste such a perpetual variety of forms of our nature [formes de notre nature]. (744)

On the one hand, we see Montaigne's typical fascination with cultural difference: These men from America, with their strange bearing, language, and apparel, seem to share little with their European counterparts. And, like Las Casas before him—though with a cutting irony foreign to the priest— Montaigne points to the way in which this difference leads to narrow-minded allegations of savagery and bestiality.[73] On the other hand, Montaigne alludes to "human nature" and implies, even in the midst of his irony, that this nature is something that takes a "pattern," a "form." It is a locus of potential, potential for language, for manner, for dress—in short, for cultural acquisition. Indeed, the French nouns that Montaigne's English translators from Florio to Frame have rendered as "pattern" and "form" are patron and forme, words closely associated with one another throughout the Essays.[74] Sayce, in discussing a particular instance of Montaigne's use of forme, writes that the word "seems to be used in the technical sense of scholastic philoso-phy: the essential shape which marks humanity and to which individual differences can be accommodated."[75] It would be precipitate, of course, to assume that the word is always employed with such a specialized denotation, but if Sayce is correct in his specific analysis, it is not beyond reasonable likelihood that the just-quoted passage from the "Apology" means to suggest that human nature is a "form" or "stamp" that readily accommodates various "patterns"—individual or cultural differences. And this, in turn, implies a unity underlying the outward human diversity upon which Montaigne places so much emphasis. There is no question, for Montaigne, that custom or habit "is a second nature [une seconde nature], and no less powerful" ("Of husbanding your will," 772), but from such a formulation we necessarily infer a "first nature" as well: a core humanity, often associated with reason and clear judgment ("Of custom, and not easily changing an accepted law," 85), and intimately connected to the intellectual genesis of cultural relativism:

> But the principal effect of the power of custom is to seize and ensnare us in such a way that it is hardly within our power to get ourselves back out of its grip and return into ourselves to reflect and reason about its ordinances. In truth, because we drink them with our milk from birth, and because the face of the world presents itself in this aspect to our first view, it seems that we are born on condition of following this course. And the common notions that we find in credit around us and infused into our soul by our fathers' seed, these seem to be the universal and natural ones. Whence it comes to pass that what is off the hinges of custom, people believe to be off the hinges of reason: God knows how unreasonably, most of the time. ("Of custom," 83)

To approach this idea from a different perspective, I now turn to several passages in which Montaigne expresses his opinion about human acquisition of cultural traits. Early in the "Apology," of course, he makes his famous assertion that "Another region, other witnesses, similar promises and threats, might imprint upon us [nous pourroyent imprimer] a contrary belief. We are Christians by the same title that we are Perigordians or Germans" (325). Leaving aside the rather subversive light in which this remark places Christianity, I stress instead Montaigne's use of the word "imprint" (imprimer); in the context, this word suggests that humans possess a receptive capacity that, while largely passive, nonetheless participates in the acquisition of customs and external traits that round out human identity—drinking them in with the milk of our birth, to adopt Montaigne's metaphor.[76] The idea, in fact, is reminiscent of Aristotle's notion that personal and civic virtues are acquired through a receptivity to their implantation with which all humans are equipped.[77] And though Montaigne is anything but the systematic thinker Aristotle is, this suggestion is further substantiated later in the "Apology" when Montaigne counterpoints his treatment of cultural inheritance with his discussion of epistemological skepticism. Speaking of the particular brand of skepticism advocated by Pyrrho and popularized by Sextus Empiricus and Diogenes Laertius,[78] Montaigne writes:

> There is nothing in man's invention that has so much verisimilitude and usefulness. It [Pyrrhonism] presents man naked and empty, acknowledging his natural weakness, fit to receive from above some outside power; stripped of human knowledge, and all the more apt to lodge divine knowledge in himself, annihilating his judgment to make more room for faith; neither disbelieving nor setting

up any doctrine against the common observances; humble, obedient, teachable, zealous; a sworn enemy of heresy, and consequently free from the vain and irreligious opinions introduced by the false sects. He is a blank tablet prepared to take from the finger of God such forms as he shall be pleased to engrave on it. (375)

Pyrrhonism, in other words, supports a view of humanity as "imprintable," though here Montaigne lays principal emphasis on the imprinting power of God rather than on that of sociocultural contexts. Elsewhere in the "Apology," however, it seems abundantly clear that the various modes or "tropes" of Pyrrhonian doubt—and in particular the tenth mode, which stresses diversity of custom, law, legendary belief, and dogmatic conception as conducive to suspension of judgment—substantially reinforce Montaigne's conviction regarding humanity's constant susceptibility to external molding.[79]

A cursory reading of the previously-quoted passage might lead one to conclude that Montaigne's talk of imprinting equates to the *tabula rasa* attitude—typical of Columbus, Martyr, and Eden—that I have discussed in chapter 1; indeed, Montaigne's phrase "fit to receive" (*propre à recevoir*) echoes similar phrases in the works of these writers, and the image of humanity as a "blank tablet" (*carte blanche*) is thoroughly consonant with the reiterated metaphor of the unpainted canvas.[80] But whereas Martyr and Columbus (and, to a lesser degree, Las Casas) maintain that American natives "have no creed" and thus, as mature adults, passively await European religious and cultural inscription, Montaigne never hesitates for a moment in conveying his implicit assumption that all peoples, everywhere, are thoroughly participatory in specific cultures. That is, there is no such thing as a pre-cultural or unaccommodated human being; the *carte blanche* image is merely a convenient theoretical entity, never the representation of a concrete reality. "Imprinting" is a complementary process, beginning—presumably—with the "drinking in" of custom at birth, and never allowing the human individual to be culturally naked or to possess blank regions as yet uninscribed by local practice or belief.[81] Moreover, Montaigne insists that "a child who had been brought up in complete solitude, remote from all association (which would be a hard experiment to make), would have some sort of speech to express his ideas" (335); these ideas—or "conceits," as Florio aptly terms them in Elizabethan parlance—would find their generation through an environmental determinism in which, paradoxically, the absence of conventional culture-conditioning itself served as a form of accommodation. One might object that such an indirect articulation of the universalist thesis is immediately nullified by Montaigne's well-known exclamation on humankind at the conclusion of the essay "Of vanity"—"There is not a single thing as empty and needy as you [humanity], who embrace the universe" (766). But this objection fails to acknowledge that the very embracing alluded to could never occur were it not for an innate human capacity to be receptive and to offer a complementary opening-up to the imprinting power inherent in external "patterns": in short, a capacity for culture acquisition. I do not deny that we see in Montaigne a trend away from the doctrinaire Christian essentialism that posits a divinely-derived self sharing a common identity with all other selves in its raison d'être as a locus of belief in God. But I reject the characterization of Montaigne as an anti-essentialist who believes that "the concept of 'man' mystifies and obscures the real historical conditions in which the actual identity of people is rooted."[82] There is room between these extremes for a more balanced and complex intermediary view, and Montaigne's *Essays* provide ample evidence that he does in fact gravitate toward such a view: never downplaying the tremendous impact of sociohistorical self-fashioning, but never relinquishing the notion that humans possess an essence, however elusive of characterization, that accommodates this fashioning.[83] "There are secret parts in the matters we handle which cannot be guessed, especially in human nature *[la nature des hommes]*— mute factors that do not show, factors sometimes unknown to their possessor himself, which are brought forth and aroused by unexpected occasions" ("Of repentance," 618).

Many of Montaigne's observations derived from historical study further substantiate this idea. As a man immersed in history—especially classical history—Montaigne frequently draws analogies between the present and the past; such a practice gestures not only toward the intellectual assimilationism that is an inevitable part of all comprehension, but also toward the hypothesis that present peoples share a common humanity with those of the past. In the essay "Of books," for example, Montaigne muses that "historians come right to my forehand. They are pleasant and easy; and at the same time, man in general *[l'homme en général]*, the knowledge of whom I seek, appears in them more alive and entire than in any other place—the diversity and truth of his inner qualities *[ses conditions internes]* in the mass and in detail, the variety of the ways he is put together, and the accidents that threaten him" (303). Such remarks do not smack of the anti-essentialist assumption. Nor does Montaigne's strong identification with the "laughing philosopher" Democritus, who, in contrast to Heraclitus, was amused rather than grieved by his meditations upon the human condition. Veering sharply toward the later pessimism of François de La Rochefoucauld and Jonathan Swift, Montaigne writes in "Of Democritus and Heraclitus" that "We are not so full of evil as of inanity; we are not as wretched as we are worthless. . . . Our own peculiar condition is that we are as fit to be laughed at as able to laugh" (221). While such an estimation of humanity is scarcely positive, we must nonetheless admit that to predicate general attributes of the human condition at all is to work from the assumption that an underlying core of being exists—and exists prior to the informing contexts and accidents that shape it.

Indeed, the assumption that this core of being exists rests at the heart of Montaigne's project as a writer. As he insists in "Of practice," "It is not my deeds that I write down; it is myself, it is my essence [c'est moy, c'est mon essence]" (274)—the implication being, here as elsewhere, that in scrutinizing himself Montaigne is at some level scrutinizing all humanity. The twenty-year essai at self-discovery pursued by Montaigne is grounded upon the assumption that others will benefit from reading it: "By my publishing and accusing my imperfections, someone will learn to fear them" ("Of the art of discussion," 703). It is an assumption borne out in the responses of many readers:

> Blaise Pascal: "It is not in Montaigne, but in myself, that I find all that I see in him."

> Ralph Waldo Emerson: "It seemed to me as if I had myself written the book, in some former life, so sincerely it spoke to my thought and experience."

> André Gide: "He [Montaigne] paints himself in order to unmask himself. And as the mask belongs more to the country and the period than to the man himself, it is above all by the mask that people differ, so that in the being that is really unmasked, it is easy to recognize our own likeness."[84]

This is by no means to ignore Montaigne's own dismissive self-appraisals— his assertion, for instance, that "all this fricassee that I am scribbling here is nothing but a record of the essays of my life" ("Of experience," 826)—or to deny the claim that he represents the human self as tremendously malleable and subject to radical change. But to believe that the self is plastic, elusive, and contradictory is not necessarily to believe that it lacks an essence; on the contrary, its essence may lie precisely in its appetitiveness, its capacity to "drink in," its potential to be the protean entity it can become.[85] One may approvingly quote Montaigne's remark that a man who was, in Florio's terms, "boldly-venturous" yesterday may appear tomorrow as a "dastardly meacocke" ("Of the Inconstancie of Our Actions," 295; cp. Frame 242), yet such a claim no more undermines the possibility of a form of human essentialism than does Montaigne's later pronouncement that "there is as much difference between us and ourselves as between us and others" (244).

Much in the same way that Edmund Spenser uses "great dame Nature" to refute the arguments of Mutabilitie in *The Faerie Queene* (Cantos of Mutabilitie, 7.57-59), Montaigne appears to regard change as an attribute of being and thus as ultimately subordinate to a non-contingent human essence. Spenser's Nature says to Mutabilitie:

> all things stedfastnes doe hate
> And changed be: yet being rightly wayd
> They are not changed from their first estate;
> But by their change their being do dilate:
> And turning to themselues at length againe,
> Doe worke their owne perfection so by fate:
> Then ouer them Change doth not rule and raigne;
> But they raigne ouer Change, and doe their states
> maintaine.[86]

Likewise, Montaigne insists that "There is no one who, if he listens to himself, does not discover in himself a pattern all his own, a ruling pattern [*une forme sienne, une forme maistresse*], which struggles against education and against the tempest of the passions that oppose it" ("Of repentance," 615). Sayce, commenting on this remark, says that Montaigne is making a case that "there is a central part of the character which remains the same, which does not move, which is separate from the passions and impervious to education, good or bad."[87] Clearly, this is an expression of essentialism, though here Montaigne is working from the assertion of an individual core of identity rather than from his more accustomed positing of a general and transcultural essence. But in the same essay he confidently observes that "Each man bears the entire form of man's estate [*la forme entiere de l'humaine condition*]" (611), a claim that simultaneously complements the suggestion of individual non-contingency and buttresses the belief that the *Essays* are not merely narcissistic trifles but penetrating meditations well worth the scrutiny of present and future readers.[88] As Edwin M. Duval has written, the *Essays* "must be considered not only in terms of an explicit relation to their *author*, but also—and perhaps even more—in terms of an implicit relation to their *reader*."[89] And such a relation implies the assumption of commonality: a stamp of nature—manifest not in cultural behavior but in culture potential—that use can never change. Frame, the translator of Montaigne's complete works, believes that it is not until Book Three of the *Essays* (1585-88) that Montaigne is convinced of "human unity and solidarity."[90] And it is indeed true that we find forceful essentialist pronouncements primarily in such Book Three essays as "Of repentance," "Of the art of discussion," "Of vanity," "Of physiognomy," and "Of experience." But even in earlier essays such as "Of the education of children," "Of cannibals," and the "Apology for Raymond Sebond" we see a strong leaning in this direction: Montaigne speaks, for instance, of assaying his "natural faculties *[facultez naturelles]*," that bend under the load of conventional study (107), and he avows that the Tupinamba natives of Brazil, unlike contemporary Europeans, are still ruled by "the laws of nature *[les loix naturelles]*" and have not yet been led astray from "the common order *[l'ordre commun]*" that they share with their transoceanic counterparts (152-53). Thus when Frame writes that Montaigne "sees clearly the fundamental unity of kings and peasants, cannibals and Europeans," he implicitly acknowledges that even as early as the 1570s (when most of Books One and Two were composed) Montaigne recognizes a human sameness that lies as a foundation beneath the changeable veneer of custom and value.[91] It is just that Montaigne's expression of this idea becomes more frequent and articulate in the later essays. In "Of vanity," for example, he claims that "Not because Socrates said it, but because it is really my feeling, and perhaps excessively so, I consider all men my compatriots, and embrace a Pole as I do a Frenchman, setting this national bond after the universal and common one" (743); and in "Of experience" he makes an oblique and metaphorical observance of essentialism in writing that "If our faces were not similar, we could not distinguish man from beast; if they were not dissimilar, we could not distinguish man from man" (819). Such articulations allow for both the surface differences that separate individuals and the deep resemblances that unite them. Similarly, when Montaigne makes the observation—clearly connected to his skeptical habit of mind—that "Others do not see you, they guess at you by uncertain conjectures; they see not so much your nature as your art" ("Of repentance," 613), his employment of the word "nature" is sufficiently ambiguous that it may refer either to an individual or a generic human essence; but in both cases, the operative assumption is that such a "nature" does indeed exist, and that it lies beneath or behind the "art" that it accommodates.

Notwithstanding, then, the implications regarding referential reading and thematic signification suggested by the discussions of several highly perceptive poststructuralist critics, Montaigne does not deny the existence of a human essence or "first nature" so much as he insists upon the difficulty or even impossibility of knowing about this core of being with any certainty. The problem, in other words, is not so much ontological as epistemological, and a confusion of the two can readily lead to the championing of Montaigne as an unwitting spokesman—if not an advocate—of anti-essentialism. It is quite true, of course, that to suspect that one can never discover single meanings in Montaigne—meanings that transcend the self-referential labyrinth the *Essays* have been made out to be—is not, of necessity, to deny that Montaigne implicitly advocates belief in a *forme maistresse*. But certainly such a conclusion follows more readily once one has adopted the deconstructive premise of non-referentiality or infringed upon the Foucaultian principle of historical discontinuity by positing thematic links between, say, the Montaignian fascination with multiplicity and the materialist rejection of pre-existential forms. On the contrary, Montaigne chooses to assume the existence of a transcultural human essence (an act that bears close comparison to the fideistic affirmation of the existence of God); he does so, in spite of his heavy emphasis on the diversity of custom, presumably because it assists him both in conceiving of people as custom- or culture-learners and in formulating and justifying his clear conviction about the fundamental equality of all peoples, whether Greek, Roman, Renaissance European, or native American. And it is precisely his *nouveau pyrrhonisme*—his unsystematic union of Pyrrhonian skepticism with fideistic affirmation—that enables him to do this.[92] Montaigne never forgets that what we call knowledge may in fact be mere opinion; thus, to read him as maintaining in a positivistic fashion that no such thing as "human nature" exists or can exist is to ignore one of the most central aspects of his thought. Montaigne is always suggestive, inquisitive, tentative, provocative—but never dogmatic.

To point to Montaigne's essentialism is to draw attention to his uniformitarian assumption that all humans share common potentials, limitations, and capacities for development: social, linguistic, moral, intellectual, spiritual. It is not to argue that he posits a Cartesian subjectivity *avant la lettre* or a comfortable and easily apprehended human nature characterized by specific transhistorical attributes. Nor is it to diminish in any way his cultural relativism or his fascination with the diversity of custom. Indeed, it is precisely Montaigne's unhesitating acceptance of the idea that cultural difference can coexist with fundamental human equality that epitomizes his essentialism. And nowhere is this more apparent than in his New World ruminations in "Of cannibals," "Of coaches," and the "Apology." Las Casas, in contrast, almost always hints that American natives are circumstantially inferior to Europeans—though essentially equal on Christian grounds—due to their heathen upbringing. And this, in turn, at least partially legitimates the criticism that Las Casas denies native Americans their *difference* by laying heavy emphasis on their shared *identity* with Europeans.[93] But Montaigne, by limiting this stress on *identity* to a conception of fundamental sameness at the level of human potential and shared capacity for culture acquisition, allows the enormous cultural *difference* of the New World to interrogate the ways of Europe. And, of course, he allows the reverse procedure as well. Accordingly—as I have argued earlier—his seldom-remarked streak of anti-primitivism lies precisely in his refusal to subscribe for any length of time to a view of either Americans or Europeans as a superior human group. Savagery and civility, for Montaigne, are attributive categories inextricably tied to a conviction that since there are countless cultural formations, there are countless ways of realizing human potential. The categories are always understood to be ethnocentric—which reveals the immense distance between Montaigne and such predecessors as Columbus, Martyr, and even Las Casas—but they are also connected to a view of the world in which, if only by faith, absolute standards of human rationality, tolerance, and decency may be imagined. And by these standards, both New and Old World peoples often fall short of the mark. The savagery of American natives, while at times the noble savagery of tradition, is more often the savagery—equally predicable of Europeans—with which people are left when they fail to attain a civility characterized by consistently humane behavior and by beliefs grounded upon an awareness of their own ignorance, presumption, and frailty.

3

Wondrous Uncertainties:
Pastoral and Primitivism in The Faerie Queene

SPENSER AND THE NEW WORLD

We have seen in chapter 2 that Michel de Montaigne's essentialism finds a parallel in Edmund Spenser's conception of Mutabilitie's defeat: The things of this world "are not changed from their first estate; / But by their change their being do dilate" (7.7.58.4-5).[1] This idea of the dilation of being—of an immutable essence enabling countless developmental variations, of "Change [as] the mode in which Permanence expresses itself"[2]—is more consistently sounded by Spenser than by Montaigne; hence, in part, Spenser's reputation as a "secure and serene poet," a poet whose certainty excuses him from the task of discovering "a sense of life he already commands."[3] But as I have demonstrated, Montaigne also assumes a human essence, an essence or *forme* that accommodates individual and cultural differences and thereby serves as a "first estate," a core of being with the potential for dilation without loss of identity. The difference is that Montaigne, in his speculation upon this essence, emphasizes its passivity and malleability, whereas Spenser, with his supreme confidence in the divine origin of the essential self, stresses its active role in identity-formation. Yet even Spenser, for all his greater serenity than Montaigne, reveals in the later parts of The Faerie Queene—and especially in Book Six—that skeptical doubts do indeed afflict him, doubts about the degree to which gentle blood and proper breeding contribute to civil behavior and about the conventionally accepted causes and boundaries of human savagery. As critics have pointed out, the end of The Faerie Queene is less self-assured, more questioning and dramatic than the beginning;[4] it is my contention that at least part of this uncertainty may be attributed to a continually growing awareness, among Spenser and his contemporaries, that the world—and in particular, the New World—provided more models of human behavior and of possible relationships between human cultures and the realm of nature than were conventionally accepted in Christian Europe. Not only Spenser's eighteen years in Ireland, but his curiosity about and apparent sympathy with England's exploratory and colonial ambitions in America, contributed to the complication of his vision of savagery and civility in *The Faerie Queene*'s sixth book.

Even if we ignore for the moment Spenser's personal acquaintance with Sir Walter Ralegh and his indubitable knowledge of the recent voyages of Martin Frobisher, Sir Francis Drake, Sir Humphrey Gilbert, Thomas Cavendish, and the Roanoke colonists, we must admit, along with Franklin McCann, that a wealth of information and speculation about the New World was readily available to English readers in the latter part of the sixteenth century: "[Eden's translation of Martyr's] *Decades* (1555) gave to any Englishman who could read his own language a rich source of information about many regions of the earth and particularly about America. By 1585 nearly all the important early Spanish and French accounts of America were available in English translation."[5] Add to this the facts that an English rendering of Bartolomé de Las Casas's *Brevisima relación* was published in 1583, a manuscript narrative of Arthur Barlowe's reconnoitering voyage to Roanoke Island was circulating late in 1584, Thomas Harriot's *A briefe and true report of the new found land of Virginia* was published in 1588, and the first edition of Richard Hakluyt's *Principal Navigations* appeared in 1589, and it becomes self-evident how prominent a topic the New World and its inhabitants must have been during the very years in which Spenser was composing *The Faerie Queene*.[6] Although Jeffrey Knapp has astutely cautioned against overestimating the excitement aroused among English writers by the American discoveries, we can usefully distinguish between a general and provocative consciousness of the New World in England and the relative slowness of this consciousness to manifest itself in the realization of colonial ambitions.[7]

But it was not only through reading travel accounts that the literate English public could learn about America. As early as 1501 English voyagers had begun to capture New World natives and ship them back to Britain, and the trend continued well into the seventeenth century. In Spenser's day, Frobisher brought back an Eskimo couple from "Meta Incognita" in 1577; the "savages" Manteo and Wanchese returned with Captain Barlowe from the Carolina coast to London in 1584; and in 1595 Ralegh transported the son of a great chief from Guiana, as well as another Indian known as Leonard Regapo.[8] Much in the same way that the Tupinamba tribesmen from coastal

Brazil caught Montaigne's attention in the 1560s, these Indians in England, we may suppose, piqued the curiosity of Spenser and his contemporaries. Regardless whether or not Spenser ever met or spoke with them, we may assume that it was partly his awareness of their existence that enabled him to write in *The Faerie Queene* of the "tawney bodies" of "sunburnt Indians" (3.12.8.3-4)—just as whether or not he ever saw the precious crown of Peruvian emeralds that Drake presented to Queen Elizabeth upon completing his circumnavigation, his knowledge of this and other New World treasures enabled him to allude, however conventionally, to "rich Oranochy," "th'Indian Peru," and the "land of gold" that for so many Elizabethans meant America (4.11.21.7; 2.Proem.2.6; 3.3.6.8; 4.11.22.6).[9]

Critics have often noted Spenser's interest in the voyagers and their discoveries.[10] More than seventy years ago Lois Whitney pointed out that "there are scattering and fragmentary references throughout *The Faerie Queene* to the voyages of the sixteenth-century seamen, to the countries new found by them, and to curious and interesting facts about the inhabitants. There is clearly an attempt to utilize bits of the current travel lore for artistic purposes."[11] Margaret T. Hodgen has stressed Spenser's "broad knowledge" of the explorers' narratives and Roy Harvey Pearce has shown that Spenser's "accounts of savages who appear to be only half men are of a piece with many such in Elizabethan voyage literature."[12] More recently, Stephen Greenblatt has suggested that in the Bower of Bliss episode in Book Two of *The Faerie Queene* Acrasia is assimilated to Irish and American forms of cultural difference, and that, moreover, the canto (2.12) echoes many of the recurrent motifs of the travel narratives: "the sea voyage, the strange, menacing creatures, the paradisal landscape with its invisible art, the gold and silver carved with 'curious imagery,' the threat of effeminacy checked by the male bond, the generosity and wantonness of the inhabitants, the arousal of a longing at once to enter and to destroy."[13] And in another discussion focused on Book Two, David T. Read has persuasively argued that in the Guyon/Mammon encounter "Spenser has carefully devised a setting that refers in numerous oblique ways to the Spanish New World; . . . Guyon participates in the inversion of native and conquistador that occurs frequently in the New World literature and places the Indian in a position of moral, even spiritual superiority to the Spaniard."[14] But despite this long-standing recognition of Spenser's debt to the voyagers' accounts, there is to my knowledge no scholarly work that connects this debt with a suggestion of just how thoroughly *The Faerie Queene* is imbued with wonder at the newly revealed potentialities of being and with uncertainty regarding conventional assumptions about proper and improper behavior. These qualities of wonder and uncertainty seem inextricably linked to the flood of information in Spenser's day about foreign lands and peoples—particularly those on the far side of the Atlantic—and nowhere is this more apparent than in Book Six, the Legend of Courtesy. But even in earlier parts of the poem we see frequent references to the New World and suggestive hints of the way that it must have impinged upon Spenser's consciousness.

There are, in the first place, the usual and thoroughly conventional Elizabethan allusions to "Ynd," "America," "fruitfullest Virginia," and "the Armericke shore" (1.6.2.7; 1.6.35.6; 2.Proem.2.9; 2.10.72.6; 5.10.3.6). There is, in addition, the urgent exhortation to the English public to acknowledge and act upon its perceived manifest destiny in Guiana:

> Ioy on those warlike women, which so long
>> Can from all men so rich a kingdom hold;
>> And shame on you, ô men, which boast your strong
>> And valiant hearts, in thoughts lesse hard and bold,
>> Yet quaile in conquest of that land of gold.
>> But this to you, ô Britons, most pertaines,
>> To whom the right hereof it selfe hath sold;
>> The which for sparing litle cost or paines,
> Loose so immortall glory, and so endlesse gaines. (4.11.22)

Ralegh had offered similar advice in recent years, and it is worth pausing to examine one of his more vehement expressions:

> To conclude, *Guiana* is a Country that hath yet her Maidenhead, never sacked, turned, nor wrought, the face of the earth hath not been torn, nor the virtue and salt of the soil spent by manurance, the graves have not been opened for gold, the mines not broken with sledges, nor their Images pulled down out of their temples. . . . For whatsoever Prince shall possess it, shall be greatest, and if the king of Spain enjoy it, he will become unresistable. Her Majesty hereby shall confirm and strengthen the opinions of all nations, as touching her great and princely actions. And where the south border of *Guiana* reacheth to the Dominion and Empire of the *Amazons*, those women shall hereby hear the name of a virgin, which is not only able to defend her own territories and her neighbors, but also to invade and conquer so great Empires and so far removed.[15]

But Spenser also reveals his interest in the New World in such telling—if less explicit—moments as the initial description of Maleger and the healing of

Timias by Belphoebe. In the former instance, we hear of a man-like creature who rides "Upon a Tygre swift and fierce" and whose arrows are "Headed with flint, and feathers bloudie dide, / Such as the Indians in their quiuers hide" (2.11.20.4; 2.11.21.4-5).[16] We are left with the impression that Maleger, like the American natives to whom he is indirectly compared, is a formidable opponent, someone with the ability to craft and shoot deadly arrows and subdue the wildest of beasts. The portrayal of Belphoebe, in contrast, draws on a more sympathetic tradition of New World reportage insofar as it shows us a woman restoring Timias to consciousness through the use of a "soueraigne weede"—quite possibly "diuine Tobacco" (3.5.33.1; 3.5.32.6).[17] Like the Salvage Man of Book Six, Belphoebe is revealed here to be at home in the natural world of the forest and well-versed in herbal remedies. She is, in fact, diametrically opposed in this respect to Duessa, who becomes utterly helpless while wandering in the "waste wildernesse": "forlorne" and "naked," she lurks in "rockes and caues farre under ground" and uses "greene mosse" to cover her "loathly filthinesse" (2.1.22.1-5).[18] Duessa's example supports the conventional wisdom that "The wood is fit for beasts" (2.3.39.9) and that those who live there inevitably become bestial; Belphoebe's, in contrast, lends credibility to the primitivistic notion that humans not only retain a distinct humanity in the natural world but have the opportunity there to learn and exercise "ciuill usage and gentility" (3.6.1.8). It is true, of course, that Belphoebe is a special case inasmuch as she partakes of the *melior natura* [superior nature] of her mother Chrysogone and her father Titan (3.6.3-7); it is also true that an anti-primitivistic predisposition on Spenser's part may be revealed by his affirmation, in *A View of the Present State of Ireland*, that "an Englishman brought up naturally in such sweet civility as England affords could find such liking in that barbarous rudeness [of Ireland] that he should forget his own nature and forgo his own nation" (48). But Spenser's willing suggestion that Belphoebe and others can thrive in the wilderness—like the astonishment he evinces at the "degenerated" nature of Englishmen in Ireland (48)—demonstrates that his anti-primitivism is by no means monolithic or untextured in character. Rather, it is qualified by uncertainties and ambiguities, many of which perhaps stem from his knowledge of New World ethnographic and travel writings.

I remarked in chapter 2 that Montaigne clearly does not subscribe to the reductive *sans roi, sans loi, sans foi* views of savagery that characterizes antipathetic chroniclers of America such as André Thevet. Spenser, in contrast, not only seems at times to subscribe to them, but occasionally draws heavily from the standard iconography of American natives—and other contemporary "primitives"—in order to fully convey a character's wildness and bestiality.

The most obvious example of this is the portrayal of the Wild Man in Book Four. As commentators have often pointed out, Spenser's description of this odious being who dwells in "saluage forrests" and "deserts wide" (4.7.2.6) owes much to the tradition of the wodewose—the medieval wild man or *homo ferus*; R. H. Goldsmith, for example, writes that this Wild Man "is fully in the [wodewose] tradition yet more fierce and monstrous than any that had gone before," and Richard Bernheimer stresses that Spenser's poem is "shot through with the mythology of the wild man."[19] But in addition to his hairiness, his aphasia, his "wreath of yuie greene," and the "tall young oake" (4.7.7.1-4) he bears in one hand—all standard elements in the representation of the wodewose, and all conducing to our impression that this creature, like Ajax in Thersites's words, is "a very land-fish, languageless, a monster" (*Tro.* 3.3.264)—the Wild Man also shares a number of characteristics most commonly associated with American natives:

> It was to weet a wilde and saluage man,
>> Yet was no man, but onely like in shape,
>> And eke in stature higher by a span, . . .
>> . . . he liu'd all on rauin and on rape
>> Of men and beasts; and fed on fleshly gore,
> The signe whereof yet stain'd his bloudy lips afore. (4.7.5.1-3,7-9)

Like the native peoples described by virtually all New World chroniclers, from the earliest to those contemporary with Spenser, this Wild Man is larger than the ordinary European; and, of course, he is cannibalistic.[20] But in an interesting twist, this cannibalism is rendered somewhat tenuous by the mystification of the Wild Man's status. If he is, as Spenser says, "no man, but onely like in shape," then, just as in the case of Polyphemus in *The Odyssey*, he is not, strictly speaking, cannibalistic—and we thus find the same conundrum that we found earlier in the antipathetic writings of Diego Alvarez Chanca and Juan Ginés de Sepúlveda, who in denying full humanity to New World natives also implicitly excused them from moral responsibility and Christian duty.[21] But Spenser also tells us that when Belphoebe shoots the Wild Man with an arrow, his "sinfull sowle / Hauing his carrion corse quite senceless left, / Was fled to hell, surcharg'd with spoile and theft" (4.7.32.3-5). Consequently—and without becoming mired in theological subtleties—it is fair to say that the Wild Man exists for Spenser in a liminal state; he is at once human and subhuman. His identity, like that of American natives generally for so many Renaissance voyagers—or that of Caliban through much of *The Tempest*—is left in profound doubt.

It may be objected that distinguishing the traits of the medieval wodewose from those peculiar to the stereotypical native American (especially in antipathetic portrayals) is virtually impossible, since the former group of characteristics almost certainly played a major role in the representation of the latter—as did such other traditions as the Golden Age myth and the Christian story of Paradise. In chapter 1, I have stressed just how thoroughly assimilative both euphoric and antipathetic portrayals of New World natives actually were. But even when we acknowledge that sixteenth-century accounts of American Indians were heavily influenced, through processes of transferral and domestication, by classical and medieval traditions concerning savagery, we must also note with Goldsmith that the same century saw a marked change in literary depictions of the wild man: "something happened in the last decade of the sixteenth century to this conventionalized figure. In the plays, romances, and poems, he suddenly emerged as the brutal and lecherous creature that his name and dress had always implied that he was."[22] Goldsmith speculates that this change may have been the result of closer links between English theater and Continental stage traditions; without disputing this, I suggest that it might also be attributable to a renewed interest in the wild man stemming from the numerous ethnographic accounts that had recently become available regarding alien peoples across the ocean. If the New World native was colored, in European eyes, by the wodewose tradition, this tradition was equally revivified by New World curiosity. The process of influence was reciprocal.

A final and fascinating example of the way in which Spenser's habit of treating savagery may have been influenced by an American awareness is the episode of Una among the satyrs in Book One. Separated from the Redcross Knight, Una is taken captive by the "Sarazin" Sansloy (1.6.8.6) and led into a "forrest wilde" (1.6.3.2) where the heathen knight plans to rape her. But her screams arouse a "troupe of Faunes and Satyres" (1.6.7.7) who dwell in the wood, and at their appearance the terrified Sansloy mounts his horse and rides away. The satyrs, gazing at Una, "stand astonied at her beautie bright" (1.6.9.8); they then prostrate themselves upon the ground and, in "wonder of her beautie soueraine," spontaneously decide to "worship her, as Queene" and later as "Goddesse of the wood" (1.6.12.6; 1.6.13.9; 1.6.16.2).[23] We are reminded by this sequence of a similar narrative trajectory in Book Four, when Artegall, disguised as a "saluage wight" and wearing a shield inscribed with the motto "Saluagesse sans finesse" (4.4.39.9), stands amazed upon discovering that the knight he has been fighting is in fact a woman, Britomart, with beautiful golden hair:

And he himselfe long gazing thereupon,
>   At last fell humbly downe vpon his knee,
>   And of his wonder made religion,
>   Weening some heauenly goddesse he did see, . . . (4.6.22.1-4)

Through Spenser's irony here we are enabled retroactively to recognize that
the satyrs in Book One also "make religion" of their wonder; in spite of Una's
efforts "To teach them truth," they persist in seeing her as "th'Image of
Idolatryes" (1.6.19.6-7). It is not until Sir Satyrane appears—himself half
satyr and half human—that Una is able to convert someone to "her discipline
of faith and veritie" (1.6.31.9) and ultimately secure an escape from the
forest.

The constellation of motifs we see in this episode—the lustful heathen;
the "saluage nation" (1.6.11.3) at once admiring, idolatrous, and ineducable;
the pagan with superior blood who recognizes and appreciates "true" religious teaching; and, above all, the evocation of wonder, and then religious
devotion, in putatively savage individuals when confronted with an exemplar of beauty and civility—all these motifs are typical of Renaissance
voyagers' accounts. We need only look to Columbus's "Letter to Santangel"
(1493) or Harriot's *Briefe and true report* (1588) to find instances of the common
tendency among New World chroniclers to represent natives as grossly
misconstruing their visitors' status: Columbus claims that the inhabitants of
Española "were very firmly convinced that I, with these ships and men, came
from the heavens"; Harriot avers that "some people could not tel whether
to thinke us gods or men."[24] And in Hakluyt's brief account of Drake's
circumnavigation (1589), we come across the telling observation that
"When they [the Miwok natives of northern California] came unto us, they
greatly wondred at the things that wee brought, but our Generall (according
to his naturall and accustomed humanitie) courteously intreated them, and
liberally bestowed on them necessarie things to cover their nakednesse,
whereupon they supposed us to be gods, and would not be perswaded to
the contrarie."[25]

Such remarks almost inevitably prompt us to entertain the sort of skepticism so well expressed by Joseph Conrad in Marlow's ironic appraisal of
Kurtz's sinister "report" in *Heart of Darkness*: "it was a beautiful piece of writing.
The opening paragraph, however, in the light of later information, strikes
me now as ominous. He began with the argument that we whites, from the
point of development we had arrived at, 'must necessarily appear to them
(savages) in the nature of supernatural beings—we approach them with the
might as of a deity,' and so on, and so on."[26] It is hard not to suspect, as

Marlow does, that these voyagers' accounts of native opinion—for all their earnestness—only barely conceal a brutal exploitation of what is either an entirely understandable misapprehension or, more likely, a convenient and reductive fabrication. For an audience in early modern Europe, the former possibility was perhaps best articulated by Francis Bacon: "Again, let a man only consider what a difference there is between the life of men in the most civilized province of Europe, and in the wildest and most barbarous districts of New India; he will feel it great enough to justify the saying that 'man is a god to man,' not only in regard to aid and benefit, but also by a comparison of condition. And this difference comes not from soil, not from climate, not from race, but from the arts."[27] As for the latter possibility, it requires little in the way of imagination. Lamentably, we can never recover the terms in which the natives represented the Europeans' arrival to themselves; what we have are the terms in which the Europeans represented what the natives thought—and these, clearly, tell us mainly about the Europeans.[28] It is true that, at least in the cases of Columbus, Drake, and Harriot, we may discover explicit acknowledgments that what I call the "divine attribution"—that is, the alleged belief among the natives that the European invaders are divine or supernatural in origin—is in fact a misperception. In other words, that which may well be a European fiction is represented as an American mistake. And this, in turn, suggests a certain unease on the part of the Europeans. But it is an unease they manage to live with; after all, their audience lies in the Old World, not in the New.

In several later accounts of native peoples produced primarily for European consumption—accounts conveniently termed "autoethnographies" by Mary Louise Pratt, and characterized as texts "in which people undertake to describe themselves in ways that engage with representations others have made of them"[29]—we see a considerable sophistication in habits of representation. In particular, we find a sort of double consciousness that allows for effective communication with readers from the dominant culture even as it facilitates subtle criticism of that culture, frequently by means of indirect or ironic expression. Among these accounts are the compendious sixteenth-century books on Mexican life and culture by the Franciscan Bernardino de Sahagún and the Dominican Diego Durán, both of whom—despite being born in Spain—spent the vast majority of their lives in Mexico, knew Nahuatl, and relied substantially on oral testimony in the composition of their histories.[30] I would argue that Spenser too, like Shakespeare after him in *The Tempest*, demonstrates something akin to the double consciousness we frequently find in Durán, Sahagún, and other New World chroniclers; in this way he moves substantially beyond the comparatively naive representations found in the writers quoted above. He engages, that is, with standard ethnographic practice in employing the "divine attribution" as a trope, but at the same time he offers ironic commentary on the frequent and seemingly unconscious European doubt about the status of those deemed "savage."[31]

In any case, we see once again in these voyagers' relations the movement from wonder to religion and the implicit association of savagery and idolatry. Bernheimer has argued that in the traditional conception of the wild man inherited by Renaissance Europe, religion played no part: "The wild man did not worship idolatrously because he did not worship at all."[32] But if this is true, we must then suppose that something happened in the Renaissance to modify this rather clear-cut perception; satyrs, after all, with their half-bestial anatomy, partake of the wild man tradition, and so do New World natives in European representation, through the processes of assimilation and cultural projection I have outlined in chapter 1.[33] It would seem, then, that the idea of the wild man itself underwent a change in the sixteenth century, a complication very likely associated with the influx of voyagers' ethnographic accounts, and particularly imbricated in a revelation of "savagery" as less constricting or limiting a condition than previously supposed. If natives of the New World had religious capacities—idolatrous or otherwise—and at the same time were involved in a reciprocal relationship with the European wodewose tradition—being inscribed by it and inscribing it in turn—it should come as no surprise that a writer such as Spenser can be found to reflect a broadened and more complicated understanding of what wildness means or could mean to his contemporaries.

Like Una among the satyrs and Britomart before the gaze of Artegall, the shepherdess Pastorella in Book Six is also the object of idolatrous admiration. The first time her future lover Calidore sees her, she is surrounded by adoring lasses and swains,

> Who her admiring as some heauenly wight,
> Did for their soueraine goddesse her esteeme,
> And caroling her name both day and night,
> The fayrest Pastorella her by name did hight. (6.9.9.6-9)

But these pastoral idolators are far removed from the comparative savagery of Una's satyrs or Artegall's assumed persona. They suggest by their presence and behavior that Spenser is interested in further exploring and limning the savage/civil binarism that he has established and evoked so often before in the poem. I turn now to Book Six of *The Faerie Queene* in order to demonstrate the extent to which Spenser narrates a set of inter-reflecting stories that assume a thorough and provocative interpenetration between the concepts of savagery and civility.

BOOK SIX, CANTOS 1–8:
SAVAGERY, CIVILITY, AND THE DEBATE OVER PRIMITIVISM

The pastoral character of Book Six—"The Legend of S. Calidore, or of Covrtesie"—is intimated as early as the third and fourth stanzas of the Proem, where Spenser speaks of the "sacred noursery / Of vertue" in which such fair flowers as courtesy are tended and brought to blossom. But not until the book's ninth canto does Spenser turn his attention fully to pastoral matters. In the meantime, his treatment of the virtue whose name he playfully derives from "Court" (6.1.1.1) takes the form of a series of elaborating and refracting episodes that, in their cumulative effect, suggest the breadth of his ideas of courtesy and discourtesy as well as their intimate connection to the related ideas of civility and savagery.

In cantos 1-3 we see Spenser repeatedly reinforce the notion that "gentle bloud will gentle manners breed" (6.3.2.2); the magical *melior natura* transmitted through aristocratic pedigree predisposes its inheritors to courtesy. Calidore, for example, is a knight "In whom, it seemes, that gentlenesse of spright / And manners mylde were planted naturall" (6.1.2.3-4), and Tristram, through a demonstration of courteous and courageous instincts, confirms Calidore's suspicion that he was "borne of noble blood" (6.2.24.6).[34] It is true that in calling Calidore's gentleness "naturall" Spenser obliquely hints that this virtue might be an innate human quality—indeed, later in the book we see Spenser further explore this idea—but the context strongly suggests that "natural" is here opposed to "artificial," and this of course implies that some people are born without a predisposition to courtesy and must work hard and be properly instructed to attain it.[35] That it may in fact be attained *solely* through education and practice is something Spenser never entirely rules out, though he clearly regards such a possibility as exceptional: "So seldome seene, that one in basenesse set / Doth noble courage shew, with curteous manners met" (6.3.1.8-9). Similarly, Spenser never states that blood alone, without training, guarantees perfect courtesy. But his repeated insistence on the gentle birth of his courteous characters tends to undermine any incipient democratic leanings we may detect in this section of *The Faerie Queene*.

At this point it seems legitimate to ask exactly what "courtesy" is, and what relationship it bears to the words "civility," "civil," and "savage," which also occur frequently in Book Six. In the book's famous first line—"Of Court it seemes, men Courtesie doe call"—Spenser provides a fanciful etymology of the word, and then tells us that courtesy is the ground "of all goodly manners . . . / And roote of ciuill conuersation" (6.1.1.5-6). Much later, in the persona of Colin Clout, he informs us that the three Graces

> on men all gracious gifts bestow,
> Which decke the body or adorne the mynde,
> To make them louely or well fauoured show,
> As comely carriage, entertainment kynde,
> Sweete semblaunt, friendly offices that bynde,
> And all the complements of curtesie:
> They teach vs, how to each degree and kynde
> We should our selues demeane, to low, to hie;
> To friends, to foes, which skill men call Ciuility. (6.10.23.1-9)

We thus have an etiology of courtesy and a sense of its closeness, in Spenser's outlook, to civility: Knowledge of "entertainment kynde" and of the "friendly offices that bynde" cannot differ greatly from knowledge of "how to each degree and kynde / We should our selues demeane."[36] The latter knowledge is perhaps slightly more comprehensive than the former, and includes our responses to foes as well as friends, but there is no question that, for Spenser, these two categories of behavior are closely allied, and the two words that designate them are nearly synonymous. This closeness is reinforced by the terms in which Calidore reprimands Briana in canto 1:

> they that breake bands of ciuilitie,
> And wicked customes make, those doe defame
> Both noble armes and gentle curtesie.
> No greater shame to man then inhumanitie. (6.1.26.6-9)

The word "inhumanitie" is crucial here: Briana, along with her "seneschall" Maleffort, has been engaged in the rather inhospitable enterprise of shearing the locks of ladies and the beards of knights in order to line a mantle she must present to Crudor if she is to earn his love. Her discourtesy thus consists of a combination of affrontery, stupidity, and arrogance, and it is precisely the breadth of this conception that reveals, by opposition, the breadth of Spenser's idea of courtesy.[37] To twentieth-century ears "discourtesy" seems an understatement for the behavior of Briana and Crudor, but the fact that Spenser also characterizes the brutal and ungenerous Turpine as a "discourteous Knight" (6.3.34.1) further reinforces the inference that lack of courtesy amounts not merely to bad manners but to inhumanity.

If we admit, then, that Spenser conceives of courtesy as a far more profound virtue than politeness—a virtue intimately connected to the concept of civility—we must also admit that at times "civility" seems to take on the broader and more progressive meaning that I spoke of in chapter 1: not merely the social condition aligned with Christianity, but any condition characterized by widespread social cooperation and established forms of behavior and authority—and not necessarily linked to Christian habits of belief. Civility, in other words, appears at times to be used by Spenser in the sense conveyed by our word "civilization," as for example in the Proem of Book Six, where courtesy is said to spread "it selfe through all ciuilitie" (6.Proem.4.5). Still, if we see hints of a Montaignian frame of mind here, we see occasional evidence elsewhere of Spenser's apparent lack of interest in distinguishing carefully and consistently between courtesy and civility: Sometimes the words differ substantially; more often they are almost synonymous. Like Las Casas, who now and then moves beyond the level of a Christian/heathen binarism in discussing American natives, Spenser is fully capable of suggesting that the virtues he treats can exist outside a Christian frame of reference; that he seldom emphasizes this is not sufficient proof that he rejects the idea.

Exemplifying this particular stratum of Spenser's thought is the hint that Tristram's courtesy, which in Spenser's initial portrayal seems almost guaranteed by his noble birth, is in fact perilously tentative. In the first place, we must note the way in which Tristram deals with the "armed knight" (6.2.3.9) who has so callously mistreated his unnamed lady (6.2.15-23). Unlike Calidore, who transforms Crudor and Briana into a courteous couple rather than killing them (6.1.39-46), Tristram summarily dispatches the rude knight (6.2.4)—so summarily, in fact, that Calidore is "inly child" (6.2.4.8) upon seeing the act. Moreover, near the close of the canto, after Calidore has agreed to take on Tristram as his squire, Tristram despoils the dead knight of his armor and feeds "his greedie eyes with the faire sight / Of the bright metall" (6.2.39.3-4). Eventually he dons the armor himself, raises the lady upon the dead knight's steed, and marches away. In this sinister metamorphosis we see Tristram "become" the knight he has slain, and we sense Spenser's suggestion that in spite of the young squire's patrician blood, his lack of proper education has prevented him from conforming to the finer points of courtesy. We begin to see the range of attitudes about nature and nurture that leads us, two cantos later, to the consideration of the Salvage Man.

Spenser invites us, in fact, to compare the Salvage Man with Tristram, inasmuch as both rescue helpless people from discourteous knights and both are ultimately revealed to be of gentle birth. Beyond this, however, the two have relatively little in common. The Salvage Man's providential appearance at the beginning of canto 4 is metaphorically likened to a "fisher barke" giving aid to "a ship with dreadfull storme long tost" (6.4.1.1-4); a sense of social hierarchy is thus immediately established, with the Salvage Man representing the meaner vessel and Calepine and Serena clearly associated with gentility and significant social status. The Salvage Man's lowliness is further indicated by his nakedness (6.4.4.4), his inability to speak (6.4.11.3-9), and his residence "Farre in the forrest" (6.4.13.5). He seems, in these qualities at least, a classic example of the wodewose; and his ignorance of "warlike instruments" (6.4.4.2) reminds us additionally of the conflation of Old World traditions with New World observations that we encounter when Columbus describes the natives of Española as having "no arms."[38] Indeed, other traces of New World iconography may also be found in the Salvage Man's portrayal: He can run "incessantly" (6.4.2.4), for example, and—like Daniel Defoe's Friday in *Robinson Crusoe*—he is "swift as any Bucke in chace" (6.4.8.3).[39] But unlike the Wild Man of Book Four, the Salvage Man represents a much more complicated blending of the wodewose and the cultural other. His apparent savagery is immediately qualified by his capacity for compassion (6.4.3.6), and the fact that he dwells in the wilderness is complicated by his generous hospitality (6.4.13-14) and his knowledge—like Belphoebe's when she heals Timias in Book Three—of the qualities and virtues of the forest's "herbes" (6.4.12.6; 6.4.16.4). Antipathetic attitudes thus give way to sympathetic portrayal; emblematic of this is the clear emphasis Spenser places upon the Salvage Man's diet: Unlike the Wild Man or the Salvage Nation presented later in Book Six, he never feeds on flesh (6.4.14.8) and is thus as far removed from cannibalism as his gentle guests.

In short, the Salvage Man—at once frightening and kind, speechless and wise—brings together the rawness associated with the natural world and the gentleness associated with good breeding; his presence suggests a breaking down of the conventional polarity of nature and culture. We can no longer credit—that is, if we ever could—the derivation of "Courtesie" from "Court." And though Spenser eventually undermines the complex suspension of elements in this depiction by informing us that the Salvage Man "was borne of noble blood" (6.5.2.7), his choice to spend much of canto 4 elaborating his portrayal before revealing this information demonstrates the extent to which he is willing to invite his readers to entertain the idea that birth may in fact make no difference, that gentleness may not necessarily be a function of blood. As if to drive this idea home, Spenser employs the last section of the same canto in contemplating blood and nurture from a different perspective: He tells us the story of the "litle babe" (6.4.18.1) rescued by Calepine and given to the childless Matilde.

Walking unarmed in the forest one day, Calepine comes upon "A cruell Beare, the which an infant bore / Betwixt his bloodie iawes, besprinckled all with gore" (6.4.17.8-9). Quite appropriately, given his status as Calidore's double in this book, Calepine finds his heart pierced with "pities point" (6.4.18.5) at the sight, and we are reminded, as he quickly contrives a way to rescue the babe, of the pity that the Salvage Man felt earlier (6.4.3.2). Thus, just as the Salvage Man saved Calepine and Serena, so Calepine saves the helpless infant; and this instance of explicit parallelism—a frequent technique in the poem—reinforces our confidence in the Salvage Man's gentle character by showing us similarly kind and courageous behavior in a knight whom we know to be trained in courtesy.

Calepine soon finds that he is lost in the forest, however, and only after a good deal of anxious wandering with the child does he come to the edge of the wood and discover the "wofull" Matilde lamenting her plight as a woman denied "the gladfull blessing of posteritie" (6.4.27.8; 6.4.31.3). Seizing his opportunity, Calepine wastes no time in presenting her with the foundling:

> Low how good fortune doth to you present
> This litle babe, of sweete and louely face,
> And spotlesse spirit, in which ye may enchace
> What euer formes ye list thereto apply,
> Being now soft and fit them to embrace;
> Whether ye list him traine in cheualry,
> Or noursle vp in lore of learn'd Philosophy. (6.4.35.3-9)

As A. Bartlett Giamatti has written, "The key word in [this] passage, and in Spenser's view of civility, is 'enchace'; that word tells how you apply form to a baby or a culture, how you create reformation or renaissance. To 'enchace' is the word that tells us what an artist does."[40] I hasten to add, though, that "enchacing" is by no means limited to aesthetic associations. If we think, for example, of Montaigne's claim that "Chaque homme porte la forme entiere de l'humaine condition" [Each man bears the entire form of man's estate], we are reminded of the complexity of Renaissance attitudes about the formation of human character.[41] "Formes" may be applied, as Spenser suggests, to an infant whose mind is a virtual *tabula rasa*, but if the form of Montaigne's "human condition" is also embedded within each person, then the claim to individual artistic shaping is substantially diminished. This is not to say that self-fashioning in the manner suggested by Calepine is improbable, but only that it may represent a naive view, a view more connected to an optimistic faith in nurture and education than to critical scrutiny of actual human development. Still, Spenser encourages in his readers here an enthusiasm for an anti-aristocratic view of gentility; Calepine tells Matilde that infants like the one he has given her, whose "linage was vnknowne," have often become "braue and noble knights" (6.4.36.2-3). It may be that Spenser intended to reveal later on, perhaps in one of the books he never composed, that the foundling, like the Salvage Man, was in fact descended from aristocratic parents. But we do not know this. What we know in canto 4 is that the Salvage Man has courteous instincts and that Calepine believes a foundling child may be brought up to courtesy. The attitudes toward gentle blood in the first three cantos of the book have been thrust aside; and while it would be an exaggeration to say that we see a kind of primitivism expressed here, it is clear that Spenser deliberately exposes us to an expanded idea of the origins of civil behavior.

But this expansion quickly contracts as we move through the next four cantos. The Salvage Man, who seems in canto 4 to be courteous by nature—though lacking in civil refinement—is revealed at the outset of canto 5 to possess the same *melior natura* shared by Tristram and Calidore. His "gentle vsage" of Serena is a "token of his gentle blood" (6.5.2.5), and Spenser marvels at the ease with which such inherited superiority may be discerned, even when "wrapt / In sad misfortunes foule deformity" (6.5.1.2-3). Of course, Spenser discerns the Salvage Man's pedigreed gentility a good deal more easily than do the characters who surround him; both Arthur and Timias, for example, assume at first that he is a villain (6.5.25.7; 6.5.27.8), and even Serena interprets his kindness as a fluke:

> In such a saluage wight, of brutish kynd,
> Amongst wilde beastes in desert forrests bred,
> It is most straunge and wonderfull to fynd
> So milde humanity, and perfect gentle mynd. (6.5.29.6-9)

We are thus exposed by this manipulation of perspectives to a range of attitudes toward the origins of courtesy—all of them conservative and aristocratic, and only Serena's admitting the possibility of natural gentility unconnected to blood. It must be acknowledged, however, that Arthur and

Timias quickly admit the Salvage Man to their company; their courtesy prevents them from scorning this man of putatively savage birth and upbring-ing. And the Salvage Man, in turn, is portrayed as "greatly growne in loue of that great pere [Arthur]" (6.5.41.8) by the end of the canto. From this we may infer, if we wish, that it is the Salvage Man's gentle blood that leads him instinctively to know whom to admire and serve; but Spenser does not insist on this. Once again, if ever so slightly, he leaves open the possibility that admirable human behavior may surface spontaneously due to innate predis-position rather than because of noble blood or gentle breeding.

It is a fleeting possibility, however. In the next three cantos, Spenser several times stresses the Salvage Man's lack of judgment and need for restraint in fighting.[42] Like Talus in Book Five (5.7.37; 5.11.65; 5.12.8), the Salvage Man seems incapable of discerning when mercy or leniency is in order, though quite fit to recognize authority, nobility, and untempered justice. We are reminded, perhaps, of the motto worn by Artegall in Book Four—"Saluagesse sans finesse" (4.4.39.9)—and of the advice given by the Hermit to Serena and Timias, both of whom have been wounded by the Blatant Beast: "First learne your outward sences to refraine / From things, that stirre vp fraile affection; . . . restraine your will, / Subdue desire, and bridle loose delight" (6.6.7.6-7; 6.6.14.5-6). The capriciousness of Serena and the impetuousness of Timias are not far removed from the passionate lack of restraint we see in the Salvage Man; and though the latter is never bitten by the Blatant Beast, Spenser's deliberate juxtaposition of the three characters' actions suggests that all of them must learn to control their "affections" if they are to attain the level of civil refinement implied by Spenser's use of "courtesy."

The least courteous of all characters in Book Six are undoubtedly the members of the Salvage Nation depicted in canto 8.[43] Dwelling in "wylde deserts," these people practice no husbandry, trade, or useful arts, but live by "stealth and spoile" (6.8.35.1-3); moreover, they "eate the flesh of men"—a custom Spenser condemns as "A monstrous cruelty gainst course of kynde" (6.8.36.2-5). Pearce has noted that "Spenser's cannibals . . . bear a particularly close resemblance to the Caribs described many times in Eden's translation of Martyr's *Decades*. . . . [people] living in the back country or on isolated islands, periodically raiding the settlements of the peaceful Indians and carrying off prisoners whom they will fatten and devour."[44] Thus, when Serena wanders innocently into the territory of the Salvage Nation, we are not surprised to see—in addition to anthropophagy—other elements of the iconography of New World natives almost spontaneously evoked. The savages are idolators, for instance, planning to sacrifice Serena "Vnto their

God" (6.8.38.6) before they eat her, and they are also helpless before their libidinous impulses:

> [Serena] being naked, to their sordid eyes
> The goodly threasures of nature appeare:
> Which as they view with lustfull fantasyes,
> Each wisheth to him selfe, and to the rest enuyes. (6.8.41.6-9)

It is only the rebuke of their priest that prevents these men from using Serena for their "beastly pleasure"; as Spenser remarks, "religion held euen theeues in measure" (6.8.43.6-9). Finally, the members of the Salvage Nation are wild carousers who play "the bagpypes and the hornes" (6.8.46.1). In this respect they principally resemble the inhabitants of the "savage nation" of Ireland where Spenser passed so much of his life—though delight in music is also a trait frequently associated with New World natives.[45] In short, the Salvage Nation's depiction relies upon a composite of largely antipathetic elements drawn from conventional Renaissance portrayals of the cultural (and religious) other. That the priest among these savages mutters secret incantations and performs "diuelish ceremonies" (6.8.45.7) is less important as an echo of specifically Irish, Roman Catholic, or Amerindian cultural practices than as an emblem of the distance these people are removed from the civility of their captive Serena or her savior Calepine.[46] And Spenser is careful to stress that they are indeed *people:* full human beings, unlike Una's satyrs with their "rough hornes" and "backward bent knees" (1.6.11.9). When Calepine slays the priest and the other men who attack him, he sends "swarmes of damned soules to hell" (6.8.49.7). This is reminiscent of the fate of the Wild Man, whose soul is "fled to hell" (4.7.32.5) when Belphoebe shoots him with an arrow, but whereas Spenser mystifies the Wild Man's status, the Salvage Nation is indisputably rendered as fully human. Thus, the entire episode may in part be regarded as a rejection of the primitivist thesis: The members of the Salvage Nation cannot claim subhuman status as either a cause or an excuse for their behavior. They are as human, if not as courteous or civil, as Calepine, Serena, and the Salvage Man.

A. S. Knowles, Jr., has written that the "contrasting natures" of the Salvage Man and the Salvage Nation "imply an unwillingness on Spenser's part to assign any one set of values to the natural man."[47] True enough in itself, this observation nonetheless fails to point to any reasons for the deeply ambiguous quality of Spenser's attitude toward the natural world and the humans most closely associated with it. On the one hand, Spenser clearly reveals an anti-primitivistic bias in his emphasis on the virtues of gentle blood and his antipathetic portrayal of such individuals as the Wild Man and the members of the Salvage Nation; Giamatti is quite right in remarking that Spenser avoided the "sentimental equation between what was primitive and what was good"—a "widely-held and much too easy conclusion."[48] On the other hand, by allowing his readers to view the Salvage Man through the eyes of Serena and Calepine, Spenser demonstrates a willingness to consider the idea that patrician birth may make no difference and that all humans possess a capacity for compassion and gentleness. It is true, of course, that the Salvage Man, like Tristram and Satyrane, lacks the civil and chivalric training of courtly life, but his instincts are good, and it is only after we have fully accepted him that we are informed of his noble blood. Moreover, the story of the infant found by Calepine reinforces the notion that one's birth matters little in comparison to one's upbringing. Spenser takes us far outside the orbit of traditional aristocratic ideas about *melior natura* before allowing us to reenter it once again.

If we are to talk of Spenser's "primitivism," then, we cannot suppose that it exists within any sort of critique of Christianity or promotion of noble savagery; but we *can* argue that it surfaces as an awareness that immersion in the natural world helps people attain humility and quiet confidence, makes them conscious of the limitations of court and courtly behavior, and encourages them to escape self-absorption and adopt what might be called an ecological perspective. This will become clearer as we consider the last four cantos of Book Six, but it is strongly implied by the cantos I have already discussed. In addition to the Salvage Man's ability—like Belphoebe's—to heal and feed people through his knowledge of "herbes" and "forrest frute" (6.4.16.4; 6.7.24.4), he also possesses a magic invulnerability (6.4.4.9) that protects him from the malevolence of "discourteous" characters like Turpine and Scorn. Refigured in the foundling child—who despite being carried in the "bloodie iawes" of a bear receives no wounds in his "tender flesh" (6.4.17.9; 6.4.23.9)—this invulnerability may well be symbolic of the virtues of a profound connection to the natural world: After all, neither the babe nor the Salvage Man has known anything else. Furthermore, it is by no means insignificant that the greatest healer of Book Six, the Hermit who cures Serena and Timias, lives alone on a plain, "Far from all neighbourhood" (6.5.34.9). Spenser clearly associates the ability to heal with the ability to avoid being wounded, and both are intimately connected with residence in wild places far from the haunts of humanity.[49]

Of course, by no means all of Spenser's characters benefit from their association with wild places. As I mentioned earlier, Duessa becomes almost bestial in the "waste wildernesse" (2.1.22.2), and her example is followed in

Book Three by Hellenore and Malbecco in their different ways (3.10-12). This regression to savagery is perhaps best expressed in Grille's choice of animality over humanity—a choice about which the Palmer can only remark to Guyon, "Let Grill be Grill, and haue his hoggish mind" (2.12.87.8). Self-evidently, then, a degeneration or Nebuchadnezzaresque lapse into the bestial is for Spenser a continual human possibility—particularly in remote and uninhabited regions;[50] as Giamatti writes, "Wild men are what we have been and can be again if, as Spenser would say, we are 'carelesse.'" I disagree with Giamatti, however, in his further assertion that none of Spenser's wild men have the potential for civility.[51] Giamatti implies that even with education and practice characters like the Salvage Man and Satyrane lack the necessary constitution to become civil in the same way that Calidore is. Yet Spenser writes in his *View of the Present State of Ireland* that "learning hath that wonderful power of itself that it can soften and temper the most stern and savage nature," and he claims, moreover, that "the rude Irish, which, being very wild at the first, are now become somewhat more civil, when as these [Englishmen in Ireland] from civility are grown to be wild and mere Irish."[52] From this it would hardly seem that Spenser denies the possibility that the savage human may become civil just as readily as the civil may become savage.[53] We can infer, then, that Spenser conceives of savagery and civility not so much as steps in an evolutionary progress as shades in a spectrum.[54] And one of the consequences of such a conception is that the two states of being may be regarded not as mutually exclusive but as interdependent and interpenetrating; Spenser has moved beyond the bounds of the limited view that savagery survives only outside the realm of civility and thus cannot coexist with civil propensities in a single human being.[55] And if, as I have argued, awareness of the New World and its inhabitants complicated the Renaissance understanding of wildness, this awareness may equally have subverted conventional ideas about the separation of nature and culture. It may, in short, have allowed Europeans such as Spenser to subject their inherited lore of courtesy to skeptical examination.[56]

Giamatti claims that for Spenser, "civility is a process of passing through the primitive in order to engage it and thus consciously to overcome it. The primitive order does not give rise to civility; it only provides the backdrop against which civility defines itself."[57] I believe, in contrast, that Spenser is much less interested in positing an adversarial relationship between savagery and civility than in suggesting their complementarity. There is no question that he believes humans must strive for the courteous and civil behavior that is learned, first and foremost, through emulation of those who already practice it. But it is by no means obvious that Spenser dismisses out of hand the possibility that this courtesy may be acquired, retained, and even refined in wild places far from court. And to the extent that people are inevitably shaped by that which surrounds them—subdued, in short, like the dyer's hand—they may be said to be representative of a complex union of the savage and the civil that defies traditional and reductive explanation. The Salvage Man feels compassion though he has grown to maturity in the wilderness; the Hermit retires to a desolate plain in order to practice and instruct a more significant courtesy than any found at court. And, in the final four cantos of Book Six, when Spenser transports us to the pastoral world of the peopled countryside, we see a further exploration of the idea that nature and culture interpenetrate in surprising and intricate ways.

BOOK SIX, CANTOS 9–12:
SPENSER'S AMBIGUOUS PASTORAL

Spenser wastes no time in introducing his readers to the rural character of the final cantos of Book Six. He does this, however, in a curious manner: Rather than employing specifically pastoral imagery at the beginning of canto 9, he uses an agricultural metaphor in which the continuing story of Calidore is likened to a stretch of as-yet-unploughed soil—"soyle both fayre and frutefull" (6.9.1.5) and thus almost certain to yield a rich harvest. Spenser then describes how Calidore has pursued the Blatant Beast in an exhausting odyssey from court to city to town, from town to country to private farm, and finally to the open field (6.9.3-4).[58] We are thus transported to the general realm of country life, but the specific character of this life—pastoral or agrarian—is left unspecified. Only when Calidore encounters shepherds with their flocks do we know for certain where we are—and even then, since the shepherds deny having seen or heard of any such "wicked feend" (6.9.6.2) as Calidore inquires about, we are left to wonder whether we are still in the Faerie Land to which we have grown accustomed from the poem's previous books. The quick courtesy of these shepherds—they immediately offer Calidore food and drink—and the seeming absence of evil from their realm briefly lure us into the attractive illusion that Calidore has stumbled into a sort of golden world where the Blatant Beast, with his slanderous malignancy, cannot penetrate, and where courteous behavior is universally practiced. Spenser's initial hesitancy in identifying this realm as pastoral perhaps indicates that he is less interested in following the precise dictates of literary convention than he is in stressing the distance of *both* pastoral and agrarian life from the life of court and city.

The common tropes of "soft" or idealizing pastoral quickly make their appearance, however. Besides "Playing on pypes, and caroling apace" (6.9.5.3), the shepherds sing "Layes of sweete loue and youthes delightfull heat" (6.9.4.4). The "swaynes" sit below the "litle hillocke" where Pastorella stands and "sing her prayses dew" (6.9.8.1-6). Meliboe, Pastorella's *de facto* father, is "a good old aged syre" with "siluer lockes" and "shepheards hooke in hand" (6.9.13.6-8); it is he who most thoroughly exemplifies the traditional hospitality of the pastoral community by inviting Calidore home and offering him food and lodging. But it is Calidore himself who, more than any of the permanent residents of this rural world, idealizes its traits. After dining with Meliboe and Pastorella, he launches into an encomium upon "the happie life, / Which Shepheards lead" (6.9.18.8-9)—a life free from "warres," "wreckes," "wicked enmitie," and "the tempests of these wordly seas" (6.9.19.4-6). He wishes that he could enjoy "such felicitie" (6.9.19.9) and that his fortunes "might transposed bee / From pitch of higher place, vnto this low degree" (6.9.28.8-9). In short, he betrays to the poem's readers through his praise of pastoral *otium* [leisure] that he knows little or nothing of rural life's realities, that his pastoralism is exactly the form described by William Empson—the "form that looks proletarian but isn't."[59] And his shallow idealism is further revealed by the fact that he continues to employ the language of hierarchy despite his newfound contempt for the court and his professed love for the superior virtues of the simple life. He comments more than once on the "lowlinesse" of Meliboe's station (6.9.27.6; 6.9.28.9), and he thinks to himself that Pastorella so far exceeds "the meane of shepheards" that she is worthy "To be a Princes Paragone" (6.9.11.3-5). As readers, we are thus exposed to a curious and apparently self-contradictory pair of ideas: that the lives of shepherds and others who possess close ties to the natural world are happier and more desirable than those of courtiers and city-dwellers, but that, at the same time, these lives are "low," "base," "meane," (6.9.28.9; 6.9.35.4; 6.9.10.9) and generally less valuable than those of people born with higher social status.

What is particularly interesting is the degree to which the actions and words of Pastorella and Meliboe corroborate these views of Calidore. Pastorella, despite her initial scorn for Calidore's "queint vsage" and "knightly seruice" (6.9.35.2-3), quickly succumbs to the charms of the courteous knight (6.9.45-46), thereby proving true Spenser's earlier characterization: "Though meane her lot, yet higher did her mind ascend" (6.9.10.9). And while Meliboe tempers the exaggerated praise of his guest by pointing out that Nature teaches one to be content with very little (6.9.20), he nonetheless seconds Calidore's praise of country life by painting his own idyllic picture of it

(6.9.21-23). Moreover, he defends the system of subordination that has placed him near the bottom of the social hierarchy, arguing that it is fitting and proper "that all contented rest / With that they hold: each hath his fortune in his brest" (6.9.29.8-9). In so doing, Meliboe perfectly exemplifies what Empson has called "the essential trick of the old pastoral": the implication of "a beautiful relation between rich and poor" through the vehicle of "simple people express[ing] strong feelings (felt as the most universal subject, something fundamentally true about everybody) in learned and fashionable language."[60] Far from being resentful of his condition, Meliboe is resentful only of Calidore's excessive courtesy—and then only mildly (6.9.33). No monarch could wish for a more dutiful, less revolutionary subject. Ultimately, then, and in spite of his more realistic view of country life and his contentedness with his station, Meliboe has a good deal in common with Calidore— above all a strong, though unstressed, consciousness of rank.

Meliboe's conservatism and mystification of class barriers fits well with Louis Montrose's persuasive view of Elizabethan pastoral as aristocratically sanctioned. Montrose argues that "The pastoral flowering of late Elizabethan and early Jacobean England . . . is dominantly aristocratic in values and style—even though the majority of its poets were of relatively humble origins and means. . . . Indeed, [pastoral] is one of that culture's characteristic forms—an authorized mode of discontent—rather than a critique made in terms of a consciously articulated oppositional culture."[61] But whereas such a view as that espoused by Montrose might logically end in an alignment of Meliboe's attitude with that of Spenser as representative of the controlling consciousness of the poem, I think Spenser undermines Meliboe's authority in both subtle and not-so-subtle ways. Just as Spenser shows us Calidore's courtly limitations in supposing rural existence to be free from care, he shows us Meliboe's moralizing complacency in praising the "lowly quiet life" (6.9.25.9). Meliboe not only accepts the status quo; he embraces it with perverse ardor. His vehement and self-satisfied remarks about forgiving "great ones" for their "follies" (6.9.22.2) and being contented without "forreine helpes" and "the worlds gay showes" (6.9.20.7; 6.9.22.1) point suspiciously to his own admission that in his "prime of years" he left the country and labored for a decade as a gardener at the Prince's court, only to see his hopes proven "idle" and his youth spent in vain (6.9.24.1; 6.9.25.2). Thus, rather than presenting a tame and easily-contained critique of hierarchy through the speech of an apparently wise and untroubled old man, Spenser may in fact be pointing here to the self-willed blindness and resignation consequent upon courtly rejection and long-harbored resentment. If so, Annabel Patterson's claim that Spenser offers "unspeakable criticism alongside . . . celebration" of the English political system may account more fully than does Montrose's argument for this peculiar undermining of Meliboe's position.[62] Spenser's practice of pastoral—equally evident, for instance, in Cuddie's responses to Piers in *The Shepheardes Calendar*'s October eclogue—may not in fact be as far removed from its classical precedents or from the famous pastoral definitions offered by Puttenham and Sidney as Raymond Williams has implied in his assertion that in Renaissance pastoral "living tensions are excised, until there is nothing countervailing, and selected images stand as themselves: not in a living world but in an enamelled one."[63] Spenser himself, like Meliboe, had spent time at court hoping for preferment, and it is by no means unthinkable that his frustrations may have found subtle and indirect expression in this portrayal of a rustic who lectures a courtier on the peace and contentment of country life.

But Spenser also devises a less subtle way of demonstrating that Meliboe's perceptions are radically limited: Late in canto 10 the "lawlesse" Brigants invade the pastoral realm (6.10.39.3). Reminiscent of the Salvage Nation depicted earlier in Book Six—though less conventionally uncivilized and far more devious—the Brigants are a non-agrarian people "That neuer vsde to liue by plough nor spade, / But fed on spoile and booty" (6.10.39.4-5), and their arrival forever destroys the "sweet peace" of Meliboe's "lowly quiet life" (6.9.25.6-9). Just a few stanzas earlier we have heard Spenser hint at a harder version of pastoral in telling us of the fierce "Tigre" that attacks Pastorella and is subsequently killed by Calidore (6.10.34.4); but with the Brigants' raid Spenser obliterates any lingering illusion that Meliboe's pastoral world is an ideal realm unconnected to the hardships and perils of Faerie Land—or, indeed, the world inhabited by *The Faerie Queene*'s readers. Like the Wild Man of Book Four, the Brigants live in caves (6.10.42.2); their "Capitaine" lusts after Pastorella with his "barbarous heart" (6.11.3.4; 6.11.4.1); and the "theeues" fight among themselves like "a sort of hungry dogs" (6.11.15.1; 6.11.17.1).[64] Ultimately they kill both Meliboe and his "aged wife" (6.11.18.4-5) and, through an ironic twist, it is only because of the Captain's lust that Pastorella survives. Calidore eventually rescues her, but though he does so dressed in "shepheards weeds" (6.11.36.2), he is well-armed and has devised a subtle strategem to gain access to the Brigants' "hellish dens" (6.11.41.2). In short, he employs tactics he never could have learned in the pastoral realm. Spenser suggests through the juxtaposition of Meliboe's death and Calidore's survival that an idealized and perhaps self-serving view of the relation between humans and the natural world is likely to lead in the end to disillusionment, even disaster. Calidore has matured in the course of his pastoral sojourn, but it is his courtly courage and shrewdness that enable him to save Pastorella's life and his own.

This process of narrative and contextual complication tends to demonstrate the truth of Helen Cooper's characterization of Spenser's attitude toward courtesy in the pastoral setting as "strangely double-edged."[65] In the trajectory from "soft" to "hard" pastoral in the late cantos of Book Six, we see a move from euphoric affirmation of the value of life close to nature to renewed recognition of the need for courtly sophistication in combatting evil. It is no accident that this move coincides with Calidore's initial evasion and subsequent resumption of his quest: the capture of the Blatant Beast. While idylling among the "perfect pleasures" (6.10.3.5) of Meliboe's realm, Calidore learns to perform country chores and temper his courteous excesses (6.9.33-46); he gains something of Pastorella's respect for simplicity and disdain of "queint" and artificial customs (6.9.35.2); and his character is deepened and complicated through his exposure to Meliboe's conviction that Nature teaches contentment (6.9.20.6-7). Spenser's overriding point in this section seems unquestionably to be that courtesy has much to gain from the natural life of the country.[66] And while this stance is far from full-fledged primitivism, it is primitivistic inasmuch as it takes us outside the charmed circle of aristocratic society and gentle blood, proposing instead a broader explanation for the genesis and development of civil behavior.

I think it is fair to say, then, that Empson somewhat misrepresents matters when he writes that "the best manners are learnt in the simple life. . . . this last is the point of Spenser's paradox about 'courtly'; the Book of Courtesy takes the reader among the Noble Savages."[67] Untrue even with respect to the Salvage Man, this claim is further contradicted by the example of Coridon, the most fully characterized shepherd after Meliboe—and anything but a noble savage. His "gealousie" of Calidore makes him "scoule, and pout, and oft complaine" (6.9.39.3; 6.9.38.7), and he is filled with "cowherd feare" when the tiger attacks Pastorella (6.10.35.3). As a representative shepherd, Coridon exemplifies the shortcomings of rural nurture as much as Meliboe and Pastorella exemplify its virtues; his depiction constitutes part of Spenser's undercutting of idealized country life in a movement toward more realistic and fully-rounded portrayal. That Meliboe himself spent ten years at court is another facet of this undercutting, as is the ultimate discovery of Pastorella's gentle birth. And yet this last revelation—withheld until the final canto of Book Six and thus reminiscent of similarly belated discoveries about Tristram and the Salvage Man—is strangely ambiguous. To learn that Pastorella, like Perdita in *The Winter's Tale*, is the long lost daughter of royal parents is perhaps to confirm one's suspicion that Spenser ultimately subscribes to aristocratic notions about hereditary superiority. At the same time, however, we must not forget that Pastorella, like Perdita, was "enchaced" in the country. And Calidore, who never learns that Pastorella's social status is equal to his own, is nonetheless content to seek and win her love. Like Florizel, who is entirely willing to give up all he has for Perdita—"I'll be thine, my fair, / Or not my father's; for I cannot be / Mine own, nor any thing to any, if / I be not thine" (WT 4.4.42-45)—Calidore embodies a similar thematic levelling, a willingness to defy custom, hierarchy, and aristocratic tradition. And this following of instincts, apparently to the promotion of chaos and disorder, is shown in the end to lead precisely to the *order* metaphorically represented by the discovery of noble birth. The nobility of Pastorella and Perdita is less important as a genealogical fact than as a stabilizing revelation in the unfolding narrative, a revelation that serves primarily as a metaphorical vehicle reaffirming a principle of order only apparently imperiled by the lovers' earlier choices. Just as in the case of the Salvage Man, then, Spenser complicates his narrative in such a way that we cannot suppose him to be unequivocally anti-primitivistic in his assumptions and speculations. The disclosure of Pastorella's gentle birth at the end of the Legend of Courtesy figures almost as an emblem of the curious lack of resolution Spenser displays as he questions the origins of savagery and civility.

Leo Marx has written that "Most literary works called pastorals . . . manage to qualify, or call into question, or bring irony to bear against the illusion of peace and harmony in a green pasture."[68] This is certainly true of Book Six of *The Faerie Queene.* Not only the presence of outsiders like the Brigants and Calidore, but that of Meliboe and Pastorella themselves complicates the simple shepherds' world. Primitivism—the belief, to a greater or lesser degree, in the sufficiency of nature and natural processes—is interrogated and found inadequate in a world where peace and harmony never reign without interruption. The courtesy and sophistication of city and court are shown to be necessary to the maintenance of social order. Yet it is in the country that Calidore finds true and faithful love, and it is there also that he is privileged to witness a "countrey lasse" (6.10.25.8) honored among the Graces in his vision on Mount Acidale. This apotheosis echoes his own union with Pastorella; that which is emblematic of natural development is placed on an equal footing with that which has been thoroughly shaped by conscious art. Once again we see the interpenetration of nature and culture which we have earlier seen in Spenser's treatment of the Salvage Man. Here, though, it is more refined, and Spenser relies on the devices of literary pastoral to demonstrate the complex synthesis of experience necessary to the formation of mature and civilized humans: on the one hand, exposure to cultural sophistication, and on the other, respect for and understanding of natural processes.

Clearly, Spenser is not the representative of a monolithic anti-primitivism that he sometimes has been taken to be—even in historically informed readings of *The Faerie Queene*.[69] Nor, of course, is he a doctrinaire primitivist, a sort of Rousseau *avant la lettre*.[70] Like Montaigne, Spenser is more complicated, more subtle. And while this subtlety may certainly be detected by other means than situating *The Faerie Queene* within the context of early modern ethnographic and geographic description of the New World, perhaps no other contextualization so clearly illuminates the poem's concern with savage and civil forms of human existence. Critics have to some extent recognized this before: Leo Marx has claimed that "It is impossible to separate the taste for pastoral and the excitement, felt throughout Europe, about the New World," and Humphrey Tonkin has stressed that European colonial expansion "led to the discovery of new communities in remote parts of the world—communities which to some European eyes seemed evidence of a more nearly perfect civilization."[71] But even beyond accepting sensible observations such as these, we may credit the idea that attention to ethnographic elements of New World description alerts us to ways in which Spenser and other Renaissance writers complicate conventional notions of the relation between savagery and civility.

For Montaigne, American natives have the potential to be as noble as the most exemplary Greeks and Romans or as foolish, presumptuous, and inhumane as the worst conquistadors, and we are more likely to apprehend this if we read his *Essays* in light of contemporary New World accounts. For Spenser, savage humans may become civil just as readily as the civil may become savage; and savagery itself is less limiting a condition than previously supposed, connected, as it unquestionably is, with all the conflicting associations of primitivism and natural sufficiency. As I have demonstrated, both writers are far from being purely primitivistic in intention; such univocalism was certainly *not* the lesson to be learned from the travel literature. But when these writers explore their primitivist curiosities—and this is frequently— they lay bare a shared assumption of crucial importance: that all people are naturally and fundamentally similar, that human capacities for intellectual, moral, and spiritual growth outweigh the accidents of particular cultural inscriptions. To suppose that Europeans could resemble Léry's Tupinamba natives if only they could escape social corruption is impossible unless one grants that both peoples share some sort of common essence, some kind of fundamental unity in their potential for development. To imagine that a man nurtured alone in the wilderness can recognize and combat inhumanity, or that a foundling infant may grow up to become more brave and noble a knight than a child born of gentle blood—such suppositions are equally essentialistic.[72] They deny the ideologically-founded distinction between common and gentle heredity; they insist upon innate qualities shared by *all* humans and upon the critical importance of nurture. And to the extent that nurture in the country or even the wilderness is divested of many of its negative stereotypes, these suppositions additionally suggest ways in which the ideas of nature and culture may be seen to overlap and lose their conventional insularity and hermetic distinctness. In Las Casas we see a first glimmering of these interconnected convictions; in Montaigne we find them supported by anecdotes, ruminations, and circuitous arguments; and in Spenser we view them refracted through the literary lenses of romance epic and pastoral.

Spenser never goes so far as to show us that there is no such thing as an "unaccommodated man"; the Wild Man of Book Four—if he *is* indeed a man—answers that description reasonably well. Naked, speechless, solitary, brutal, and nasty, he certainly bears a greater resemblance to a "bare, fork'd animal" than *Lear*'s Poor Tom or *The Tempest*'s Caliban. But in other portrayals of "natural" humans in *The Faerie Queene*—portrayals less deeply indebted to the literary tradition of the wodewose—Spenser veers in the direction that Montaigne took earlier; he suggests, as Montaigne did so remarkably in "Of cannibals," that the idea of human beings wholly without cultural trappings is a myth, a medieval hangover, an untenable reduction.[73] The satyrs have traces of civility in their capacity—however idolatrous—to transform wonder into religion; the Salvage Man has acquired gentleness, healing power, and a rudimentary moral sense; and even the Salvage Nation, though cruelly discourteous, is characterized by its musicality and respect for individual authority. Spenser certainly does not follow the pattern of writers such as Columbus and Martyr, who represent the savage predominantly as a *tabula rasa*: devoid of cultural traits and eminently available for Christian and European inscription. Rather, he adopts an attitude congruent with the methods of Las Casas and especially Montaigne in incorporating the details of contemporary ethnography into a complex synthesis, thereby placing inherited ideas of savagery and civility in a new and comparatively unconventional light. He is not, of course, the epistemological skeptic that Montaigne is, nor an impassioned defender of fundamental human rights and Christian essentialism like Las Casas, but he nonetheless shares important beliefs and operant presuppositions with these writers. Above all—and in spite of his reputation as a poet's poet, serene, confident, and ideologically conservative—Spenser is a brilliant observer of contemporary habits of thought and ideation, and often a more shrewd and subtle critic of them than many of his commentators have acknowledged.

4
—

Shakespearean Accommodation and New World Ethnography

MEN OF INDE AND COLONIAL DISCOURSE

Audiences and scholars have long recognized that the plays of William Shakespeare, like Edmund Spenser's *Faerie Queene,* allude in various places and various ways to the New World. Many of these allusions are wholly conventional, signalling nothing more than a repetition of standard Renaissance stereotypes about America; among these may be counted lighthearted references to the mineral wealth of the New World in *The Comedy of Errors, The Merchant of Venice, Henry the Fourth, Part One, As You Like It, The Merry Wives of Windsor,* and *Twelfth Night,* and metaphors in which love is likened to Amerindian sun worship in *Love's Labor's Lost* and *All's Well That Ends Well.*[1] Others, such as the mention of the "strange Indian with the great tool" in *Henry VIII* (5.3.34), are perhaps equally stereotypical but at the same time more suggestive of familiarity with individual New World natives; long ago Sidney Lee speculated that Shakespeare "doubtless caught a glimpse" of most of the natives of Virginia, Guiana, and New England who were brought to London in the late sixteenth and early seventeenth centuries.[2] Still others constitute examples of linguistic borrowing, such as "hurricanoes" in *King Lear* (3.2.2), "potato" in *Troilus and Cressida* (5.2.56), "cannibals" in *Henry the Sixth, Part Three* (1.4.152, 5.5.61) and *Othello* (1.3.143), and, more indirectly, "Setebos" in *The Tempest* (1.2.373, 5.1.261).[3] Finally, there are dramatic allusions, allusions dependent not so much upon explicit references to the "Indies," "Mexico," or "Bermoothes" as upon situations resonant with contemporary New World associations. A particular abundance of these may be found in *The Tempest*—at least according to an ever-growing number of critics—and as a result, readings of the play in which the European consciousness of America serves as a contextual ground have become increasingly common in recent years.

As Alden T. Vaughan has pointed out, "The 'Americanist' reading" of *The Tempest*, while "only one of many that have flourished in the past three and a half centuries, . . . has dominated twentieth-century interpretations."[4] Prospero's assumption of rulership, Gonzalo's imagined "plantation," and Caliban's slavery and rebellion are just a few of the facets of this drama that make it, in Leo Marx's words, Shakespeare's "American fable."[5]

Discussion of Shakespeare's sources for *The Tempest* and for his New World allusions in other plays has taken interesting directions in recent years, resulting, among other things, in a critical revaluation of conventional source study of the past. No one denies that a reference such as that in *Twelfth Night* to "the new map, with the augmentation of the Indies" (3.2.79-80) provides persuasive evidence that Shakespeare had glanced through the second edition of Richard Hakluyt's *Principal Navigations* (1598-1600), or that certain passages in *The Tempest* bear strong witness to Shakespeare's acquaintance with John Florio's 1603 translation of Michel de Montaigne and the Bermuda narratives of William Strachey and Silvester Jourdain.[6] But source study relying on parallel passages and grounded on the principle of a writer's actual familiarity with source texts quickly loses its air of objectivity and shades into varying degrees of speculativeness, as the investigations of Margaret T. Hodgen and Robert Ralston Cawley clearly reveal.[7] Thus it should come as no surprise that we find more recent commentators abandoning all pretense of demonstrating that Shakespeare "knew" a given text; instead, we discover an increasing interest in models and in informing discursive contexts. Charles Frey, for example, while noting curious parallels between incidents in *The Tempest* and in narratives of early circumnavigations such as those of Ferdinand Magellan, Sir Francis Drake, and Thomas Cavendish, nonetheless points out that "Whether or not Shakespeare had read Eden's narrative of Magellan's voyage, such accounts can inform or illuminate *The Tempest* because they provide models of Renaissance experience in the New World. . . . We need to read the voyage literature, therefore, not necessarily to find out what Shakespeare read, but what Shakespeare and his audience together would have been likely to know—what they would have gathered from a variety of sources."[8] Similarly, Francis Barker and Peter Hulme, drawing on Julia Kristeva's articulation of intertextuality, argue that what they term "contextualization" "differs most importantly from source criticism when it establishes the necessity of reading *The Tempest* alongside congruent texts, irrespective of Shakespeare's putative knowledge of them, and when it holds that such congruency will become apparent from the constitution of discursive networks to be traced independently of authorial 'intentionality'."[9] In defense of traditional source criticism, it is only fair to note that even such conventional practitioners as Cawley and Hodgen occasionally advance beyond the stage of unproblematic attribution; Cawley suggests that certain texts that postdate *The Tempest* are also valuable inasmuch as they "illustrate the general spirit of the times"; Hodgen argues convincingly that if Shakespeare had never read Montaigne's "Of cannibals," Gonzalo's "plantation" speech might well have been written anyway, perhaps very much as it now exists.[10] Similarly, Maynard Mack cautions us, in discussing the sources of *King Lear*, against "ignoring larger, admittedly vaguer, but equally cogent influences, which frequently determine the way in which the specific source is used."[11] In short, an awareness of textual "congruencies" is by no means unique to poststructuralist critics. In contrast to their predecessors, however, these critics have much more satisfactorily articulated the theoretical grounds for such an awareness, principally on the basis of discursive networks and practices; and, in addition, they have contended that all texts, whether construed generically as "poetry," "history," "travel writing," or otherwise, are equally permeable by ideology and by cultural norms and presuppositions.

The discourse most frequently brought forth as an informing context for *The Tempest* is English colonialism in the late sixteenth and early seventeenth centuries. And perhaps no passage from canonical English literature better characterizes the spirit of such critical contextualization than the following, in which Lemuel Gulliver, returned from his sojourn among the Houyhnhnms, offers a cynical précis of British overseas activities:

> For instance, A Crew of Pyrates are driven by a Storm they know not whither; at length a Boy discovers Land from the Top-mast; they go on Shore to rob and plunder; they see an harmless People, are entertained with Kindness, they give the Country a new Name, they take formal possession of it for the King, they set up a rotton Plank or a Stone for a Memorial, they murder two or three dozen of the Natives, bring away a Couple more by Force for a Sample, return home, and get their Pardon. Here commences a new Dominion acquired with a Title by *Divine Right*. Ships are sent with the first Opportunity; the Natives are driven out or destroyed, their Princes tortured to discover their Gold; a free License given to all Acts of Inhumanity and Lust; the Earth reeking with the Blood of its Inhabitants: And this execrable Crew of Butchers employed in so pious an Expedition, is a *modern Colony* sent to convert and civilize an idolatrous and babarous People.[12]

Colonial contextualization, of course, has been more or less implicit in many twentieth-century readings and productions of *The Tempest*; witness, for instance, the procolonial production mounted in 1904 by Herbert

Beerbohm-Tree, the anticolonial production by Jonathan Miller in 1970, and the suggestive remarks of such politically divergent writers as A. L. Rowse, Roberto Fernández Retamar, and Leslie Fiedler.[13] But only in the past dozen or fifteen years has there been a concerted effort to locate the play explicitly within the complicated network of ideas, preconceptions, goals, schemes, rhetoric, and propaganda that constitutes colonial discourse. Barker and Hulme, for example, see *The Tempest* as "imbricated within the discourse of colonialism," and Paul Brown writes that the play "serves as a limit text in which the characteristic operations of colonialist discourse may be discerned—as an instrument of exploitation, a register of beleaguerment and a site of radical ambivalence."[14] One of the interesting consequences of this explicit contextualization is that recent critics have found a means whereby to demonstrate the extent to which earlier commentators either occluded or missed altogether the text's "anxieties" about colonialism due to their sympathy—conscious or unconscious—with colonialist ambitions and ideology.[15] In contrast, and without pursuing at length this sort of *ad hominem* criticism, such writers as Barker, Hulme, and Brown have drawn attention to the ways in which *The Tempest* illuminates common tropes of colonialist discourse and offers resistance both to procolonial and antihistorical readings. Brown argues, for instance, that Prospero "produces" Caliban as a dangerous and threatening other, and that the containment of Caliban, Stephano, and Trinculo unifies Prospero and Alonso's party in their colonial and aristocratic hegemony.[16] And Hulme makes the useful point that "Prospero is [a] colonial historian, and such a convincing and ample historian that other histories have to fight their way into the crevices of his official monument."[17] All three writers demonstrate an acute awareness that "truths" about Caliban, Ariel, and the beginnings of Prospero's rule on the island have too often been conflated with Prospero's own allegations. As Hulme puts it, critics have time and again shown an "uncritical willingness to identify Prospero's voice as direct and reliable authorial statement, and therefore to ignore the lengths to which the play goes to dramatize its problems with the proper beginnings of its own story."[18] In a strange way, then, it would appear that emphatic historical contextualization has allowed recent readers of *The Tempest* to make valuable contributions to what in the past has emphatically *not* been considered an activity deeply dependent upon this sort of historical knowledge—reading the play as a *play*, a dramatic construct that continually comments upon its own existence and assertions through its inherently dialogic nature.

A sampling of the interchanges and dramatic incidents in *The Tempest* that tend to receive greater attention in colonialist considerations might begin with the following pair of speeches: Stephano's remark to Trinculo that "the King and all our company else being drown'd, we will inherit here" (2.2.174-75), and Prospero's reminiscence to Alonso and others that "most strangely / Upon this shore . . . was [I] landed, / To be the lord on't" (5.1.159-62). The first of these pronouncements is uttered in the presence of Caliban (clearly a more rightful "inheritor" than Stephano, if only on the grounds of prior inhabitation), and both reveal a complete obliviousness to the idea that indigenous non-Europeans might have a legitimate claim to lands upon which Europeans have stumbled. Yet the idea was not foreign to European jurists of the period—Francisco de Vitoria offers one of its classic statements in his *De Indiis recenter inventis, relectio prior [On the Indians Lately Discovered]* (1539)[19]—and even Drake delayed claiming Nova Albion (northern California) for England until after a ceremony in which the native king "made several orations, or rather supplications, that hee [Drake] would take their province and kingdome into his hand, and become their King, . . . which thing our Generall thought not meete to reject, because he knew not what honour and profit it might be to our Countrey."[20] Stephano's further remark to Caliban, "Trinculo and thyself shall be viceroys" (3.2.108), reminds us that viceregal government was the standard form of colonial rule in Spanish America; and Prospero's command, "Let them be hunted soundly" (4.1.262), immediately follows the stage direction "Enter divers Spirits in shape of dogs and hounds, hunting them about; Prospero and Ariel setting them on," thereby reinforcing the sense in which the punishment of Caliban and the Neapolitan drunkards recapitulates the many early modern accounts of New World natives being terrorized by dogs.[21]

Other incidents highlighted by situating *The Tempest* within colonialist discourse might include the initial reciprocity of relations between Prospero and Caliban (1.2.332-38); the disagreement among Gonzalo, Adrian, Antonio, and Sebastian as to the nature of the island (1.2.35-58); Trinculo and Stephano's talk of transporting Caliban to Europe in a get-rich-quick scheme (2.2.27-33, 2.2.76-78); Stephano's use of liquor to inspire Caliban's devotion (2.2.82-188); Ariel's exclamation "Thou liest" as a veiled suggestion that *he*, in fact, is the rightful ruler of the island (3.2.45); Gonzalo's articulation of entrenched European ignorance regarding the wondrousness and variety of the things of this world (3.3.42-49);[22] Prospero's excessive discomposure upon suddenly remembering Caliban's feeble plot against his life (4.1.139-42); Sebastian's and Antonio's comments on buying and marketing Caliban (5.1.265-66); and, above all, the various ways in which Caliban is demonized and his status as a human being mystified or otherwise rendered uncertain. Because this last aspect of the play constitutes my principal subject in the second section of this chapter, I will say no more about it here. I will add, however, that inasmuch as Caliban's attempted rape of Miranda is adduced as justification for his enslavement and proof of his unregeneracy (1.2.344-62), Prospero's "colonial rule" may rely, in part, upon a rhetorical process of selective forgetting: Many men in Prospero's Milan might also have attempted to violate the honor of his child, but such behavior would not necessarily have stigmatized them as incapable of civility or wholly irredeemable. Prospero, however, occupies an ideal position from which to "forget" this fact, since Caliban has no cognizance of it and thus no compelling reason to contradict Prospero's construction of reality or characterization of him as one upon "whose nature / Nurture can never stick" (4.1.188-89).

Perhaps the major problem with recent colonialist readings of *The Tempest* is that they tend to categorically condemn other readings as ahistorical while remaining dogmatic in their own insistence that, as Barker and Hulme put it, "The ensemble of fictional and lived practices, which for convenience we will simply refer to here as 'English colonialism', provides *The Tempest's* dominant discursive con-texts" [sic].[23] Rather than positing colonialism as a useful and illuminating discursive frame for the play, critics in this vein imply that *The Tempest* remains, in many important respects, unintelligible without the particular historical imbrication that they bring to it. Brown claims, for instance, that Prospero's rule is "after all a colonialist regime on the island," yet in saying so he ignores several crucial facts: There is never any indication that the island is perceived as the permanent property of Milan, there was no initial intent to "plant" or colonize it, and Prospero obviously does not wish to remain there. Brown also asserts that "Stephano the 'drunken butler' and the 'jester' Trinculo obviously represent . . . 'masterless men', whose alliance with the savage Caliban provides an antitype of order, issuing in a revolt requiring chastisement and ridicule."[24] But while this claim is valuable insofar as it extends the political discourse of colonialism so as to include the class discourse of masterlessness, its schematic dogmatism is highly limiting.[25] Even Terence Hawkes, a critic generally more nuanced than Brown in his speculations upon Prospero and Caliban, argues that the "roots" of their relationship "find their true nourishment in the ancient home-grown European relationships of master and servant, landlord and tenant"—which is simply a way of abandoning colonialism for another and perhaps less controversial historical contextualization.[26] In short, colonialist readings tend to fail through narrowness of focus just as they succeed through acuity. And while their grounding in historical process and detail prompts fascinating interpretive speculations, moral and sociopolitical agendas often predetermine their conclusions. Hawkes, in the previously quoted passage, remains historicist in method but eschews colonial contextualization in favor of a class discourse undoubtedly more familiar to Shakespeare and equally amenable to contemporary Marxist/materialist interpretation. I suggest that one may retain the New World context and the historicist approach without necessarily committing oneself to the near-dogmatism that seems endemic to colonialist readings. Such a strategy has been recently employed by Jeffrey Knapp, who, in a book remarkable for its complex presentation of relations between English colonialism and English literature, claims that Shakespeare "wants to recommend American colonies as essential to England's well-being, and essential precisely because of the dangerous treasure those colonies may secure," but adds that in so doing Shakespeare "must 'remove' such motives and even America itself from direct consideration in order to promote the temperate homebodiedness without which, he believes, a colony cannot last."[27] I propose that the strategy also becomes possible by shifting the contextual ground from the highly politicized discourse of colonialism to the more taxonomic, speculative, polyvalent, and autonomous discourse of ethnography. This is by no means to imply that ethnographic contextualization is apolitical; clearly it is not. But just as clearly, ethnography is bound by no necessary ties to the familiar and seemingly unalterable dynamic of exploration, domination, plantation, surveillance, and containment that—at least according to many recent accounts—constitutes a core structure of the colonialist project.

Obviously, the incidental or inchoate ethnography of the early modern period may be construed as merely one more facet of the vast network of thoughts, words, and deeds that we call "colonialism." David B. Quinn hints at this when he writes that "The earliest stages of contact between Englishmen and non-English cultures were likely to be governed by the desire to define and limit their inferiority (or non-Englishness) and to find ways of forcing them into a new English pattern, reforming them or obliterating them." But Quinn acknowledges that there also existed "the tendency to observe alien cultures for their own sake," and, at least in the case of England and Ireland, "The making of notes, the taking of an interest—scornful or superior, earnest or objective—led from casual observation to some measure of systematic study of Irish life and Irish society, to an elementary ethnology, if not precisely to a social anthropology."[28] The same holds true more generally, I maintain, in the case of Europe and the New World; the accounts of such writers as Ramon Pané, Bartolomé de Las Casas, Toribio Motolinía, Alvar Nuñez Cabeza de Vaca, Jacques Cartier, Diego Durán, Bernardino de Sahagún, Jean de Léry, Arthur Barlowe, Thomas Harriot, and John Smith—to name just a few—exhibit in varying degrees and varying ways the kinds of

interest in and description of alien cultures that may be considered legiti-
mately ethnographic.[29] And while Quinn's supposition that this interest can
be "objective" is rendered false by the inevitable subjective assimilationism
that accompanies the interpretation of any alterological encounter, his larger
point remains valid: Cultural description separable from overt colonial aims
and emanating primarily from curiosity and the desire to record and contemplate the unfamiliar may be found in the Renaissance.[30] The significance of
this is that one may utilize early ethnography as a distinct contextual ground
within which to locate *The Tempest* or any other relevant text: Colonial
discourse, in and of itself, has no intrinsic superiority as a historical frame,
but is simply one of many "force-fields" we can "bring to the play to disclose
its meanings."[31] An ethnographic contextualization is likely to prove valuable
precisely because of its lack of strict connection to political ends. This is not
to say that it is wholly disassociated from ideology; we should never forget,
for example, that Pané assembled his ethnographic notes because Columbus
commanded him to do so, or that Las Casas, Motolinía, Durán, and Sahagún
were zealous Christian missionaries, or that Barlowe and Harriot were
employees of Ralegh in one of his grand colonial schemes.[32] At the same
time, though, we must acknowledge that the documents of these writers—
and numerous other forms of reportage such as the glossaries of Eden, Léry,
and Smith—emblematize a genuine European curiosity about alien cultures
that would almost certainly have manifested itself under any historical
circumstances.[33] Inasmuch as Renaissance ethnography is primarily a descriptive rather than a manipulative or hegemonic discourse—fully capable of
registering curiosity, ambivalence, confusion, and even self-condemnation
in representing and attempting to understand the cultural other—employing
it as a discursive context promises to yield readings less dogmatic or pro-
grammatic than those typically brought forth by colonialist critics. In what
follows, therefore, I propose to situate *The Tempest* within the context of this
inchoate Renaissance ethnography, and in particular to examine the extent
to which Caliban may be perceived as a product of conflicting accounts
regarding the savagery or civility of New World natives.

MAN-MONSTERS: *THE TEMPEST* AND *MUCEDORUS*

Throughout *The Tempest* an air of ambiguity surrounds Caliban. His name—
almost certainly an anagram of "cannibal"—appears in the First Folio's cast
list among the play's human characters (as opposed to its "Spirits") and above
those of Trinculo and Stephano, but he is described there as "a salvage and

deformed slave."[34] And when Prospero first mentions Caliban to Ariel in Act One, it is difficult to decide whether the bestial or the human plays a greater role in his constitution:

> Then was this island
> (Save for the son that [she] did litter here,
> A freckled whelp, hag-born), not honor'd with
> A human shape. (1.2.281-84)

Although Hulme cites these lines as proof of Prospero's "grudging admittance of Caliban's humanity" and rails against those who seize upon the last six words as "'evidence' of Caliban's lack of human shape,"[35] I think rather that a sense of uncertainty is exquisitely balanced here, that "litter," "whelp," "hag-born," and the parenthetical exception play off against "son" and the main clause in such a way as to reveal Prospero's own deep confusion about Caliban's status. Later in this chapter I will argue that *The Tempest* moves gradually—almost inexorably—toward affirming Caliban as a man, but in the play's earlier scenes his status is deliberately mystified. However, unlike many colonialist readers, who interpret this mystification as Prospero's ruse to justify usurpation, I think its presence is due primarily to the genuine uncertainty regarding the human status of cultural aliens that emerges as a pervasive motif in the early modern period. Again and again in the travel literature, ethnographic description reveals a deep-seated ambivalence toward ethnic otherness and perceived savagery, and while this ambivalence is undoubtedly exploited at times by conquerors and colonists, its initial presence does not appear to be a necessary function of the European will to power.

Take, for example, Richard Johnson's 1609 description of the natives of Virginia near the colony at Jamestown: "[The region] is inhabited with wild and savage people, that live and lie up and downe in troupes like heards of Deere in a Forrest: they have no law but nature, their apparell skinnes of beasts, but most goe naked, . . . they are generally very loving and gentle, and do entertaine and relieve our people with great kindnesse; they are easy to be brought to good, and would fayne embrace a better condition."[36] Here we see a people likened to "heards of Deere" and alleged to have "no law but nature," yet we also hear that they are capable of "great kindnesse" and—like Caliban when he claims that he will "be wise hereafter, / And seek for grace" (5.1.295-96)—desire to "embrace a better condition." Similarly, in the writings of Captain John Smith we encounter such seemingly contradictory portrayals of the Chesapeake Algonquians as that, on the one hand, they are "sterne Barbarians," "fiends," "inconstant Salvages," and "naked Divels," and that, on the other, they "have amongst them such government, as that their Magistrates for good commanding, and their people for due subjection, and obeying, excell many places that would be counted very civill."[37] It is as if the authors of these passages can relinquish neither their wonder at the seemingly "natural" or "bestial" condition of American natives nor their ever-recurring recognition—or suspicion, at any rate—that these people, like Europeans, possess genuine forms of "civility." And while such a comment as Johnson's that the Virginians "would fayne embrace a better condition" may certainly be read within the frame of colonial discourse as a projection of the colonists' desire for defensible hegemony, it also may reflect a more concrete kind of observation—perhaps of the sort we see in Thomas Harriot when he tells us that despite the coastal Algonquians' clear exhibition of spiritual culture, "they were not so sure grounded, nor gave such credite to their traditions and stories, but through conversing with us they were brought into great doubts of their owne, and no small admiration of ours."[38]

Critics who have touched, however perfunctorily, upon the presentation of Caliban as in some way indebted to New World ethnography have tended either to trace a speculative genealogy through specific travel accounts or to allude somewhat unassuredly to the sort of ambivalence reflected in the above quotations. The former inclination has been present at least since the time of Edmund Malone—who claimed in 1821 that Caliban was Shakespeare's version of a Patagonian—and perhaps reached its apogee in Fiedler's pronouncement that "Caliban seems to have been created, on his historical side, by a fusion in Shakespeare's imagination of Columbus's first New World savages with Montaigne's Brazilians, Somers's native Bermudans, and those Patagonian 'giants' encountered by Pigafetta during his trip around the world with Magellan, strange creatures whose chief god was called, like Caliban's mother's, 'Setebos'."[39] The latter tendency, however, while relatively common, has provoked few interesting observations beyond the rather obvious generality that Caliban's portrayal relies upon a conflation of contradictory descriptions and evaluations of cultural otherness—particularly American otherness. Geoffrey Bullough, for example, writes that "the ambiguity of travelers' opinions about the American natives affects Shakespeare's handling of Caliban," and Hulme goes so far as to say that "Caliban, as a compromise formation, can exist only within discourse: he is fundamentally and essentially beyond the bounds of representation."[40] But few critics have, to my knowledge, explored the ambiguity or the "compromise formation" of Caliban at any length. Many seem inclined, after acknowledging ambivalence, to settle upon rather reductive conclusions; a representative example is the claim that "By every account in the play, Caliban is something less than a man. . . . He is an American savage, clearly humanoid though not fully human."[41]

Two commentators, however, have come close to focusing on the sort of ambivalence to which I want to draw attention. In stressing the distinction between the European views that, on the one hand, "Indian language was deficient or non-existent" and that, on the other, "there was no serious language barrier," Stephen Greenblatt anticipates Tzvetan Todorov's useful schematization of European perceptions of native Americans as either acknowledging *difference* and concluding *inferiority*, or acknowledging *equality* and concluding *identity*.[42] Greenblatt writes, for instance, that the tensions of this dichotomy "either push the Indians toward utter difference—and thus silence—or toward utter likeness—and thus the collapse of their own, unique identity."[43] And in a slightly different vein, Richard Marienstras has observed that Caliban possesses a "dubious ontological status"; he "can be seen as a complete and irreducible contradiction or, alternatively, as having two positive but separate natures, each stemming from a different scale of values."[44] What Greenblatt and Marienstras do not do, however, is point toward a middle range of perception that either acknowledges *difference* without immediately concluding *inferiority* or acknowledges *equality* without positing *identity*. Yet we see views within this range implicitly expressed, for example, by various early writers in their recognition and description of distinctly different tribes and social groups among native American peoples:

Alvar Nuñez Cabeza de Vaca (1542): The inhabitants of all this region [Malhado] go naked. The women alone have any part of their persons covered, and it is with a wool that grows on trees. The damsels dress themselves in deerskin. The people are generous to each other of what they possess. They have no chief. All that are of a lineage keep together. They speak two languages; those of one are called Capoques, those of the other, Han. They have a custom when they meet, or from time to time when they visit, of remaining half an hour before they speak, weeping; and, this over, he that is visited first rises and gives the other all he has, which is received, and after a little while he carries it away, and often goes without saying a word. They have other strange customs; but I have told the principal of them, and the most remarkable, that I may pass on and further relate what befel us.

Jean de Léry (1578): Although like other Brazilians [the Ouetaca] go entirely naked, nonetheless, contrary to the most ordinary custom of the men of that country (who, as I have already said and will later expand upon, shave the front of their head and clip their locks in the back), these wear their hair long, hanging down to the buttocks. . . . The Margaia, Cara-ia, or Tupinamba (which are the names of the three neighboring nations), or one of the other savages of that country, without trusting or approaching the Ouetaca, shows him from afar what he has—a pruning-hook, a knife, a comb, a mirror, or some other kind of wares brought over for trade—and indicates by a sign if he wants to exchange it for something else.

José de Acosta (1589): It is a popular error to treat the affairs of the Indies as if they were those of some farm or mean village and to think that, because the Indies are all called by a single name, they are therefore of one nature and kind. . . . The nations of Indians are innumerable, and each of them has its own distinct rites and customs and needs to be taught in a different way. I am not properly qualified to handle the problem, since a great many peoples are unknown to me, while even if I knew them well it would be an immense task to discuss them all one by one. I have therefore thought it proper to speak primarily of the Peruvians in this work.

Walter Ralegh (1596): This island [Trinidad] is called by the people thereof *Cairi*, and in it are divers nations: those about *Parico* are called *Iaio*, those at *Punto Carao* are of the *Arwacas*, and between *Carao* and *Curiapan* they are called *Salvaios*, between *Carao* and *Punto Galera* are the *Nepoios*, and those about the Spanish City term themselves *Carinepagotos*: Of the rest of the nations, and of other ports and rivers I leave to speak of here, being impertinent to my purpose, and mean to describe them as they are situate in the particular plot and description of the Island, three parts whereof I coasted with my barge, that I might the better describe it.

William Strachey (1612): [T]hus it may appear how they are a people who have their several divisions, provinces, and princes, to live in and to command over, and do differ likewise (as amongst Christians) both in stature, language, and condition; some being great people, as the Susquehannas, some very little, as the Wicocomocos; some speaking likewise more articulate and plain, and some more inward and hollow, as is before remembered; some courteous and more civil, others cruel and bloody; Powhatan having large territories and many petty kings under him, as some have fewer.

John Smith (1624): Upon the head of the Powhatans are the Monacans, whose chiefe habitation is at Rasauweak, unto whom the Mowhemenchughes, the Massinnacacks, the Monahassanughs, the Monasickapanoughs, and other nations pay tributes. Upon the head of the river of Toppahanock is a people called Mannahoacks. To these are contributers the Tauxanias, the Shackaconias, the Ontponeas, the

Tegninateos, the Whonkenteaes, the Stegarakes, the Hassinnungaes, and divers others, all confederates with the Monacans, though many different in language, and be very barbarous, living for the most part of wild beasts and fruits [sic]. Beyond the mountaines from whence is the head of the river Patawomeke, the Salvages report inhabit their most mortall enemies, the Massawomekes, upon a great salt water, which by all likelihood is either some part of Cannada, some great lake, or some inlet of some sea that falleth into the South sea.[45]

To the extent that these descriptions register plurality and allow a varied yet specific cultural inheritance to the natives introduced they represent anti-*tabula rasa* views and thus stand in opposition to such bald and overarching characterizations as Samuel Purchas's that American natives are "bad people, having little of Humanitie but shape, ignorant of Civilitie, of Arts, of Religion; more brutish then the beasts they hunt, more wild and unmanly then that unmanned wild countrey, which they range rather then inhabite."[46] Yet to the extent that they point explicitly to differences among these natives—and implicitly to differences between them and Europeans—they resist both the easy conclusion of inferiority and the more insidious one of identity. In short, they fall outside the polarizing rubric suggested by Greenblatt and Todorov. Rather than countering claims that native Americans are subhuman *tabulae rasae* by wholly assimilating them into European-ness, these descriptions—and others like them—allow the natives their difference and in fact stress their cultural diversity. Thus they provide a more subtle contrast than that proposed by Greenblatt, a contrast more relevant to *The Tempest*. If we can admit that early modern ethnography allows for an ambivalence not solely between the binary opposites of subhumanity and virtual identity, but also among the range that includes subhumanity, identity, and cultural—but fully human—difference, we can sharpen our account of the way this ambivalence sheds light on the characterization of Caliban.

An interesting way of producing this account lies in situating Caliban within an ethnographic context and then contrasting him with another curiously ambiguous character from English Renaissance drama: the "wild man" Bremo in the anonymous and highly popular play *Mucedorus*.[47] Caliban has been connected to Bremo before, notably by Frank Kermode in his eclectic genealogy of Caliban's character; but while Kermode points to Bremo's conventionality as a wodewose or salvage man, he does not dwell on the association with Caliban.[48] Yet there is much of interest to focus on, particularly given an ethnographic contextualization.

Like the Wild Man in Book Four of *The Faerie Queene*, Bremo lives in a cave in the woods (7.7, 17.94), carries a club (7.5,21,29), and is lustful and cannibalistic (11.16-19, 11.21, 11.25-30, 15.59-60); but unlike Spenser's Wild Man (or, for that matter, the Salvage Man of Book Six), Bremo possesses language and demonstrates an ability to relent and to recognize changes within himself (11.38-54, 15.105). Moreover, he is represented as having the capacity to fall in love (11.37-55, 15.1-55), though exactly what this love means to him remains unclear.[49] Finally, like Caliban, he is poetic, particularly in the description of his immediate surroundings (15.23-55): He knows the forest's oaks, quail, partridges, blackbirds, larks, thrushes, nightingales, springs, violets, cowslips, marigolds, and deer, and if his catalog strikes us as more conventional and symbolic than realistic, it nonetheless suggests a genuine love of place. Bremo seems, therefore, a rather more attractive character than the standard wodewose or *homo ferus*, and certainly less violent and lecherous than the type described as common in the late sixteenth century by R. H. Goldsmith.[50] Yet Bremo is duped and then brutally killed onstage by Mucedorus late in the play (17.35-67), and nothing in the response of Amadine or Mucedorus to the murder invites us to regard it as anything more consequential than the slaughter of an offending beast. Bremo is dismissed as a "tyrant" and "wicked wight" (17.68,74); that he has grown progressively more sympathetic and dies in the act of providing instruction to Mucedorus (17.51-67) is utterly forgotten. The play seems to tell us that a wild man, regardless of his apparent capacity for improvement or potential for civility, is subhuman and may be killed without remorse or consequence.

Contrast this with Caliban's portrayal in *The Tempest*. Like Bremo, who is called a "cruel cutthroat" and a "bloody butcher" (17.6,27), Caliban is the target of many dubious allegations: Prospero terms him a "demi-devil" (5.1.272) and a "poisonous slave, got by the devil himself / Upon thy wicked dam" (1.2.319-20); Miranda reviles him as an "Abhorred slave, / Which any print of goodness wilt not take, / Being capable of all ill!" (1.2.351-53). Yet much more than *Mucedorus*, *The Tempest* offers forms of resistance to these allegations, both in the speeches of Caliban and in the words and actions of other characters. For every suggestion that Caliban is not fully human, a counter-suggestion emerges that he *is*; Miranda's dual attitude (1.2.445-46; 3.1.50-52) becomes emblematic of this tendency. Moreover, in opposition to the view that Caliban is devoid of goodness, we have the uncontested claim of Caliban himself that his initial relationship with Prospero was thoroughly reciprocal:

> When thou cam'st first,
> Thou strok'st me and made much of me, wouldst give me
> Water with berries in't, and teach me how

To name the bigger light, and how the less,
That burn by day and night; and then I lov'd thee
And show'd thee all the qualities o' th' isle,
The fresh springs, brine pits, barren place and fertile.
Curs'd be I that did so! (1.2.332-39)[51]

Caliban goes on to point out that he is now Prospero's subject, when earlier he was "mine own king" (1.2.342), and of course Prospero responds to this implied charge of usurpation by making the counter-accusation that Caliban attempted to rape Miranda and thus deserves his subjugation. But if, as Stephen Orgel has suggested, Caliban's unrepentant attitude toward this attempted rape may be partly explained by the fact that "free love in the New World is regularly treated [in Renaissance travel narratives] not as an instance of the lust of savages, but of their edenic innocence,"[52] Prospero's allegation that Caliban is a "slave / Whom stripes may move, not kindness!" (1.2.344-45) loses much of its persuasiveness. Indeed, the problems of subordination and rebellion highlighted by the Prospero/Caliban relation may be usefully contrasted with the relative absence of such problems in the Prospero/Ariel interdependence; Ariel's nearly perfect modelling of subservience and service-ultimately-rewarded may be possible precisely because Ariel, quite explicitly, is *not* human. Such behavior, and such social relations, are far more problematic for Caliban.

Many Renaissance descriptions of New World natives have been adduced as sources or models of the subhuman or near-human element of Caliban's characterization, among them Peter Martyr's depiction of "certeyne wyld men" in Española who "neuer . . . wyll by any meanes becoome tame. . . . [and] are withowte any certaine language" and Robert Fabian's portrayal of three Eskimos who "spake such speach that no man could understand them, and in their demeanour like to bruite beastes."[53] But far fewer descriptions have been produced in support of another side of this characterization: Caliban as fully human, though radically different. Giovanni Verrazzano's observation that the native peoples of Florida "did not desire cloth of silke or of golde, much lesse of any other sort, neither cared they for things made of steele and yron" is perhaps typical of these descriptions in that it serves as an analogue of a specific incident in *The Tempest*: Caliban's rejection of the "glistering apparel" so attractive to Stephano and Trinculo (4.1.222-54).[54] But there are other anti–*tabula rasa* ethnographic views available in the Renaissance, views less likely to be seen as pertinent to *The Tempest* because they are broader in scope and not as easily associated with particular passages in the play. And I refer not only to the writings of Las Casas and Montaigne discussed in earlier chapters. Léry, for instance, emphasizes the social harmony of the Tupinamba even as he exposes the conceptual limitations attendant upon his own religious bias: "As for the civil order of our savages, it is an incredible thing—a thing that cannot be said without shame to those who have both divine and human laws—how a people guided solely by their nature, even corrupted as it is, can live and deal with each other in such peace and tranquility."[55] José de Acosta describes the Incas' indigenous form of literacy: "Unbelievable as it may seem, the Peruvians made up for their lack of letters with so much ingenuity that they were able to record stories, lives, laws, and even the passage of time and numerical calculations by means of certain signs and aids to the memory which they had devised and which they call *quipos*. Our people with their letters are commonly unable to match the skill of the Peruvians with these devices. I am not at all certain that our written numerals make counting or dividing more accurate than their signs do."[56] Alexander Whitaker writes that the inhabitants of Virginia are "lustie, strong, and very nimble: they are a very understanding generation, quicke of apprehension, suddaine in their dispatches, subtile in their dealings, exquisite in their inventions, and industrious in their labour. . . . there is a civill government amongst them which they strictly observe"; William Strachey characterizes the elaborate dressing and ornamentation of a Virginian queen as "ceremonies which I did little look for, carrying so much presentment of civility"; and Thomas Harriot, in a passage to which I will return, avers of the Algonquians, "Some religion they have alreadie, which although it be farre from the trueth, yet being as it is, there is hope it may be the sooner and easier reformed. They beleeve that there are many Gods."[57] It is true that Léry's and Whitaker's remarks, like those of Las Casas, emanate from a Christian essentialist perspective; this emerges explicitly in Whitaker's opinion that "One God created us, they have reasonable soules and intellectuall faculties as well as wee; we all have *Adam* for our common parent: yea, by nature the condition of us both is all one, the servants of sinne and slaves of the divell."[58] It is true as well that Acosta's "Unbelievable as it may seem" and Harriot's "farre from the trueth" disclose the strongly ethnocentric tendencies of these early ethnographic accounts. But as I have argued earlier, some degree of subjective assimilationism is inevitable in any description of a cultural other; the preceding quotations—and others like them—are remarkable in the degree to which they avoid the easy conclusion of *identity* and insist upon a measure of *difference*. And if such views as these played a role in the evolution of Caliban's character, it is not hard to understand why Caliban seems far less "unaccommodated" than *Mucedorus*'s Bremo. Even Bremo's portrayal reveals certain suggestions of contemporary ethnographic influence, but by and large his conventionality as a wodewose preempts the possibility of any lasting ambivalence in his character: Like Chanca's New World natives, he is essentially less than fully human; like them, easy to kill without remorse. But Caliban, whose depiction relies heavily on Renaissance ethnography—and particularly on the ambivalences I have stressed between the other as subhuman, identical, and human but different—is thereby rendered far less easy to dismiss. If he is a "salvage" man, his savagery is nonetheless treated by Shakespeare with more tolerance and more respect for its potential or concealed civility than is Bremo's by his anonymous creator.

A final word about *Mucedorus*. The play's *dramatis personae* not only lists the characters but provides instructions for the doubling (and tripling) of parts; thus, for example, Bremo is to be played by the same actor who plays Tremelio and Envy.[59] I find this intriguing for several reasons. Tremelio is a would-be assassin, a captain persuaded by the jealous Segasto to kill Mucedorus (6.62-82). In fact, precisely the opposite occurs: Mucedorus kills *him* in self-defense, calling him a "Vile coward" (6.81). And Envy, a figure who appears only in the Induction and Epilogue, is constantly reviled by his allegorical counterpart, Comedy, as, among other things, a "monster" (Ind. 16), an "ugly fiend" (Ind. 75), a "hellhound" (Epi. 24), a "Nefarious hag" (Epi. 26), and a "bloody cur, nursed up with tiger's sap" (Ind. 35). In short, the trio of Bremo, Tremelio, and Envy—all playable by the same actor—represents something like a principle of monstrosity or unnaturalness, and these characters' purpose in the play is perhaps indirectly suggested by Comedy's urgent wish that Envy "mix not death 'mongst pleasing comedies" (Ind. 50). In fact, death *is* present in *Mucedorus*, and the play is more a tragicomedy than a simple comedy treating "naught else but pleasure and delight" (Ind. 51). In spite of the play's happy ending, Envy insists to Comedy, "yet canst thou not conquer me" (Epi. 12) and threatens that in the future he will overthrow her by the following strategem:

> From my study will I hoist a wretch,
> A lean and hungry neger cannibal,
> Whose jaws swell to his eyes with chawing malice;
> And him I'll make a poet. (Epi. 34-37)

This implies that if an outcast or "native monster" (Epi. 20) of the sort Envy describes had the linguistic command of a poet, he would represent a true threat to Comedy's complacence; he would have the power of subversion. And while Comedy dismisses this threat as nonsense and easily manages to subdue Envy by the Epilogue's end, the description of a poetic "neger cannibal" nonetheless has a strangely prophetic ring for readers familiar with *The Tempest*. In spite of Caliban's alleged aphasia at the initial contact with Prospero, he learns language—learns it astonishingly well—and this acquisition, perhaps more than any other trait, marks his humanity and signals his potential menace to the intruding Europeans. Envy's threat, with its suggestion that characters such as Bremo and the "neger cannibal" are necessary to the workings of comedy even as they endanger its survival and structural integrity, prefigures in a peculiar way Prospero's elusive remark about Caliban: "this thing of darkness I / Acknowledge mine" (5.1.275-76). Comedy cannot thrive without the dangerous potency of Envy: *Mucedorus* needs Bremo and Tremelio just as *The Tempest* needs Alonso, Antonio, and Sebastian—and just as Prospero needs Caliban.

One of *The Tempest's* most explicit mystifications of Caliban's status lies in Stephano's reference to him as "My man-monster" (3.2.12). Clearly, such a phrase would be less appropriate with respect either to Bremo, notwithstanding his command of language, or to *The Faerie Queene's* Salvage Man, in spite of his aphasia; but for Caliban—especially at this point in the play—it seems a perfect designation, emblematic of the pervasive ambivalence regarding his condition that the play has created. Stephano utters it early in the second of four scenes in which he and Trinculo appear with Caliban. In the first of these scenes, Trinculo makes the thoroughly ambiguous remark—after coming upon Caliban wrapped in his gaberdine—that in England "would this monster make a man; any strange beast there makes a man" (2.2.30-31); Stephano seconds this ambiguity by alluding to "salvages and men of Inde" (2.2.58) and marvelling that the composite Caliban/Trinculo is "some monster of the isle with four legs, ... Where the devil should he learn our language?" (2.2.65-67). Interestingly, however, this uncertainty regarding Caliban is mirrored by Caliban's own uncertainty regarding the Neapolitans—especially Stephano. And it is in this pair of corresponding and reinforcing ambivalences that we begin to see perhaps the greatest value of locating *The Tempest* within an ethnographic context.

Prompted by his drinking of Stephano's sack—itself an action resonant with contemporary New World associations—Caliban exclaims to himself, "These be fine things, and if they be not sprites. / That's a brave god, and bears celestial liquor. / I will kneel to him" (2.2.116-18). This is followed by such exclamations as "Hast thou not dropp'd from heaven? . . . I do adore thee. . . . I prithee, be my god. . . . Thou wondrous man" (2.2.137-64). Like *The Faerie Queene's* Artegall when he meets Britomart—or the satyrs in their encounter with Una—Caliban "makes religion" of his wonder.[60] It is true that he swears allegiance to Stephano, and true also that this willing subordination is often interpreted as proof of his natural slavishness.[61] But Shakespeare makes it clear that Caliban is inebriated before he takes Stephano for a "brave god" (2.2.117), and that, in turn, Caliban succumbs to the man/god confusion *before* he promises to be Stephano's "true subject" (2.2.125). Thus, notwithstanding the comic mode of the scene or its status as subplot in the play's larger design, Caliban does not necessarily reveal an abject propensity to be a slave. Stephen Greenblatt has written, in a discussion of the *Diario*, that Columbus occasionally demonstrates a recognition of "reverse wonderment" among the native Americans he encounters in the Caribbean;[62] Caliban's behavior here suggests a literary transformation of that wonderment. His subservience, initially, is not that of man-monster to man, but of man-monster to man-god; and while it is in some respects comic, it merits far more than ridicule.[63] We must not forget, for example, that Caliban possesses a concept of divinity or godhead: His references to his "dam's" god, Setebos, make this clear (1.2.373, 5.1.261). And since it is virtually beyond dispute that Shakespeare takes "Setebos" from Pigafetta's account of Magellan's voyage, it bears noting that in an adjacent passage, Pigafetta describes the reaction of a Patagonian native confronted by Europeans: "When he sawe the capitayne with certeyne of his coompany abowte hym, he was greatly amased and made signes holdynge vppe his hande to heauen, signifyinge therby that owre men came from thense."[64] Indeed, as demonstrated in chapter 3, the motif of native Americans regarding Europeans as gods is common in the voyagers' accounts.[65] And while this representation, due to its utter one-sidedness, is clearly unreliable as a descriptive characterization, its implicit reliance upon the idea that idolatry can evolve into "true" religion suggests that at its core lies the accurate perception, among European observers, that the native inhabitants of America practiced forms of devotion that could only be categorized as "religious" and only construed as proof of full humanity. Harriot, in a passage quoted earlier, expresses this best: "Some religion they have alreadie, which although it be farre from the trueth, yet being as it is, there is hope it may be the easier and sooner reformed."[66] The Europeans' very theory of evangelization—or, at any rate, their most successful theory—relied upon the premise that what they deemed idolatry was in fact a conclusive indication of humanity and a positive step toward Christian conversion.[67] The ability to confuse men for gods, as Caliban does, is thus a confirmation of the views expressed in the anti–*tabula rasa* descriptions quoted above. When American natives are represented as overestimating the status of Europeans, they are simultaneously—if indirectly—represented as fully human in status and as possessing cultural forms of their own. They are not blank pages, not unaccommodated.

The emphasis that Shakespeare gives to the ambivalences just discussed both highlights the play's debt to voyagers' accounts and propels it toward its romantic conclusion. Stephano cannot decide whether Caliban is monster or man; Caliban, equally, cannot decide whether Stephano is man or god. And, as if in sympathy with these uncertainties, Miranda wonders whether Ferdinand is human or divine (1.2.410-20), and neither Ferdinand nor Alonso can initially decide whether Miranda is a maid or a goddess (1.2.422-29, 5.1.185-88).[68] Gradually, however, the uncertainties are resolved, the multiple possibilities collapsed. Prospero assures Miranda that Ferdinand "eats, and sleeps, and hath such senses / As we have" (1.2.413-14); Miranda describes herself to Ferdinand as "No wonder, sir, / But certainly a maid" (1.2.427-28); Ferdinand tells his father that Miranda "is mortal" (5.1.188); and Caliban curses himself for his error: "What a thrice-double ass / Was I to take this drunkard for a god, / And worship this dull fool!" (5.1.296-98). And while no explicit recognition surfaces in Stephano or Trinculo that Caliban is human, there remains the far more significant remark by Prospero that "this thing of darkness I / Acknowledge mine" (5.1.275-76). As Greenblatt has pointed out, Prospero "may intend these words only as a declaration of ownership, but it is difficult not to hear in them some deeper recognition of affinity, some half-conscious acknowledgment of guilt."[69] Affinity and guilt indeed; many years ago, assuming the persona of Caliban and addressing a composite Prospero/Shakespeare, W. H. Auden character-ized this recognition as follows:

> Striding up to Him in fury, you glare into His unblinking eyes and stop dead, transfixed with horror at seeing reflected there, not what you had always expected to see, a conquerer smiling at a conquerer, both promising mountains and marvels, but a gibbering fist-clenched creature with which you are all too unfamiliar, for this is the first time indeed that you have met the only subject that you have, who is not a dream amenable to magic but the all too solid flesh you must acknowledge as your own; at last you have come face to face with me, and are appalled to learn how far I am from being, in any sense, your dish; how completely lacking in that poise and calm and all-forgiving because all-under-standing good nature which to the critical eye is so wonderfully and domestically present on every page of your published inventions.[70]

Prospero's acknowledgment may imply that Caliban is what he—Prospero —can become, or what his nurture may, in the end, amount to; in either case, his remark hints at the same interpenetration of the conventionally savage and civil suggested by the portrayal of *The Faerie Queene*'s Salvage Man. Perhaps Prospero is also implicitly admitting that Caliban possesses a perceptive subjectivity and thus stands in a dialogic relationship with him. At all events, this acknowledgment—coming as it does from the character who, more than anyone else, has been responsible for the mystification of Caliban's identity—goes far toward finally drawing Caliban within the bounds of humanity.

Throughout *The Tempest* we look at Caliban much in the way that Renaissance explorers must have looked at New World natives. In some ways he seems bestial; but in others—among them his intimate knowledge of the isle, his initial nurturing of Prospero and Miranda, his later resentment of Prospero's rule, his capacity for forming warm attachments, his vulnerability, and his dreamy, reflective poetry—he seems entirely human. Above all, there is his decision, late in the play, to "be wise hereafter, / And seek for grace" (5.1.295-96).[71] Perhaps this means that he will seek Christian prevenient grace—the divine favor of God—or perhaps the pardon or indulgence of Prospero.[72] But in this particular instance, the word "grace" need not necessarily refer either to divine dispensation or human forgiveness; it *could* be being used in the alternative sense of "virtue," as it is twice elsewhere in the play (3.1.45, 5.1.70), and in such other instances as John Donne's famous lines about "man, this world's vice-emperor, in whom / All faculties, all graces are at home," or the passage from *Macbeth* when Malcolm speaks of "The King-becoming graces" and mentions, among other traits, "justice," "temp'rance," "lowliness," "Devotion," and "patience" (4.3.91-94).[73] Caliban, in vowing to "seek for grace," may very well be vowing not submission (and thus containment by the dominant culture) but rather an independent project of self-betterment; the virtue he may be seeking is that of proper judgment, so that in the future he will not again make his past mistake of confusing humans and gods. In any case, though Shakespeare never explicitly resolves the matter of Caliban's status, he suggests—to the extent that he gradually allows the play's other uncertainties about character identity to dissolve into thin air—that Caliban, like Ferdinand, Miranda, and Stephano, is a fully human being. And this suggestion is reinforced by *The Tempest*'s thorough contradiction of Prospero's allegation that Caliban is ineducable, "a born devil, on whose nature / Nurture can never stick" (4.1.188-89); the same could be said, after all, of Antonio and Sebastian, neither of whom—unlike Caliban—show any sign of repentance for their conspiracy, though both have had the advantage of more refined and extended nurture. One might even argue that Caliban, in his initial and fully reciprocal relation with

Prospero, demonstrates a nurture that, far from failing to "stick" to his nature, lies at its very essence.

Placing *The Tempest* within an ethnographic context goes far toward explaining why Caliban cannot be discarded in the way that Bremo can, for example, in *Mucedorus*. Caliban is not merely a "wild man," a sinister, shadowy figure derived from European folklore and Medieval tradition; he remains far more complex and distinct, and though his portrayal certainly reveals bestial elements, it is also vivified by an audience acknowledgment of the existence of culturally alien humans across the ocean. Like the ambivalences of New World ethnography, the ambivalences of *The Tempest* gradually move toward human inclusiveness. And this levelling tendency, which shows the failings of aristocrats as well as the admirable traits of an alleged "demi-devil," bears a resemblance both to movements in other late plays of Shakespeare and to the ideals of what I will refer to as "Montaignian pastoral"—a more radical pastoral than that typical of Spenser, more informed by the speculative and critical spirit that characterizes the *Essays*. As the whoreson and the Bedlam beggar must be acknowledged in *King Lear* (1.1.24, 3.4.28-180), and the strange Tupinamba in Montaigne, so too must Caliban.

MONTAIGNIAN PASTORAL AND THE THING ITSELF

> My Dear One is mine as mirrors are lonely,
> As the poor and the sad are real to the good king,
> And the high green hill sits always by the sea.
>
> —W. H. Auden, 'The Sea and the Mirror'

Like the New World, the island of *The Tempest* is experienced differently by its different foreign observers; it is, in effect, a complex Rorschach blot that exposes its observers' habitual presuppositions. Among the court party, for example, Sebastian and Antonio claim that the island's air is "rotten" and stinks as if "perfum'd by a fen" (2.1.48-49), while Adrian finds that it breathes "most sweetly" (2.1.47). Adrian also asserts that the island is "of subtle, tender, and delicate temperance" despite its "desert" and "Uninhabitable" appearance (2.1.35-43). The most positive view advanced, however, is that of Gonzalo, who exclaims "How lush and lusty the grass looks! How green!" (2.1.53-54) and alludes in his famous plantation speech to the "foison" and "abundance" of nature on the isle (2.1.163-64). Because this speech also echoes—in more than a dozen places—a passage from Florio's 1603 trans-

lation of Montaigne's "Des cannibales," critics have often assumed that
Gonzalo's perception of the isle's utopian potential owes its feeling to the
spirit of that essay and especially to Montaigne's "primitivism." Accordingly,
they have argued that the logical failings of his speech—not to mention its
skeptical reception by Antonio and Sebastian—express Shakespeare's "extreme antipathy to the [Montaigne] passage."[74] Lee, for instance, writes that
"Shakespeare cherished none of Montaigne's amiable dreams of the primitive state of man in America," and Fiedler adds that "the very words
[Shakespeare] attributes to Gonzalo he has lifted from Florio's translation
of the French skeptic, whose skepticism seems to have failed him for once
in his essay 'Of the Cannibals.'"[75] I believe, on the contrary, that much more
than amiable dreams were lifted from Florio. Not only Gonzalo's enthusiasm, but Sebastian and Antonio's ironic skepticism, and, indeed, some of the
very ambivalences at the core of *The Tempest*—ambivalences that contribute
to the play's peculiar pastoralism—all these may be traced in part to
Montaigne's complex ruminations.

First, though, it is just as well to acknowledge that unqualified enthusiasm
of the sort attributed to Gonzalo may be found as readily in any number of
voyagers' accounts as in Montaigne. Gonzalo's emphasis on the imagined
"abundance" of the island's natural provision, for instance, is reminiscent of
the effusive descriptions of Guiana and Roanoke Island provided, respectively, by Ralegh and Barlowe:

> I never saw a more beautiful country, nor more lively prospects, hills so raised
> here and there over the valleys, the river winding into divers branches, the plains
> adjoining without bush or stubble, all fair green grass, the ground of hard sand
> easy to march on, either for horse or foot, the deer crossing in every path, the
> birds towards the evening singing on every tree with a thousand several tunes,
> cranes and herons of white, crimson, and carnation perching on the river's side,
> the air fresh with a gentle easterly wind, and every stone that we stooped to take
> up, promised either gold or silver by his complexion.

> Wee viewed the lande about us, being whereas we first landed, very sandie, and
> lowe towards the water side, but so full of grapes, as the very beating, and surge
> of the Sea overflowed them, of which we founde such plentie, as well there, as
> in all places else, both on the sande, and on the greene soile on the hils, as in the
> plaines, as well on every little shrubbe, as also climing towardes the toppes of
> the high Cedars, that I thinke in all the world the like aboundance is not to be
> founde: . . . This Island had many goodly woods, and full of Deere, Conies, Hares,
> and Fowle, even in the middest of Summer, in incredible abundance. . . . The

earth bringeth foorth all things in aboundance, as in the first creation, without toile or labour.[76]

And Barlowe's description, in turn, may have found its way into parts of Michael Drayton's ode "To the Virginian Voyage" (1606):

> . . . Virginia,
> Earth's only paradise,
>
> Where nature hath in store
> Fowl, venison, and fish,
>   And the fruitful'st soil
>   Without your toil
> Three harvests more,
> All greater than your wish.
>
> And the ambitious vine
> Crowns with his purple mass,
>   The cedar reaching high
>   To kiss the sky,
> The cypress, pine,
> And useful sassafras.
>
> To whose the golden age
> Still nature's laws doth give,
>   No other cares that tend,
>   But them to defend
> From winter's age,
> That long there doth not live.[77]

Similarly, Cartier—though somewhat less euphorically than Barlowe—provides us with an account of a new land ripe for European domestication: "the Countrey is as fayre and as pleasaunte as possiblye can bee seene, being leauell, smoothe, and verye playne, fitte to be husbanded and tilled."[78] Finally, Silvester Jourdain's concluding impression of Bermuda may have served Shakespeare as a model: "my opinion sincerely of this lland is, that whereas it hath been, and is still accounted, the most dangerous infortunate, and most forlorne place of the world, it is in truth the richest, healthfullest, and pleasing land . . . as ever man set foot upon."[79] Particularly in its contrastive structure, where a prevailing opinion is acknowledged only to be supplanted by a contrary truth, Jourdain's description seems to anticipate the reaction of Gonzalo to the "several strange Shapes" who provide an illusory banquet to the wandering courtiers (3.3.19 s.d.):

> If in Naples
> I should report this now, would they believe me?
> If I should say I saw such [islanders]
> (For, certes, these are people of the island),
> Who though they are of monstrous shape, yet note
> Their manners are more gentle, kind, than of
> Our human generation you shall find
> Many, nay, almost any. (3.3.27-34)

Even more explicitly, monstrous shape is belied by gentle manners in John Brereton's 1602 depiction of New England natives: "These people are of tall stature, broad and grim visage, of a blacke swart complexion, their eiebrowes painted white; . . . they are exceeding courteous, gentle of disposition, and well-conditioned, excelling all others that we haue seene."[80] But for the extravagant quality of Gonzalo's praise—in which the gentleness of the "monstrous" islanders not only matches, but exceeds that of "Our human generation"—we must turn again to Barlowe, who claims that the Roanoke natives are "goodly people, and in their behaviour as mannerly, and civill, as any of Europe. . . . most gentle, loving, and faithfull, . . . such as lived after the manner of the golden age. . . . a more kinde, and loving people, there can not be found in the world, as farre as we have hitherto had triall."[81] In short, we need not rely upon Montaigne's exclamations regarding the "great abundance of fish and flesh" in Brazil or upon the contentment of the Tupinamba "with what nature afoordeth them" and knowledge of "how to enjoy their condition happily" in order to account for Gonzalo's enthusiasm.[82] If anything, we do ourselves a disservice by such reliance, since we thereby occlude much else that lies in Montaigne's essay. That Shakespeare "lifted" a particularly euphoric passage from "Of the Caniballes" and momentarily subjected it to skeptical scrutiny by no means implies that he rejected wholesale the constellation of ideas expressed in this and other essays dealing with the New World. It is one thing to argue that Shakespeare mocked a bit of enthusiastic hyperbole; it is quite another to argue that in doing so he mocked Montaigne.

A number of critics have acknowledged this distinction and taken steps toward a more careful consideration of the relation between *The Tempest* and Montaigne. Kermode, for instance, points out that "It is over-simple to assume that this perennial theme [Gonzalo's ideal commonwealth] is destroyed by the cheap jeers of Antonio and Sebastian," and stresses that "There are points in the play at which Shakespeare uses Caliban to indicate how much baser the corruption of the civilized can be than the bestiality of the natural, and in these places he is using his natural man as a criterion of civilized corruption, as Montaigne had done."[83] Similarly, Leo Marx writes that "To conclude that Prospero's triumph is a triumph of art over nature does not square with our full experience of the play."[84] Both critics, in short, suggest that *The Tempest* invites us to entertain the primitivist thesis of natural sufficiency more seriously than Antonio and Sebastian entertain Gonzalo's daydream. Kermode recognizes that Shakespeare does more with Caliban than merely provide a possible authentication of Prospero's allegations, and Marx takes seriously the claims of nature in the play, thereby arriving at his ultimate conclusion that *The Tempest* asserts a pastoral ideal and is "a comedy in praise neither of nature nor civilization, but of a proper balance between them."[85] In the end, however, neither Kermode nor Marx acknowledges the full complexity of Montaigne; they readily admit that his "primitivism" is not as lightly dismissed by Shakespeare as other critics have maintained, but they neglect to show that he also articulates a tempering anti-primitivism that goes far toward suggesting a ground for *The Tempest*'s ambivalences about nature. I argued in Chapter 2 that Montaigne not only poses New World natives as a foil to "civilized" Europeans, but also stresses their failings—particularly in regard to "reasons rules" ("Of cannibals," 156) and imagined absolutes of civility; he criticizes them, in short, even as he praises them. Likewise, Shakespeare points to Caliban's humanity even as he allows him to be represented by others as bestial and subhuman. The balances between these portrayals are different, clearly, but the terms are fundamentally the same: Both Montaigne and Shakespeare wrestle with the relative degrees of savagery and civility they may attribute to their "natives."

Such wrestling is largely dismissed in statements like Kermode's that Caliban "represents the natural man" or Marx's that he "embodies the untrammelled wildness or cannibalism at the heart of nature."[86] And while I agree with the assertion that "Caliban is anything but a Noble Savage," I seriously question the related conclusion that "Caliban has almost nothing in common with the prelapsarian savages described in Montaigne's essay 'Of the Cannibals,' from which Gonzalo's Utopia is, in Florio's translation, almost verbatim derived."[87] In the first place, Montaigne's savages are hardly "prelapsarian"; if anything, they are *post*lapsarian in their imperfection and *extra*lapsarian in the total lack of interest Montaigne shows in placing them within a Christian context. But in addition, it is simply not true that Caliban has essentially nothing in common with the New World natives Montaigne describes. Like them, he behaves in ways that place him at a far remove from conventional civility (he attempts rape and plots assassination; they burn enemies alive and flay the skins of women in human sacrifice); like them, he possesses other traits that distance him equally from conventional savagery (he speaks poetry and chooses to seek for grace; they compose songs that show no barbarity and believe that the souls of good and evil people receive different treatment in eternity).[88] Above all, though, both Caliban and Montaigne's natives are revealed as human beings with characteristic human potentials: emotional, intellectual, spiritual. They are not unaccommodated. It is true that Montaigne habitually operates from a clear assumption of sociocultural accommodation, while Shakespeare only gradually allows the mystification of Caliban's status to resolve itself into an affirmation of simultaneous humanity and difference; but in the end, both writers offer us portrayals of beings who are at once savage and civil, at once fully human and distinctly non-European.

If we agree, then, that Montaigne is not the sentimental primitivist he has often been made out to be, and that Shakespeare is not satirizing his views in *The Tempest* but rather exploring and exploiting the ambivalences he produces, we can begin to see ways in which *The Tempest* might be said to embody not merely the pastoral ideal that Marx speaks of, but a specifically Montaignian pastoral ideal.[89] I believe Marx is quite correct in claiming that *The Tempest* involves "a redemptive journey away from society in the direction of nature," and that "the entire fable unquestionably affirms the impulse of civilized man to renew himself by immersion in the simple, spontaneous instinctual life." Moreover, he aptly points out that most pastoral texts contain "counter-forces" that call into question the harmony of the green world—counter-forces lying both in the realm of nature and in that of civilization.[90] But Marx locates the counter-force against which *The Tempest*'s pastoral ideal is defined much more prominently in the natural realm than in the civilized—and particularly, in Caliban. His conclusion about Prospero's pastoralism, in other words, is only possible given his unproblematic view of this "salvage and deformed slave." If, however, we decide through ethnographic contextualization and close attention to Montaigne that Caliban is not an embodiment of "wildness" and "cannibalism" but an accommodated man, part savage and part civil, we must refine Marx's notion accordingly. Rather than supposing Gonzalo's utopian speech to reflect Montaigne's alleged primitivism, and Caliban, in turn, to serve dramatically as a representation of this view's inadequacy, I propose that we read Montaigne as situating complex counter-forces both in the civilized and the natural worlds. He acknowledges civil barbarity *and* civil virtue, the sufficiency of nature *and* the chaos of nature. Montaigne's opinions, if primitivistic at all, constitute a substantially qualified and "hard" version of primitivism. Like "hard" pastoral, in which the harsher realities of rural life are not obscured or glossed over, hard primitivism points to the limitations of life lived in a state of nature even as it praises its virtues. Moreover, both hard primitivism and hard pastoral— unlike their "soft" and idealizing counterparts—achieve much of their effect through aggressively challenging conventional notions about the inevitable superiority of art, civilization, and gentle blood over the common natural inheritance of humans. Thus, for example, Montaigne stresses the savagery of Europeans in the New World quite as much as he does the mingled civility and savagery of its native inhabitants. And Shakespeare, though he adjusts the balances somewhat, does likewise: He exposes the criminality of Alonso, Sebastian, and Antonio while pointing simultaneously to the potential decency and proven indecency of Caliban. It is fair to say, then, that if a kind of levelling is achieved in hard primitivism or pastoral, it is achieved not by casting a romantic veil over class, ethnic, and educational differences but by forcefully drawing attention to the failings (and occasional virtues) of the contrasting groups in which those differences are embodied. This is the method practiced by Montaigne, and to the extent that it is also practiced by Shakespeare, the pastoral ideal ultimately asserted in *The Tempest* may be usefully characterized as Montaignian.

An alternate way of expressing this is to say that *The Tempest*'s version of pastoral is already to a large extent implied by Montaigne's hard primitivism and by Shakespeare's treatment of nature as refracted through the portrayal of Caliban. I claimed earlier that Caliban must be acknowledged just as are the Tupinamba in Montaigne and the bastard Edmund in *King Lear;* I propose moreover that this acknowledgment carries the force of an authentic critique of society and not merely that of an "authorized mode of discontent."[91] Montaigne, after all, allows the Tupinamba cannibals to voice a trenchant charge against French economic policy and social injustice: "Second (they have a way in their language of speaking of men as halves of one another) they had noticed that there were among us men full and gorged with all sorts of good things, and that their other halves were beggars at their doors, emaciated with hunger and poverty; and they thought it strange that these needy halves could endure such an injustice, and did not take the others by the throat, or set fire to their houses" ("Of cannibals," 159). I do not deny that much may be said for the idea, expressed in varying ways by William Empson, Louis Montrose, and others, that Elizabethan pastoral is a literary form largely sanctioned by the aristocracy inasmuch as it tends to mystify class differences and present commoners as attractive through their wisdom and equanimity. This idea holds true, for example, in *Mucedorus*; but it is not borne out in *Lear* or *The Tempest*. In *Mucedorus*, the lip-service paid to pastoral levelling in the hero's charming assertion that "shepherds are men, and kings are no more" (9.30) works to conceal the fact that egalitarianism is undermined by the fate of Bremo and by Amadine's evasive answer to Mucedorus's question as to whether she would be content as a shepherdess:

> It shall not need; if Amadine do live,
> Thou shalt be crownéd King of Aragon. (17.150-51)

But in *King Lear*, as in Montaigne's "Of Cannibals," articulations of egalitarian ideas are organically bound to bitter attacks on the violation of moral (and specifically royal) responsibility. Much as in Sir Philip Sidney's *Arcadia*—particularly in the King of Paphlagonia episode whence Shakespeare derived the Gloucester subplot[92]—pastoral in *Lear* is inseparable from political critique:

> Poor naked wretches, wheresoe'er you are,
> That bide the pelting of this pitiless storm,
> How shall your houseless heads and unfed sides,
> Your looped and windowed raggedness, defend you
> From seasons such as these? O, I have ta'en
> Too little care of this! Take physic, pomp;
> Expose thyself to feel what wretches feel,
> That thou mayst shake the superflux to them,
> And show the heavens more just. (3.4.28-36)

> Heavens, deal so still!
> Let the superfluous and lust-dieted man,
> That slaves your ordinance, that will not see
> Because he does not feel, feel your pow'r quickly;
> So distribution should undo excess,
> And each man have enough. (4.1.68-73)

Similarly, in *The Tempest*, Prospero's ultimate acknowledgment of Caliban most certainly "insinuates and glances at greater matters" in the fashion described by Puttenham.[93] As I argued earlier, this acknowledgment draws Caliban within the bounds of humanity—albeit humanity perceived as deeply flawed and vicious just as much as noble and generous.[94] Miranda's "brave new world" of Old World humanity, after all, is immediately circumscribed by Prospero in his laconic "'Tis new to thee" (5.1.183-84); he knows too well that its beauty, bravery, and wondrousness are accompanied by elements of duplicity and corruption that make Caliban seem tame by comparison. Marx neglects to mention Prospero's acknowledgment of Caliban when he argues for *The Tempest's* assertion of a pastoral ideal; to do so, presumably, would be to suggest a greater affinity between the realms symbolized by Caliban and Prospero than Marx is willing to risk.[95] But such an acknowledgment is central to the play's thematic structure. Moreover, it is representative of a true levelling in which differences based on culture or rank are subverted through the dramatic exposure of aristocratic villains and the sublime recognition of human fellowship between a wise if pessimistic old man and a "salvage and deformed slave."[96] When Prospero, in the play's Epilogue, asks the audience in conventional terms for applause—"As you from crimes would pardoned be, / Let your indulgence set me free"—he perhaps hints one final time at his own self-recognition and at his very human need for mercy and grace.

For citizens of early modern Europe, noble birth, high rank, gentle blood, and, more generally, inscription by Christian and aristocratic culture are claims to status and authority based on historical circumstance and powerfully reinforced by tradition. Shakespeare, like Montaigne—and more than Spenser—seems willing to question these claims, to demonstrate ways in which they may be besieged and undermined. And though he is not as eager as Montaigne to advance the counter-claims of cultural otherness or perceived savagery, the complexity of his portrayal of Caliban nonetheless suggests the seriousness with which he undertakes the project of representing non-aristocratic and non-European peoples and points of view. Those who are conventionally or apparently unaccommodated turn out, on closer inspection, to be just as endowed with the potential for cultural conditioning as those who judge them. And if the levelling implied by this discovery appears, in the case of *The Tempest*, to move ever downward, so that humans seem united in their failings rather than in their virtues, we should perhaps not be particularly surprised. After all, *The Tempest's* author also left us such plays as *The Merchant of Venice, Troilus and Cressida, Measure for Measure, Timon of Athens* and, of course, *King Lear.* Like *The Tempest, Lear* is deeply concerned with the conflicting claims of nature and culture. Both plays, moreover, involve challenges to authority that, though ultimately suppressed, carry persuasive articulations of their legitimacy. Finally, *Lear*, like *The Tempest* (and *Timon* too, for that matter), is obsessively concerned with human unaccommodation and with the category of the monstrous; its characters bandy about the allegation of monstrosity much in the same manner that Prospero and Miranda mystify Caliban's human status.[97]

Both the genuine and the falsely perceived affronts to authority in *Lear* are condemned as "unnatural" and "monstrous." The King of France, for instance, hearing that Cordelia is "new adopted" to Lear's hate (1.1.203), marvels that she could "in this trice of time / Commit a thing so monstrous, . . . Sure her offense / Must be of such unnatural degree / That monsters it" (1.1.216-20). Gloucester, likewise, learning from Edmund of Edgar's supposed plot against his life, exclaims "He cannot be such a monster" (1.2.102); Edmund, in turn, speaks to his father of Edgar's "unnatural purpose" (2.1.50). Regarding Goneril's plan to kill Albany and marry Edmund, Albany responds "Most monstrous!" (5.3.160); earlier, after hearing of Gloucester's blinding, he has wondered if "Humanity must perforce prey upon itself, / Like monsters of the deep" (4.2.49-50). And Lear, of course, shrieks that Goneril's ingratitude is "More hideous . . . than the sea-monster" (1.4.267-68): Inhospitality becomes "Monster ingratitude!" (1.5.40). In short, for Lear and Gloucester, disloyalty, cruelty, and ungratefulness are unnatural—and that which is unnatural is, ipso facto, monstrous. For Edmund, on the other hand, only instincts and appetites are natural; the vast remainder of human behavior may be attributed to "The curiosity of nations" and "the plague of custom" (1.2.1-4).[98] Neither view is borne out as correct by the play. Lear and especially Gloucester are easily deceived because they cannot draw the sharp line that Edmund can between pure appetite and customary usage. For them, such phenomena as primogeniture, social subordination, patriarchalism in its varied forms, and a king's possession of authority and power are "natural"—as much a part of nature as mutual love between father and child. Edmund, on the other hand, sees through this aristocratic ideology—the arrogation to nature of those things that are in fact cultural constructs—but at the same time, in his devotion to a radically stripped-down conception of "nature," his life truly becomes "cheap as beast's" (2.4.267). Indeed, much more than the brother whom he victimizes, Edmund—through his own choosing—is the unaccommodated man in *King Lear*.[99]

Literally speaking, of course, Poor Tom is unaccommodated as well: He is without shelter and clothes, without social position, without reason, without true name. His own father cannot recognize him, and in fact tells the Old Man that "I' th' last night's storm I such a fellow saw, / Which made me think a man a worm" (4.1.32-33). But as I pointed out in the Prologue, Poor Tom is imaged not only as a beast but also as someone who uses language evocatively, someone Lear can wish to learn from and emulate. And in this more important sense, Tom is far from being unaccommodated: He is not void and cultureless, not a *tabula rasa*. The "nothing" of "Edgar I nothing am" (2.3.21) is no more hollow than Cordelia's earlier "nothings" (1.1.89,91).

If Poor Tom is "the thing itself" (3.4.106), there is nonetheless an unmistakable suggestion in Lear's speech that "the thing itself" is perhaps not such a bad thing after all—a suggestion that the "three on's [who] are sophisticated" (3.4.105-06) may deserve equal, if not greater, censure. If he is but a "fellow" in the eyes of Gloucester and Kent (3.4.177-80), there is nonetheless a sense in which he unites his companions in a fellowship of misery.[100] Lear has travelled an immense distance from the absolutism of his "Reason not the need" speech (2.4.264-70); he may call Tom a "poor, bare, forked animal" (3.4.107-08), but his actions belie his words. And if, as I suspect, Shakespeare is drawing upon his familiarity with Montaignian habits of thought in this passage, he may well have an ironic or undercutting intent in mind as he conceives Lear's lines. Montaigne implies that despite appearances, human status is not so readily lost as Lear supposes, that in fact it can never be lost because humans can never be pre-cultural. This is, after all, one of the principal lessons of The Tempest if we locate the play's representation of Caliban within the discursive realm of New World ethnography. It should come as no surprise that both Montaigne in "Of cannibals" and Shakespeare in Lear allude to ancient philosophers ("Lycurgus and Plato" [153]; "learned Theban" and "good Athenian" [3.4.160,183]) immediately upon their consideration of humans putatively regarded as "savage" (152) or "near to beast" (2.3.9); neither writer has trouble associating the conventionally unaccommodated with the conventionally wise and cultured.

Lear's reference to Poor Tom as a "learned Theban" may signal something else as well: a half-conscious recognition that Tom's "art"—a manifestation of his status as a cultural being—is in part responsible for his "natural" appearance. Like Montaigne's Tupi love-lyric or Prospero's tempest, both of which emblematize the interpenetration of art and nature so predominant as a motif in the works where they appear, Edgar's assumed identity as Poor Tom brings into question exactly what "the thing itself" is. Can a human be unaccommodated? Can nature be separated from art and culture? Or, on the contrary, are these ideas inextricably connected? Both the epistemological observation that nature is a conceptual construct and thus cultural and the seemingly contradictory ontological notion that all art and culture ultimately derive from nature suggest that a decisive and convincing separation of the ideas is impossible. If this is true, then the Renaissance ideas of savagery and civility are equally inseparable, since they gain their conventional force as descriptive attributions through their respective association with conceptions of nature and art. As I have argued throughout this study, Montaigne, Spenser, and Shakespeare appear to acknowledge this inextricable connectedness—though in differing manners and to differing degrees. Montaigne recognizes the astonishing promise of nature, but never wholly endorses its sufficiency, for he knows as well that humans are culture-learning beings who benefit from their arts. Spenser employs the device of literary pastoral to exhibit human connectedness to the natural world, and though he never verges on full-fledged primitivism, he creates characters such as the Salvage Man who go far beyond their literary predecessors in suggesting the limitations of traditional ideas of savagery and civility. And Shakespeare, through the representation of beings perceived as uncertain or marginal in their humanity, demonstrates how allegations of monstrosity, bestiality, and unnaturalness reflect back upon those who make them as much as they identify and characterize their intended objects. In all cases, this explicit or implied interpenetration of ideas of nature and culture is foregrounded when the writings in which it occurs are contextualized within the ethnographic discourse of the Renaissance—and above all, the consideration of New World peoples.

Polixenes tells Perdita in *The Winter's Tale* that the source of life she refers to as "great creating Nature" (4.4.88) is "made better by no mean / But Nature makes that mean; . . . the art itself is Nature" (4.4.89-97). And while Polixenes himself, at this point in the play, represents dubious or even unworthy authority, his words nonetheless suggest a possible and deeply satisfying resolution to a profoundly difficult matter—a resolution perhaps also inchoate in Lear's mind when, during his madness, he mutters to himself, "Nature's above art in that respect" (4.6.86). In a rather different vein, Spenser, in the *Cantos of Mutabilitie,* offers us a portrayal of "great dame Nature" (7.5.1), a figure who defends an expansive view of being and identity against the allegation of radical flux and inconstancy.[101] What unites these two conceptions is that both presuppose a nature that is fundamentally generous and accommodating. To suggest, as Polixenes does, that art and culture emanate from nature and thereby "change" it (4.4.96) is not at all far from claiming, as Spenser's Nature does, that

> all things stedfastnes doe hate
> And changed be: yet being rightly wayd
> They are not changed from their first estate;
> But by their change their being doe dilate: (*Mut.* 7.58.2-5)

This view of nature as an accommodating force is also distinctly Montaignian inasmuch as it stresses the sublime potential of nature while, at the same time, recognizing and valuing the diversity of that which nature gives rise to—diversity in the form of custom and culture. For Montaigne, as for us, New

World ethnographies such as those of Columbus, Pané, Las Casas, Léry, Durán, Sahagún, Harriot, Acosta, and Smith offer varied and conflicting accounts of the "savagery" of American natives. But in Montaigne's meditations, thoughts about this savagery and cultural otherness inevitably become intertwined with reflections upon the ongoing debate over nature and art, and one of the principal results is that savagery is accorded greater complexity and respect than in any previous Renaissance consideration. Montaigne refuses to resort to reductive explanations or models; he eschews the wild man and the Arcadian innocent, the noble and the ignoble savage. And in this respect he is followed by his English successors. It is obvious that Spenser and Shakespeare differ enormously—in their indebtedness (or lack thereof) to Montaigne, their interest in and reliance upon literary tradition, their employment of travel writing for source material, their choice of literary venues, and their ultimate thematic concerns—but it is evident nonetheless that in their treatments of savagery and civility they reflect the same fundamental reluctance to rely upon inherited ideas that we see in Montaigne. Renaissance accounts of New World peoples serve both to alert us to the sensitivity with which these authors represent savage and civil humanity and to suggest one of the principal means by which this sensitivity may have been achieved. The very human tendency to regard certain other humans as unaccommodated did not end, of course, with Lear on the heath or Prospero on the isle, but in the acknowledgment these characters finally make of the genuine accommodation of others lies the beginning of one of the great lessons to be learned in any encounter between an old world and a new.

Epilogue
Acoma Pueblo, March 1986

In March 1986 I spent a week visiting friends in New Mexico. One day we drove out from Albuquerque to Acoma, a pueblo built upon a rocky fortress-like mesa that towers above the high desert stretching west into Arizona. Acoma is reputed to be the oldest continuously inhabited city in the United States; archaeologists date its initial occupation to the twelfth century A.D. Its original settlers—and, by generational extension, its present-day inhabitants—may well be descendants of the Anasazi, whose culture as evidenced at such sites as Mesa Verde and Chaco Canyon represents one of the most remarkable flowerings of architectural, agricultural, and artistic achievement among native North American peoples.

It was at Acoma that I first imagined writing a book along the lines of the one I have now finished. I was not aware at the time that in 1540, when Francisco de Coronado "discovered" the pueblo, Montaigne was just seven years old, studying Latin, and being awakened each morning by gentle music, or that the Acoma Indians had dwelt at their city for roughly 400 years before Spenser and Shakespeare were born. But the large Catholic mission at one edge of the mesa forced me to acknowledge an Old World presence in this strikingly New World place. Far from the Atlantic realm of hurricanes and sargassos, of Brazil and Virginia and the Spanish Main, wandering Europeans of the Renaissance had once again emphatically instituted a principal facet of their cultural inheritance.

It is not, apparently, that the Spaniards were unimpressed by the Acomas' fine three-story houses, their abundant supplies of maize and beans, and their ingenious method of collecting and preserving water in rock cisterns atop the mesa. It is simply that no matter *how* impressed they may have been, they were also participating in an age-old dynamic of foreign contact, conquest, and conversion that was reenacting itself, with their complicity, yet another time. In 1598 the Spaniards fought and defeated the Acomas, and some years later a Franciscan friar named Juan Ramirez began constructing the mission. By 1640, one hundred years after Coronado's arrival, it was completed.

There is, however, something strangely arresting about this mission. I was aware before I saw it that transplanted cultural forms often take on trappings from their new locales—indeed, anthropologists regard this as a truism—but the mission at Acoma manifests this syncretistic tendency with uncommon vividness. In its spare design, its adobe-brick and plaster construction, its flat roof, trapezoidal towers, massive *vigas* and beige sandstone hue, it resembles the native architecture in every respect except size. From a distance—from a neighboring mesa, say—it appears very much of a piece with the pueblo's other buildings. And inside, one of its paintings depicts a beardless Christ with dark skin and straight black hair.

That Europeans conquered the native peoples of North and South America is a stark and incontrovertible truth, as is the consequent fact that these peoples and their cultures were in many cases erased from existence through ethnocidal acts we cannot afford to forget. But equally undeniable is our knowledge that despite this erasure, traces of New World custom, belief, and practice continue to survive—not only in the hybrid cultures of America, but in post-conquest Old World cultures as well. This may be, as at Acoma Pueblo, in the relatively direct form of cross-cultural transference and mutual assimilation; or it may be, as in the Americas at large, in the more indirect form of revolutionary rethinking about the relation between human beings and their natural environment. In the European writings I have discussed, this survival is principally a matter of geographical allusions, scattered linguistic borrowings, and reflections of the way that Renaissance ethnography impinges upon the thematics of pastoral literature and the conventional means of representing ethnic and cultural otherness. But even when the influence of the New World is traced—as in this study—through Old World perceptions and Old World literary texts, this influence nonetheless suggests the intrinsic limitations to ideas about the purity and hermeticism of European culture and works of art. By extension, I think the impingement of the New World upon the Old points toward the inescapable interdependence of literature and history, of artistic endeavor and political reality, and of the world's varied cultural traditions—traditions we must cherish, and never cease to cherish.

Notes

Prologue

1. *King Lear*, 3.4.128-39. Unless otherwise noted, quotations from the plays and poems of Shakespeare are drawn from *The Riverside Shakespeare*, ed. G. Blakemore Evans, et al. (Boston: Houghton Mifflin, 1974). I have retained the brackets indicating editorial choices among variant texts.

2. Autolycus himself, who claims to have served a prince and worn "three-pile" before falling "out of service" (4.3.13-14), possesses a past similar in outline to that imagined by Edgar for Poor Tom.

3. "A Letter addressed to the Chapter of Seville," *Four Voyages*, 66.

4. For example, Antonio Pigafetta writes in his account of Magellan's circumnavigation (1519-22) that the natives of Patagonia, whom he describes variously as "giantes" and "beastes," "lyve of raw flesshe and a certeyne sweete roote which they caule *capar*" (*Decades*, 219-20). Similarly, the Spanish friar Tomaso Ortiz is quoted by Peter Martyr as saying that natives of the North American mainland are "incapable of learning. . . . They eat fleas, spiders and worms raw, whenever they find them. They exercise none of the human arts or industries" (*De Orbe Novo*, 7.4.275). Francisco López de Gómara claims that "the chiefest foode" of certain New World natives is "flesh, and that oftentimes they eate rawe, . . . They eate the fatte as they take it out of the Oxe, and drinke the blood hotte, and die not therewithall" (*Principal Navigations*, vol. 9, 167). And the anonymous *True Declaration of the Estate of the Colonie in Virginia* (1610) states that the Virginian natives are "humane beasts," no more to be trusted than "Lions, Beares, and Crocodiles" (*Tracts*, vol. 3, 6).

5. I have used the terms "Indian," "American Indian," and "Amerindian" in this study almost as frequently as "native American"; similarly, I often rely on "New World" rather than "America" or "the Americas." I recognize the difference between these

sets of terms—though all of them are ultimately Eurocentric—and employ the former as well as the latter so as to stress my interest in early modern European perceptions of America and its indigenous inhabitants.

6. On the Sepúlveda/Las Casas disputation see the second section of chapter 1.

7. For translated quotations from Montaigne's *Essais* (including essay titles) I have relied primarily upon the elegant rendering by Donald M. Frame (*The Complete Essays of Montaigne* [Stanford: Stanford University Press, 1958]); in-text page numbers refer to this edition.

8. See Frame, *The Complete Essays*, 698, 150, and J. H. Elliott, *The Old World and the New* (Cambridge: Cambridge University Press, 1970) 13.

9. In this regard Montaigne resembles one of the best of the early ethnographers, the Spanish Franciscan Bernardino de Sahagún. Describing the condition of Tenochtitlan's inhabitants during the siege of Cortés, Sahagún writes that "all the common folk suffered torments of famine. Many died of hunger. No more did they drink pure, clean water—only brackish water did they drink. Of it many people died, and many people therefore suffered from a bloody flux, of which they died. And all was eaten—lizards and swallows; and maize straw, and salt-grass. And they ate *colorin* wood, and they ate the glue orchid, and the frilled flower; and tanned hides, and buckskin, which they roasted, baked, toasted, or burned, so that they could eat them; and they gnawed sedum, and mud bricks. Never had there been such suffering" (*Florentine Codex: General History of the Things of New Spain*, trans. Arthur J. O. Anderson and Charles E. Dibble [Santa Fe and Salt Lake City: School of American Research and University of Utah Press, 1955-82] Book 12, 100).

Chapter 1

1. *The Fall of Natural Man*, rev. ed. (Cambridge: Cambridge University Press, 1986) 6.

2. See, for example, Bernard McGrane, *Beyond Anthropology* (New York: Columbia University Press, 1989) chapter 1; McGrane claims that during the early modern period the "actions and behavior [of foreign peoples] were experienced as being manifestations of barbarism and savage degeneracy—a hybrid composite of Christian 'nature' and Christian 'evil'" (17).

3. Mircea Eliade, "The Myth of the Noble Savage or, the Prestige of the Beginning," in *Myths, Dreams, and Mysteries* (New York: Harper and Row, 1960) 39. Mary Louise Pratt discusses continuities between pre-twentieth-century travel writing and contemporary ethnographic practice in "Fieldwork in Common Places," *Writing Culture*, ed. James Clifford and George E. Marcus (Berkeley: University of California Press, 1986) 27-50.

4. In her introduction to an issue of *Ethnohistory* devoted to exploring connections between travel writing and ethnography, Caroline B. Brettell points out that

"Although the majority of travelers in the past clearly did not view themselves as professional ethnographers, modern ethnohistorians and historical anthropologists have frequently used their accounts as a source of ethnographic data" ("Introduction: Travel Literature, Ethnography, and Ethnohistory," *Ethnohistory* 33:2 [1986]: 127). Similarly, Karen Ordahl Kupperman writes that "work by ethnohistorians on the Algonquians of eastern North America has made many of [John Smith's] descriptions of Indian life and culture seem more realistic; he is now considered an important source on those cultures" (Introduction, *Captain John Smith: A Select Edition of His Writings* [Chapel Hill: University of North Carolina Press, 1988] 3). In corroboration of these claims, see, for example, the fine ethnohistorical studies of James Axtell, particularly *The European and the Indian* (Oxford: Oxford University Press, 1981) and *After Columbus* (Oxford: Oxford University Press, 1988), and Kupperman's own *Settling with the Indians* (Totowa, NJ: Rowman and Littlefield, 1975).

5. Octavio Paz, "The Power of Ancient Mexican Art," *NYRB* 37:19 (December 6, 1990) 18; J. H. Elliott, *The Old World and the New* (Cambridge: Cambridge University Press, 1970) 35; Anthony Pagden, *The Fall of Natural Man*, 122; David B. Quinn, *The Elizabethans and the Irish* (Ithaca: Cornell University Press, 1966) 20. See also Bernard G. Hoffmann, *From Cabot to Cartier* (Toronto: University of Toronto Press, 1961); Margaret T. Hodgen, *Early Anthropology in the Sixteenth and Seventeenth Centuries* (Philadelphia: University of Pennsylvania Press, 1964); two articles by John Howland Rowe: "Ethnography and Ethnology in the Sixteenth Century" (*KASP* 30 [1964]: 1-19) and "The Renaissance Foundations of Anthropology" (*AA* 67 [February 1965]: 1-20); Michael T. Ryan, "Assimilating New Worlds in the Sixteenth and Seventeenth Centuries," *CSSH* 23:4 (October 1981): 519-38; J. Jorge Klor de Alva, "Sahagún and the Birth of Modern Ethnography: Representing, Confessing, and Inscribing the Native Other," in *The Work of Bernardino de Sahagún*, ed. Klor de Alva, et al. (Austin: University of Texas Press, 1988) 31-52; Mary B. Campbell, "The Illustrated Travel Book and the Birth of Ethnography: Part I of De Bry's *America*," in *The Work of Dissimilitude*, ed. David G. Allen and Robert A. White (Newark: University of Delaware Press, 1992) 177-95; Karl W. Butzer, "From Columbus to Acosta: Science, Geography, and the New World," *Annals of the Association of American Geographers* 82:3 (1992): 543-65; and Arnold Krupat, *Ethnocriticism* (Berkeley: University of California Press, 1992) 49-80.

6. See Rowe, "Ethnography and Ethnology," 2, 11-15, and "The Renaissance Foundations of Anthropology," 12-20. A possible addition to this list is William Harrison's *The Description of England* (London, 1577, 1587), though neither "ethnography" nor "autoethnography" is quite accurate as a generic characterization of Harrison's work. On "autoethnography" see chapter 3, notes 29 and 31.

7. Léry's book has been famously referred to as "the anthropologist's breviary" by Claude Lévi-Strauss (*Tristes Tropiques*, trans. John and Doreen Weightman [New

York: Atheneum, 1975] 81). Léry's most recent English translator, Janet Whatley, writes in her introduction that Léry's "vivid and subtle ethnography of the Tupinamba Indians and his minute description of the marvelous abundance of their natural setting provide one of the most detailed and engaging of the reports we have of how the New World looked while it was indeed still new" (*History of a Voyage to the Land of Brazil* [Berkeley: University of California Press, 1990] xv).

8. *History of a Voyage*, lxi.

9. "Of the Caniballes," in *The Essayes of Montaigne*, trans. John Florio [London, 1603; New York: Modern Library, 1933] 163.

10. On Santo Tomás, see Elliott, *The Old World and the New*, 34; on Molina, Pagden, *The Fall of Natural Man*, 17; on Sagard, M. Trudel, *The Beginnings of New France, 1524-1663* (Toronto: University of Toronto Press, 1973) 155-59. See also Michel de Certeau's semiotic examination of Léry's *colloque* in *The Writing of History* (New York: Columbia University Press, 1988) 209-43.

11. Rowe, "Ethnography and Ethnology," 1.

12. For a classic expression of the tripartite model, see chapter 14 of Pierre d'Ailly's *Imago Mundi* [ca. 1410] trans. Edwin F. Keever (Wilmington, NC: Linprint, 1948). On the persistence—well into the seventeenth century—of this model, see William Shakespeare's reference to "the three-nook'd world" in *Antony and Cleopatra* (4.6.5); Elizabeth Cary's to "the triple earth" in *The Tragedy of Mariam, The Fair Queen of Jewry*, ed. Barry Weller and Margaret W. Ferguson (Berkeley: University of California Press, 1994) 3.3.175; and Sir Thomas Browne's to "this triple Continent" in *Religio Medici* (*Sir Thomas Browne: Selected Writings*, ed. Sir Geoffrey Keynes [Chicago: University of Chicago Press, 1968] 29). The Latin tract *Mundus novus* (Basel, ca. 1503-05)—based on a letter of Amerigo Vespucci's to Lorenzo di Pietro de' Medici—was "the first printed and published account of an authentic expedition (1501-02) to a continental landmass across the Atlantic," according to David B. Quinn in "New Geographical Horizons: Literature" (*First Images of America*, ed. Fredi Chiappelli [Berkeley: University of California Press, 1976] vol. 2, 639). In fact, as Quinn and others have pointed out, either Vespucci or his Florentine friends fabricated an account of an earlier voyage to the American mainland in order to take away the honor of its "discovery" from Christopher Columbus. The account is now recognized for what it is—a sham—but its existence demonstrates that Vespucci was aware of the "newness" of the American lands in a way that Columbus was not. See Quinn, 639-47; F. J. Pohl, *Amerigo Vespucci: Pilot Major* (New York: Columbia University Press, 1944) chapters 5 and 10; Samuel Eliot Morison, *The European Discovery of America: The Southern Voyages* (New York: Oxford University Press, 1974) 276-97, 304-12; Carlo Ginzburg, *The Cheese and the Worms* (Harmondsworth: Penguin, 1982) 82; and William Brandon, *New Worlds for Old* (Athens: Ohio University Press, 1986) 39.

13. Stephen Greenblatt, *Marvelous Possessions* (Chicago: University of Chicago Press, 1991) 86. It is well known that Norse colonists from Greenland settled briefly at "Vinland" (perhaps in Newfoundland) around the year 1000, and Greenlandic Norse continued to harvest timber from the Labrador coast until around 1350. On pre-Columbian European contacts with the New World, see Samuel Eliot Morison, *The European Discovery of America: The Northern Voyages* (New York: Oxford University Press, 1971); Anne and Helge Ingstad, *The Discovery of a Norse Settlement in America* (Oslo, 1977); Jan Carew, *Fulcrums of Change* (Trenton, NJ: Africa World Press, 1988) 3-48; and Barry Fell, *America, B.C.* (New York: Pocket Books, 1989).

14. On the term "Indians" for American natives see Robert F. Berkhofer, Jr., *The White Man's Indian* (New York: Vintage, 1979) 4-6. The "dirty dog/noble savage" dichotomy is from Lewis Hanke, *All Mankind is One* (DeKalb: Northern Illinois University Press, 1974) 9. Frank Kermode, in his *English Pastoral Poetry*, discusses the connection between this dual view of American natives and "the two opinions about natural men" held in the Renaissance: "one holding that they were virtuous because unspoilt, and the other that they were vicious because they belonged to what the theologians called the state of nature as opposed to the state of grace" (London: George G. Harrap, 1952) 40. Likewise, C. S. Lewis points out that the American "Natural man" might be regarded either as "ideally innocent" or as "brutal, subhuman" (*English Literature in the Sixteenth Century* [Oxford: Oxford University Press, 1954] 17). See also Berkhofer, 27-28.

15. Entry for Thursday, October 11, 1492 (as interpolated by Bartolomé de Las Casas) in the *Diario*, 65-69. Columbus did in fact take six natives back to Spain, where they were baptized and presented to the court of Ferdinand and Isabella; see Samuel Eliot Morison, *Admiral of the Ocean Sea* (Boston: Little, Brown, 1942) 360.

16. Tzvetan Todorov, *The Conquest of America* (New York: Harper and Row, 1984) 39. Mircea Eliade makes the same point in his "The Myth of the Noble Savage or, the Prestige of the Beginning" (39).

17. Those who *did* make it alive were usually put on display when they arrived in the Old World. Cortés, for instance, brought "a large party of native Mexicans to Spain with him in 1528, including two princes, eight jugglers, and twelve ball players. The jugglers were sent on to Rome where they performed for the Pope. Fifty Tupinamba [from coastal Brazil] were taken to Rouen in 1550 to participate in a pageant put on by the city in honor of the King of France." See Rowe, "Ethnography and Ethnology in the Sixteenth Century," 3; Sidney Lee, "The American Indian in Elizabethan England," *Elizabethan and Other Essays*, ed. F. S. Boas (London: Oxford University Press, 1929) 263-301; Jan Carew, *Fulcrums of Change*, 37-38; and Steven Mullaney, "Strange Things, Gross Terms, Curious Customs: The Rehearsal of Cultures in the Late Renaissance," *Representing the English Renaissance*, ed. Stephen Greenblatt (Berkeley: University of California Press, 1988) 65-92.

18. Entry for December 16, 1492 in the *Diario*, 235-37.

19. Entry for December 25, 1492 in the *Diario*, 281.

20. Todorov, 42-43.

21. Deborah Root, in an incisive critique of Todorov's book ("The Imperial Signifier: Todorov and the Conquest of Mexico," *Cultural Critique* [Spring 1988]: 197-219), argues that the binarism of Todorov's categories contributes in part to his "racialist" (215) and dehistoricized explanation of the Spanish conquest of Mexico. Root does not deal with Todorov's discussion of Columbus, but her claim that "in *The Conquest of America* the voice of the "Other" is evoked only to be, again, silenced" (219) suggests that she would find his generalized typology of alterity inadequate. See also Rolena Adorno's discussion of Todorov in "Arms, Letters and the Native Historian in Early Colonial Mexico," *HI* 4 (1989), esp. 202-08; Inga Clendinnen's comments on Todorov's account of the Mexican conquest in "'Fierce and Unnatural Cruelty': Cortés and the Conquest of Mexico," *REP* 33 (Winter 1991): 65-100, esp. 66; and Gananath Obeyesekere's brief critique of Todorov in *The Apotheosis of Captain Cook* (Princeton: Princeton University Press, 1992) 16-19.

22. *The Invention of Culture*, rev. ed. (Chicago: University of Chicago Press, 1981) 4.

23. Edward Said, *Orientalism* (New York: Vintage, 1979) 272. For a different formulation of this idea—a formulation grounded in the work of Heidegger and Gadamer—see John Keber, "Sahagún and Hermeneutics: A Christian Ethnographer's Understanding of Aztec Culture" (in *The Work of Bernardino de Sahagún* [Austin: University of Texas Press, 1988]): "Prejudices are necessary, in other words, because they supply the structure in which the act of interpretive knowledge takes place. . . . Put more simply, it is only as members of a tradition that we can think at all. The irony of human knowing is that the very tradition that empowers us to think also threatens to seal us in" (54). And see Arnold Krupat, *Ethnocriticism* (Berkeley: University of California Press, 1992) 6.

24. Todorov, 42-43. As we will see, Todorov makes the same claim about Montaigne in "L'Etre et L'Autre: Montaigne," *YFS* 64 (1983): 125. On this, see chapter 2.

25. Ibid, 132.

26. The two myths, Christian and classical, had so thoroughly interpenetrated one another by this time that they were often conflated in the accounts of individual writers. Again and again we see reference to the perpetually mild and springtime climate of the New World, the fruitful soil, the bountiful garden-like flora, and the gentle peace-loving natives. Likewise, a clear distinction between these two versions of early humanity and the idyllic pastoral world of Arcadia was seldom maintained. The myths, through their inherent sketchiness, merged into one another and provided convenient frames through which the New World could be perceived. Many writers have discussed this theme; see, for example, Elliott's *The Old World and the New*; Harry Levin, *The Myth of the Golden Age* (Bloomington: Indiana

University Press, 1969); Henri Baudet, *Paradise on Earth* (New Haven: Yale University Press, 1965); A. Bartlett Giamatti, *The Earthly Paradise and the Renaissance Epic* (Princeton: Princeton University Press, 1966); Howard Mumford Jones, *O Strange New World* (New York: Viking, 1964); Mircea Eliade, *Myths, Dreams, and Mysteries* (New York: Harper and Row, 1960); H. C. Porter, *The Inconstant Savage* (London: Duckworth, 1979); Bernard W. Sheehan, *Savagism and Civility* (Cambridge: Cambridge University Press, 1980); Antonello Gerbi, *Nature in the New World* (Pittsburgh: University of Pittsburgh Press, 1986); and Germán Arciniegas, *America in Europe* (San Diego: Harcourt Brace, 1986).

27. *Decades*, 1.3.18. Cf. this description by Vasco de Quiroga of the native Americans' resemblance to men of the Golden Age as imaged in Lucian's *Saturnales*: "They have the same customs and manners, the same quality, simplicity, goodness, obedience and humility, the same festivities, games, pleasures, drinking, idling, pastimes, and nudity, and lacked but the poorest of household goods nor had any desire for better, and had the same clothing, footwear and food, all such as was provided free by the fertility of the soil and almost without labor, care, or seeking on their part." Quiroga, the bishop of Michoacán in Mexico and a man profoundly influenced by Thomas More's representation of an ideal state in *Utopia* (1516), is quoted by Todorov in *The Conquest of America*, 194. See Silvio Zavala, "Sir Thomas More in New Spain: A Utopian Adventure of the Renaissance" (in *Essential Articles for the Study of Sir Thomas More*, ed. Richard S. Sylvester and G. P. Marc'hadour [Hamden: Archon, 1977] 302-11); see also Levin's discussion of Quiroga in *The Myth of the Golden Age*, 93.

28. Marc Lescarbot, for instance, devotes the sixth book of his *Histoire de la Nouvelle France* (1609) to delineating correspondences among the myths and customs of the Canadian Indians of Acadia and the Greeks and Romans. See the translation by W. L. Grant, *History of New France*, 3 vols. (Toronto: University of Toronto Press, 1907-14).

29. *Decades*, 1.9.45. See also Edward Gaylord Bourne, "Columbus, Ramon Pane and the Beginnings of American Anthropology," *PAAS* 17 (April 1906): 310-48, esp. 343. Bourne accurately observes that Pané's account "is not only the first treatise ever written in the field of American Antiquities, but to this day remains our most authentic record of the religion and folk-lore of the long since extinct Tainos, the aboriginal inhabitants of Hayti" (311).

30. *Letters from Mexico*, trans. and ed. Anthony Pagden (New Haven: Yale University Press, 1986) 108. As J. H. Elliott writes in *The Old World and the New*, Cortés "attempts to bring the exotic into the range of the familiar by writing of Aztec temples as mosques, or by comparing the marketplace of Tenochtitlán with that of Salamanca" (19). And in *Nature in the New World*, Antonello Gerbi remarks that "In Cortés, the conquistador, the prevailing theme is the Europeanness or actual Hispanism of America" (96). To a certain extent this tendency is excusable, since the highlands of Mexico bear a far

greater resemblance to the Old World landscapes Cortés knew than do the tropical islands of the Caribbean. But it is worth noting that Bernal Díaz del Castillo, one of Cortés's soldiers and the author of *The Conquest of New Spain*, wrote that "When we saw all those cities and villages built in the water, and other great towns on dry land, and that straight and level causeway leading to Mexico [Tenochtitlán], we were astounded. These great towns and *cues* [temples] and buildings rising from the water, all made of stone, seemed like an enchanted vision from the tale of Amadis. Indeed, some of our soldiers asked whether it was not all a dream. . . . It was all so wonderful that I do not know how to describe this first glimpse of things never heard of, seen or dreamed of before" (Harmondsworth: Penguin, 1963) 214.

31. On Oviedo, see Pagden, *The Fall of Natural Man*, 25; Harriot, *A briefe and true report of the new found land of Virginia* (1588), in *Virginia Voyages*, 67. Harriot also writes that the "Virginian" Indians kill fish "with poles made sharpe at one end, by shooting them into the fish after the maner as Irish men cast darts" (64). William Strachey, in his *History of Travel into Virginia Brittannia* (written 1612, published 1625), exemplifies a somewhat more "objective" style of ethnographic description—though in the end equally assimilationist—when he writes that "the word *werowance*, which we call and construe for a king, is a common word whereby they call all commanders" (excerpted in *Elizabethans*, 208).

32. *The Fall of Natural Man*, 17.

33. Gante is quoted in Spanish in Lewis Hanke's *The First Social Experiments in America* (Gloucester, MA: Peter Smith, 1964) 4n; the translation is mine.

34. Richard Hakluyt, "A generall and briefe description of the Countrey, and condition of the people, which are found in Meta Incognita," *Principal Navigations*, vol. 7, 370.

35. "Of the newe landes and of ye people founde by the messengers of the kynge of portyngale named Emanuel" (ca. 1510-11; author unknown, but the passage appears to be a précis of Vespucci's *Mundus novus* of 1503-05), in *First Three Books*, xxvii; *Decades*, 3.3.104.

36. Columbus first mentions cannibalism in his entry for November 23, 1492; see the *Diario*, 167. Peter Hulme discusses the alleged cannibalism of the Caribs in detail in his *Colonial Encounters* (London: Methuen, 1986), particularly chapters 1 and 2. The term "anti-image" is drawn from Jones's *O Strange New World* (New York: Viking, 1964) 35ff.

37. *A Collection of Essays by George Orwell* (San Diego: Harcourt, Brace, Jovanovich, 1946) 181.

38. The phrase "stereotypical dualism" is from Hulme, 50. Urs Bitterli, for instance, illustrates this dualism when he writes that European opinion "alternated between placing the Indians just above the beasts and regarding them virtually as inhabitants of Eden" (*Cultures in Conflict* [Stanford: Stanford University Press, 1989] 75-76).

39. *The Old World and the New*, 15. Sidney Lee was perhaps thinking along these lines when he wrote, forty years earlier, that "American ethnology was destined to startle

and unsettle orthodox European beliefs in a greater degree than any marvels of inanimate nature in the New World" (*Elizabethan and Other Essays* [London: Oxford University Press, 1929] 265). Similarly, J. R. Hale has claimed that "The 'ethnicks' of the Americas had a special, though delayed, power to jolt the Europeans into taking fresh stock of themselves" ("Sixteenth-Century Explanations of War and Violence," *Past and Present* 51 [1971]: 6).

40. Tzvetan Todorov implies this in his discussion of Las Casas and Sepúlveda, 167ff. Deborah Root goes so far as to argue that "Although Todorov claims to deplore the 'value judgements' he finds in most Spanish colonial texts, his own complicity with these writings may be traced in the discursive structure of his discussion of Sepúlveda's view of Aztec society" (209).

41. On Montesinos and his effect upon Las Casas, see Anthony Pagden's introduction to Las Casas's *A Short Account of the Destruction of the Indies*, trans. Nigel Griffin (Harmondsworth: Penguin, 1992) xx-xxi.

42. Anthony Pagden, *The Fall of Natural Man* (Cambridge: Cambridge University Press, 1986) 21-22; Samuel Eliot Morison, *Admiral of the Ocean Sea* (Boston: Little, Brown, 1942) 51. For a short biography of Las Casas, see George Sanderlin's introduction to *Las Casas: A Selection of His Writings* (New York: Knopf, 1971) 3-25. On the Dominican friar Montesinos and his influential 1511 sermons, see Las Casas's *Historia*, Book Three, chapters 4 and 5; see also Lewis Hanke, *The Spanish Struggle for Justice in the Conquest of America* (Philadelphia: University of Pennsylvania Press, 1949), chapter 1.

43. J. H. Elliott, *The Old World and the New* (Cambridge: Cambridge University Press, 1970) 42.

44. Carl Ortwin Sauer, *The Early Spanish Main* (Berkeley: University of California Press, 1966) 38.

45. *The Devastation of the Indies: A Brief Account*, trans. Herma Briffault (New York: Seabury Press, 1974; rpt. Baltimore: Johns Hopkins University Press, 1992) 28-29. Other translations of Las Casas's famous *Brevisima relación de la destruccion de las Indias* (Seville, 1552) include *The Spanish Colonie* (rendered by "M.M.S." and published in London in 1583; rpt. Ann Arbor: University Microfilms, 1966) and *A Short Account of the Destruction of the Indies*, trans. Nigel Griffin (Harmondsworth: Penguin, 1992).

46. The full text of the papal bull may be found in *New Iberian World*, vol. 1, 386-88. See also Lewis Hanke, "Pope Paul III and the American Indians," *Harvard Theological Review* 30 (1937): 65-102; and Germán Arciniegas, *America in Europe* (San Diego: Harcourt, Brace, 1986) 100, 276.

47. Las Casas himself uses the phrase *tablas rasas* in his *Apologética historia*, ii, 262. Bernard W. Sheehan briefly touches on Las Casas in his *Savagism and Civility* (Cambridge: Cambridge University Press, 1980), claiming that "His Indian society lacked the elemental signs of a real culture" (26); but Sheehan appears to contradict himself by

also pointing to Las Casas's "eye for the constituent parts of native culture" (30). Margaret T. Hodgen writes that Las Casas provided "an immense service in integrating the Indian with the human race. But all in all, the missionary's opinion of savagery differed little from that of the fault-finding layman" (*Early Anthropology in the Sixteenth and Seventeenth Centuries* [Philadelphia: University of Pennsylvania Press, 1964] 369).

48. See, for example, his *Diario* entries for October 11 and 16, November 1 and 12, 1492; see also the famous "Letter to Santangel" of 1493 ("Letter of Columbus, describing the results of his first voyage," in *The Journal of Christopher Columbus*, trans. Cecil Jane [London: Anthony Blond, 1968] 196).

49. *Decades*, 2.1.52. Richard Eden, in his "Preface to the Reader" before his translation of Martyr, writes that "these simple gentiles lyuing only after the lawe of nature, may well bee lykened to a smoothe and bare table vnpaynted, or a white paper vnwritten, vpon the which yow may at the fyrst paynte or wryte what yow lyste, as yow can not vppon tables alredy paynted, vnlesse yow rase or blot owt the fyrste formes" (*Decades*, Preface).

50. Edmundo O'Gorman, *The Invention of America* (Bloomington: Indiana University Press, 1961) 138-39.

51. "Utopian Ethnology in Las Casas's *Apologética*," *HI* 4 (1989): 275.

52. Todorov, *The Conquest of America* (New York: Harper and Row, 1984) 168.

53. Todorov admires Sahagún and Durán for their knowledge of Nahuatl and other New World languages; Las Casas, it is said, never learned a native American tongue. Todorov also praises these men for what Clifford Geertz might call their "thick description" of Mexican culture and religion. And regarding Sahagún, Todorov writes, "One detail nicely illustrates the difference between Las Casas and Sahagún: for Las Casas, it will be remembered, all the Indians give evidence of the same qualities—there is no difference among peoples, not to mention individuals; Sahagún, for his part, refers to his individual informants by their own names" (*The Conquest of America*, 240). Still, I think that the difference between Las Casas and these other ethnographic writers is one of degree rather than of kind. The latters' perceptions may be more nuanced than those of Las Casas, but ultimately they too are engaged in an assimilative project—and cannot help but be so.

54. See, for example, Lewis Hanke, *All Mankind is One* (DeKalb: Northern Illinois University Press, 1974) and *Aristotle and the American Indians* (London: Hollis and Carter, 1959); Pagden, *The Fall of Natural Man* (Cambridge: Cambridge University Press, 1986) 109-45 and "Introduction" to Las Casas's *A Short Account of the Destruction of the Indies*, trans. Nigel Griffin (Harmondsworth: Penguin, 1992) xxvii-xxx; and Stafford Poole's translation of Las Casas's *In Defense of the Indians* (DeKalb: Northern Illinois University Press, 1974). Also noteworthy are H. C. Porter, *The Inconstant Savage* (London: Duckworth, 1979) 153-80; Tzvetan Todorov, *The Conquest of America*, 151-82; and Jan Carew, *Fulcrums of Change* (Trenton, NJ: Africa World Press, 1988) 28-31.

55. Aristotle writes that "all men who differ from others as much as the body differs from the soul, or an animal from a man (and this is the case with all whose function is bodily service, and who produce their best when they supply such service)—all such are by nature slaves, and it is better for them, on the very same principle as in other cases just mentioned, to be ruled by a master. A man is thus by nature a slave if he is capable of becoming (and this is the reason why he also actually becomes) the property of another, and if he participates in reason to the extent of apprehending it in another, thought destitute of it himself. . . . it is nature's intention also to erect a physical difference between the body of the freeman and that of the slave, giving the latter strength for the menial duties of life, but making the former upright in carriage" (*The Politics of Aristotle*, trans. Ernest Barker [Oxford: Clarendon Press, 1946] 1254-b, 13).

56. *The hystorie of the Weste Indies*, wrytten by Gonzalus Ferinandus, in *Decades*, 210. Montaigne may have been relying upon this "information" when he alluded, in his "Apology for Raymond Sebond," to lands where "the head and the skin of [the people's] forehead is so hard that iron cannot cut it and is blunted by it" (*The Complete Essays of Montaigne*, trans. Donald M. Frame [Stanford: Stanford University Press] 391). See also Oviedo's *Natural History of the West Indies*, trans. and ed. Sterling A. Stoudemire (Chapel Hill: University of North Carolina Press, 1959) 43.

57. Quoted in Lewis Hanke, *The First Social Experiments in America* (Cambridge: Harvard University Press, 1935) 20, and translated from Sepúlveda's *Democrates segundo, o de las justas causas de la guerra contra los indios* (ca. 1544), ed. Angel Losada (Madrid, 1951) 33.

58. Hanke, *All Mankind is One*, 17. Oviedo, for example, was termed by Las Casas "a deadly enemy of the Indians" (34).

59. I take these dates from Anthony Pagden, "*Ius et Factum:* Text and Experience in the Writings of Bartolomé de Las Casas," *REP* 33 (Winter 1991) 151, and H. C. Porter, *The Inconstant Savage*, chapter 8. José Rabasa claims that "the bulk of the *[Apologética]* as we know it was written between 1556 and 1559" ("Utopian Ethnology," 267).

60. *In Defense of the Indians*, 28.

61. *Apologética historia*, ii, 531; also quoted in Elliott's *The Old World and the New*, 45. See also Pagden, *The Fall of Natural Man*, 135. Elliott points out that Sepúlveda countered Las Casas's instances of the Indians' artistic and architectural ability by claiming that many animals—spiders, for instance—can create things that humans cannot duplicate.

62. *Apologética historia*, chapter 62, as excerpted in Sanderlin, *Las Casas: A Selection*, 128. For Las Casas's reliance, in the *Apologética historia*, upon the ethnographic descriptions of Alvar Núñez Cabeza de Vaca, see Rolena Adorno, "The Discursive Encounter of Spain and America: The Authority of Eyewitness Testimony in the Writing of History," *William and Mary Quarterly* 49:2 (April 1992): 220-27.

63. *The Conquest of America*, 188-92, 172-75. In terms of my earlier summary of Todorov's schematization, "perspectivism" amounts to acknowledging *equality* and concluding *identity*, while nonetheless recognizing that the values held by the other are "true"

from the perspective of the other's cultural presuppositions, if not "absolutely true." In this construction, of course, "absolute truth" still resides with the perceiving subject—in this case, the European Las Casas.

64.   Sanderlin, 144. Montaigne writes, in "Of cannibals" (1579-80), that "there is nothing barbarous and savage in that nation [Brazil], from what I have been told, except that each man calls barbarism whatever is not his own practice; for indeed it seems we have no other test of truth and reason than the example and pattern of the opinions and customs of the country we live in" (*The Complete Essays of Montaigne*, trans. Donald M. Frame [Stanford, 1958] 152).

65.   *Apologética historia*, i, 339; quoted (and translated) by José Rabasa in "Utopian Ethnology," 282.

66.   Todorov, *The Conquest of America*, 132.

67.   Historians agree that Las Casas is often guilty of exaggeration in his accounts of Spanish atrocities and in his claims about the numbers of natives who died in Mexico and the Caribbean during the first fifty years of the post-Columbian era. Still, even if Las Casas's estimate that more than twenty million Indians died as the result of murder, starvation, overwork, suicide, or disease is inaccurate, the "Black Legend" *[La Leyenda Negra]* nonetheless represents one of the most massive ethnocides in history. For discussions of this issue, see Porter, *The Inconstant Savage*, chapter 8; Hanke, *All Mankind is One*; Charles Gibson, *Spain in America* (New York: Harper and Row, 1966) 43-47; Benjamin Keen, "The Black Legend Revisited: Assumptions and Realities," *Hispanic American Historical Review* 49 (November 1969): 703-19; Sherburne Cook and Woodrow W. Borah, *Essays in Population History* (Berkeley: University of California Press, 1971) 376-411; Roberto Fernández Retamar, "Against the Black Legend" (1976), in *Caliban and Other Essays* (Minneapolis: University of Minnesota Press, 1989) 56-73; William Brandon, *New Worlds for Old* (Athens: Ohio University Press, 1986) 158-61; Jan Carew, *Fulcrums of Change*, 20, 28; Urs Bitterli, *Cultures in Conflict* (Stanford: Stanford University Press, 1989) 33-34, 79-80; and the Introduction to Las Casas's *The Devastation of the Indies*, trans. Herma Briffault (New York, 1974). William S. Maltby, however, writes that Las Casas's "allegation that anywhere from thirty to fifty million Indians were slain by the Spaniards is patently absurd" (*The Black Legend in England* [Durham: Duke University Press, 1971] 18); Maltby's book attempts to show, among other things, that anti-Hispanism in England grotesquely distorted the perception of Spanish activities in the New World.

68.   *Apologética historia*, chapter 48, as excerpted in Sanderlin, 201-02.

69.   See Pagden, *The Fall of Natural Man*, 140-45.

70.   For a critique of the developmental model which aligns non-European "primitives" with European children, see Richard A. Shweder, "On Savages and Other Children," *AA* 84 (1982): 354-66.

71.   Hodgen, *Early Anthropology*, 361. I believe that, on the balance, Hodgen is correct in this judgment, though as I have pointed out, euphoric accounts and sympathetic

estimations of New World natives were fairly common in the early years after Columbus's discovery. See also Robert F. Berkhofer, Jr., *The White Man's Indian* (New York: Vintage, 1979); Anthony Pagden, "The Savage Critic: Some European Images of the Primitive," *Yearbook of English Studies*, 1983, 32; and Richard Marienstras, *New Perspectives on the Shakespearean World* (Cambridge: Cambridge University Press, 1985) chapter 7. Berkhofer claims that "no one argued that the Indian was as good as the European in this early period [roughly the first half of the sixteenth century]" (10); Marienstras writes that "From the fifteenth century up until the mid-seventeenth most travellers manifested indifference or hostility toward the cultures of primitive peoples" (163).

72. I take these now-familiar critical designations from the following sources: "new historicism" (Stephen Greenblatt, Introduction to "The Forms of Power and the Power of Forms in the Renaissance," *Genre* 15:1 and 15:2 [1982] 5); "poetics of culture" (ibid., 6, and Greenblatt, *Shakespearean Negotiations* [Berkeley: University of California Press, 1988] 5); "cultural materialism" (Jonathan Dollimore, "Shakespeare, cultural materialism and the new historicism," in *Political Shakespeare*, ed. Dollimore and Alan Sinfield [Ithaca: Cornell University Press, 1985] 2). Dollimore borrows the phrase "cultural materialism" from the works of Raymond Williams, particularly *Marxism and Literature* (Oxford: Oxford University Press, 1977) and *Problems in Materialism and Culture* (London: New Left, 1980); Williams defines "cultural materialism" as "a theory of the specificities of material cultural and literary production within historical materialism" (*Marxism and Literature* 5). See also the collections of essays in *The New Historicism*, ed. H. Aram Veeser (New York: Routledge, 1989) and *Redrawing the Boundaries*, ed. Stephen Greenblatt and Giles Gunn (New York: MLA, 1992).

73. Michel Foucault, *The Order of Things* (New York: Vintage, 1970) 387.

74. Ibid, 310-11.

75. Jonathan Dollimore, "Shakespeare, cultural materialism, and the new historicism," 2-17; and *Radical Tragedy* (Chicago: University of Chicago Press, 1984) 153-81. But see, in addition, Gerald Graff's comments on essentialism in "Co-optation" (in *The New Historicism*, ed. H. Aram Veeser, 168-81). Graff stresses that the standard critique of essentialism ignores that the idea's meaning is dependent upon its use in particular social conjunctures; "Appealing to essences (or to the natural, the objective, etc.) is often a way of rationalizing coercive social practices, but not necessarily always. In the recent American and South African racial struggles, to take just one example, the idea that there is an essential human nature that racist regimes violate has had an important 'oppositional' effect" (174).

76. *Radical Tragedy*, 155.

77. Ibid, 17, 155. In a similar way, Antonio Gramsci discusses connections between Niccolò Machiavelli and Karl Marx in *Selections From Prison Notebooks*, trans. and ed. Quintin Hoare and Geoffrey Nowell Smith (London: Lawrence and Wishart, 1971).

78. "The New Historicism in Renaissance Studies," *ELR* 16 (1986): 22.

79. Michel Foucault, *The Archaeology of Knowledge* (New York: Pantheon, 1972) 169. Hayden White stresses Foucault's emphasis upon "ruptures" and "disjunctions" in his essay "Foucault Decoded" (*Tropics of Discourse* [Baltimore: Johns Hopkins University Press, 1978] 234).

80. Fredric Jameson goes so far as to intimate the desirability of this state of affairs; he writes in *The Political Unconscious* (Ithaca: Cornell University Press, 1981) that "our readings of the past are vitally dependent upon our experience of the present" (11). See also Robert D'Amico, *Historicism and Knowledge* (New York: Routledge, 1989) xiii, 116; and, on what anthropologists call "upstreaming," see Inga Clendinnen, *Ambivalent Conquests* (Cambridge: Cambridge University Press, 1987) 133.

81. "Introduction: Partial Truths," in *Writing Culture*, ed. James Clifford and George E. Marcus (Berkeley: University of California Press, 1986) 22. See also Arnold Krupat's *Ethnocriticism* (Berkeley: University of California Press, 1992) 49-80.

82. I rely here on a pair of recent and eminently sensible definitions of "subjectivity" in articles by Louis Montrose and David Simpson: "Professing the Renaissance: The Poetics and Politics of Culture" (in *The New Historicism*, 15-36), and "Literary Criticism and the Return to 'History'" (*CI* 14:4 [Summer 1988]: 721-47). Montrose claims that "my invocation of the term 'Subject' is meant to suggest an equivocal process of *subjectification*: on the one hand, shaping individuals and loci of consciousness and initiators of action—endowing them with *subjectivity* and with the capacity for agency; and, on the other hand, positioning, motivating, and constraining them within—*subjecting them to*—social networks and cultural codes that ultimately exceed their comprehension or control" (21); Simpson writes that "Subjectivity can now be thought of as, instead, made up of both idiosyncracy and intersubjectivity. . . . Subjectivity must rather be imagined as the site of determinate (if not always visible) forces inclining us to decisions that range between relatively unconstrained and highly constrained" (744-45).

83. *Shakespearean Negotiations*, 20.

84. I use "appropriative" here in a less pejorative sense than that employed, for example, by Alan Sinfield in "Against Appropriation" (*Essays in Criticism* 31 [July 1981]: 181-95); Sinfield is more sanguine than I am about the possibility of avoiding projections of the present into the past.

85. See *Radical Tragedy*, 17-18, 154, 252, 257-58, 269-70. Dollimore acknowledges that Montaigne's word "custom" (*coutume*) is different from Althusser's "ideology," but still claims that "the Renaissance possessed a sophisticated concept of ideology if not the word" (18).

86. Dollimore treats Kant explicitly in *Radical Tragedy*, 255-56, and consistently rejects idealist forms of philosophy in favor of materialism; the association of idealism with essentialism is maintained throughout.

87. *The Complete Essays of Montaigne,* trans. Donald M. Frame (Stanford: Stanford University Press, 1958) 453-54. See also "Of Democritus and Heraclitus": "Things in themselves may have their own weights and measures and qualities; but once inside, within us, she [the soul] allots them their qualities as she sees fit" (220). Apropos of this discussion, Paul de Man treats Montaigne as a precursor to phenomenology in "Montaigne and Transcendence," *Critical Writings,* 1953-1978, ed. Lindsay Waters (Minneapolis: University of Minnesota Press, 1989): 3-11.

88. *Prolegomena to any Future Metaphysics,* trans. Peter G. Lucas (Manchester: Manchester University Press, 1953) 9. Kant stresses that his reading of the British empiricists—especially David Hume—was a major reason for his movement away from the Continental tradition of rationalism typified by René Descartes and G. W. Leibniz. One would think that Dollimore, for example, would find the notion of Kant's "Copernican Revolution" sympathetic to his own continuation of the project of decentering man. It seems to me no coincidence that Kant chose as an analogy to his hypothesis that objects conform to the human faculty of intuition the astronomical theory proposing that earth-bound spectators rather than heavenly bodies are in motion—a theory that decentered the earth from the solar system. See the *Critique of Pure Reason,* trans. Norman Kemp-Smith (New York: St. Martin's Press, 1965) 22-25. See also Perry Anderson, *Considerations on Western Marxism* (London: Verso, 1979) 59-67; Anderson demonstrates that not only G. W. F. Hegel and Ludwig Feuerbach, but also Immanuel Kant, Jean-Jacques Rousseau, Hume, Galileo Galilei, and Niccolò Machiavelli have been identified by various theorists as philosophical precursors of Marx.

89. *Prolegomena,* 75-76; *Critique of Pure Reason,* 29. Kant did, of course, believe that knowledge about the conditions of experience was possible, but he agreed with Hume that metaphysical knowledge—knowledge of what transcends experience (God, the soul, the real world beyond appearances)—was unattainable. See Richard H. Popkin's remarks on Kant in his article "Skepticism" in *The Encyclopedia of Philosophy* (New York: Macmillan and Free Press, 1967) vol. 7, 456-58.

90. Dominick LaCapra, for example, has argued that at times a text "has its own self-questioning 'voices' or tendencies that engender resistances to our desires for meaning or nonmeaning and that qualify our attempts at a critical exchange" ("On the Line: Between History and Criticism," *Profession* 89 [1989]: 8).

91. "How to Recognize a Poem When You See One," in *Is There a Text in This Class?* (Cambridge: Harvard University Press, 1980) 336.

92. "Resonance and Wonder," in *Learning to Curse* (New York: Routledge, 1990) 169.

93. "The New Historicism and Its Discontents: Politicizing Renaissance Drama," *PMLA* (May 1987): 300. Pechter, however, does not sufficiently distinguish between new historicist and cultural materialist *practice,* treating both approaches as fundamentally equal in their degree of political awareness and activism. He does not, for example, stress cultural materialism's concern with discovering and exposing con-

temporary appropriations of the past that serve to support or legitimate particular ideologies, nor does he emphasize new historicism's easier compatibility with various formalist approaches and its less explicitly political agenda. See, for further distinctions, Louis Montrose, "Renaissance Literary Studies and the Subject of History," *ELR* 16 (1986): 7.

94. On definitions of fideism, and in particular on Saint Augustine, Michel de Montaigne, Blaise Pascal, Sören Kierkegaard, and others as fideists in their approaches to determining the truth value of propositions by means of reason and faith, see Richard H. Popkin, *The History of Scepticism from Erasmus to Spinoza* (Berkeley: University of California Press, 1979) xviii-xxii.

95. *Tropics of Discourse*, 82.

96. On Althusser's concept of ideology see his essay "Ideology and Ideological State Apparatuses" in *Lenin and Philosophy and Other Essays* (New York: Monthly Review Press, 1971) 127-86. See also Williams's discussion of ideology in *Marxism and Literature*, 55-71; Dollimore's in *Radical Tragedy*, 9-19; Terry Eagleton's in "Ideology and Scholarship" (in *Historical Studies and Literary Criticism*, ed. Jerome J. McGann [Madison: University of Wisconsin Press, 1985] 114-25); Jean Howard's in "The New Historicism in Renaissance Studies," 28-29; and James H. Kavanagh's in *Critical Terms for Literary Study*, ed. Frank Lentricchia and Thomas McLaughlin (Chicago: University of Chicago Press, 1990) 306-20.

97. I am thinking, specifically, of Homer's characterization of the Scythians in Book Thirteen of *The Iliad*, Herodotus's portrayal of the Persians, Egyptians, and Scythians in Books One, Two, and Four of his *Histories*, and Tacitus's depiction of the Germans in his *Germania*.

98. Hayden White has argued in *Tropics of Discourse* that a key part of the historian's task is to provide a "plot structure for a sequence of events so that their nature as a comprehensible process is revealed by their figuration as a *story of a particular kind*" (58). White stresses the degree to which historians rely on the conventions of literary art; and though he asserts, in agreement with Foucault, that "we require a history that will educate us to discontinuity more than ever before; for discontinuity, disruption, and chaos is our lot" (50), his emphasis upon the employment of "mythoi" (60) in historical narrative-writing implies an acceptance of a different form of continuity and points to the inevitable intrusion of the historian's own cultural/historical present in his depiction of the past. In a similar vein, James Clifford, Mary Louise Pratt, and others have discussed the fictive and self-conscious elements of ethnographic writing in *Writing Culture*; and see Clifford Geertz, *The Interpretation of Cultures* (New York: Basic Books, 1973) esp. chapter 1.

99. I refer to Geertz's leaning toward explicit acknowledgment of the interpretive dimension of ethnography, as evidenced, for instance, in *The Interpretation of Cultures*, 9-10, 15-16, and elsewhere.

100. For a discussion of interpretation as inevitably entailing acts of appropriation, see Tony Bennett, *Formalism and Marxism* (London: Methuen, 1979) 142.

101. *Hakluytus Posthumous*, vol. 19, 62.

102. For an illuminating discussion of "barbarity," see Pagden, *The Fall of Natural Man*, 15-26. See also José de Acosta's tripartite division of barbarity in *How to procure the salvation of the Indians* (1589), as excerpted and translated by Rowe ("Ethnography and Ethnology in the Sixteenth Century," *KASP* 30 [1964]: 16-19).

103. The *OED* lists as the two primary denotations of "savagery" (1) "The quality of being fierce or cruel; savage disposition, conduct, or actions" and (2) "The condition of being wild or uncivilized; the characteristics of savages; the savage state of human society." A Renaissance usage in accordance with the former denotation is exemplified by a quotation from Shakespeare's *King John* (4.3.48); the earliest usage matching the latter meaning is claimed to be a passage in Coleridge's *Literary Reminiscences*. However, frequent quotations from Shakespeare, Gascoigne, Puttenham, Ralegh and other Renaissance authors are adduced in support of the use of "savage" (both adjective and noun) as meaning "existing in the lowest stage of culture" and "A person living in the lowest state of development or cultivation; an uncivilized, wild person." In Johnson's *Dictionary* (London, 1755) the noun "savage" is defined as "A man untaught and uncivilized; a barbarian." In the great eighteenth-century French *Encyclopédie* (Paris and Neufchâtel, 1751-65) the noun *sauvage* is defined as "peuples barbares qui vivent sans loix, sans police, sans religion, & qui n'ont point d'habitation fixe." The adjective *sauvage*, however, has fewer connotations of ferocity than its English cognate; it can mean "natural" and "wild" as well as "uncivilized": wildflowers, for example, are *fleurs sauvages*.

104. See chapters 9 and 10 of Hodgen, *Early Anthropology*.

105. Hodgen, *Early Anthropology*, chapters 9 and 10; Roy Harvey Pearce, *The Savages of America* (Baltimore: Johns Hopkins University Press, 1965) 3-49; Edward William Tayler, *Nature and Art in Renaissance Literature* (New York: Columbia University Press, 1964) 80-88.

106. Las Casas, as we have seen, relies upon this notion from time to time. For example, after admitting that American Indians have occasionally committed vengeful acts against the Spaniards, he writes, "their hardness and impetuosity would be that of children, of boys ten or twelve years old" (*The Devastation of the Indies*, 41).

107. See chapters 1 and 2 of Leo Marx's *The Machine in the Garden* (London: Oxford University Press, 1964) especially 3-46. See also the prologue and first two chapters of Roderick Nash's *Wilderness and the American Mind*, rev. ed. (New Haven: Yale University Press, 1973).

108. Dionyse Settle, *A true reporte of the laste voyage into the West and Northwest regions, etc, 1577, worthily atchieued by Capteine Frobisher* (Amsterdam, 1969) sig. C1v; James I, *Daemonologie* (Edinburgh, 1966) 69.

109. According to the *OED*, it was not until the latter part of the nineteenth century that the noun "culture" came to acquire—probably by metaphorical evolution from its earlier sense of "cultivation"—denotations close to those we are familiar with today; in 1891 Edward B. Tylor defined "culture" as "that complex whole which includes knowledge, belief, art, morals, law, custom, and any other capabilities and habits acquired by man as a member of society" (quoted in Stephen Greenblatt's essay "Culture" in *Critical Terms for Literary Study*, ed. Frank Lentricchia and Thomas McLaughlin, 225). Robert F. Berkhofer, Jr., discusses the evolution of modern ideas of "culture"—including those of Tylor, Franz Boas, Ruth Benedict, Alfred Kroeber, and Clyde Kluckhohn—in *The White Man's Indian* (New York: Vintage, 1979) 51-54, 62-69. For illuminating treatments of sixteenth-century anthropology, see Rowe's "Ethnography and Ethnology in the Sixteenth Century," *KASP* 30 (1964): 1-19 and "The Renaissance Foundations of Anthropology," *AA* 67 (February 1965): 1-20.

110. *The Captive* (Cambridge, MA, 1682; Tucson: American Eagle Publications, 1990) 6, 63-64.

111. Jefferson, "In Congress, July 4, 1776. A Declaration by the Representatives of the United States of America, in General Congress Assembled."

112. There were, of course, many Renaissance proponents of the view that true civility depended not upon breeding but upon gentle blood, upon an inherited and presumably God-given *melior natura* that set apart a small minority of humans from the rest of their kind. See, for example, the arguments of Count Lodovico Canossa in the First Book of Castiglione's *Courtier* (Harmondsworth: Penguin, 1976) 52-59, and Frank Kermode's Introduction to the Arden *Tempest* (London: Methuen, 1954) xliii-li.

113. Thomas P. Roche, in glossing Spenser's use of "civility" in *The Faerie Queene* (6.10.23.9), defines the word as "social order, and the kind of behaviour which perpetuates social order" (New Haven: Yale University Press, 1981) 1227. L. G. Salingar, in his essay on "The Social Setting" in *The New Pelican Guide to English Literature*, emphasizes that the English Renaissance use of "civility" "implied not only polish or good breeding, but the sobriety and mutual deference of men associated in well-governed cities and corporations" (London: Penguin, 1982) vol. 2, 19.

114. "Civil" is defined in the *OED* as "Of or belonging to citizens; . . . In that social condition which accompanies and is involved in citizenship or life in communities; not barbarous; civilized; advanced in the arts of life." Numerous Renaissance writers are quoted, including Shakespeare, Richard Hooker, John Florio, and Richard Eden in his *A treatyse of the newe India*. The first non-obsolete definition of "civility," borrowed from Samuel Johnson, is "The state of being civilized; freedom from barbarity." Subsequent denotations, however, grow weaker, tending toward more specific characterizations of behavior, such as "Behavior proper to the intercourse of civilized people; ordinary courtesy or politeness, as opposed to rudeness of

behavior; decent respect, consideration" and "decency, seemliness." Renaissance quotations are adduced for all denotations.

115. Sir Walter Ralegh, *The History of the World*, 6 vols. (Edinburgh, 1820) vol. 2, 491.

116. "Civilization" is defined in *Webster's Third New International Dictionary*, for example, as "a relatively high level of cultural and technological development; . . . the stage of cultural development at which writing and the keeping of written records is attained . . . the culture characteristic of a particular time or place."

117. Quoted in Etienne Grisel, "The Beginnings of International Law and General Public Law Doctrine: Francisco de Vitoria's *De Indiis prior*." In *First Images of America*, ed. Fredi Chiappelli (Berkeley: University of California Press, 1976) vol. 1, 309.

118. *Oroonoko: Or, the Royal Slave* (London, 1688; New York: Norton, 1973) 43.

119. "On Monday, March 23 [1772], I found him [Johnson] busy, preparing a fourth edition of his folio Dictionary. . . . He would not admit *civilization*, but only *civility*. With great deference to him, I thought *civilization*, from *to civilize*, better in the sense opposed to *barbarity*, than *civility*" (*The Life of Samuel Johnson*, LL.D. [London: Oxford University Press, 1953] 466). See also p. 775, where Johnson explains to John Wilkes how he has been educating Boswell: "I turned him loose at Lichfield, my native city, that he might see for once true civility: for you know he lives among savages in Scotland, and among rakes in London."

120. *The New Founde Worlde, or Antarctike* (Amsterdam, 1971) chapter 27, sig. G3. Thevet, a Franciscan friar and geographer who accompanied Villegagnon on his expedition to colonize Brazil in the mid-1550s, published his *Les singularitéz de la France antarctique* at Paris in 1558. Along with Jean de Léry's *Histoire d'un voyage fait en la Terre du Bresil* (La Rochelle, 1578), this account of French exploration and expansionism was widely read throughout Europe. Montaigne certainly knew both books.

121. In Thomas Harriot's *A briefe and true report of the new found land of Virginia* (1588), for example, we read that the Algonquian natives of the Roanoke region "may in short time be brought to civilitie, and the imbracing of true religion" (*Virginia Voyages*, 68). And George Abbot writes, in his *Briefe Description of the Whole Worlde* (London, 1599): "At the first arriving of the Spaniardes, . . . they founde in those partes nothing shewing trafique of knowledge of any other Nation, but the people naked, uncivill, some of them devourers of mans flesh, ignorant of shipping, without all kinde of learning, having no rememberance of history or writing among them, never having heard of any such religion as in other places of the worlde is knowne: but being utterly ignorant of Scripture, or Christ, or Moyses, or any God" (quoted by Margaret T. Hodgen in "Montaigne and Shakespeare Again," *HLQ* 16 [1952]: 34). On the widely assumed connection between civility and Christianity in the Renaissance, see also Rowe, "Ethnology and Ethnography in the Sixteenth Century," 5-7, and W. R. Jones, "The Image of Barbarians in Medieval Europe," *CSSH* 13:4 (October 1971): 376-401.

122. "Of the inconsistency of our actions," 244. Compare François de La Rochefoucauld's maxim 135: "At times we are as different from ourselves as we are from others" (*Maxims*, trans. Leonard Tancock [Harmondsworth, 1959] 54). Elsewhere, Montaigne writes that "Others do not see you, they guess at you by uncertain conjectures; they see not so much your nature as your art" ("Of repentance," 613).

Chapter 2

1. Unless otherwise noted, quotations from Montaigne's *Essays* (including essay titles) are drawn from Donald M. Frame's fine English translation (*The Complete Essays of Montaigne* [Stanford: Stanford University Press, 1958]); for the passages above, see p. 154. Hereafter I will use in-text citations to this translation. Because I am also interested in preserving the character of Montaigne's essays as encountered by Tudor and Stuart audiences, I will occasionally quote from the 1603 English rendering by John Florio, *The Essayes of Michael Lord of Montaigne* (New York: Modern Library, 1933). Florio's translation is not always completely reliable, however, so when I cite it I will also include corresponding page references to Frame's version. Quotations in the original French are drawn from Michel de Montaigne, *Les Essais*, ed. Pierre Villey, and reissued under the direction of V. L. Saulnier, 2d ed., 3 vols. (Paris: Presses Universitaires de France, 1992).

2. See, for example, Pierre Villey, *Les Sources et L'Évolution des Essais de Montaigne*, 2 vols. (Paris: Hachette, 1908); Gilbert Chinard, *L'exotisme américain dans la littérature française au XVIe siècle* (Paris: Hachette, 1911) esp. chapters 8-10; Roland Lebel, *Histoire de la Littérature Coloniale en France* (Paris: Larose, 1931); Geoffroy Atkinson, *Les Nouveaux Horizons de la Renaissance Française* (Paris: Droz, 1935); Marcel Bataillon, *Etudes sur Bartolomé de las Casas* (Paris: Institut d'Etudes Hispanique, 1965) xxxvii; Bernard Weinberg, "Montaigne's Readings for 'Des Cannibales'," in *Renaissance and Other Studies*, ed. George Bernard Daniel, Jr. (Chapel Hill: University of North Carolina Press, 1968) 261-79; Benjamin Keen, *The Aztec Image in Western Thought* (New Brunswick: Rutgers University Press, 1971) 157-58; Richard Sayce, *The Essays of Montaigne* (London: Weidenfeld and Nicolson, 1972) 91; Germán Arciniegas, *America in Europe* (San Diego: Harcourt Brace, 1986) esp. chapter 5; William Brandon, *New Worlds for Old* (Athens: Ohio University Press, 1986); and Tom Conley, "Montaigne and the Indies: Cartographies of the New World in the *Essais*, 1580-88," *HI* 4 (1989) esp. 225-27, 251-52.

3. See Weinberg, "Montaigne's Readings for 'Des Cannibales'," for a thorough compilation of parallel passages.

4. Brandon, 21, 37-39. Thomas Hackett translated Thevet's book into English in 1568 as *The New Founde Worlde, or Antarctike*. Ronsard wrote a poem entitled "Les Isles

Fortunées" (1554) which may have been partly inspired by the Villegagnon expedition.

5. *The New Founde Worlde*, chapter 61, sig. O1v; chapter 29, sig. G6.

6. Frame dates "Of cannibals" to 1578-80.

7. *History of a Voyage to the Land of Brazil*, trans. Janet Whatley (Berkeley: University of California Press, 1990) 198.

8. *History of a Voyage*, 147, 150.

9. "The Philosopher's Breviary: Jean de Léry in the Enlightenment," *REP* 33 (Winter 1991): 203.

10. *History of a Voyage*, 67-68, 131-32, 168.

11. Girolamo Benzoni's book (Venice, 1565) received the French title *Histoire nouvelle du nouveau monde* (Geneva, 1579); Francisco López de Gómara's account (Saragossa, 1552) was translated as *Histoire générale des Indes Occidentales et Terre Neuves* (Paris, 1569). Montaigne also drew from Cravalix's Italian translation of Gómara's *Historia de la conquista de México* (Venice, 1576); see Conley, 232-33, 254n. Most of the allusions to the New World that appear to be drawn from Gómara are found either in the second edition of the *Essais* (1588) or in the post-1588 additions to this edition; this perhaps explains why the essay "Of coaches" (1585-88) contains both more positive estimations of the civility and more scathing opinions of the savagery of New World natives than does "Of cannibals." See Conley, 244-45; Brandon, 40-42; Sayce, 26, 193; Keen, 160; Chinard, 209-10; and Villey, vol. 1, 270.

12. Giovanni Ramusio published Italian translations of Jacques Cartier's two narratives in his *Delle Navigationi et Viaggi* (Venice, 1556); Hans Staden's book, whose original German title was *Wahrhaftige Historie und Beschreibung eyner Landschafft der Wilden, Nacketen, Grimmigen, Menschfresser Leuten, in der Newen Welt America gelegen*, was published in Marburg in 1557. For a good summary account of French and German (as well as Spanish and Portuguese) geographical literature of the Renaissance, see Boies Penrose, *Travel and Discovery in the Renaissance* (New York: Atheneum, 1962) chapter 17.

13. He concludes, for example: "They required of them [the natives] victualles for their nourishment; and some gold for the behoofe of certaine Physicall experiments. Moreover, they declared unto them, the beleeving in one onely God, and the trueth of our religion, which they perswaded them to embrace, adding thereto some minatorie threats" (823; F695). For the text of the "Requerimiento," see *New Iberian World*, vol. 1, 288-90.

14. *Histoire générale des Indes Occidentales et Terre Neuves*, folio 24v. Quoted by Sayce, 193.

15. "Des cannibales," *Les Essais de Michel de Montaigne*, vol. 1, 267. Montaigne repeats this formula when, in "Des coches," he claims that it hasn't been fifty years since the peoples of the New World "ne sçavoit ny lettres, ny pois, ny mesure, ny vestements, ny bleds, ny vignes" ["knew neither letters, nor weights and measures, nor clothes, nor wheat, nor vines"] (vol. 3, 166).

16. In her essay "Montaigne and Shakespeare Again" (*HLQ* 16 [1952]: 23-42), Margaret
     T. Hodgen cites a number of early sources—*loci communes*, in effect—from which
     both Montaigne and Shakespeare might have derived the formulaic device of
     characterizing non-European peoples and cultures in terms of negation (itemizing
     what they lacked) rather than positive attribution. Herman Melville participated in
     this tradition as well, judging from his description in *Typee* of Marquesan society:
     "There were no foreclosures of mortgages, no protested notes, no bills payable, no
     debts of honor in Typee; no unreasonable tailors and shoemakers, unreasonably
     bent on being paid; no duns of any description; no assault-and-battery attorneys to
     foment discord, backing their clients up to a quarrel, and then knocking their heads
     together; no poor relations, everlastingly occupying the spare bedchamber, and
     diminishing the elbowroom at the family table; no destitute widows with their
     children starving on the cold charities of the world; no beggars; no debtors' prisons;
     no proud and hardhearted nabobs in Typee; or to sum up all in one word—no
     Money!" (*Typee* [1846; New York: Signet, 1964] 146). See also Hodgen's *Early
     Anthropology* (Philadelphia: University of Pennsylvania Press, 1964) 194-201, Rich-
     ard G. Cole's "Sixteenth-Century Travel Books as a Source of European Attitudes
     Toward Non-White and Non-Western Culture," *PAPS* 116 (February 1972): 59-67,
     Robert F. Berkhofer, Jr., *The White Man's Indian* (New York: Vintage, 1979) 25-27,
     and Martin Orkin's "Othello and the 'plain face' of Racism," *SQ* 38:2 (1987): 168.

17. See Sayce, 26, 91-95, 129, 141, 193, 274, 311.

18. Villey, vol. 1, 59-242; Keen, 157-58; Weinberg, 261-79; Bataillon, xxxvii;
     Arciniegas, 106. Chinard is vague, admitting that Montaigne's "connaissance
     d'ouvrages comme ceux de Las Casas or de Gómara le met en présence des crimes
     commis par les Espagnols dans les Indes Occidentales" [acquaintance with works
     like those of Las Casas or Gómara exposed him to the crimes committed by the
     Spaniards in the West Indies], but never pointing to any parallel passages (*L'exotisme
     américain*, 193-94). Conley writes that "In the moving, mystical element of writing
     which creates a present past of living relations through its own means, 'De la
     moderation,' 'Des cannibales,' and 'Des coches' appear to bond an unconscious
     rapport with Las Casas through an absolute identity of viewpoint" (252); I agree
     entirely with Conley's inference of rapport, though I am not sure it is "unconscious"
     and am certain that it does not amount to an "identity of viewpoint."

19. In its French version, Las Casas's book (Seville, 1552) went by the fashionably
     anti-Castilian title *Tyrannies et Cruautés des Espagnols*. The first English translation, by
     "M.M.S." (London, 1583), was entitled, rather less sensationally, *The Spanish Colonie,
     or Briefe Chronicle of the Acts and gestes of the Spaniards in the West Indies*. A later translation
     by John Phillips, *The Tears of the Indians: Being an Historical and true Account of the Cruel
     Massacres and Slaughters of above Twenty Millions of innocent people* (London, 1656), once
     again exploited anti-Catholic and anti-Spanish sentiments; it was dedicated to

Oliver Cromwell, and aligned the Lord Protector in its opening pages with justice and the cause of native Americans in opposition to popish tyranny.

20. *The Spanish Colonie*, sig. A4.

21. *The Devastation of the Indies*, trans. Herma Briffault (New York: Seabury Press, 1974; rpt. Baltimore: Johns Hopkins University Press, 1992) 34-35. See, for comparison, *The Spanish Colonie*, sigs. A3v-A4.

22. *The Devastation of the Indies*, 37; compare *The Spanish Colonie*, sig. B1.

23. A similar revulsion, incidentally, may be found in Benzoni's book in the French version by Urbain Chauveton. As Brandon writes, the *Histoire nouvelle du nouveau monde* "lost none of its critical passion in translation" (*New Worlds for Old*, 42).

24. *Las Casas: A Selection of His Writings*, trans. and ed. George Sanderlin (New York: Knopf, 1971) 144.

25. *Life and Labor in Ancient Mexico*, (trans. by Benjamin Keen of *Breve y sumaria relación de los señores de la Nueva España* [New Brunswick: Rutgers University Press, 1963] 173); Zorita's book was probably written sometime before 1570, though it was not published until the nineteenth century.

26. I quote here from the Authorized King James Version of 1611.

27. "*The Tempest* and the New World," *SQ* 30:4 (Winter 1979): 34. Francis Barker and Peter Hulme, elaborating on this idea and fusing it with Julia Kristeva's notion of "intertextuality" in their article "Nymphs and reapers heavily vanish: the discursive con-texts of *The Tempest*," assert that "Intertextuality, or con-textualization, differs most importantly from source criticism when it establishes the necessity of reading *The Tempest* alongside congruent texts, irrespective of Shakespeare's putative knowledge of them, and when it holds that such congruency will become apparent from the constitution of discursive networks to be traced independently of authorial 'intentionality'" (*Alternative Shakespeares*, ed. John Drakakis [London: Methuen, 1985] 196).

28. Bernard Sheehan, *Savagism and Civility*, 29; Tzvetan Todorov, "L'Etre et L'Autre: Montaigne," *YFS* 64 (1983): 125.

29. Jean Howard (writing of Todorov) in "The New Historicism in Renaissance Studies," *ELR* 16 (1986): 22.

30. Florio, trans., *The Essayes of Montaigne*, 822; for comparison, see Frame, 694.

31. *History of a Voyage*, 67.

32. "Amorous canzonet" and "sufficiencie" are from Florio, 170.

33. Todorov, "L'Etre et L'Autre: Montaigne," 124-26. Georges van den Abbeele recognizes that Montaigne's strategies of cultural representation in "Des cannibales" and "Des coches" serve as "important early moments in the defense of autochthonous American cultures," but he places greater emphasis than I do on "their hermeneutics of analogical recuperation (whereby the other's threatening otherness is domesticated by the systematic recoding of cultural differences as veiled similarities)" (*Travel as Metaphor from Montaigne to Rousseau* [Minneapolis: University of Minnesota Press, 1992] 36).

34. *Essays in the History of Ideas* (Baltimore: Johns Hopkins University Press, 1948) 238.

35. See Frank Kermode's Introduction to the Arden *Tempest* (London: Methuen, 1954) xxxiv-v; Edward William Tayler, *Nature and Art in Renaissance Literature* (New York: Columbia University Press, 1964) 36-37; Leo Marx, *The Machine in the Garden* (New York: Oxford University Press, 1964) 49; Jan Kott, *Shakespeare Our Contemporary* (New York: Norton, 1964) 332; Henri Baudet, *Paradise on Earth* (New Haven: Yale University Press, 1965) 29; Leslie Fiedler, *The Stranger in Shakespeare* (New York: Stein and Day, 1972) 230; Philip Edwards, *Shakespeare: A Writer's Progress* (Oxford: Oxford University Press, 1987) 175; Sheehan, *Savagism and Civility* (Cambridge: Cambridge University Press, 1980) 26-29.

36. In an otherwise judicious and balanced account of Montaigne's thought, particularly that of the "Apology," Louis I. Bredvold claims that "After 1576 Montaigne became the supreme exponent of Naturalism, the libertine Naturalism of the Renaissance" (*The Intellectual Milieu of John Dryden* [Ann Arbor: University of Michigan Press, 1934] 34). Tayler corroborates this view by calling Montaigne a "naturalist" and suggesting that his devaluation of art in favor of nature was a stance well removed from the Christian humanists' attitude that art may redeem nature (*Nature and Art*, 36-37).

37. *Paradise on Earth*, 29.

38. *The New Found Worlde, or Antarctike*, trans. Thomas Hackett (London, 1568; Amsterdam: Theatrum Orbis Terrarum, 1971) chapter 27, sig. G3.

39. *Of the Interchangeable Course, or Variety of Things in the whole World* [London, 1594], trans. by "R. A." of *De la Vicissitude ou Variété des Choses en l'Univers* [Paris, 1575], sig. F3v.

40. *Les Essais de Michel de Montaigne*, vol. 1, 277. Florio renders this rather laboriously as "All that is not verie ill; but what of that? They weare no kinde of breeches nor hosen" (171).

41. Montaigne, of course, was frequently under fire in seventeenth- and eighteenth-century France for being an atheist, or, at best, a rather lukewarm Christian; Blaise Pascal writes in the *Pensées*, for instance, that the *Essays* suggest "an indifference about salvation" (*Pascal's Pensées* [New York: Dutton, 1958] 15 [fragment 63]). The view that Montaigne was a committed non-believer has been revived in the twentieth century by Don Cameron Allen in *Doubt's Boundless Sea* (Baltimore: Johns Hopkins University Press, 1964) and implied by Jonathan Dollimore in *Radical Tragedy* (Chicago: University of Chicago Press, 1984).

42. "A Note on Montaigne's 'Des Cannibales' and the Humanist Tradition," *First Images of America*, ed. Fredi Chiappelli (Berkeley: University of California Press, 1976) vol. 1, 66.

43. See, for example, Richard L. Regosin, *The Matter of My Book* (Berkeley: University of California Press, 1977) 39-40, and Stephen Orgel's introduction to the Oxford Shakespeare edition of *The Tempest* (Oxford: Oxford University Press, 1987) 35.

44. *The Agricola and the Germania*, trans. H. Mattingly, rev. S. A. Handford (Harmondsworth: Penguin, 1970) 113-30; 105.

45. *The Agricola and the Germania*, 113, 134.

46. Elsewhere, after describing how the Tupinamba have learned to imitate the Portuguese fashion of torturing prisoners by burying them up to the waist and then shooting them with arrows, Montaigne comments "I am not sorry that we note the barbarous horror of such acts" ("Of cannibals," 155).

47. George Boas, *Primitivism and Related Ideas in Antiquity* (Baltimore: Johns Hopkins University Press, 1935) 366. The Caesar reference is to *De Bello Gallico*, VI, 21-23.

48. For valuable commentary on the connections between ethnographic characterization and moral evaluation see Robert F. Berkhofer, Jr., *The White Man's Indian* (New York: Vintage, 1979) 25-31. Berkhofer claims, for instance, that "most of the White studies of Indian culture(s) were (and are) also examinations of Indian moral character. . . . eye-witness description prior to this century and so much still in our time combines moral evaluation with ethnographic detail, and moral judgments all too frequently passed for science in the past according to present-day understanding" (27).

49. Arthur O. Lovejoy and George Boas, in *Primitivism and Related Ideas in Antiquity* (Baltimore: Johns Hopkins University Press, 1935) make a useful distinction between chronological and cultural primitivism—the former concerning the time at which "the most excellent condition of human life, or the best state of the world in general, must be supposed to occur" (1), the latter being "the belief of men living in a relatively highly evolved and complex cultural condition that a life far simpler and less sophisticated in some or all respects is a more desirable life" (7). Technically, then, I am speaking here of chronological primitivism, though it seems clear that the two forms overlap and are thus not mutually exclusive.

50. *The Machine in the Garden*, 55.

51. Aldo Scaglione, "A Note on Montaigne's 'Des Cannibales'," 68. Scaglione argues that Montaigne is a humanist in the Italian tradition of Petrarch and others; I agree that Montaigne's classicism allows him to look with a skeptical eye on contemporary achievements, but I believe, in contrast to Scaglione, that it is precisely this sort of pessimism that marks Montaigne's variance from mainstream Renaissance humanism. He seems, at best, a grudging humanist.

52. Florio, *The Essayes of Michael Lord of Montaigne* (New York: Modern Library, 1933) 822-23.

53. Sheehan, *Savagism and Civility*, 27.

54. For an incisive discussion of Montaigne's treatment of the nature/art opposition within the domain of language, see Terence Cave, *The Cornucopian Text* (Oxford: Clarendon Press, 1979) 299-302.

55. Ben Jonson, *Timber, or Discoveries* (London, 1640-41) in *Ben Jonson*, ed. C. H. Herford and Percy and Evelyn Simpson (Oxford: Clarendon Press, 1925-52) vol. 8, 639.

56. It is interesting to note that Peter Martyr tries to excuse the existence of warfare in the New World by suggesting that it also existed in the Golden Age: "these naked

people also are tormented with ambition for the desyre they haue to enlarge their dominions: by reason wherof they kepe warre & destroy one an other: from the which plage I suppose the golden world was not free" (*Decades*, 1.2.8). Since Martyr cannot change the apparent facts, he changes the myth; Montaigne's realism is quite evident by comparison.

57. Edwin M. Duval is a notable exception; in a fine discussion of the different perspectives on barbarism that Montaigne adopts in "Of cannibals," he writes that "Even if the Brazilians are barbarous in absolute terms, then, they cannot be considered to be barbarous by comparison with us" ("Lessons of the New World: Design and Meaning in Montaigne's 'Des Cannibales' [I:31] and 'Des Coches' [III:6]," *YFS* 64 [1983]: 97). See also Tom Conley, "Montaigne and the Indies: Cartographies of the New World in the *Essais*, 1580-88," *HI* 4 (1989): 235-36.

58. Frame, in his "Editor's Note" to the "Apology for Raymond Sebond" (*Montaigne's Essays and Selected Writings: A Bilingual Edition* [New York: St. Martin's Press, 1963] 196) writes that "The extreme skepticism of the famous *Que sçay-je?* was accepted for centuries as Montaigne's central position, though recent scholarship sees it rather as a step toward the convictions of Book Three." Regosin observes that "Montaigne's attitudes align him with the Pyrrhonians—those, he claims, still in search of the truth. But to regard him merely as a Skeptic is to mistake his means for his end, to misjudge his effort to delineate the proper area of human inquiry" (*The Matter of My Book,* 56).

59. Hayden White, in his article "The Forms of Wildness: Archaeology of an Idea" (in *The Wild Man Within*, ed. Edward Dudley and Maximilian E. Novak [Pittsburgh: University of Pittsburgh Press, 1972] 3-38) argues that primitivism is essentialistic: "basic to it is the conviction that men are really the same throughout all time and space but have been made evil in certain times and places by the imposition of social restraints upon them. Primitivists set the savage, both past and present, over against civilized man as a model and ideal; but instead of stressing the qualitative differences between them, they make of these differences a purely quantitative matter, a difference in degree of corruption rather than in kind" (26). I agree with this statement and would argue that what I have called Montaigne's "anti-primitivism" likewise shares this essentialist assumption.

60. See Theodore Spencer, *Shakespeare and the Nature of Man*, 2d ed. (Cambridge, MA: Harvard University Press, 1949) esp. chapters 1 and 2; Hiram Haydn, *The Counter-Renaissance* (New York: Charles Scribner's Sons, 1950) *passim;* and Rosalie L. Colie, *Paradoxia Epidemica: The Renaissance Tradition of Paradox* (Princeton: Princeton University Press, 1966) esp. 374-95. On essentialism, see Michel Foucault's discussion of "man" as the designation for a fundamentally unified humanity, a human race whose every member is endowed with "primary reality," "density," and a transhistorical, self-generative core of being (*The Order of Things: An Archaeology of the Human Sciences*,

trans. Alan Sheridan [New York: Vintage, 1973] esp. 310-11, 387); see also Jonathan Dollimore's distinction between Christian essentialism and essentialist humanism in *Radical Tragedy: Religion, Ideology and Power in the Drama of Shakespeare and His Contemporaries* (Chicago: University of Chicago Press, 1984) esp. 153-81.

61. *The Matter of My Book: Montaigne's Essais as the Book of the Self* (Berkeley: University of California Press, 1977) 51; "The Boundaries of Interpretation: Self, Text, Contexts in Montaigne's *Essays*," in *Renaissance Rereadings: Intertext and Context*, ed. Maryanne Cline Horowitz, et al. (Urbana: University of Illinois Press, 1988) 19, 29.

62. Gérard Defaux, "Readings of Montaigne," trans. John A. Gallucci, *Yale French Studies* 64 (1983): 73, 77-79, 82-84, 91-92. The Derrida quotation is from *Of Grammatology* (Paris, 1967), trans. Gayatri Chakravorty Spivak (Baltimore: Johns Hopkins University Press, 1976) 158.

63. Terence Cave, *The Cornucopian Text: Problems of Writing in the French Renaissance* (Oxford: Clarendon Press, 1979) 271-321; Antoine Compagnon, "A Long Short Story: Montaigne's Brevity," *YFS* 64 (1983): 24-50; Antoine Compagnon, *Nous, Michel de Montaigne* (Paris: Editions de Seuil, 1980); Jules Brody, *Lectures de Montaigne* (Lexington, KY: French Forum, 1982); André Tournon, "Self-Interpretation in Montaigne's *Essais*," *YFS* 64 (1983): 51-72.

64. *The Cornucopian Text*, 321; *Nous, Michel de Montaigne, passim*, esp. 230.

65. "L'Etre et L'Autre: Montaigne," *Yale French Studies* 64 (1983): 125, 144.

66. Jean Starobinski, *Montaigne in Motion* (Chicago: University of Chicago Press, 1985) x, 293, 307; Dollimore, *Radical Tragedy*, 17-18, 169-70.

67. *Radical Tragedy* 17, 18, 155.

68. Steven Rendall, *Distinguo: Reading Montaigne Differently* (Oxford: Clarendon Press, 1992) vii, 126.

69. "Montaigne and the Subject of Polity," in *Literary Theory/Renaissance Texts*, ed. Patricia Parker and David Quint (Baltimore: Johns Hopkins University Press, 1986) 116, 144-46.

70. Dollimore, for instance, claims that "Montaigne's scepticism is central to Jacobean tragedy whereas his fideism is not" (*Radical Tragedy*, 21). In the fine introduction to his recent translation of Montaigne's "Apology," M. A. Screech argues convincingly for the essential Christian orthodoxy of Montaigne's defense of Sebond's *Theologia naturalis* (1487), though he attaches an opprobrium to the interpretation of Montaigne as a fideist, a notion that I find somewhat puzzling; I do not view fideism, as Screech appears to, as strident anti-rationalism deriving from the prior conviction "that all depends on unfettered faith—faith as trust and faith as credulity" (Introduction, *An Apology for Raymond Sebond* [Harmondsworth: Penguin, 1987] xx). Montaigne's earlier translator, Donald M. Frame, has written that "Montaigne's scepticism is used not to cast doubt on Catholicism but to support it by placing it beyond the reach of reason. His is the position of the fideist, who humbles reason

in religious matters to the advantage of faith" (*Montaigne's Essais: A Study* [Englewood Cliffs: Prentice-Hall, 1969] 25). See also Colie, *Paradoxia Epidemica*, 412; Frame, *Montaigne: A Biography* (New York: Harcourt Brace, 1965) 170; D. P. Walker, *The Ancient Theology* (Ithaca: Cornell University Press, 1972) 140; Richard H. Popkin, *The History of Scepticism from Erasmus to Spinoza* (Berkeley: University of California Press, 1979) xviii-xxii; and Zachary S. Schiffman, "Montaigne and the Rise of Skepticism in Early Modern Europe: A Reappraisal," *Journal of the History of Ideas* 45 (1984): 514.

71. *Paradoxia Epidemica*, 378.

72. See, for example, "Of custom, and not easily changing an accepted law," "Of husbanding your will," and "Of experience." Robert Ornstein offers succinct and valuable observations about Montaigne's attitude toward human reason and his view of custom as second nature in *The Moral Vision of Jacobean Tragedy* (Madison: University of Wisconsin Press, 1960) 39-40. See also Donald R. Kelley, "'Second Nature': The Idea of Custom in European Law, Society, and Culture," in *The Transmission of Culture in Early Modern Europe*, ed. Anthony Grafton and Ann Blair (Philadelphia: University of Pennsylvania Press, 1990) 131-72; and, for variations of the proverb that custom is second nature, Morris Palmer Tilley, *The Proverbs of England in the Sixteenth and Seventeenth Centuries* (Ann Arbor: University of Michigan Press, 1950) 136.

73. Bartolomé de Las Casas writes, for instance, at the conclusion of his *Apologética historia* that "A man is apt to be called barbarous, in comparison with another, because he is strange in his manner of speech and mispronounces the language of the other. . . . According to Strabo, Book XIV, this was the chief reason the Greeks called other peoples barbarous, that is, because they were mispronouncing the Greek language. But from this point of view, there is no man or race which is not barbarous with respect to some other man or race. . . . Thus, just as we esteemed these peoples of the Indies barbarous, so they considered us, because of not understanding us" (*Bartolomé de Las Casas: A Selection of His Writings*, trans. and ed. George Sanderlin [New York: Knopf, 1971] 144). Compare Montaigne in "Of cannibals": "Now, to return to my subject, I think there is nothing barbarous and savage in that nation [Brazil], from what I have been told, except that each man calls barbarism whatever is not his own practice" (152).

74. Here, for example, is Florio elsewhere in the *Essays*: "I would willingly excuse our people for having no other patterne *[patron]* or rule of perfection, but his owne customes, his owne fashions" ("Of Ancient Customes," 256); "Every man beareth the whole stampe *[forme]* of humane condition" ("Of Repenting," 726); Europeans were "divers in language, in habite, in religion, in behaviour, in forme *[forme]*, in countenance" from the Mexicans and Peruvians whom they conquered ("Of Coaches," 822). All citations are from *The Essayes of Michael Lord of Montaigne*, trans. John Florio (London, 1603; New York: Modern Library, 1933); compare Frame, *The*

Complete Essays, 215, 611, 694. Because *forme* is an obvious cognate, Florio normally translates it as the English "form" (usually spelled "forme"); on occasion, however, he substitutes the English word "stampe."

75. *The Essays of Montaigne: A Critical Exploration* (London: Weidenfeld and Nicolson, 1972) 113. Sayce is speaking of the word as employed in "Du repentir": "Chaque homme porte la forme entiere de l'humaine condition." Sayce's claim is seconded by Starobinski, *Montaigne in Motion*, 96.

76. Montaigne's use of *imprimer*, with its suggestion of a reciprocity between that which is imprinted and that which imprints, is suggestive of Spenser's use of "enchace" in Book Six of *The Faerie Queene* (Canto 4, stanza 35).

77. Aristotle, *Nichomachean Ethics*, trans. Martin Ostwald (New York: Macmillan, 1962) Book Two, chapter 1, 1103a. Aristotle claims that "the virtues are implanted in us neither by nature nor contrary to nature: we are by nature equipped with the ability to receive them, and habit brings this ability to completion and fulfillment" (33).

78. Montaigne rejects the other major variety of skepticism derived from Classical philosophy—Academic skepticism—on the grounds that in following Socrates's remark that "All I know is that I know nothing" this doctrine amounts to a negative dogmatism. Pyrrhonism, in contrast, encourages doubt even of the claim that nothing can be certainly known; it is completely non-committal with regard to knowledge claims and thus completely non-dogmatic. See the "Apology," 370-74; Sextus Empiricus, *Outlines of Pyrrhonism*, trans. R. G. Bury (Cambridge, MA: Harvard University Press, 1955); Diogenes Laertius, *Lives of Eminent Philosophers*, trans. R. D. Hicks (London: Heinemann, 1925); Popkin, *The History of Scepticism*; Don Cameron Allen, *Doubt's Boundless Sea: Skepticism and Faith in the Renaissance* (Baltimore: Johns Hopkins University Press, 1964); and Myles Burnyeat, ed., *The Skeptical Tradition* (Berkeley: University of California Press, 1983).

79. On the modes of Pyrrhonian doubt, see Sextus Empiricus, *Outlines of Pyrrhonism*, 25-93; regarding the tenth mode, Sextus tells us that "since by means of this Mode also so much divergency is shown to exist in objects, we shall not be able to state what character belongs to the object in respect of its real essence, but only what belongs to it in respect of this particular rule of conduct, or law, or habit, and so on with each of the rest. So because of this Mode also we are compelled to suspend judgment regarding the real nature of external objects" (93).

80. Peter Martyr, for example, writes in his *De orbe novo* (Basel, 1533) that "lyke as rased or vnpaynted tables, are apte to receaue what formes soo euer are fyrst drawen theron by the hande of the paynter, euen soo these naked and simple people, doo soone receaue the customes of owre Religion, and by conuersation with owre men, shake of theyr fierce and natiue barbarousnes" (Richard Eden, *The Decades of the newe worlde or west India* [London, 1555; facsimile rpt. Ann Arbor: University Microfilms, 1966] Decade 2, Book 1, page 52). And in his "Preface to the Reader" immediately

preceding the translation of Martyr, Eden writes that "these simple gentiles lyuing only after the lawe of nature, may well bee lykened to a smoothe and bare table vnpaynted, or a white paper vnwritten, vpon the which yow may at the fyrst paynte or wryte what yow lyste, as yow can not vppon tables alredy paynted, vnlesse yow rase or blot owt the fyrste formes" (*Decades*, Preface). See also Bartolomé de Las Casas's *The Spanish Colonie* ("M.M.S.'"s 1583 translation of the *Brevisima relacion de la destruccion de las Indias occidentales* [Seville, 1552; facsimile rpt. Ann Arbor: University Microfilms, 1966]): "They haue their understanding very pure and quicke, being teachable and capable of all good learning, very apt to receiue our holy Catholique faith" (sigs. A1-A1v).

81. Time and again in the *Essays* Montaigne rejects any suggestion that American natives are culturally empty or lack religious beliefs in the way hinted at by Columbus, Martyr, and other early writers. He claims, for instance, in "Of cannibals" that the Tupinamba "believe that souls are immortal, and that those who have deserved well of the gods are lodged in that part of heaven where the sun rises, and the damned in the west" (154). And in "Of coaches" he writes that "As for one single God, the account had pleased them, but they did not want to change their religion, having followed it so advantageously for so long, and they were not accustomed to take counsel except of their friends and acquaintances. . . . There we have an example of the babbling of this infancy" (695-96).

82. *Radical Tragedy*, 153.

83. See Timothy J. Reiss, "Montaigne and the Subject of Polity," for an alternative view. Reiss argues that the "Cartesian idea of the subject is not to be found in Montaigne" and that the "universal being" implied by such phrases as *estre universel* ("Of repentance," 611) is "universal by virtue of its movement and inconstancy" (133). I agree that Montaigne does not articulate a subjectivity based on innate and identifiable structures of the mind, but he assumes, nonetheless, an essentialism grounded on common human potentials. On human self-fashioning of such potentials, see the "Apology," p. 371: "They [men who exemplify "man in his highest estate"] have fashioned their soul *[ont manié leur ame]* to all directions and all angles, supported and propped it with all the outside assistance that was fit for it, and enriched and adorned it with all they could borrow, for its advantage, from the inside and the outside of the world; it is in them that the utmost height of human nature *[de l'humaine nature]* is found."

84. Pascal, *Pensées* (New York: Dutton, 1958) 15 (fragment 64); Emerson, "Montaigne; Or, the Skeptic," in *Selections from Ralph Waldo Emerson*, ed. Stephen E. Whicher (Boston: Houghton Mifflin, 1957) 290; Gide, "Montaigne," in *The Living Thoughts of Montaigne* [London: Cassell and Company, 1939] 5.

85. Compare Giovanni Pico della Mirandola's response, in his "Oration on the Dignity of Man," to the Chaldean saying that "Man is a being of varied, manifold, and

inconstant nature": "But why do we emphasize this? To the end that after we have
been born to this condition—that we can become what we will—we should
understand that we ought to have especial care to this, that it should never be said
that against us that, although born to a privileged position, we failed to recognize
it and became like unto wild animals and senseless beasts of burden" (*The Renaissance
Philosophy of Man*, ed. Ernst Cassirer, Paul Oskar Kristeller, and John Herman
Randall, Jr. [Chicago: University of Chicago Press, 1948] 227).

86. Spenser, *The Faerie Queene* [London, 1590, 1596] ed. Thomas P. Roche, Jr., with the
    assistance of C. Patrick O'Donnell, Jr. (New Haven: Yale University Press, 1981):
    7.7.58.2-9.

87. *The Essays of Montaigne*, 116.

88. Florio renders this famous line as follows: "Every man beareth the whole stampe of
    humane condition" (*Essayes*, 726).

89. "Montaigne's Conversions: Compositional Strategies in the *Essais*," *French Forum* 7
    (1982): 18. See also Colie, *Paradoxia Epidemica*, 383.

90. Introduction, *The Complete Essays of Montaigne*, xiii.

91. *Montaigne's Discovery of Man: The Humanization of a Humanist* (New York: Columbia
    University Press, 1955) 108.

92. On the *nouveau pyrrhonisme* as a distinct intellectual movement in the late sixteenth
    and early seventeenth centuries, see Popkin's *History of Scepticism*, chapters 3 and 4;
    I use the term here in a rather looser sense. See Frame's sensible discussion of
    Montaigne's Pyrrhonian period (*Montaigne: A Biography*, 175-80).

93. I refer to the critique of Las Casas produced by Tzvetan Todorov in *The Conquest of
    America* (Paris, 1982; New York: Harper and Row, 1984); see, in particular, 168-82.
    See also Sheehan, *Savagism and Civility* (Cambridge: Cambridge University Press,
    1980) 29.

Chapter 3

1. All quotations from *The Faerie Queene* (London, 1590, 1596) are drawn from the
   edition by Thomas P. Roche, Jr., with the assistance of C. Patrick O'Donnell, Jr.
   (New Haven: Yale University Press, 1981). Quotations from *A View of the Present State
   of Ireland* (composed ca. 1596; Dublin, 1633) are from the W. L. Renwick edition
   (Oxford: Clarendon Press, 1970).

2. C. S. Lewis, *The Allegory of Love* (London: Oxford University Press, 1938) 356.

3. Roger Sale, *Reading Spenser* (New York: Random House, 1968) 13-14, 26.

4. Paul Alpers, for instance, writes in *The Poetry of The Faerie Queene* (Princeton: Princeton
   University Press, 1967) that "The fact that dramatic action is inherent in the subjects
   of the last three books of *The Faerie Queene* is the fundamental reason that they are

more uneven than the first three" (299); Sale claims that "The world on which the poem looks in Book VI is a far more 'dramatic' place than the Faerie Land of the earlier parts of the poem" (*Reading Spenser*, 13). Michael O'Connell has likened Book Five of *The Faerie Queene* to William Shakespeare's *2 Henry IV* and *Henry V* in its "political skepticism," and Book Six—with its "freer, ampler world of romance"—to the last plays of Shakespeare, where "considerations of history and probability are left far behind" (*Mirror and Veil* [Chapel Hill: University of North Carolina Press, 1977] 187).

5. Franklin T. McCann, *English Discovery of America to 1585* (New York: King's Crown Press, 1952) 189. McCann stresses the large number of copies of the *Decades* that must have been printed in the first edition (136).

6. Writing in the same period, Christopher Marlowe refers often to the New World, as for example in *Doctor Faustus* (1.1.83, 1.1.85, 1.1.122, 1.1.132), *Tamburlaine, Part One* (3.3.255, 3.3.264-65, 5.2.457), *Edward II* (1.4.50), and *The Jew of Malta* (3.5.5). Other contemporary references may be found in Thomas Kyd's *The Spanish Tragedy* (3.14.9) and Sir Philip Sidney's *Apologie for Poetrie* (James Harry Smith and Edd Winfield Parks, eds., *The Great Critics* [New York: Norton, 1967] 226, 229). Later significant references to the New World occur—among other places—in Thomas Dekker's *The Shoemaker's Holiday* (5.5.73); John Marston's *The Malcontent* (2.4.11); Cyril Tourneur's *The Atheist's Tragedy* (5.2.193) and *The Revenger's Tragedy* (1.3.87, 2.1.251); Ben Jonson's *Volpone* (2.1.257-58), *The Alchemist* (2.1.2, 2.1.36, 3.2.49), and *Bartholomew Fair* (Induction.12, 2.6.24); John Webster's *The Duchess of Malfi* (3.2.267); and Thomas Middleton's *Women Beware Women* (1.2.62). (All citations here are to Russell A. Fraser and Norman Rabkin, eds., *Drama of the English Renaissance* [New York: Macmillan, 1976].) For an exhaustive list of late sixteenth- and early seventeenth-century English dramatic references to America see the final section of Robert Ralston Cawley's *The Voyagers and Elizabethan Drama* (Boston: Modern Language Association, 1938).

7. Jeffrey Knapp, *An Empire Nowhere* (Berkeley: University of California Press, 1992) 19.

8. "We brought home also two of the Savages being lustie men" writes Barlowe at the end of his "Narrative of the 1584 Voyage" (*Virginia Voyages*, 12); Sidney Lee chronicles the practice of bringing New World natives to England in his article "The American Indian in Elizabethan England," *Elizabethan and Other Essays*, ed. F. S. Boas (London: Oxford University Press, 1929) 263-301.

9. On the Peruvian crown and other examples of American wealth that Drake brought back to England, see Warren L. Hanna, *Lost Harbor* (Berkeley: University of California Press, 1979) 22. Donne demonstrates a similarly conventional awareness of America's riches in such lines as "O my America, my new found land, / My kingdom, safeliest when with one man manned, / My mine of precious stones, my empery"; "tell me, / Whether both th'Indias of spice and mine / Be where thou left'st them, or

lie here with me"; and "she whose rich eyes, and breast, / Gilt the West Indies, . . . that rich Indy which doth gold inter" ("Elegy 19," "The Sun Rising," and "An Anatomy of the World" in A. J. Smith, ed., *John Donne: The Complete English Poems* [Harmondsworth: Penguin, 1973] 125, 80, 276). Jonson, in *The Alchemist* (2.1.2, 2.1.36), has Sir Epicure Mammon speak to Surly of "the rich Peru" and "perfect Indies" (Russell A. Fraser and Norman Rabkin, eds., *Drama of the English Renaissance* [New York: Macmillan, 1976] vol. 2, 153).

10. See, for instance, the editors' notes in *The Variorum Spenser* (Baltimore: Johns Hopkins University Press, 1932-57), vol. 2, 185, and vol. 5, 248.

11. Lois Whitney, "Spenser's Use of the Literature of Travel in *The Faerie Queene*," *MP* 19 (1921): 143.

12. Margaret T. Hodgen, *Early Anthropology in the Sixteenth and Seventeenth Centuries* (Philadelphia: University of Pennsylvania Press, 1964) 365; Roy Harvey Pearce, "Primitivistic Ideas in *The Faerie Queene*," *JEGP* 44 (1945): 139.

13. Stephen Greenblatt, *Renaissance Self-Fashioning from More to Shakespeare* (Chicago: University of Chicago Press, 1980) 181-82.

14. "Hunger of Gold: Guyon, Mammon's Cave, and the New World Treasure," *ELR* 20:2 (Spring 1990): 227, 231. See also Jeffrey Knapp, "Error as a Means of Empire in *The Faerie Queene* 1," *ELH* 54:4 (Winter 1987): 801-34; Thomas Cain, *Praise in* The Faerie Queene (Lincoln: University of Nebraska Press, 1978) 91-101; and John N. Wall, Jr., "'Fruitfullest Virginia': Edmund Spenser, Roanoke Island, and the Bower of Bliss," *Renaissance Papers* (1984): 1-17.

15. *The Discoverie of the Large, Rich and Beautiful Empire of Guiana* (London, 1596), in *Sir Walter Ralegh: Selected Writings*, ed. Gerald Hammond (Manchester: Carcanet Press, 1984) 120, 123.

16. The emphasis on feathers is repeated in the description of Fancy in Cupid's Masque: "Like as the sunburnt Indians do aray / Their tawney bodies" with "painted plumes, in goodly order dight" (3.12.8.2-4). In Eden's translation of Martyr's *De orbe novo*, we find the following remarks about the inhabitants of "Guadalupea" in the West Indies: "Owre men furthermore, founde there . . . fardelles of dyuers kyndes of fethers wherof they make them selues crestes and plumes after the maner of owre men of armes: also certeine clokes whiche they esteeme as moste cumly ornamentes. They founde lykewyse an innumerable multitude of bowes and arrowes. . . . and . . . clokes of fethers, with faire plumes and crestes of variable colours" (*Decades*, 3.5.117). In Thomas More's *Utopia* (1516), Raphael Hythloday describes a Utopian priest as wearing "a robe of many colors . . . decorated with the feathers of different birds so skillfully woven together that the value of the handiwork far exceeds the cost of the most precious materials" (trans. Robert M. Adams [New York: Norton, 1992] 80-81); More is known to have been familiar with Amerigo Vespucci's *Four Voyages* (in *Cosmographiae Introductio* [St. Die, 1507]), which at one point describes a group of

New World natives whose most valued possessions include "birds' plumes of many colors" (Vespucci, "The First Voyage," excerpted in *Utopia*, 107). Jean de Léry's *History of a Voyage* (1578) details the Tupinamba custom of making clothing from birds' feathers (60-61). Francis Bacon, in *The New Atlantis* (1622), describes the natives of America as taking "great pride and delight in the feathers of birds" (London, n.d.) 221. Milton, describing Adam and Eve's need, after the Fall, to cover themselves (*Paradise Lost*, 9.1116-17), writes that "Columbus found th' American so girt / With feather'd Cincture" (Merritt Y. Hughes, ed., *John Milton: Complete Poems and Major Prose* [Indianapolis: Bobbs-Merrill, 1957] 404). And Voltaire, in *Candide* (1759), informs us that Candide and Cacambo were "dressed in robes woven of hummingbird feathers" upon their arrival in Eldorado (*Candide*, trans. Robert M. Adams, in *The Norton Anthology of World Masterpieces*, ed. Maynard Mack, et al., 6th ed. [New York: Norton, 1992] vol. 2, 368).

17. The supposedly beneficent qualities of tobacco could have been brought to Spenser's attention through a number of late sixteenth-century writings, among them Thomas Harriot's *A brief and true report* (1588). Harriot writes, for instance, that Algonquian natives of the Roanoke area "are notably preserved in health, and know not many grievous diseases" due to their custom of smoking tobacco leaves; tobacco "purgeth superfluous fleame and other gross humors, and openeth all the pores and passages of the body." He also relates that he and his fellow colonists "found many rare and woonderful experiments of the vertues" of tobacco (*Virginia Voyages*, 58). See Jeffrey Knapp, "Elizabethan Tobacco," *Rep* 21 (1988): 27-66, esp. 27-30, 40-41.

18. Interestingly, Spenser has Irenius employ precisely the same phrase—"loathly filthiness"—in describing the Irish custom of wearing "glibs" (*View*, 53).

19. R. H. Goldsmith, "The Wild Man on the English Stage," *MLR* 53 (1958): 488; Richard Bernheimer, *Wild Men in the Middle Ages* (Cambridge: Harvard University Press, 1952) 2. See also G. M. Pinciss, "The Savage Man in Spenser, Shakespeare, and Renaissance English Drama," *The Elizabethan Theatre VIII*, ed. G. R. Hibbard (Port Credit: P. D. Meany, 1982): 69-89. Of the conventional wild man's perceived existence, Bernheimer writes that it is "a life of bestial self-fulfillment, directed by instinct rather than volition, and devoid of all those acquired tastes and patterns of behavior which are part of our adjustment to civilization" (*Wild Men*, 4).

20. Largeness of stature is often overlooked as a common attribute of the American native in Renaissance portrayal. Christopher Columbus, for example, writes that the people of Guanahaní "are of good-sized stature" (*Diario*, 67); Antonio Pigafetta describes a Patagonian native as being "of stature as bigge as a giante" (*Decades*, 219); Dionyse Settle characterizes the natives of Baffin Island as "men of a large corpora-ture, and good proportion" (*A true reporte of the laste voyage into the West and Northwest regions* [Amsterdam: Theatrum Orbis Terrarum, 1969] sig. C5); Richard Hakluyt, in his description of Sir Francis Drake's landing in California, states that "the people

that inhabited round about came downe, and amongst them the King himselfe, a
man of a goodly stature, & comely personage, with many other tall and warlike men"
("The famous voyage of Sir Francis Drake into the South sea" [London, 1589], in
Principal Navigations, vol. 11, 120); and Captain John Smith marvels at the
"Sasquesahanock" Indians he meets: "Such great and well proportioned men are
seldome seene, for they seemed like Giants to the English" (from *The Generall Historie
of Virginia* [London, 1624], in *The Complete Works of Captain John Smith*, ed. Philip L.
Barbour (Chapel Hill: University of North Carolina Press, 1986) vol. 2, 106.

21. Diego Alvarez Chanca claimed that the natives of Española exhibited a bestiality
"greater than that of any beast upon the face of the earth" ("A Letter addressed to
the Chapter of Seville," in *Four Voyages*, 66). Sepúlveda cited, as "proof of their
savage life, like that of wild beasts," the American Indians' alleged habit of "devour-
ing human flesh" (quoted by Tzvetan Todorov, *The Conquest of America* [New York:
Harper and Row, 1984] 156).

22. Goldsmith, "The Wild Man on the English Stage," 485.

23. A contemporary example of the wild man's conventional propensity to be tamed by
a beautiful and virtuous woman may be found in a speech written by John Lyly and
spoken by a "wild man" at an entertainment for Queen Elizabeth in Cowdray, Sussex
on August 17, 1591: "my untamed thoughts waxe gentle, & I feele in my selfe civility,
a thing hated, because not knowen, and unknown, because I knew not you. Thus
vertue tameth fiercenesse, Beauty, madnesse. Your Maiesty on my knees will I
followe, bearing this Club, not as a Salvage, but to beate downe those that are" (*The
Complete Works of John Lyly*, ed. R. W. Bond [London, 1902; Oxford: Clarendon Press,
1967] vol. 1, 425, 472). See also the encounter of Bremo and Amadine (scene xi) in
the popular Elizabethan play *Mucedorus* (*Drama of the English Renaissance*, ed. Russell A.
Fraser and Norman Rabkin, [New York: Macmillan, 1976] vol. 1, 472-73); Paul
Brown's discussion of Elizabeth's encounter with an "Hombre Salvagio" at an
entertainment at Kenilworth in 1575 ("'This thing of darkness I acknowledge mine':
The Tempest and the Discourse of Colonialism," *Political Shakespeare*, ed. Jonathan
Dollimore and Alan Sinfield [Ithaca: Cornell University Press, 1985] 54); and
Bernheimer, *Wild Men in the Middle Ages*, 135-55.

24. "Letter of Columbus, describing the results of his first voyage," in *The Journal of
Christopher Columbus*, trans. Cecil Jane (London: Anthony Blond, 1968) 196; Harriot,
A briefe and true report (*Virginia Voyages*, 73). See also Pigafetta's claim that a Patagonian
"giante," upon seeing Magellan and his company, "was greatly amased and made
signes holdynge uppe his hande to heauen, signifyinge therby that owre men came
from thense" (*Decades*, 219). Or, as a final example, consider the following story
related by Bernal Díaz del Castillo, who accompanied Cortés in the campaign to
conquer Mexico: In 1519, *en route* to Tenochtitlan, Cortés seized five of Moctezuma's
imperial tax-gatherers and ordered the local natives to suspend payment of any

further tributes to the emperor. This act of insubordination so astonished the natives that, according to Díaz, "they said no human beings dared to do such a thing, and it must be the work of *Teules.* Therefore from that moment they called us *Teules,* which means gods or demons." A few months later, after a battle with another group of natives, Díaz reports that "we buried [our] dead in one of the Indians' underground houses, so that they should not see we were mortal but believe that we were indeed *Teules,* as they called us" (*The Conquest of New Spain* [Harmondsworth: Penguin, 1963] 112, 150).

25. "The famous voyage of Sir Francis Drake into the South sea," *Principal Navigations,* vol. 11, 119. In *The World Encompassed* (1628), an account of Drake's voyage by his nephew, we read that when the Miwok approached Drake and his men, they stood "as men ravished in their mindes, with the sight of such things as they never had seene or heard of before that time: their errand being rather with submission and feare to worship us as Gods, then to have any warre with us as with mortall men" (Francis Drake, *The World Encompassed,* ed. N. M. Penzer [London: Argonaut Press, 1926] 369). Indeed, as Pearce has written, "accounts of primitive, instinctive worship such as Una receives from the satyrs are common in Elizabethan voyage literature" ("Primitivistic Ideas in *The Faerie Queene,*" *JEGP* 44 (1945): 146).

26. Joseph Conrad, *Heart of Darkness* (in *The Portable Conrad,* ed. Morton Dauwen Zabel [Harmondsworth: Penguin, 1976] 561).

27. *The New Organon* [London, 1620], ed. Fulton H. Anderson (Indianapolis: Bobbs-Merrill, 1960), 118 (Book One, aphorism 129).

28. Because of this, we should be wary of such speculations as the following: "Caliban will be so quick at a later stage to take Stephano for a god that we may fairly assume that he had earlier taken Prospero for one. Thus the Indians in the earlier days had been disposed to view the white man" (D. G. James, *The Dream of Prospero* [Oxford: Oxford University Press, 1967] 110). See my discussion of this topic in chapter 4; see also Inga Clendinnen's fine chapter, "Finding out," in *Ambivalent Conquests* (Cambridge: Cambridge University Press, 1987) 131-38.

29. "Arts of the Contact Zone," *Profession 91* (1991): 35. Mary Louise Pratt cites the 1613 *Chronicle* of Felipe Guaman Poma de Ayala as a representative example of Renaissance autoethnography (33-37); Guaman Poma was an indigenous Peruvian who wrote both in Quechua and Spanish, and whose book offers a revisionist and potentially subversive account of the Spanish conquest. It was not published (unsurprisingly) until 1937.

30. Sahagún's account, *La Historia general de las cosas de Nueva España,* was first published in 1829, roughly two hundred fifty years after its completion; Durán's book, *La Historia de las Indias de Nueva España,* first saw publication in 1867, nearly three hundred years after its composition. For examples of the sort of sophisticated and double-edged representation of native opinions that I have just spoken of, see Sahagún,

Florentine Codex, Book 12 (Santa Fe and Salt Lake City: School of American Research and the University of Utah, 1955), *passim;* and Durán, *The Aztecs: The History of the Indies of New Spain* (New York: Orion Press, 1964), esp. chapters 68-78.

31. For an extended discussion of these and related matters, see my essay "Attributions of Divinity in Renaissance Ethnography and Romance; Or, Making Religion of Wonder," *JMRS* 24:3 (1994): 415-47.

32. Bernheimer, *Wild Men in the Middle Ages*, 12.

33. A. Bartlett Giamatti, for example, has no hesitation in including satyrs among his catalogue of Spenser's wild men in "Primitivism and the Process of Civility in Spenser's *Faerie Queene*," *First Images of America*, ed. Fredi Chiappelli (Berkeley: University of California Press, 1976) vol. 1, 73.

34. Tristram, who is also "tall and faire of face" (6.2.5.4), exemplifies the common romance convention—also connected to Neoplatonic doctrine—that blood will tell: Good bodies reveal good pedigrees. See, in addition, Belphoebe's recognition of gentility in the "person" of Timias (4.8.14.3). Peter Laslett, in his fascinating sociological study, provides persuasive evidence for a factual basis to this convention when he writes that "The privileged [in sixteenth- and seventeenth-century Europe] were no doubt taller, heavier and better developed than the rest just as they were in Victorian times. In the Elizabethan age, and in pre-industrial times generally, gentlemen may have had beards and broken voices earlier than the rest, and ladies may have become full women more quickly" (*The World We Have Lost, Further Explored*, 3d ed. [New York: Scribner's, 1984] 89).

35. The idea that courtesy might be "natural" or innate among entire groups of people is suggested, among other places, in the account by David Ingram of his remarkable journey on foot from Mexico to Nova Scotia in 1568-69: "They [the Indians of what is now the southeastern United States] are naturally very courteous, if you do not abuse them, either in their persons or goods, but use them courteously" (*The Relation of Dauid Ingram of Barking* [London, 1589; Ann Arbor: University Microfilms, 1966] 558). Ingram also writes, however, that the same Indians "are so brutish & beastly, that they wil not forbeare the use of their wiues in open presence" (558). In Arthur Barlowe's account of his voyage to the North Carolina coast, we read that the local Indians are "very handsome, and goodly people, and in their behaviour as mannerly, and civill, as any of Europe. . . . Wee found the people most gentle, loving, and faithfull, void of all guile, and treason, and such as lived after the manner of the golden age" ("Narrative of the 1584 Voyage," in *Virginia Voyages*, 4, 8-9). And Sir Walter Ralegh, describing the Orenoqueponi king Topiawari, writes that he "marvelled to find a man of that gravity and judgment, and of so good discourse, that had no help of learning nor breed" (*The Discoverie of the Large, Rich and Beautiful Empire of Guiana* [London, 1596] in *Sir Walter Ralegh: Selected Writings*, ed. Gerald Hammond [Manchester: Carcanet Press, 1984] 108).

36. Roche, editor of the Yale edition of *The Faerie Queene*, glosses "Ciuility" (6.10.23.9) as "social order, and the kind of behavior which perpetuates social order" (1227).

37. Michael O'Connell recognizes this breadth when he writes that for Spenser, "courtesy is close to the very basis of human intercourse" (*Mirror and Veil* [Chapel Hill: University of North Carolina Press, 1977] 162). See also C. S. Lewis, who states in *The Allegory of Love* (London: Oxford University Press, 1938) that "it [courtesy] is a combination of charity and humility, in so far as these are social, not theological, virtues" (350).

38. Entries for October 11 and December 16, 1492 (*Diario*, 67, 235).

39. Pigafetta writes that Ferdinand Magellan and his men see "certeyne Canibales" in Patagonia who are "so swyfte of foote" that Europeans cannot overtake them (*Decades*, 219); Léry describes the Ouetaca tribe of Brazil as "so swift of foot . . . that not only do they evade all risk of death when they are pressed and pursued by their enemies . . . , but also when they hunt they catch certain wild animals—kinds of stags and does—by running them down" (*History of a Voyage*, 28-29); and in *The World Encompassed* (1628) we read that the Miwok Indians whom Drake encounters in California in 1578 are "exceeding swift in running, and of long continuance, the use wherof is so familiar with them, that they seldome go, but for the most part runne" (quoted in Warren L. Hanna, *Lost Harbor* [Berkeley: University of California Press, 1979] 377). Defoe describes Friday as so fast afoot that "he went like the wind; for sure never man or horse run like him" (*The Life and Adventures of Robinson Crusoe*, ed. Angus Ross [Harmondsworth: Penguin, 1965] 240).

40. Giamatti, "Primitivism and the Process of Civility in Spenser's *Faerie Queene*," in *First Images of America*, ed. Fredi Chiappelli (Berkeley: University of California Press, 1976) vol. 1, 78.

41. "Du repentir," *Les Essais de Michel de Montaigne*, ed. Pierre Villey, 3 vols. (Paris, 1923-24) vol. 3, 27. The translation is Frame's (in *The Complete Essays of Montaigne*, 611).

42. See especially 6.6.39-40 and 6.8.28-29. In these cantos Spenser also employs animal imagery more frequently in describing the Salvage Man; he likens him, for instance, to "a fell Lion" (6.6.22.4) and "a greedy kight" (6.8.28.4).

43. "Nation," according to the *OED*, carries the primary denotation of "An extensive aggregate of persons, so closely associated with each other by common descent, language, or history, as to form a distinct race or people, usually organized as a separate political state and occupying a definite territory"; Shakespeare employs the word in this sense when he has Shylock claim, in soliloquy, that Antonio "hates our sacred nation" (*MV*, 1.3.48). But the word has the secondary suggestion of "heathen society," as, for example, in its denotations (II.5.c and II.5.d) as "An Irish clan" and "A tribe of North American Indians," and in its plural form (I.2.a) as "The heathen nations, the Gentiles." An example of the latter may be found in the King James Bible (1611), where we read that "the Lord shall scatter you among the nations, and ye shall be left few in number among the heathen, whither the Lord shall lead you"

(Deuteronomy 4:27). See also Robert F. Berkhofer, Jr., *The White Man's Indian* (New York: Vintage, 1979) 16.

44. Pearce, "Primitivistic Ideas in *The Faerie Queene*," *JEGP* 44 (1945): 150. Pearce quotes a passage from Eden (*First Three Books*, 66; see also pp. 50, 148-49, and 177). Martyr's description of "certeyne wyld men whiche lyue in the caues & dennes of the montaynes, . . . men [who] neuer used the companye of any other: . . . without any certaine dwellynge places, and with owte tyllage or culturynge of the grounde . . . [and] withowte any certaine language" (*Decades*, 3.8.134) serves as a possible source not only for Spenser's Salvage Nation but for his Wild Man (Book Four) and his Salvage Man (Book Six).

45. In the first sentence of *A View of the Present State of Ireland*, Eudoxius observes to Irenius: "But if that country of Ireland whence you lately came be so goodly and commodious a soil as you report, I wonder that no course is taken for the turning thereof to good uses, and reducing that savage nation to better government and civility" (*View*, 1). Further evidence that Spenser had Ireland in mind as he wrote cantos 7 and 8 of Book Six of *The Faerie Queene* may be found in the description of Disdain, who wears a jacket of "checklaton" (6.7.43.4); Roche, in the notes to his edition of the poem, quotes Spenser's *View* as defining "checklaton" as "that kind of gilded leather which they [the Irish] use to embroider their irish jackets" (*The Faerie Queene*, 1222). On the love of music evidenced by New World inhabitants, see, for example, Drake's *The World Encompassed*, where the Miwok natives are said to have taken "such pleasure in our singing of Psalmes, that whensoeuer they resorted to vs, their first request was commonly this, *Gnaáh*, by which they intreated that we would sing" (Hanna, *Lost Harbor* [Berkeley: University of California Press, 1979] 372).

46. Eudoxius explicitly equates "barbarous nations" with "ceremonies and superstitious rites" (*View*, 7), thereby corroborating the commonplace notion that while "savages" may have religion, they do not have the *right* religion.

47. A. S. Knowles, Jr., "Spenser's Natural Man," *Renaissance Papers 1958, 1959, 1960*, ed. G. W. Williams and P. G. Phialas, (Durham: Duke University Press, 1961) 7.

48. "Primitivism and the Process of Civility in Spenser's *Faerie Queene*," 72.

49. Donald Cheney finds an even stronger primitivistic impulse in Book Six than I do; he writes, for instance, that the Salvage Man's "presence suggests that in order to create and maintain a flourishing society, man must make use not merely of his higher powers but of his lower powers as well. He must unite his brutish and gentle natures to achieve a cultured mildness of manner which is constantly being invigorated, strengthened, and defended by contact with the rigors of nature" (*Spenser's Image of Nature* [New Haven: Yale University Press, 1966] 210-211). While I consider this view intriguing, I think Cheney ends up with a slightly wrong emphasis, isolating the "brutish" and "gentle" natures in such a way as to obscure the possibility that they interpenetrate and are perhaps ultimately inseparable.

50. Compare God's speech to Adam as imagined by Giovanni Pico della Mirandola in his "Oration on the Dignity of Man" (ca. 1486): "Thou shalt have the power to degenerate into the lower forms of life, which are brutish. Thou shalt have the power, out of thy soul's judgment, to be reborn into the higher forms, which are divine" (*The Renaissance Philosophy of Man*, ed. Ernst Cassirer, Paul Oskar Kristeller, and John Herman Randall, Jr. [Chicago: University of Chicago Press, 1948] 225).

51. "Primitivism and the Process of Civility in Spenser's *Faerie Queene*," 74. Giamatti writes that the "primitive order" has no self-consciousness or art but only instinct: "And good though instinct may be—it can be far better than what is misshapen by art, for instance—it is in itself not enough for true civility" (73).

52. *View*, 159, 151. The first observation is made by Irenius (who has recently returned from Ireland), the second by his interlocutor Eudoxius. Frank Kermode, in his introduction to the Arden *Tempest* (London: Methuen, 1954), provides a seventeenth-century corroboration of Spenser's idea in the theory of Edward Phillips, a nephew of John Milton: "that noble thing call'd Education . . . raiseth beauty even out of deformity, order and regularity out of Chaos and confusion . . . [and is] able to civilize the most savage natures, & root out barbarism and ignorance from off the face of the Earth" (xlvi).

53. Bernheimer echoes this idea in claiming that "The state of the wild man was thus reached not by a gradual ascent from the brute, but by a descent. . . . the state of wildness was usually not regarded as irrevocable, but as amenable to change through acculturation" (*Wild Men in the Middle Ages* [Cambridge: Harvard University Press, 1952] 8). See also Walter J. Ong, "Spenser's *View* and the Tradition of the 'Wild' Irish" (*MLQ* 3:4 [1942]: 561-71) and David T. Read's discussion of Philotime and Disdayne (from Book Two of *The Faerie Queene*) in "Hunger of Gold," 225-26.

54. It is quite true, as Greenblatt points out, that Spenser often "sees the Irish as living in certain respects as the English did before the civilizing influence of the Norman Conquest" (*Renaissance Self-Fashioning* [Chicago: University of Chicago Press, 1980] 302, note 45), but this evolutionary model serves Spenser only to a limited degree, and is more effective as a means of conveying a general impression than it is precise as an ethnographic characterization. For a visual recapitulation of this model, see John White's five drawings of ancient Picts appended to his illustrations for the 1590 Theodor de Bry edition of Harriot's *A briefe and true report of the new found land of Virginia* (New York: Dover, 1972).

55. Indeed, Bernheimer sees the notion of the wild man as a response to a persistent psychological urge: "the need to give external expression and symbolically valid form to the impulses of reckless physical self-assertion which are hidden in all of us, but are normally kept under control" (*Wild Men in the Middle Ages*, 3).

56. Paul Brown, in his article "'This thing of darkness I acknowledge mine': *The Tempest* and the Discourse of Colonialism," argues similarly that "The same discourse which allows

for the transformation of the savage into the civil also raises the possibility of a reverse transformation" (*Political Shakespeare*, ed. Jonathan Dollimore and Alan Sinfield [Ithaca: Cornell University Press, 1985] 57). The prevailing view that Spenser has little tolerance for the Irish, and little good to say about them, is contested by David B. Quinn in *The Elizabethans and the Irish* [Ithaca: Cornell University Press, 1966] 20, 30.

57. Giamatti, "Primitivism," 76.

58. Here we see Spenser elaborating upon the conventional trio of possible locales for human habitation: court, city, country. For comparable expressions of this topos, see *As You Like It*, 2.1.59, and Tourneur's *The Atheist's Tragedy*, 4.4.44 (in *Jacobean Tragedies*, ed. A. H. Gomme [Oxford: Oxford University Press, 1969] 220); and for an interesting expression of the equally common court/country duality, see Bianca's soliloquy at 4.1.24-42 in Middleton's *Women Beware Women* (*Jacobean Tragedies*, 374).

59. William Empson, *Some Versions of Pastoral*, (London, 1935; rpt. Norfolk, CT: New Directions, 1960) 6. Empson goes on to contrast pastoral literature with fairy stories, claiming that the latter are "'by' and 'for,' [but] not 'about' [the people]; whereas pastoral though 'about' is not 'by' or 'for'" (6). Similarly, Kermode stresses that "The first condition of Pastoral is that it is an urban product" (*English Pastoral Poetry* [London: George G. Harrap, 1952] 14). But we must not forget the dimension of pastoral imagining so memorably expressed by C. S. Lewis: "Some readers cannot enjoy the shepherds [of *The Faerie Queene*, Book Six] because they know (or they say they know) that real country people are not more happy or more virtuous than any one else; but it would be tedious here to explain to them the many causes (reasons too) that have led humanity to symbolize by rural scenes and occupations a region in the mind which does exist and which should be visited often. If they know that region, let them try to people it with tram conductors and policemen, and I shall applaud any success they may have; if not, who can help them?" (*The Allegory of Love* [London: Oxford University Press, 1938] 352-53).

60. Empson, *Some Versions of Pastoral*, 11.

61. Louis Adrian Montrose, "Of Gentlemen and Shepherds: The Politics of Elizabethan Pastoral Form," *ELH* 50 (1983): 426-27. Humphrey Tonkin somewhat anticipates Montrose when he suggests, in *Spenser's Courteous Pastoral* (Oxford: Clarendon Press, 1972), that "pastoral is actually the least egalitarian of literary modes" and that "Pastoral . . . reinforces a social structure which must have looked a little rickety in places by Spenser's day. . . . [pastoral's] workings suggest that the natural world itself approves and reinforces the social hierarchy: for all that it may look otherwise, the social system is rooted in natural laws" (115, 291).

62. Patterson, *Pastoral and Ideology: Virgil to Valéry* (Berkeley: University of California Press, 1987) 131.

63. Raymond Williams, *The Country and the City* (New York: Oxford University Press, 1973) 18. Puttenham writes in his *Arte of English Poesie* (London, 1589) that "the Poet

devised the Eglogue . . . not of purpose to counterfait or represent the rusticall manner of loves and communications, but under the vaile of homely persons, and in rude speeches to insinuate and glaunce at greater matters, and such as perchance had not bene safe to have disclosed in any other sort" (Cambridge, 1936) 38-39. Sidney's *Apologie for Poetrie* (London, 1595) suggests that "the Pastorall Poem . . . can shewe the miserie of people, under hard Lords, or ravening Souldiours . . . [and] under the prettie tales of Wolves and Sheepe, can include the whole considerations of wrong dooing and patience" (*The Great Critics*, ed. James Harry Smith and Edd Winfield Parks [New York: Norton, 1967] 209).

64. The Brigants' caves are located on "a little Island" covered with "shrubby woods" and "ouergrowen gras" (6.10.41.6-9); the "coastes" near the isle are frequented by "merchants" who traffic in "slaues" (6.11.9.2-6). This wild coastal setting—complete with its allusion to the slave trade—is reminiscent of many such in the voyagers' accounts, including those of Martin Frobisher (1576-78) as described by Richard Hakluyt, where Indians "live in Caves of the earth, and hunt for their dinners or praye, even as the beare or other wild beastes do" (*Principal Navigations*, vol. 7, 370). The Brigants' civil war echoes another common motif of Renaissance ethnography; Arthur Barlowe, for instance, writes that the wars of the Roanoke people "are very cruell, and bloodie, by reason whereof, and of their civill dissentions, which have happened of late yeeres amongst them, the people are marvelously wasted, and in some places, the Countrey left desolate" ("Narrative of the 1584 Voyage," in *Virginia Voyages*, 10).

65. Helen Cooper, *Pastoral: Mediaeval into Renaissance* (Ipswich: D. S. Brewer, 1977) 164.

66. Humphrey Tonkin makes a rather similar point in a rather different way—employing a more conventionally allegorical reading of Book Six—when he argues that the union of Arthur and the Salvage Man in defeating Turpine demonstrates that "the proper running of society depends on close contact with the natural world" (*Spenser's Courteous Pastoral*, 181). Michael O'Connell observes that Book Six of *The Faerie Queene*, along with *Cymbeline*, *The Winter's Tale*, and *The Tempest*, involve "'returns' to the pastoral world, where characters discover, or perhaps rediscover, things vitally important to human civility" (*Mirror and Veil*, 187).

67. Empson, *Some Versions of Pastoral*, 20. Pearce answers this claim by asserting that "at no moment does Spenser have any illusions. Even though he praises the pastoral life, he portrays no truly noble savages" ("Primitivistic Ideas in *The Faerie Queene*," *JEGP* 44 [1945]: 140). Relying on the definition of "cultural primitivism" given by Lovejoy and Boas in *Primitivism and Related Ideas in Antiquity* (Baltimore: Johns Hopkins University Press, 1935), Pearce goes on to argue that Spenser "is drawn to that aspect of cultural primitivism which posits the idea of the essential goodness of a simple, pastoral life. Yet he finds fearful that aspect of cultural primitivism which would make the lives of savages good, and he contrasts that life often with the

ordered, rational life of his heroes" (142). I agree with this assessment, though Pearce neglects to distinguish carefully between pastoral-ness and wildness, thereby leaving much room for confusion in interpreting Book Six.

68. *The Machine in the Garden* (London: Oxford University Press, 1964) 25.

69. See, for example, Sheehan's commentary on Spenser in *Savagism and Civility* (Cambridge: Cambridge University Press, 1980) 74-78.

70. Hayden White suggests this in his article "The Forms of Wildness: Archaeology of an Idea," *The Wild Man Within*, ed. Edward Dudley and Maximilian E. Novak (Pittsburgh: University of Pittsburgh Press, 1972) 28. White relies heavily on Bernheimer's characterization of the Salvage Man in *Wild Men in the Middle Ages*, 7, 11, 25, 112-13; significantly, Bernheimer doesn't treat the Wild Man of Book Four.

71. *The Machine in the Garden*, 38; *Spenser's Courteous Pastoral*, 192.

72. White, in distinguishing "primitivism" from "archaism," claims that primitivism is essentialistic in the way I have just argued ("The Forms of Wildness," 26).

73. Mark Archer, without arguing that Spenser used Montaigne as a source, quotes Montaigne frequently in demonstrating that he read and considered Cicero and Seneca much in the way that Spenser must have; Spenser's treatment of courtesy and grace owes much to these classical authors, as does Montaigne's. See "The Meaning of 'Grace' and 'Courtesy': Book Six of *The Faerie Queene*," *SEL* 27:1 (Winter 1987): 17-34. See also the final pages of Jonathan Goldberg's *Endlesse Worke: Spenser and the Structures of Discourse* (Baltimore: Johns Hopkins University Press, 1981); Goldberg, in claiming that "No matter how far 'back' into nature the poem recedes, there is always a text, a sign of civilization, before nature, and not merely in the cannibals and brigands. . . . Behind nature there is always civilization and its texts" (169-70), goes further than I would in emphasizing textual/artificial primacy in Book Six, but I agree with his impulse to demonstrate the complex qualifications of the art/nature binarism.

Chapter 4

1. See *Err.* 3.2.132-37, *MV* 1.3.19-20, *1H4* 3.1.166-67, *AYL* 3.2.88-89, *Wiv.* 1.3.69-72, *TN* 2.5.13-14, *LLL* 4.3.218-21, and *AWW* 1.3.204-7. All quotations from the plays and poems of William Shakespeare are drawn from *The Riverside Shakespeare*, ed. G. Blakemore Evans, et al. (Boston: Houghton Mifflin, 1974). I have retained the brackets indicating editorial choices among variant readings.

2. Sidney Lee, "The American Indian in Elizabethan England," *Elizabethan and Other Essays*, ed. F. S. Boas (London: Oxford University Press, 1929) 285. Lee claims that Shakespeare's "strange Indian" was in fact the New Englander known as "Epenow" who was exhibited about London—for money—in 1611 (284).

3. For "hurricano," see also *Tro.* 5.2.172; for "potatoes," *Wiv.* 5.5.19; for "Hannibal" as a malapropism for "cannibal," *MM* 2.1.174; for "Cannibals" as a malapropism for "Hannibals," *2H4* 2.4.180. "Hurricane" is derived, through Spanish, from the Arawakan word "hurakan," according to Peter Hulme in *Colonial Encounters* (London: Methuen, 1986) 95; see also Hulme's "Hurricanes in the Caribbees: The Constitution of the Discourse of English Colonialism," in *1642: Literature and Power in the Seventeenth Century,* ed. Francis Barker, et al. (Colchester: University of Essex Press, 1981) 77, note 9. "Potato," according to the *OED,* is derived from the Haitian (i.e., Taino) "batata"; Richard Eden (1555) and John Hawkins (1565) are cited as having used variant forms. "Cannibal" derives, ultimately, from Columbus's *Diario,* which characterizes the people of "Caniba" as anthropophagous; see, for instance, the entries for November 23 and 26, 1492. The *OED* cites English appropriations of the Spanish "canibales" beginning with Eden (1553 and 1555). "Setebos," as *Tempest* commentators have long known, comes from Antonio Pigafetta's account of Ferdinand Magellan's circumnavigation in 1519-22; two Patagonians who were deceived and captured by Magellan's men "cryed vppon theyr greate deuyll *Setebos* to helpe them" (*Decades,* 220). See also the references to "Settaboth" and "Settaboh" in the *Notes* of Francis Fletcher, Sir Francis Drake's chaplain on the 1577-80 circumnavigation (*The World Encompassed,* ed. N. M. Penzer [New York: Argonaut Press, 1969] 115).

4. "Shakespeare's Indian: The Americanization of Caliban," *SQ* 39:2 (Summer 1988): 137. See also Alden T. Vaughan and Virginia Mason Vaughan, *Shakespeare's Caliban: A Cultural History* (Cambridge: Cambridge University Press, 1991); chapters 2, 5, and 6 provide excellent overviews of various "Americanist" readings of *The Tempest.*

5. "Shakespeare's American Fable" is the title of chapter 2 of Leo Marx's *The Machine in the Garden* (London: Oxford University Press, 1964).

6. The first volume of the second (and enlarged) edition of Richard Hakluyt's *Principal Navigations* was accompanied by a world map based on the Mercator projection. Further evidence that Shakespeare knew this collection of travel narratives is suggested by a speech of one of *Macbeth's* Witches: "Her husband's to Aleppo gone, master o' th' Tiger" (1.3.7); we read in "The voyage of M. Ralph Fitch . . . in the yeere of our Lord 1583" of "a ship of London called the Tyger, wherein we went for Tripolis in Syria: & from thence we tooke the way for Aleppo" (*Principal Navigations,* vol. 5, 465). William Strachey's account of the 1609 Bermuda shipwreck of the *Sea Venture,* bound for the new English colony at Jamestown, is titled *A True Repertory of the Wrack and Redemption of Sir Thomas Gates;* it was first published in Samuel Purchas's *Hakluytus Posthumous* (London, 1625), but circulated in manuscript around London in 1610. Silvester Jourdain's account of the same voyage, *A Discovery of the Barmudas, Otherwise Called the Isle of Devils,* was published in London in 1610. On Shakespeare and John Florio, see Eleanor Prosser, "Shakespeare, Montaigne, and the *Rarer Action,*" *ShakS* 1 (1965): 261-64.

7. See Margaret T. Hodgen, "Montaigne and Shakespeare Again," *HLQ* 16 (1952): 23-42, and Robert Ralston Cawley, "Shakspere's Use of the Voyagers in *The Tempest*," *PMLA* 41 (1926): 688-726. Cawley greatly extends and further catalogues his study of source material in *The Voyagers and Elizabethan Drama* (Boston: Modern Language Association, 1938) and *Unpathed Waters* (Princeton: Princeton University Press, 1940).

8. "*The Tempest* and the New World," *SQ* 30:4 (Winter 1979): 34.

9. "Nymphs and reapers heavily vanish: the discursive con-texts of *The Tempest*," *Alternative Shakespeares*, ed. John Drakakis (London: Methuen, 1985) 196. Barker and Hulme cite Julia Kristeva's *Le Texte du roman* (The Hague, 1970) as their source for the concept of intertextuality. In a separate work, Hulme quotes Charles Frey approvingly as a critic who "rejects the idea of an autotelic text" in favor of careful study of *The Tempest*'s "discursive milieux" (*Colonial Encounters*, 93).

10. Cawley, "Shakspere's Use of the Voyagers," 688n; Hodgen, "Montaigne and Shakespeare Again," 40.

11. *King Lear in Our Time* (Berkeley: University of California Press, 1965) 49.

12. Jonathan Swift, *Gulliver's Travels*, in *The Writings of Jonathan Swift*, ed. Robert A. Greenberg and William Bowman Piper (New York: Norton, 1973) 258.

13. On the Herbert Beerbohm-Tree and Jonathan Miller productions, see Virginia Mason Vaughan, "'Something Rich and Strange': Caliban's Theatrical Metamorphoses," *SQ* 36:4 (1985): 390-405, Trevor R. Griffiths, "'This Island's mine': Caliban and Colonialism," *Yearbook of English Studies 13*, ed. G. K. Hunter and C. J. Rawson (London: Modern Humanities Research Association, 1983) 159-80, and Anthony B. Dawson, *Watching Shakespeare* (New York: St. Martin's Press, 1988) 231-41. See also, for a discussion of earlier productions, Michael Dobson, "'Remember / First to Possess his Books': The Appropriation of *The Tempest*, 1700-1800," *SbS* (1991): 99-108. A. L. Rowse writes that "perhaps in the subconscious corridors of the mind we think of what happened to the redskins" (*The Elizabethans and America* [New York: Harper and Brothers, 1959] 197-98); Roberto Fernández Retamar argues, in the tradition of José Martí and Frantz Fanon, that *The Tempest* aids us in articulating a Marxist critique of European and Yankee imperialism in Latin America: Ariel is a Gramscian intellectual and Caliban is a symbol of the oppressed proletariat ("Caliban: Notes Toward a Discussion of Culture in Our America" [1971], in *Caliban and Other Essays* [Minneapolis: University of Minnesota Press, 1989] esp. 39-45); Leslie Fiedler claims that by the end of *The Tempest*, "the whole history of imperialist America has been prophetically revealed to us in brief parable: from the initial act of expropriation through the Indian wars to the setting up of reservations, and from the beginnings of black slavery to the first revolts and evasions" (*The Stranger in Shakespeare* [New York: Stein and Day, 1972] 238). See also Dominique Octave Mannoni, *Prospero and Caliban: The Psychology of Colonization* (New York: Praeger, 1956); Philip Mason, *Prospero's Magic* (London: Oxford University Press, 1962); D.

G. James, *The Dream of Prospero* (Oxford: Oxford University Press, 1967); Harry Berger, Jr., "Miraculous Harp: A Reading of Shakespeare's *Tempest*," *ShakS* 5 (1969): 353-83; John Gillies, "Shakespeare's Virginian Masque," *ELH* 53 (1986): 673-707; and, most recently, Jeffrey Knapp, "Distraction in *The Tempest*," in *An Empire Nowhere* (Berkeley: University of California Press, 1992) 220-42.

14. Barker and Hulme, "Nymphs and reapers," 204; Paul Brown, "'This thing of darkness I acknowledge mine': *The Tempest* and the discourse of colonialism," *Political Shakespeare*, ed. Jonathan Dollimore and Alan Sinfield (Ithaca: Cornell University Press, 1985) 68.

15. "Anxiety" in this sense is drawn from Barker and Hulme, 198. Barker and Hulme offer a critique of Frank Kermode's introduction to the Arden *Tempest* (London, 1954), 195-96. See also Terence Hawkes's remarks on the English critic Sir Walter Raleigh in *That Shakespeherian Rag* (London: Methuen, 1986) 51-72, and Meredith Anne Skura's brief mention of G. Wilson Knight in "Discourse and the Individual: The Case of Colonialism in *The Tempest*," *SQ* 40:1 (Spring 1989): 46.

16. "'This thing of darkness'," 53.

17. *Colonial Encounters*, 125.

18. *Colonial Encounters*, 124. Richard Marienstras makes a similar point when he argues that because Prospero knows more than any other character, spectators "see and judge events from his point of view"; he adds, however, that "it is not possible, in the conflict between [Prospero] and Caliban, entirely to eliminate or discredit the reasoning of the latter" (*New Perspectives on the Shakespearean World* [Cambridge: Cambridge University Press, 1985] 171).

19. Francisco de Vitoria writes that the title to possession of a given territory, when based upon the discovery of that territory, is legitimate in certain cases (prior lack of inhabitation, for instance); but such a title is *not* legitimate in most parts of America: "the barbarians were true owners, both from the public and from the private standpoint. Now the rule of the law of nations is that what belongs to nobody is granted to the first occupant" (quoted in Stephen Greenblatt, *Marvelous Possessions* [Chicago: University of Chicago Press, 1991] 61).

20. "The famous voyage of Sir Francis Drake into the South sea," *Principal Navigations*, vol. 11, 121-22. Apropos of this, Louis B. Wright has accurately observed that "the doctrine that particular regions [of the New World] had been set aside until such time as Englishmen might need to emigrate . . . helped to create an English version of the belief in Manifest Destiny which profoundly influenced colonial enterprise in the seventeenth century" (*Religion and Empire* [Chapel Hill: University of North Carolina Press, 1943] 85-86).

21. See, for example, Bartolomé de Las Casas's *The Spanish Colonie* (Ann Arbor: University Microfilms, 1966) sig. A4, and Michel de Montaigne's "Of cannibals" (*Essays*, 155). Sister Corona Sharp argues in her article "Caliban: The Primitive Man's Evolution"

that "Shakespeare could hardly have missed hearing about [Las Casas'] *The Spanish Colonie*, and the numerous passages in this work that are analogous to portions of *The Tempest* are worth noting" (*ShakS* 14 [1981]: 279). See also Skura's "Discourse and the Individual," 51.

22. On this, compare Montaigne in "Of coaches": "Our world has just discovered another world (and who will guarantee us that it is the last of its brothers, since the daemons, the Sibyls, and we ourselves have up to now been ignorant of this one?) no less great, full, and well-limbed than itself" (*Essays*, 693).

23. Barker and Hulme, "Nymphs and reapers," 198. Skura points to this limitation in colonialist readings when she writes that "the exploitative and self-justifying rhetoric [of colonialism] is only one element in a complex New World discourse" ("Discourse and the Individual," 54).

24. Brown, "'This thing of darkness,'" 60, 52-53.

25. For a useful and balanced critique of Brown's article and the view that Shakespeare endorsed the colonial project, see Deborah Willis, "Shakespeare's *Tempest* and the Discourse of Colonialism," *SEL* 29 (1989): 277-89. See also Russ McDonald, "Reading *The Tempest*," *ShS* 43 (1991): 15-28, esp. 15-17.

26. Hawkes, *That Shakespeherian Rag*, 3.

27. *An Empire Nowhere*, 235.

28. David B. Quinn, *The Elizabethans and the Irish* (Ithaca: Cornell University Press, 1966) 20.

29. Jack Beeching observes in his Introduction to Hakluyt's *Voyages and Discoveries* (Harmondsworth: Penguin, 1972) that "Shipmen breaking in upon more primitive, hitherto untouched societies for the purposes of trade had a faculty of observing and recording curious customs with the lack of prejudice which distinguishes the anthropologist, who is their historical legatee" (12); while the claim that these accounts reveal a "lack of prejudice" is certainly naive, Beeching's point is still pertinent.

30. On Renaissance ethnography see, among other studies, Margaret T. Hodgen, *Early Anthropology In the Sixteenth and Seventeenth Centuries* (Philadelphia: University of Pennsylvania Press, 1964); two articles by John Howland Rowe: "Ethnography and Ethnology in the Sixteenth Century" (*KASP* 30 [1964]: 1-19) and "The Renaissance Foundations of Anthropology" (*AA* 67 [February 1965]: 1-20); Michael T. Ryan, "Assimilating New Worlds in the Sixteenth and Seventeenth Centuries," *CSSH* 23:4 (October 1981): 519-38; Caroline B. Brettell, "Introduction: Travel Literature, Ethnography, and Ethnohistory," *Ethnohistory* 33:2 [1986]: 127; and Mary B. Campbell, "The Illustrated Travel Book and the Birth of Ethnography: Part I of De Bry's *America*," in *The Work of Dissimilitude*, ed. David G. Allen and Robert A. White (Newark: University of Delaware Press, 1992) 177-95. See also chapter 1 of this monograph.

31. Charles Frey contrasts the idea of "sources" with that of "linguistic and narrative force-field[s]" in "*The Tempest* and the New World," 33. Alden T. Vaughan cites Frey's

article, along with Greenblatt's "Learning to Curse: Aspects of Linguistic Colonialism in the Sixteenth Century" (*First Images of America*, ed. Fredi Chiappelli, [Berkeley: University of California Press, 1976] vol. 2, 561-80), as a forerunner in "the new interest in historical contexts" ("Shakespeare's Indian: The Americanization of Caliban," 151n).

32. Indeed, Greenblatt has brilliantly argued that what appears in Thomas Harriot's *Briefe and true report* to be "a conversation among equals, as if all meanings were provisional, as if the signification of events stood apart from power" is in fact "part of the process whereby Indian culture is constituted as a culture and thus brought into the light for study, discipline, correction, and transformation" ("Invisible Bullets," in *Shakespearean Negotiations* [Berkeley: University of California Press, 1988] 36-37). I am, I suppose, more sanguine than Greenblatt in my conviction that Renaissance ethnography, by and large, is only loosely tied to colonial aims; one encounters, I believe, abundant instances of disinterested description.

33. Richard Eden, "The Indian language," in *Decades*; Jean de Léry, *History of a Voyage*, chapter 20; John Smith, *A Map of Virginia* (London, 1612), in *The Complete Works of Captain John Smith*, ed. Philip L. Barbour (Chapel Hill: University of North Carolina Press, 1986) vol. 1, 136-39. See also Jacques Cartier, "The language that is spoken in the Land newly discouered, called new Fraunce" and "The names of the chiefest partes of man, and other wordes necessarie to be knowen," in *A Shorte and briefe narration of the two Nauigations and Discoueries to the Northweast partes called Newe Fravnce*, trans. John Florio (London, 1580; Ann Arbor: University Microfilms, 1966) 27, 79-80. Greenblatt contends that "In Cartier, as in almost all early European accounts, the language of the Indians is noted not in order to register cultural specificity but in order to facilitate barter, movement, and assimilation through conversion" (*Marvelous Possessions*, 104); while there is certainly a good measure of truth to this, I think that such documents as Cartier's and Léry's glossaries inevitably *do* register cultural specificity and difference, thereby both demonstrating European interest in the other and providing a discourse in which that interest may perpetuate itself.

34. As Skura points out, these words appear in the Folio's "Names of the Actors"; Shakespeare may or may not have written them ("Discourse and the Individual: The Case of Colonialism in *The Tempest*," *SQ* 40:1 [Spring 1989]: 48).

35. *Colonial Encounters* (London: Methuen, 1986) 114.

36. *Nova Brittania* (London, 1609), in *Tracts*, vol. 1, no. 6, 11.

37. *The Generall Historie of Virginia* (London, 1624), in *The Complete Works of Captain John Smith*, ed. Philip L. Barbour (Chapel Hill: University of North Carolina Press, 1986) vol. 2, 152, 183, 189, 198, 125-26.

38. *A briefe and true report* (London, 1588), in *Virginia Voyages*, 70.

39. Edmund Malone, *The Plays and Poems of William Shakespeare* 21 vols. (London, 1821) vol. 15, 11-14; Leslie Fiedler, *The Stranger in Shakespeare* (New York: Stein and Day,

1972) 233. Sidney Lee also points to the varied ethnographic roots of Caliban, including the Guianans described by Sir Walter Ralegh, but he curbs his enthusiasm enough to recollect—unlike Fiedler—that there were no "native Bermudans" ("The American Indian in Elizabethan England," in *Elizabethan and Other Essays*, ed. F. S. Boas [London: Oxford University Press, 1929] 263-301).

40. Geoffrey Bullough, *Narrative and Dramatic Sources of Shakespeare* (London: Routledge and Kegan Paul, 1975) vol. 8, 257; Hulme, *Colonial Encounters*, 108. See also Cawley, who argues that Caliban is not a mélange of types but a representation of the changing attitudes toward native Americans held by the colonists ("Shakspere's Use of the Voyagers in *The Tempest*," *PMLA* 41 [1926]: 719n); Sharp, who writes that Caliban's character "took shape under the influence of conflicting opinions held on the American Indians during Shakespeare's lifetime" ("Caliban: The Primitive Man's Evolution," *ShakS* 14 [1981]: 267); and Karen Flagstad, who adds that "the savage Caliban conflates contradictory stereotypes" ("'Making this Place Paradise': Prospero and the Problem of Caliban in *The Tempest*," *ShakS* 18 [1986]: 221).

41. Bernard Sheehan, *Savagism and Civility* (Cambridge: Cambridge University Press, 1980) 85, 87.

42. Greenblatt, "Learning to Curse: Aspects of Linguistic Colonialism in the Sixteenth Century," in *First Images of America*, ed. Fredi Chiappelli (Berkeley: University of California Press, 1976) vol. 2, 574; Tzvetan Todorov, *The Conquest of America* (New York: Harper and Row, 1984) 42-43. See also chapter 1.

43. "Learning to Curse," 575.

44. *New Perspectives on the Shakespearean World* (Cambridge: Cambridge University Press, 1985) 169-70. I disagree with Marienstras, however, when he asserts that Caliban's uncertain status "gives the reader a feeling of instability that remains with him through to the end of the play" (170).

45. Cabeza de Vaca, *Relation of Nuñez Cabeza de Vaca*, trans. Buckingham Smith (New York, 1871; Ann Arbor: University Microfilms, 1966) 82; Léry, *History of a Voyage to the Land of Brazil*, trans. Janet Whatley (Berkeley: University of California Press, 1990) 29; Acosta, *How to procure the salvation of the Indians*, excerpted in John Howland Rowe, "Ethnography and Ethnology in the Sixteenth Century," *KASP* 30 (1964): 16; Ralegh, *The Discovery of the Large, Rich and Beautiful Empire of Guiana* (London, 1596; Manchester: Carcanet Press, 1984) 81; Strachey, *Historie of Travell into Virginia Britannia*, excerpted in *Elizabethans*, 215; Smith, *Generall Historie*, in *The Complete Works of Captain John Smith*, vol. 2, 119.

46. "Virginias Verger," in *Hakluytus Posthumous*, vol. 19, 231. For other, earlier, examples of what I have called *tabula rasa* views of American natives, see chapter 1.

47. All quotations from *Mucedorus* (London, 1598) are drawn from *Drama of the English Renaissance*, ed. Russell A. Fraser and Norman Rabkin (New York: Macmillan, 1976) vol. 1, 463-80. *Mucedorus* was published in seventeen separate editions between 1598

and 1658. It was performed by the King's Men in 1610 "before the King's majesty at Whitehall on Shrove-Sunday night" (Fraser and Rabkin, 463); thus Shakespeare probably knew the play, and may have acted in it.

48. Introduction to the Arden *Tempest* (London: Methuen, 1954) xxxviii-ix. Norman Rabkin writes that "Bremo the wild man is something of a forerunner of Caliban, suggesting the interest of an age of exploration in the phenomenon of natural man while ensuring that the play remains fairy tale" (Introduction to *Mucedorus*, 463). See also G. M. Pinciss, "The Savage Man in Spenser, Shakespeare, and Renaissance English Drama," *The Elizabethan Theatre VIII*, ed. G. R. Hibbard (Port Credit: P. D. Meany, 1982): 72-78.

49. Bremo's encounter with Amadine in scene 11 reveals obvious similarities to the conventional motif of the wild man's transformation to civility in the presence of a beautiful and virtuous woman. But this particular encounter is presented as a more sentimental and less thoroughly transforming experience.

50. R. H. Goldsmith, "The Wild Man on the English Stage," *MLR* 53 (1958): 481-91.

51. This speech, with its indication of Caliban's intelligence and appreciation of Prospero's gifts, echoes numerous accounts of New World natives, among them James Rosier's 1605 description of Indians along the New England coast: "They seemed all very civil and merry, showing tokens of much thankfulness for those things we gave them. We found them then (as after) a people of exceeding good invention, quick understanding, and ready capacity" (*A True Relation of the Most Prosperous Voyage Made This Present Year 1605 by Captain George Weymouth*, excerpted in *Elizabethans*, 149). On George Weymouth's voyage, see Sidney Lee, "The American Indian in Elizabethan England," 282.

52. Stephen Orgel, Introduction to the Oxford *Tempest* (Oxford: Oxford University Press, 1987) 34. Sharp takes this view even further in calling the attempted rape "Caliban's failure in European sexual ethics" ("Caliban: The Primitive Man's Evolution," *ShakS* 14 [1981]: 273). And Paul Brown asserts that Caliban's "inability to discern a concept of private, bounded property concerning his own dominions is reinterpreted as a desire to violate the chaste virgin, who epitomizes courtly property" ("'This thing of darkness I acknowledge mine': *The Tempest* and the discourse of colonialism," *Political Shakespeare*, ed. Jonathan Dollimore and Alan Sinfield [Ithaca: Cornell University Press, 1985] 62). See also Orgel's "Shakespeare and the Cannibals," in *Cannibals, Witches, and Divorce*, ed. Marjorie Garber (Baltimore: Johns Hopkins University Press, 1987) 55.

53. *Decades*, 3.8.134; *Principal Navigations*, vol. 7, 155. The three Eskimos Fabian describes were brought by Sebastian Cabot to England from the North American Arctic in 1502 and presented to Henry VII. See Sidney Lee, "The American Indian in Elizabethan England," in *Elizabethan and Other Essays*, ed. F. S. Boas (London: Oxford University Press, 1929) 270.

54. "The relation of John de Verrazzano a Florentine, of the land by him discovered in the name of his Majestie. Written in Diepe the eight of July, 1524," *Principal Navigations*, vol. 8, 433.

55. *History of a Voyage*, 158.

56. *How to procure the salvation of the Indians*, 17.

57. Alexander Whitaker, *Good Newes from Virginia* (London, 1613; New York: Scholars' Facsimiles and Reprints, 1936) 26-27; Strachey, *Historie of Travel into Virginia Britannia* (London, 1612), excerpted in *Elizabethans*, 212; Harriot, *A briefe and true report* (London, 1588), in *Virginia Voyages*, 68.

58. *Good Newes from Virginia*, 24.

59. Alan C. Dessen discusses this role-doubling as "a means to call attention to structural or thematic analogies" in "Conceptual Casting in the Age of Shakespeare: Evidence from *Mucedorus*," *SQ* 43:1 (Spring 1992): 67-70.

60. *The Faerie Queene*, ed. Thomas P. Roche, Jr. (New Haven: Yale University Press, 1981) 4.6.22 and 1.6.7-19.

61. Richard Marienstras, for example, writes that Caliban "rushes into servitude even when striving for freedom" (*New Perspectives*, 175).

62. *Marvelous Possessions: The Wonder of the New World* (Chicago: University of Chicago Press, 1991) 77.

63. For a fascinating and sustained example of native Americans confronting Europeans whom they cannot, at first, satisfactorily categorize, see Diego Durán, *The Aztecs: The Indies of New Spain* (New York: Orion Press, 1964), esp. chapters 69-74. Durán claims, for instance, that Moteczoma and his ministers plotted various strategies of resistance to Cortés and the other conquistadors even while alluding to them as immortal beings: "'I do not know' [said Moteczoma] 'what measures to take to prevent these gods from reaching the city or seeing my face. Perhaps the best solution will be the following: let there be gathered enchanters, sorcerers, sleep-makers and those who know how to command snakes, scorpions and spiders, and let them be sent to enchant the Spaniards. Let them be put to sleep, let them be shown visions, let the little beasts bite them so that they die.' . . . 'O powerful lord' [responded Tlillancalqui] 'your decision seems good to me, but if they are gods who will be able to harm them? However, nothing will be lost in the attempt'" (276).

64. *Decades*, 219. And see the references to "Settaboth" and "Settaboh" in the *Notes* of Francis Fletcher (*The World Encompassed*, ed. N. M. Penzer [New York: Argonaut Press, 1969] 115).

65. Drake's men found that the Miwok natives of California "supposed us to be gods, and would not be perswaded to the contrary" (Hakluyt, "The famous voyage of Sir Francis Drake into the South sea," *Principal Navigations*, vol. 11, 119). And Harriot writes of the Indians near the Roanoke Colony, "some people could not tel whether to thinke us gods or men" (*A briefe and true report*, in *Virginia Voyages*, 73). See also

Cawley, *The Voyagers and Elizabethan Drama* (Boston: Modern Language Association, 1938) 385-88. In one of the classic English fictions dealing with the encounter of European and native American, Daniel Defoe exploits this motif in portraying the relationship between Crusoe and the "savage" Friday: "I believe, if I would have let him, he would have worshipped me and my gun" (*The Life and Adventures of Robinson Crusoe*, ed. Angus Ross [Harmondsworth: Penguin, 1965] 214). For a further exploration of this motif, see my essay "Attributions of Divinity in Renaissance Ethnography; Or, Making Religion of Wonder," *JMRS* 24:3 (1994): 415-47.

66. *A briefe and true report*, 68.

67. See, for instance, John Calvin, *Institutes of the Christian Religion*, trans. John Allen, 2 vols. (Philadelphia: Presbyterian Board of Christian Education, 1936) 1:54 (Book 1, chapter 3); Richard Hooker, *Of the Laws of Ecclesiastical Polity*, in *The Folger Library Edition of the Works of Richard Hooker*, ed. W. Speed Hill et al., 4 vols. (Cambridge: Harvard University Press, 1977) 2:19 (Book 5, chapter 1, section 3); and the early chapters of Paul's epistle to the Romans. Bacon, in his essay "Of Atheism," writes that "The Indians of the West have names for their particular gods, though they have no name for God: as if the heathens should have had the names Jupiter, Mars, etc., but not the word *Deus*—which shows that even those barbarous people have the notion, though they have not the latitude and extent of it. So that against atheists the very savages take part with the very subtlest philosophers" (*The Essays* [London, 1597, 1612] ed. John Pitcher [Harmondsworth: Penguin, 1985] 109). For a non-theological expression of this idea, see *The Travels of Sir John Mandeville*, trans. C. W. R. D. Mosely (Harmondsworth: Penguin, 1983) chapter 18, esp. p. 121.

68. On connections between Miranda and the American native Pocahontas, see Morton Luce's Arden edition of *The Tempest* (London: Methuen, 1902) 169-70; Geoffrey Bullough's *Narrative and Dramatic Sources*, vol. 8, 241; and Jeffrey Knapp, *An Empire Nowhere* (Berkeley: University of California Press, 1992) 240-41.

69. *Shakespearean Negotiations* (Berkeley: University of California Press, 1988) 157. See also Skura, "Discourse," 66; Knapp, *An Empire Nowhere*, 239; Lynda E. Boose, "The Father and the Bride in Shakespeare," *PMLA* 97:3 (1982): 341; and Gananath Obeyesekere, *The Apotheosis of Captain Cook* (Princeton: Princeton University Press, 1992) 11-12. When Ferdinand speaks to Prospero of "our worser genius" as a force that can potentially "melt . . . honor into lust" (4.1.27-28), he anticipates Prospero's "thing of darkness" speech inasmuch as he suggests that a principle of wildness or savagery lies within all humans.

70. "The Sea and the Mirror," in *The Collected Poetry of W. H. Auden* (New York: Random House, 1945) 387-88.

71. In claiming that he will "be wise hereafter, / And seek for grace" (5.1.295-96), Caliban is almost certainly *not* speaking ironically; the tone of self-annoyance in which he castigates himself for taking the drunkard Stephano for a god and worshipping the "dull fool" Trinculo (5.1.297-98) seems strongly to preclude this.

72. On prevenient grace, see Article 10 of the Church of England's Thirty-nine articles (1571): "The condition of man after the fall of Adam is such, that he cannot turn and prepare himself, by his own natural strength and good works, to faith and calling upon God: Wherefore we have no power to do good works pleasant and acceptable to God, without the grace of God preventing us, that we may have a good will, and working with us, when we have that good will" (from Thomas Rogers, *The Faith, Doctrine, and Religion, Professed and Protected in the Realm of England . . . Expressed in 39 Articles* [Cambridge, 1607; rpt. New York: Johnson Reprint Corporation, 1968] 103). If Caliban is capable of seeking prevenient grace, the presumption is strong that he is fully human.

73. John Donne, "An Anatomy of the World: The First Anniversary" (lines 161-62) in *John Donne: The Complete English Poems*, ed. A. J. Smith (Harmondsworth: Penguin, 1973) 274. See also *As You Like It*, 3.2.11 and 3.2.17, and *Hamlet*, 4.7.21. The *OED* defines this meaning of "grace" as "In persons: Virtue; an individual virtue; sense of duty or propriety" (II.13.b).

74. A. O. Lovejoy, "On the Discrimination of Romanticisms," *Essays in the History of Ideas* (Baltimore: Johns Hopkins University Press, 1948) 238n. The passage in question is not merely the short section that Shakespeare apparently plagiarizes, but the entire central part of the essay—all of which treats the contrast between the "natural" lives of the Tupi natives and the "artificial" lives of Europeans. See chapter 2 of this study.

75. Lee, "The American Indian in Elizabethan England," 295; Fiedler, *The Stranger in Shakespeare*, 231. Lee continues by writing that "Shakespeare's American is not the Arcadian innocent with whom Montaigne identifies him" (296). Terence Hawkes, in *Shakespeare's Talking Animals* (Totowa, NJ: Rowman and Littlefield, 1973), offers a more qualified assessment: "The audience is invited, in short, to agree with Antonio's verdict 'The latter end of his commonwealth forgets the beginning,' and to pass it in the name of fallible humanity upon all such Utopian fantasy" (199-200).

76. *The Discovery of the Large, Rich and Beautiful Empire of Guiana* (London, 1596; Manchester: Carcanet Press, 1984) 110; "Narrative of the 1584 Voyage" (London, 1589), in *Virginia Voyages*, 2-3, 8. Compare Ralph Lane's comment on the Roanoke region: "we have discovered the maine to be the goodliest soyle under the cope of heaven, so abounding with sweete trees, that bring such sundry rich and pleasant gummes, grapes of such greatnesse, yet wilde, as France, Spaine, nor Italie have no greater, . . . it is the goodliest and most pleasing Territorie of the world" ("An extract of Master Ralph Lanes letter to M. Richard Hakluyt Esquire" [September 1585] in *Principal Navigations*, vol. 8, 319).

77. *Poetry of the English Renaissance, 1509-1660*, ed. J. William Hebel and Hoyt H. Hudson (New York: Appleton-Century-Crofts, 1929) 297. Leo Marx has pointed to the "obvious debt" of Drayton's ode to Barlowe's account (*The Machine in the Garden* [London: Oxford University Press, 1964] 38-39); see also Hawkes, *Shakespeare's*

Talking Animals, 197-98. Andrew Marvell's "Bermudas," with its stress upon the "eternal spring" (13) of the islands and their abundance of "fowl," "pom'granates," "figs," "melons," "apples," "cedars," and "ambergris" (15-28) may also owe a debt to Barlowe, as it does, according to Elizabeth Story Donno, to Waller's "The Battle of the Summer Islands" (1645) and possibly to Captain John Smith's *Generall Historie of Virginia* (London, 1624). See Elizabeth Story Donno's *Andrew Marvell: The Complete Poems* (Harmondsworth: Penguin, 1972) 116, 266.

78. *A Short And briefe narration of the two Nauigations and Discoueries to the Northweast partes called Newe Fravnce,* trans. John Florio (London, 1580; Ann Arbor: University Microfilms, 1966) 54.

79. *A Discovery of the Barmudas* (London, 1610), excerpted in the Arden *Tempest,* ed. Frank Kermode (London: Methuen, 1954) 141.

80. *A Briefe and true Relation of the Discouerie of the North part of Virginia* (London, 1602; Ann Arbor: University Microfilms, 1966) 4, 10; John Brereton's account is also excerpted in *Elizabethans,* 137, 143. Brereton's is the earliest English eye-witness account of native Americans from the New England region.

81. "Narrative of the 1584 Voyage," 4, 8-9.

82. "Of the Caniballes," in John Florio, trans., *The Essayes of Michael Lord of Montaigne* (London, 1603; New York: Modern Library, 1933) 164, 167-68; compare Donald M. Frame, trans., *The Complete Essays of Montaigne* (Stanford: Stanford University Press, 1958) 153, 156.

83. Introduction to the Arden *Tempest,* xxxviii.

84. *The Machine in the Garden,* 57-58.

85. *The Machine in the Garden,* 65.

86. Introduction to *The Tempest,* xxxviii; *The Machine in the Garden,* 69.

87. Greenblatt, "Learning to Curse," 570; Stephen Orgel, Introduction to the Oxford *Tempest* (Oxford: Oxford University Press, 1987) 35. Greenblatt goes on to support his assertion by claiming that "Shakespeare does not shrink from the darkest European fantasies about the Wild Man; indeed he exaggerates them: Caliban is deformed, lecherous, evil-smelling, idle, treacherous, naive, drunken, rebellious, violent, and devil-worshipping" (570).

88. I allude here not only to "Of cannibals" (154, 158), but also to the essay immediately preceding it in Book One of the *Essays,* "Of moderation" (149).

89. Leo Marx takes Gonzalo's commonwealth vision and Prospero's wedding masque as emblematic of two contrasting ideals bodied forth in the play; "The difference between the masque and the plantation speech, finally, is the difference between a pastoral and a primitive ideal" (*The Machine in the Garden,* 65).

90. *The Machine in the Garden,* 69, 60, 25.

91. The phrase is Louis Adrian Montrose's, from his essay "Of Gentlemen and Shepherds: The Politics of Elizabethan Pastoral Form" (*ELH* 50 [1983]: 427).

92. See *The Countess of Pembroke's Arcadia*, ed. Maurice Evans (Harmondsworth: Penguin, 1977) Book Two, chapter 10, 275-83; the blind king, after hearing his son's relation of their collective travails to Pyrocles and Musidorus, exclaims "Ah, my son, . . . how evil an historian are you that leave out the chief knot of all the discourse, my wickedness, my wickedness!" (277). For an excellent recent discussion of subversive political ideas in *Lear*, see Margot Heinemann, "'Demystifying the Mystery of State': *King Lear* and the World Upside Down," *ShS* 44 (1992): 75-83.

93. *The Arte of English Poesie* (London, 1589), ed. G. D. Willcock and A. Walker (Cambridge: Cambridge University Press, 1936) 39.

94. On this point I disagree with Greenblatt, who writes that "By no means is Caliban accepted into the family of man; rather, he is claimed as Philoctetes might claim his own festering wound" ("Learning to Curse," 570).

95. Leo Marx, 57-65. Marx *does* mention the acknowledgment later on in his chapter (69), but only briefly, and in a different context.

96. Cosmo Corfield points to suggestions of commonality between Prospero and Caliban in a brief discussion of Prospero's "Caliban-like diction"; see "Why Does Prospero Abjure His 'Rough Magic'?" *SQ* 36:1 (Spring 1985): 36-37, 42-43.

97. See James Black's fine exploration of this theme in "The Monster in Shakespeare's Landscape," *The Elizabethan Theatre VIII*, ed. G. R. Hibbard (Port Credit: P. D. Meany, 1982) 51-68.

98. Many critics have noted a dual view of nature in this play; Irving Ribner, for example, expresses it in the following way: "There are two concepts of nature at war with one another within the play. One is the orthodox nature of Richard Hooker's Christian humanism, of Cordelia, Kent, and Edgar; the other is the nature of Renaissance skepticism, of Edmund, Goneril and Regan. While he is cut off from God's order by his sins, Lear swears by the nature of Edmund; at the end of the play he is won back to that of Cordelia" ("The Gods Are Just: A Reading of *King Lear*," *TDR* 2:3 (May 1958): 39. Ribner relies, in turn, upon John F. Danby, *Shakespeare's Doctrine of Nature* (London: Faber and Faber, 1948), esp. Part One, "The Two Natures."

99. The treatment of nature and monstrousness in *Lear* helps us to understand allegations of "natural" and "unnatural" behavior in *The Tempest*. In calling his brother Antonio "Unnatural" (5.1.79), for instance, Prospero follows the conventional usage employed by Lear and Gloucester; he does the same when he criticizes Antonio for expelling "nature" (5.1.76 and 79). But in condemning Caliban's "nature" (4.1.188), Prospero reveals his double standard: Caliban's rebellion may be attributed to his "nature" and is thus "natural," while Antonio's rebellion is "unnatural." For Prospero, then, nature is fundamentally good in an aristocrat, but in Caliban it is depraved. However, insubordination aligned with natural forces has been powerfully represented—and legitimized—earlier in the play (1.1). Prospero thus restricts "nature" too severely; it is broader and more potentially subversive than he is willing to allow.

Later, when Prospero acknowledges Caliban as "mine" (5.1.276), he is perhaps implicitly admitting that his double standard was incorrect.

100. Compare the speeches of Flavius and the Servants in *Timon of Athens* 4.2, especially lines 16-29.

101. See also Guyon's encounter with Acrasia in the Bower of Bliss (*The Faerie Queene* 2.12).

Bibliography

Primary Materials

Acosta, José de. *The Natural and Moral History of the Indies.* [London, 1604]. Trans. by Edward
    Grimston of *Historia natural y moral de las Indias.* [Seville, 1590]. Ed. Clements R.
    Markham. 2 vols. London: Hakluyt Society, 1880.

————. *How to procure the salvation of the Indians.* Partial trans. by John Howland Rowe of
    De natura novi orbis libri duo, et de promulgatione evangelii, apud barbaros, sive de produranda
    inforum salute libri sex. [Ca. 1576-77; Salamanca, 1589]. In Rowe, "Ethnography and
    Ethnology in the Sixteenth Century." *Kroeber Anthropological Society Papers* 30 (1964):
    16-19.

Ailly, Pierre d'. *See* D'Ailly, Pierre.

Aristotle. *Nichomachean Ethics.* Trans. Martin Ostwald. New York: Macmillan, 1962.

————. *The Politics of Aristotle.* Trans. Ernest Barker. Oxford: Clarendon Press, 1946.

Bacon, Sir Francis. *The New Atlantis.* [London, 1622]. London: Routledge, n.d.

————. *The New Organon and Related Writings.* [London, 1620]. Ed. Fulton H. Anderson.
    Indianapolis: Bobbs-Merrill, 1960.

————. "Of Plantations." In *The Essayes or Counsels, Civill and Morall.* [London, 1597; rev.
    eds. 1612, 1625]. Ed. Michael Kiernan. Oxford: Clarendon Press, 1985. 106-08.

Barlowe, Arthur. "Arthur Barlowe's Narrative of the 1584 Voyage." [London, 1589]. In
    Quinn, ed., *Virginia Voyages,* 1-12.

Behn, Aphra. *Oroonoko: or, the Royal Slave.* [London, 1688]. New York: Norton, 1973.

Benzoni, Girolamo. *History of the New World.* Trans. by W. H. Smyth of *La Historia del Mondo*
    Nuovo. [Venice, 1565]. 1st Series, vol. 21. Hakluyt Society. London: Hakluyt
    Society, 1857.

Boemus, Joannes. *The Fardle of facions, conteining the aunciente maners, customes, and Lawes, of the*
    peoples enhabiting the two partes of the earth, called Affrike and Asie. [London, 1555]. Trans.
    by William Watreman of *Omnium gentium mores leges et ritus ex multis clarissimis rerum*
    scriptoribus. [1520]. Facsimile edition. Amsterdam: Theatrum Orbis Terrarum, 1970.

————. *The manners lawes and customs of all nations.* [London, 1611]. Trans. by E. Aston of *Omnium gentium mores leges et ritus ex multis clarissimis rerum scriptoribus.* [1520].

Boswell, James. *The Life of Samuel Johnson, LL.D.* [London, 1791; rev. 1793, 1799]. London: Oxford University Press, 1953.

Brereton, John. *A Briefe and true Relation of the Discovery of the North part of Virginia.* [London, 1602]. Excerpted in Wright, ed., *The Elizabethans' America,* 137-44.

————. *A Briefe and true Relation of the Discovery of the North part of Virginia.* [London, 1602]. March of America Facsimile Series, 16. Ann Arbor: University Microfilms, 1966.

Brotherston, Gordon. *Image of the New World: The American continent portrayed in native texts.* Trans. Gordon Brotherston and Ed Dorn. London: Thames and Hudson, 1979.

Browne, Sir Thomas. *Religio Medici.* [Ca. 1636; London, 1642, 1643]. In *Sir Thomas Browne: Selected Writings.* Ed. Sir Geoffrey Keynes. Chicago: University of Chicago Press, 1968.

Cabeza de Vaca, Alvar Nuñez. *Relation of Nuñez Cabeza de Vaca.* [New York, 1871]. Trans. by Buckingham Smith of *La relación que dio Alvar Nuñez Cabeza de Vaca de lo acaescido en las Indias en la armada donde yua por gobernador Pánfilo de Narváez desde el año de veynte y siete* . . . . [1542; Madrid, 1555]. March of America Facsimile Series, 9. Ann Arbor: University Microfilms, 1966.

Cartier, Jacques. *A Shorte And briefe narration of the two Nauigations and Discoueries to the Northwest partes called Newe Fravnce.* [London, 1580]. Trans. by John Florio of Giovanni Ramusio's Italian translation of Cartier's French original. [Venice, 1556]. March of America Facsimile Series, 10. Ann Arbor: University Microfilms, 1966.

Cary, Elizabeth. *The Tragedy of Mariam, The Fair Queen of Jewry,* with *The Lady Falkland, Her Life,* by one of her daughters. Ed. Barry Weller and Margaret W. Ferguson. Berkeley: University of California Press, 1994.

Casas, Bartolomé de las. *See* Las Casas, Bartolomé de.

Castañeda, Pedro de, et al. *The Journey of Coronado.* Trans. by George Parker Winship of *Relacion de la jornada de Cibola compuesta por Pedro de Castañeda de Nacera donde se trata de todos aquellos poblados y ritos, y costumbres, la cual fue el año de 1540.* San Francisco: Grabhorn Press, 1933. Rpt. New York: Dover Publications, 1990.

Castiglione, Baldesar. *The Book of the Courtier.* Trans. by George Bull of *Il Cortegiano.* [Venice, 1528]. Harmondsworth: Penguin, 1967.

Chanca, Diego Alvarez. "A Letter addressed to the Chapter of Seville." Trans. by R. H. Major of "La Carta del Doctor Chanca." [Ca. 1494]. In Columbus, et al., *Four Voyages to the New World: Letters and Selected Documents.* Bilingual edition. Trans. and ed. R. H. Major. Gloucester, MA: Peter Smith, 1978. 18-68.

————. "The Letter of Doctor Diego Alvarez Chanca, Dated 1494." Trans. Fernandez de Ybarra. *Smithsonian Miscellaneous Collections* 48 (1907): 428-57.

Chapman, George. "De Guiana, Carmen Epicum." In *The Poems of George Chapman.* Ed. Phyllis Brooks Bartlett. New York: Modern Language Association of America, 1941. 353-57.

Cieza de León, Pedro de. *La crónica del Perú.* [Seville, 1553]. BAE, Vol. 26. Madrid: M. Rivadeneyra, 1879.

Columbus, Christopher. *The Diario of Christopher Columbus's First Voyage to America, 1492-1493.* Abstracted by Fray Bartolomé de las Casas. Trans. and transcribed Oliver Dunn and James E. Kelley, Jr. Norman: University of Oklahoma Press, 1989.

————. *Four Voyages to the New World: Letters and Selected Documents.* Bilingual edition. Trans. and ed. R. H. Major. Gloucester, MA: Peter Smith, 1978.

————. *Journals and Other Documents on the Life and Voyages of Christopher Columbus.* Trans. and ed. Samuel Eliot Morison. New York: Heritage Press, 1963.

————. *The Journal of Christopher Columbus.* Trans. Cecil Jane. London: Anthony Blond, 1968.

————. *The Log of Christopher Columbus.* Trans. Robert H. Fuson. Camden, ME: International Marine, 1987.

Columbus, Ferdinand. *The Life of the Admiral Christopher Columbus by his Son Ferdinand.* Trans. by Benjamin Keen of *Historie . . . delle vita, & de' fatti dell'Ammiraglio D. Cristoforo Colombo.* [Venice, 1571]. New Brunswick: Rutgers University Press, 1959.

Conrad, Joseph. *Heart of Darkness.* [London, 1902]. In *The Portable Conrad.* Rev. ed. Ed. Morton Dauwen Zabel; revised Frederick R. Karl. Harmondsworth: Penguin, 1976. 490-603.

Cortés, Hernán. *Letters from Mexico.* Trans. and ed. Anthony Pagden; introduction by J. H. Elliott. New Haven: Yale University Press, 1986.

D'Ailly, Pierre. *Imago Mundi by Petrus Ailliacus.* [Ca. 1410.] Trans. Edwin F. Keever. Wilmington, NC: Linprint, 1948.

Defoe, Daniel. *The Life and Adventures of Robinson Crusoe.* [London, 1719]. Ed. Angus Ross. Harmondsworth: Penguin, 1965.

Díaz del Castillo, Bernal. *The Conquest of New Spain.* Trans. by J. M. Cohen of *Historia verdadera de la conquista de la Nueva-España.* [Ca. 1568; Madrid, 1632]. Harmondsworth: Penguin, 1963.

Donne, John. *The Complete English Poems.* Ed. A. J. Smith. Harmondsworth: Penguin, 1971.

Drake, Sir Francis (nephew of the admiral). *The World Encompassed.* [London, 1628]. March of America Facsimile Series, 11. Ann Arbor: University Microfilms, 1966.

———— *The World Encompassed by Sir Francis Drake, Being his next Voyage to that to Nombre de Dios, collated with an unpublished manuscript of Francis Fletcher, chaplain to the expedition.* Ed. W. S. W. Vaux. London: Hakluyt Society, 1854. Rpt. New York: Burt Franklin, n.d.

Drama of the English Renaissance. Ed. Russell A. Fraser and Norman Rabkin. 2 vols. New York: Macmillan, 1976.

Drayton, Michael. "Ode to the Virginian Voyage." In *Poetry of the English Renaissance, 1509-1660.* Ed. J. William Hebel and Hoyt J. Hudson. New York: Appleton-Century-Crofts, 1929. 296-97.

Durán, Fray Diego. *The Aztecs: The History of the Indies of New Spain.* Trans. by Doris Heyden and Fernando Horcasitas of Part One of *Historia de las Indias de Nueva España e Islas de Tierra Firme.* [Ca. 1581; Mexico City, 1867 and 1880]. New York: Orion Press, 1964.

————. *Book of the Gods and Rites and The Ancient Calendar*. Trans. by Fernando Horcasitas and Doris Heyden of Parts Two and Three of *Historia de las Indias de Nueva España e Islas de Tierra Firme*. [Ca. 1581; Mexico City: 1867 and 1880]. Norman: University of Oklahoma Press, 1971.

————. *Historia de las Indias de Nueva España e Islas de la Tierra Firme*. Ed. Angel Ma. Garibay K. 2 vols. Mexico City: Editorial Porrua, 1967.

Eden, Richard. *The Decades of the newe worlde or west India*. [London, 1555]. Trans. by Richard Eden of Decades 1-3 of Peter Martyr's *De orbe novo decades*. [Ca. 1511-30; Alcalá, 1516; Basel, 1533]. March of America Facsimile Series, 4. Ann Arbor: University Microfilms, 1966. Also in Arber, ed., *The first Three English books on America*. Birmingham, 1885.

————. *A Treatyse of the newe India*. [London, 1553]. Trans. by Richard Eden of part of the fifth book of Sebastian Münster's *Cosmographiae universalis*. [1544]. March of America Facsimile Series, 3. Ann Arbor: University Microfilms, 1966. Also in Arber, ed., *The first Three English books on America*. Birmingham, 1885.

The Elizabethans' America: A Collection of Early Reports by Englishmen on the New World. Ed. Louis B. Wright. Cambridge: Harvard University Press, 1965.

Emerson, Ralph Waldo. "Montaigne; Or, the Skeptic." [Ca. 1844-45]. In *Representative Men*. [Boston, 1850]. Rpt. in *Selections from Ralph Waldo Emerson: An Organic Anthology*. Ed. Stephen E. Whicher. Boston: Houghton Mifflin, 1957. 284-301.

English Sixteenth-Century Verse: An Anthology. Ed. Richard S. Sylvester. New York and London: Norton, 1984.

"The famous voyage of Sir Francis Drake into the South sea, and therehence about the whole Globe of the earth, begun in the yeere of our Lord, 1577." In Richard Hakluyt, *Principal Navigations*, vol. 11, 101-33.

The first Three English books on America, being chiefly Translations, Compilations, &c., by Richard Eden. Ed. Edward Arber. Birmingham, 1885.

Fuller, Thomas. "Of Plantations." In *The Holy State and the Profane State*. [London, 1642]. Ed. Maximilian Graff Walten. Vol. 2. New York: Columbia University Press, 1938. 193-94.

Garcilaso de la Vega, El Inca. *The Florida of the Inca*. Trans. by John Grier Varner and Jeannette Johnson Varner of *La Florida del Ynca: Historia del Adelantado Hernando de Soto, Governador y capitan general del Reyno de la Florida, y de otros heroicos cavalleros Españoles è Indios*. [Lisbon, 1605]. Austin: University of Texas Press, 1962.

————. *The Incas: The Royal Commentaries of the Inca Garcilaso de la Vega, 1539-1616*. Trans. by Maria Jolas of *Comentarios reales de los Incas*. [Lisbon, 1609; Cordova, 1617]. New York: Orion Press, 1961.

————. *Royal Commentaries of the Incas*. Trans. by H. V. Livermore of *Comentarios reales de los Incas*. [Lisbon, 1609; Cordova, 1617]. 2 vols. Austin: University of Texas Press, 1966.

The Geneva Bible: A Facsimile of the 1560 Edition. Intro. by Lloyd E. Berry. Madison and Milwaukee: University of Wisconsin Press, 1969.

Gilbert, Sir Humphrey. *A Discovrse of a Discouerie for a new Passage to Cataia.* [London, 1576]. Facsimile edition. Amsterdam: Theatrum Orbis Terrarum, 1968.

Gómara, Francisco López de. *The Pleasant Historie of the Conquest of Weast India.* [London, 1578]. Trans. and abridgment by Thomas Nicholas of the second part of *La Historia de las Indias y Conquista de México.* [Saragossa, 1552]. March of America Facsimile Series, 6. Ann Arbor: University Microfilms, 1966.

————. *Cortés: The Life of the Conqueror by His Secretary.* Trans. by Lesley Byrd Simpson of the second part of *La Historia de las Indias y Conquista de México.* [Saragossa, 1552]. Berkeley: University of California Press, 1964.

Gray, Robert. "A Good Speed to Virginia." [London, 1609]. *The Genesis of the United States.* Ed. Alexander Brown. Vol. 1. New York: Russell and Russell, 1964. 293-302.

Greene, Robert. *The Spanish Masquerado.* [London, 1589]. In *The Life and Complete Works in Prose and Verse of Robert Greene, M.A.* Ed. Alexander B. Grosart, LL.D. Vol. 5. London, 1881-86. Rpt. New York: Russell and Russell, 1964. 235-88.

Guaman Poma de Ayala, Felipe. *El primer nueva corónica y buen gobierno.* [Ca. 1613]. Ed. John Murra and Rolena Adorno. Mexico City: Siglo XXI, 1980.

Hakluyt, Richard (the elder). "Inducements to the liking of the voyage intended towards Virginia." [Ms. 1585]. In John Brereton's *A Briefe and true Relation of the Discouerie of the North part of Virginia.* [London, 1602]. Ann Arbor: University Microfilms, 1966. 25-36.

————. "Notes framed by a Gentleman heretofore to bee giuen to one that prepared for a discouerie." [Ca. 1578]. In *Divers voyages touching the discouerie of America.* Ed. Richard Hakluyt. [London, 1582]. Ann Arbor: University Microfilms, 1966. Folios K-K3.

Hakluyt, Richard (the younger). *Divers voyages touching the discouerie of America.* [London, 1582]. March of America Facsimile Series, 5. Ann Arbor: University Microfilms, 1966.

————. *The Principal Navigations Voyages Traffiques and Discoveries of the English Nation.* [London, 1589-90, 1598-1600]. 12 vols. Glasgow: J. MacLehose and Sons, 1903-1904. Rpt. New York: AMS Press, 1965.

————. *Voyages and Discoveries.* Ed. and abridged Jack Beeching. Harmondsworth: Penguin, 1972.

Harcourt, Robert. *A Relation of a Voyage to Guiana.* [London, 1613].

Harriot, Thomas. *A briefe and true report of the new found land of Virginia.* [London, 1588]. In Quinn, ed., *Virginia Voyages,* 46-76.

————. *A briefe and true report of the new found land of Virginia.* [Frankfurt, 1590]. With engravings by Theodor de Bry based on drawings by John White. Ed. Paul Hulton. New York: Dover Publications, 1972.

Harrison, William. *The Description of England.* [London, 1577, 1587]. Ed. Georges Edelen. Ithaca: Cornell University Press, 1968.

Herodotus. *The Histories.* Trans. Aubrey de Sélincourt; rev. A. R. Burn. Harmondsworth: Penguin, 1972.

Hobbes, Thomas. *Leviathan.* [London, 1651]. Ed. C. B. Macpherson. Harmondsworth: Penguin, 1968.

Homer. *The Iliad.* Trans. Robert Fitzgerald. New York: Anchor Doubleday, 1974.

———. *The Odyssey.* Trans. Robert Fitzgerald. New York: Anchor Doubleday, 1963.

Ingram, David. *The Relation of Dauid Ingram of Barking* (as presented by Richard Hakluyt in the first edition of *Principal Navigations*). [London, 1589]. March of America Facsimile Series, 14. Ann Arbor: University Microfilms, 1966.

Jacobean Tragedies. Ed. A. H. Gomme. Oxford: Oxford University Press, 1969.

James I. *Daemonologie.* [Edinburgh, 1597]. Edinburgh: Edinburgh University Press, 1966.

The Jamestown Voyages under the First Charter, 1606-1609. Ed. Philip L. Barbour. Hakluyt Society, 2d Series. 2 vols. Cambridge: Hakluyt Society, 1969. 136-37.

Jonson, Ben. "Newes from the New World Discover'd in the Moone. A Masque, as it was presented at covrt before King James. 1620." In *Ben Jonson.* Ed. C. H. Herford and Percy and Evelyn Simpson. Vol. 7. Oxford: Clarendon Press, 1925-52. 511-25.

———. *Sejanus.* [London, 1605]. Ed. Jonas A. Barish. New Haven: Yale University Press, 1965.

———. *Timber, or Discoveries.* [London, 1640-41]. In *Ben Jonson.* Ed. C. H. Herford and Percy and Evelyn Simpson. Vol. 8. Oxford: Clarendon Press, 1925-52. 555-649.

Jourdain, Silvester. *A Discovery of the Barmudas, Otherwise Called the Isle of Devils.* [London, 1610]. In Wright, *A Voyage to Virginia in 1609.*

Kant, Immanuel. *Critique of Pure Reason.* [Riga, 1781, 1787]. Trans. Norman Kemp Smith. New York: St. Martin's Press, 1965.

———. *Proloegomena to any Future Metaphysics That Will Be Able to Present Itself as a Science.* [1783]. Trans. Peter G. Lucas. Manchester: Manchester University Press, 1953.

Keymis, Laurence. *A Relation of the Second Voyage to Guiana.* [London, 1596].

La Rochefoucauld, François de. *Maxims.* Trans. by Leonard Tancock of *Réflexions ou sentences et maximes morales.* [Paris, 1665]. Harmondsworth: Penguin, 1959.

Landa, Diego de. *The Maya. Diego de Landa's "Account of the Affairs of Yucatán".* Trans. by A. R. Pagden of *Relación de las cosas de Yucatán.* [Ca. 1566; Paris, 1864]. Chicago: J. Philip O'Hara, 1975.

Las Casas, Bartolomé de. *The Devastation of the Indies: A Brief Account.* Trans. by Herma Briffault of *Brevísima relación de la destrucción de las Indias occidentales.* [Seville, 1552]. New York: Seabury Press, 1974. Rpt. Baltimore: Johns Hopkins University Press, 1992.

———. *History of the Indies.* Trans. by Andrée Collard of *Historia de las Indias.* [Ca. 1559; Madrid, 1875]. Ed. Andrée Collard. New York: Harper and Row, 1971.

———. *In Defense of the Indians: The Defense of the Most Reverend Lord, Don Fray Bartolomé de Las Casas, of the Order of Preachers, Late Bishop of Chiapa, Against the Persecutors and Slanderers of the Peoples of the New World Discovered Across the Seas.* Trans. and ed. by Stafford Poole, C.M., of the *Apologia.* [Ca. 1550]. DeKalb: Northern Illinois University Press, 1974.

————. "The 'Only Method' of Converting the Indians." Trans. by George Sanderlin of *Del unico modo de atraer a todos los pueblos a la verdadera religión*. [1537]. In *Bartolomé de Las Casas: A Selection of His Writings*. Trans. and ed. George Sanderlin. New York: Knopf, 1971. 157-63.

————. *Bartolomé de Las Casas: A Selection of His Writings*. Trans. and ed. George Sanderlin. New York: Knopf, 1971.

————. *A Short Account of the Destruction of the Indies*. Trans. by Nigel Griffin of *Brevísima relación de la destrucción de las Indias occidentales*. [Seville, 1552]. Intro. by Anthony Pagden. Harmondsworth: Penguin, 1992.

————. *The Spanish Colonie, or Briefe Chronicle of the Acts and gestes of the Spaniards in the West Indies*. [London, 1583]. Trans. by M. M. S. of the French version [Antwerp, 1579] of *Brevísima relación de la destrucción de las Indias occidentales*. [Seville, 1552]. March of America Facsimile Series, 8. Ann Arbor: University Microfilms, 1966.

————. *The Tears of the Indians*. [London, 1656]. Trans. by John Phillips of *Brevísima relación de la destrucción de las Indias occidentales*. [Seville, 1552]. Stanford: Academic Reprints, n.d.

The Last Voyage of Thomas Cavendish, 1591-1592. Ed. David Beers Quinn. Chicago: University of Chicago Press, 1976.

Last Voyages: Cavendish, Hudson, Ralegh: The Original Narratives. Ed. Philip Edwards. Oxford: Clarendon Press, 1988.

Le Roy, Louis (Regius). *Of the Interchangeable Course, or Variety of Things in the whole World . . . Written in French by Loys le Roy called Regius: and Translated into English by R. A*. [London, 1594]. Trans. of *De la vicissitude ou varieté des choses en l'univers*. [Paris, 1575].

Léry, Jean de. *History of a Voyage to the Land of Brazil, Otherwise Called America*. Trans. by Janet Whatley of *Histoire d'un voyage faict en la terre du Bresil, autrement dite Amérique*. [Geneva, 1578]. Berkeley: University of California Press, 1990.

Lescarbot, Marc. *History of New France*. Trans. by W. L. Grant of *Histoire de la Nouvelle France*. [Paris, 1609]. 3 vols. Toronto, 1907-14.

————. *Nova Francia: A Description of Acadia*. [1606]. London: Routledge, 1928.

Lyly, John. *The Complete Works of John Lyly*. Ed. R. Warwick Bond. 3 vols. [London, 1902]. Oxford: Clarendon Press, 1967.

Machiavelli, Niccolò. *The Prince*. Trans. by Christian E. Detmold of *Il Principe*. [1513; Rome, 1532]. New York: Washington Square Press, 1963.

————. *The Prince*. Trans. by Robert M. Adams of *Il Principe*. [1513; Rome, 1532]. New York: Norton, 1977.

Magellan's Voyage, A Narrative Account of the First Circumnavigation, by Antonio Pigafetta. Trans. of a French version, by R. A. Skelton. 2 vols. New Haven: Yale University Press, 1969.

Magellan's Voyage Around the World. Ed. James Alexander Robinson. Cleveland: Arthur Clarke, 1906.

Martyr, Peter (Pietro Martire d'Anghiera). *The Decades of the newe worlde or west India*. [London, 1555]. Trans. by Richard Eden of Decades 1-3 of *De orbe novo decades*. [Ca.

1511-30; Alcalá, 1516; Basel, 1533]. In Arber, ed., *The first Three English books on America*. Birmingham, 1885. 43-398.

———. *The Decades of the newe worlde or west India*. [London, 1555]. Trans. by Richard Eden of Decades 1-3 of *De orbe novo decades*. March of America Facsimile Series, 4. Ann Arbor: University Microfilms, 1966.

———. *De Orbe Novo: The Eight Decades of Peter Martyr D'Anghera*. Trans. by Francis Augustus MacNutt of Decades 1-8 of *De orbe novo decades*. 2 vols. New York: Putnam's, 1912. Rpt. New York: Burt Franklin, 1970.

———. *De Orbe Novo or the Historie of the West Indies, etc., comprised in eight decades. Whereof three have beene formerly translated into English by R. Eden, whereunto the other five are newly added by the industries and painfull Travails of M. Lok*. London, 1612.

Marvell, Andrew. *The Complete Poems*. Ed. Elizabeth Story Donno. Harmondsworth: Penguin, 1972.

Melville, Herman. *Typee: A Peep at Polynesian Life During a Four Months' Residence in a Valley of the Marquesas*. [London, 1846]. New York: Signet, 1964.

Milton, John. *Paradise Lost*. [London, 1667, 1674]. In *John Milton: Complete Poems and Major Prose*. Ed. Merritt Y. Hughes. Indianapolis: Bobbs-Merrill, 1957.

Monardes, Nicolas. *Joyfull Newes out of the Newe Worlde*. [London, 1577]. Trans. by John Frampton of *Segunda parte de las Indias Occidentales*. [Seville, 1571]. Ed. Stephen Gaselee. 2 vols. London, 1925. Rpt. New York: AMS, 1967.

Montaigne, Michel de. *An Apology for Raymond Sebond*. [Ca. 1575-76]. Trans. M. A. Screech. Harmondsworth: Penguin, 1987.

———. *The Complete Essays of Montaigne*. Trans. Donald M. Frame. Stanford: Stanford University Press, 1957.

———. *Les Essais*. [Bordeaux, 1580; Paris, 1588]. Ed. Pierre Villey, and reissued under the direction of V. L. Saulnier. 2d ed. 3 vols. Paris: Presses Universitaires de France, 1992.

———. *The Essayes of Michael Lord of Montaigne*. Trans. John Florio. [London, 1603]. New York: The Modern Library, 1933.

———. *Montaigne's Essays and Selected Writings: A Bilingual Edition*. Trans. and ed. Donald M. Frame. New York: St. Martin's Press, 1963.

———. *Oeuvres complètes*. Ed. Albert Thibaudet and Maurice Rat. Bibliothèque de la Pléiade. Paris: Éditions Gallimard, 1962.

More, Thomas. *The Complete Works of St. Thomas More*. Ed. J. H. Hexter and E. Surtz. 4 vols. New Haven: Yale University Press, 1965.

———. *Utopia*. [Louvain, 1516]. Trans. and ed. Robert M. Adams. 2d ed. New York: Norton, 1992.

Motolinía, Fray Toribio de Benavente. *Motolinía's History of the Indians of New Spain*. Trans. by Elizabeth Andros Foster of *Historia de los Indios de la Nueva España*. [Ca. 1541; 1858]. Berkeley: Cortés Society, Bancroft Library, 1950.

Mucedorus. [London, 1598, 1610]. In *Drama of the English Renaissance.* Ed. Russell A. Fraser and Norman Rabkin. Vol. 1. New York: Macmillan, 1976. 463-80.

Münster, Sebastian. *See* Eden, Richard.

New Iberian World: A Documentary History of the Discovery and Settlement of Latin America to the Early 17th Century. Ed. John H. Parry and Robert G. Keith. 5 vols. New York: Times Books, 1984.

The New World. The First Pictures of America . . . With Contemporary Narratives. Ed. and annotated Stefan Lorant. New York: Duell, Sloane and Pearce, 1946.

"Of the newe landes and of ye people founde by the messengers of the kynge of portyngale named Emanuel." [Antwerp, no later than 1511]. In Edward Arber, ed., *The first Three English books on America.* Birmingham, 1885.

Ovid. *The Metamorphoses of Ovid.* Trans. Mary M. Innes. Harmondsworth: Penguin, 1955.

Oviedo y Valdés, Gonzalo Fernández de. *La historia general y natural de las Indias, islas y Tierra-Firme del mar Océano.* [Seville, 1535]. Ed. Juan Perez de Tudela Bueso. In *Biblioteca de Autores Españoles Desde la Formacion del Lenguaje Hasta Nuestros Dias.* Madrid: Ediciones Atlas, 1959. Vols. 117-20.

————. *The hystorie of the Weste Indies, wrytten by Gonzalus Ferdinandus.* Trans. by Richard Eden of selected passages from *Crónica de las Indias: La historia general y natural de las Indias, islas y Tierra-Firme del mar Océano, primera parte.* [Seville, 1535]. In *The Decades of the newe worlde or west India.* [London, 1555]. Ann Arbor: University Microfilms, 1966. 174-215.

————. *Natural History of the West Indies.* Trans. and ed. by Sterling A. Stoudemire of *Crónica de las Indias: La historia general y natural de las Indias, islas y Tierra-Firme del mar Océano, primera parte.* [Seville, 1535]. University of North Carolina Studies in the Romance Languages and Literature, No. 32. Chapel Hill: University of North Carolina Press, 1959.

Pané, Ramon. "Treatise of Friar Ramon on the Antiquities of the Indians Which He as One Who Knows Their Language Diligently Collected by Command of the Admiral." Trans. by Edward Gaylord Bourne of "Relación acerca de las antigüedades de los Indios." [Ca. 1493-96]. In "Columbus, Ramon Pane and the Beginnings of American Anthropology." *Proceedings of the American Antiquarian Society* 17 (April 1906): 310-48.

Pascal, Blaise. *Pascal's Pensées.* [Ca. 1660-62]. Trans. W. S. Trotter. Introduction by T. S. Eliot. New York: Dutton, 1958.

Pico della Mirandola, Giovanni. "Oration on the Dignity of Man." [Ca. 1486]. Trans. Elizabeth Livermore Forbes. In *The Renaissance Philosophy of Man.* Ed. Ernst Cassirer, Paul Oskar Kristeller, and John Herman Randall, Jr. Chicago: University of Chicago Press, 1948. 223-54.

Pigafetta, Antonio. "A briefe declaration of the vyage or nauigation made abowte the worlde. Gathered owt of a large booke wrytten hereof by master Antonie Pygafetta Vincentine, knyght of the Rhodes." In Richard Eden, *Decades,* 217-33. Also in Edward Arber, ed., *First Three Books,* 249-62.

Poetry of the English Renaissance, 1509-1660. Ed. J. William Hebel and Hoyt J. Hudson. New York: Appleton-Century-Crofts, 1929.

Pope Alexander VI. "The Bull of Donation." [Rome, 1493]. In Richard Eden, *The Decades of the newe worlde or west India.* [London, 1555]. March of America Facsimile Series, 4. Ann Arbor: University Microfilms, 1966. 167-73.

Pope Paul III. "The Bull *Sublimis Deus.*" [Rome, 1537]. In Francis Augustus MacNutt, *Bartholomew De Las Casas: His Life, His Apostolate, His Writings.* New York and London: Putnam's, 1909. 426-31.

Portuondo, Fernando, ed. *El Segundo Viaje del Descubrimiento.* Havana: Ciencias Sociales, 1977.

Purchas, Samuel. *Hakluytus Posthumous, or Purchas His Pilgrimes.* [London, 1625]. 20 vols. Glasgow: MacLehose, 1905-07.

Puttenham, George. *The Arte of English Poesie.* [London, 1589]. Ed. G. D. Willcock and A. Walker. Cambridge: Cambridge University Press, 1936.

Ralegh, Sir Walter. *The Discoverie of the Large, Rich and Beautiful Empire of Guiana.* [London, 1596]. In *Sir Walter Ralegh: Selected Writings.* Ed. Gerald Hammond. Manchester: Carcanet Press, 1984. 76-123.

———. *The History of the World.* [London, 1614]. 6 vols. Edinburgh: Archibald Constable, 1820.

Ramusio, Giovanni Battista. *Delle Navigationi et Viaggi.* [Venice, 1556]. 3 vols. Facsimile edition. Amsterdam: Theatrum Orbis Terrarum, 1970.

Rastell, John. *The Interlude of the Four Elements: An Early Moral Play.* [Ca. 1518]. Ed. J. O. Halliwell. Vol. 22 of *Early English Poetry.* London: Percy Society, 1848.

"The Requirement." Trans. by Lewis Hanke of the "Requerimiento." [Ca. 1513]. In *History of Latin American Civilization: Sources and Interpretations.* Ed. Lewis Hanke. Vol. 1. Boston: Little, Brown, 1967. 123-25. Rpt. in *New Iberian World, vol. 1,* 288-90.

Rich, Richard. *Newes from Virginia: The Lost Flocke Triumphant.* [London, 1610]. In *The Genesis of the United States.* Ed. Alexander Brown. Vol. 1. New York: Russell and Russell, 1964. 420-26.

Rogers, Thomas. *The Faith, Doctrine, and Religion, Professed and Protected in the Realm of England, and Dominions of the Same, Expressed in 39 Articles.* [Cambridge, 1607]. Rpt. as *The Catholic Doctrine of the Church of England: An Exposition of the Thirty-Nine Articles.* [Cambridge, 1854]. Rpt. New York: Johnson Reprint, 1968.

Rosier, James. *A True Relation of the most prosperous voyage made this present year 1605 by Captaine George Waymouth in the Discovery of the land of Virginia.* [London, 1605]. Excerpted in Wright, *The Elizabethans' America,* 144-54.

———. *A True Relation of the most prosperous voyage made this present year 1605 by Captaine George Waymouth in the Discovery of the land of Virginia.* [London, 1605]. March of America Facsimile Series, 17. Ann Arbor: University Microfilms, 1966.

Rousseau, Jean-Jacques. *Discourse on the Origin of Inequality.* Trans. of *Discours sur l'origin de l'inégalité parmi les hommes.* [Amsterdam, 1754]. In *Jean-Jacques Rousseau: The Basic Political Writings.* Trans. and ed. Donald A. Cress. Indianapolis: Hackett, 1987. 23-109.

Rowlandson, Mary. *The Captive: The True Story of the Captivity of Mrs. Mary Rowlandson Among the Indians and God's Faithfulness to her in her Time of Trial.* [Cambridge, 1682]. Tucson: American Eagle, 1990.

Sahagún, Fray Bernardino de. *Florentine Codex: General History of the Things of New Spain.* Trans. and ed. Arthur J. O. Anderson and Charles E. Dibble of the Nahuatl text of *Historia general de las cosas de Nueva España* [Ca. 1547-77]. 13 vols. Santa Fe and Salt Lake City: School of American Research and University of Utah, 1955-82.

———. *Historia general de las cosas de Nueva España.* [Ca. 1547-77; Mexico City, 1829]. Ed. Miguel Acosta Saignes. 3 vols. Mexico City: Editorial Nueva España, 1946.

———. *A History of Ancient Mexico.* Trans. by Fanny R. Bandelier of Carlos Maria de Bustamante's transcription of Sahagún's *Historia general de las cosas de Nueva España.* Glorieta, NM: Rio Grande Press, 1976.

Schouten, Willem Cornelisz. *The Relation of a Wonderfull Voiage made by William Cornelison Schouten.* [London, 1619]. Trans. by William Philip of *Journal ofte Beschryvinghe van de wonderlicke reyse ghedaen door Willem Cornelisz Schouten.* [Amsterdam, 1618]. Cleveland: World Publishing, 1966.

Select Documents Illustrating the Four Voyages of Columbus. Trans. and ed. Cecil Jane. London: Hakluyt Society, 2d Series, nos. 65 and 70, 1930-32.

Sepúlveda, Juan Ginés de. *Democrates segundo, o de las justas causas de la guerra contra los indios.* [Ca. 1544]. Ed. Angel Losada. Madrid: Consejo Superior de Investigaciones Cientifícas, Instituto Francisco de Vitoria, 1951.

Settle, Dionyse. *A true reporte of the laste voyage into the West and Northwest regions, etc., 1577, worthily atchieued by Capteine Frobisher.* [London, 1577]. Facsimile edition. Amsterdam: Theatrum Orbis Terrarum, 1969.

Seventeenth Century Poetry. The Schools of Donne and Jonson. Ed. Hugh Kenner. New York: Holt, Rinehart and Winston, 1964.

Shakespeare, William. *The Parallel King Lear, 1608-1623.* Prepared by Michael Warren. Berkeley: University of California Press, 1989.

———. *The Riverside Shakespeare.* Ed. G. Blakemore Evans, et al. Boston: Houghton Mifflin, 1974.

———. *The Tempest.* Ed. Frank Kermode. London: Methuen, 1954.

———. *The Tempest.* Ed. Stephen Orgel. Oxford: Clarendon Press, 1987.

Sidney, Sir Philip. "An Apologie for Poetrie." [Ca. 1580-82; London, 1595]. In *The Great Critics.* Ed. James Harry Smith and Edd Winfield Parks. New York: Norton, 1967. 187-232.

———. *The Countess of Pembroke's Arcadia.* [Ca. 1580-84; London, 1593]. Ed. Maurice Evans. Harmondsworth: Penguin, 1977.

Smith, Captain John. *The Complete Works of Captain John Smith (1580-1631).* Ed. Philip L. Barbour. 3 vols. Chapel Hill: University of North Carolina Press, 1986.

———. *Captain John Smith: A Select Edition of His Writings.* Ed. Karen Ordahl Kupperman. Chapel Hill: University of North Carolina Press, 1988.

Spenser, Edmund. *The Faerie Queene*. [London, 1590, 1596, 1609]. Ed. Thomas P. Roche, Jr., with the assistance of C. Patrick O'Donnell, Jr. New Haven: Yale University Press, 1981.

———. *A View of the Present State of Ireland*. [Ca. 1596; Dublin, 1633]. Ed. W. L. Renwick. Oxford: Clarendon Press, 1970.

———. *The Works of Edmund Spenser: A Variorum Edition*. Ed. Edwin Greenlaw, Charles Grosvenor Osgood, Frederick Morgan Padelford, and Ray Heffner. 12 vols. Baltimore: Johns Hopkins University Press, 1932-57.

Staden, Hans. *Hans Staden: The True History of His Captivity*. Trans. by Malcolm Letts of *Warhaftig Historia und Beschreibung eyner Landtschafft der wilden, nacketen, grimmigen, Menschfressen Leuthen, in der Newenwelt America gelegen*. [Marburg, 1557]. London: Routledge, 1928.

Strachey, William. *The Historie of Travell into Virginia Britannia*. [London, 1612]. Ed. Louis B. Wright and Virginia Freund. Hakluyt Society, 2d Series, no. 103. London: Hakluyt Society, 1953.

———. *A true repertory of the wracke, and redemption of Sir Thomas Gates Knight*. [Ca. 1610]. In Samuel Purchas, *Hakluytus Posthumous*, vol. 19, 5-67. Rpt. in Wright, *A Voyage to Virginia in 1609*.

Swift, Jonathan. *The Writings of Jonathan Swift: Authoritative Texts, Background, Criticism*. Ed. Robert A. Greenberg and William Bowman Piper. New York: Norton, 1973.

Tacitus, Cornelius. *The Agricola and the Germania*. Trans. by Harold Mattingly (with revisions by S. A. Handford) of *De origine et situ Germanorum*. [Ca. a.d. 98]. Harmondsworth: Penguin, 1970.

Thevet, André. *André Thévet's North America: A Sixteenth-Century View*. Ed. Roger Schlesinger and Arthur P. Stabler. Kingston and Montréal: McGill-Queen's University Press, 1986.

———. *The New Found Worlde, or Antarctike*. [London, 1568]. Trans. by Thomas Hacket of *Les singularitéz de la France antarctique, autrement nommée Amerique*. [Paris, 1558]. Facsimile edition. Amsterdam: Theatrum Orbis Terrarum, 1971.

The Three Voyages of Martin Frobisher. Ed. Vilhjalmur Stefansson. 2 vols. London: Argonaut Press, 1938. Rpt. New York: Da Capo Press, 1971.

Tracts and Other Papers, Relating Principally to the Origin, Settlement, and Progress of the Colonies in North America. Ed. Peter Force. 4 vols. New York: Peter Smith, 1947.

A True Declaration of the Estate of the Colonie in Virginia. [London, 1610]. In Force, *Tracts*, vol. 3.

Vaca, Alvar Nuñez Cabeza de. *See* Cabeza de Vaca, Alvar Nuñez.

Vega, Garcilaso de la (El Inca). *See* Garcilaso de la Vega, El Inca.

The Voyages of Giovanni da Verrazano, 1524-1528. Ed. Lawrence C. Wroth. New Haven and London: Yale University Press, 1970.

Vespucci, Amerigo. *The Letters of Amerigo Vespucci and Other Documents Illustrative of his Career*. Trans. Clements R. Markham. Hakluyt Society, 1st Series, number 90. London: Hakluyt Society, 1894.

———. *Mundus Novus: Letter to Lorenzo Pietro di Medici.* Trans. by George T. Northrup of *Mundus Novus Albericus Vespucius Laurentio Petri de Medicis.* [Basel, 1503-05]. Vol. 5 of *Vespucci Reprints, Texts, and Studies.* Princeton: Princeton University Press, 1916.

Vico, Giambattista. *The New Science of Giambattista Vico.* [3d ed, Naples, 1744]. Trans. Thomas Goddard Bergin and Max Harold Fisch. Ithaca: Cornell University Press, 1968.

Virginia richly valued, By the description of the maine land of Florida. [London, 1609]. Trans. by Richard Hakluyt (the younger) of the anonymous *Relaçam verdadeira dos trabalhos.* [Evora, Portugal, 1557]. March of America Facsimile Series, 12. Ann Arbor: University Microfilms, 1966.

Virginia Voyages from Hakluyt. Ed. David B. Quinn and Alison M. Quinn. London: Oxford University Press, 1973.

A Voyage to Virginia in 1609: Two Narratives. Ed. Louis B. Wright. Charlottesville: University Press of Virginia, 1964.

The Voyages of Colonising Enterprises of Sir Humphrey Gilbert. Ed. David B. Quinn. Hakluyt Society, 2d Series, nos. 83-84. London: Hakluyt Society, 1940.

Waldseemüller, Martin. *Cosmographiae Introductio.* [St. Dié, 1507]. Trans. Joseph Fischer and Franz von Wieser. March of America Facsimile Series, 2. Ann Arbor: University Microfilms, 1966.

Whitaker, Alexander. *Good Newes from Virginia.* [London, 1613]. New York: Scholars' Facsimiles and Reprints, 1936.

The World Encompassed and Analogous Contemporary Documents Concerning Sir Francis Drake's Circumnavigation of the World. Ed. N. M. Penzer. [London, 1926]. New York: Cooper Square, 1969.

Zárate, Augustín de. *The Discovery and Conquest of Peru.* Trans. by J. M. Cohen of *Historia del descubrimiento y conquista del Peru.* [Antwerp, 1555; English trans. by Thomas Nicholas, London, 1581]. Harmondsworth: Penguin, 1968.

Zorita, Alonso de. *Life and Labor in Ancient Mexico: The Brief and Summary Relation of the Lords of New Spain.* Trans. by Benjamin Keen of *Breve y sumaria relación de los señores de la Nueva España.* [Ca. 1570; Mexico City, 1891]. New Brunswick: Rutgers University Press, 1963.

Secondary Materials

Adorno, Rolena. "Arms, Letters and the Native Historian in Early Colonial Mexico." *Hispanic Issues 4: 1492-1992: Re/Discovering Colonial Writing* (1989): 201-24.

———. "The Negotiation of Fear in Cabeza de Vaca's *Naufragios.*" *Representations 33* (Winter 1991): 163-99.

Allen, Don Cameron. *Doubt's Boundless Sea: Skepticism and Faith in the Renaissance.* Baltimore: Johns Hopkins University Press, 1964.

Alpers, Paul. "The Eclogue Tradition and the Nature of Pastoral." *College English 34* (1972): 352-71.

————. "Empson on Pastoral." *New Literary History* 10 (1978): 101-23.

————. *The Poetry of* The Faerie Queene. Princeton: Princeton University Press, 1967.

————. "What is Pastoral?" *Critical Inquiry* 8 (1982): 437-60.

Althusser, Louis. *Lenin and Philosophy and Other Essays*. Trans. Ben Brewster. New York: Monthly Review Press, 1971.

Anderson, Perry. *Considerations on Western Marxism*. London: Verso, 1979.

Andrews, K. R., N. P. Canny, P. E. H. Hair, eds. *The Westward Enterprise: English Activities in Ireland, the Atlantic, and America, 1480-1650*. Liverpool: Liverpool University Press, 1978.

Annas, Julia, and Barnes, Jonathan. *The Modes of Scepticism: Ancient Texts and Modern Interpretations*. Cambridge: Cambridge University Press, 1985.

Archer, Mark. "The Meaning of 'Grace' and 'Courtesy': Book Six of *The Faerie Queene*." *Studies in English Literature, 1500-1900* 27:1 (Winter 1987): 17-34.

Arciniegas, Germán. *America In Europe: A History of the New World in Reverse*. [1975]. Trans. Gabriela Arciniegas and R. Victoria Arana. San Diego: Harcourt, Brace, Jovanovich, 1986.

————. *Amerigo and the New World: The Life and Times of Amerigo Vespucci*. Trans. H. de Onís. New York: Knopf, 1955.

Atkinson, Geoffroy. *The Extraordinary Voyage in French Literature Before 1700*. New York: Columbia University Press, 1920.

————. *Les Nouveaux Horizons de la Renaissance Française*. Paris: Librairie E. Droz, 1935.

Auden, W. H. "The Sea and the Mirror: A Commentary on Shakespeare's *The Tempest*." In *The Collected Poetry of W. H. Auden*. New York: Random House, 1945. 351-404.

Axtell, James. *After Columbus: Essays in the Ethnohistory of Colonial North America*. New York: Oxford University Press, 1988.

————. *The European and the Indian: Essays in the Ethnohistory of Colonial North America*. New York: Oxford University Press, 1981.

————. *The Invasion Within: The Contest of Cultures in North America*. Oxford: Oxford University Press, 1985.

Barber, C. L. *Shakespeare's Festive Comedy: A Study of Dramatic Form and its Relation to Social Custom*. Princeton: Princeton University Press, 1959.

Barker, Francis, and Peter Hulme. "Nymphs and reapers heavily vanish: the discursive con-texts of *The Tempest*." In *Alternative Shakespeares*. Ed. John Drakakis. London: Methuen, 1985. 191-205.

Bataillon, Marcel. *Etudes sur Bartolomé de las Casas*. Paris: Centre de Recherches de l'Institut d'Etudes Hispaniques, 1965.

Baudet, Henri. *Paradise on Earth: Some Thoughts on European Images of Non-European Man*. Trans. Elizabeth Wentholt. New Haven: Yale University Press, 1965.

Bausum, Henry. "Edenic Images of the Western World: A Reappraisal." *South Atlantic Quarterly* 67 (Autumn 1968): 672-87.

Bennett, Tony. *Formalism and Marxism.* London: Methuen, 1979.

Berger, Jr., Harry. "Miraculous Harp: A Reading of Shakespeare's *Tempest.*" *Shakespeare Studies* 5 (1969): 353-83. Rpt. in Berger, *Second World and Green World: Studies in Renaissance Fiction-Making.* Berkeley: University of California Press, 1988. 147-85.

————. "A Secret Discipline: *The Faerie Queene,* Book VI." In *Form and Convention in the Poetry of Edmund Spenser.* Ed. William Nelson. English Institute Essays. New York: Columbia University Press, 1961. 35-75.

Berkhofer Jr., Robert F. *The White Man's Indian: Images of the American Indian from Columbus to the Present.* New York: Vintage Books, 1979.

Bernal, Ignacio. *Mexico Before Cortez: Art, History and Legend.* Trans. Willis Barnstone. Garden City, NY: Dolphin Books, 1963.

Bernheimer, Richard. *Wild Men in the Middle Ages: A Study in Art, Sentiment, and Demonology.* Cambridge: Harvard University Press, 1952.

Bhabha, Homi K. "Difference, discrimination and the discourse of colonialism." In *The Politics of Theory.* Ed. Francis Barker, Peter Hulme, Margaret Iverson, and Diana Loxley. Colchester: University of Essex, 1983.

————. "Of mimicry and man: The ambivalence of colonial discourse." *October* 28 (1984): 125-33.

Bitterli, Urs. *Cultures in Conflict: Encounters Between European and Non-European Cultures, 1492-1800.* [Munich, 1986]. Trans. Ritchie Robertson. Stanford: Stanford University Press, 1989.

Black, James. "The Monster in Shakespeare's Landscape." *The Elizabethan Theatre VIII.* Ed. G. R. Hibbard. Port Credit: P. D. Meany, 1982. 51-68.

Boas, George. *Essays on Primitivism and Related Ideas in the Middle Ages.* Baltimore: Johns Hopkins University Press, 1948.

Boon, James A. "Comparative De-enlightenment: Paradox and Limits in the History of Ethnology." *Daedalus* 109:2 (Spring 1980): 73-91.

Boose, Lynda E. "The Father and the Bride in Shakespeare." *PMLA* 97:3 (May 1982): 325-47.

Bourne, Edward Gaylord. "Columbus, Ramon Pane and the Beginnings of American Anthropology." *Proceedings of the American Antiquarian Society* 17 (April 1906): 310-48.

Brandon, William. *New Worlds for Old: Reports from the New World and their effect on the development of social thought in Europe, 1500-1800.* Athens: Ohio University Press, 1986.

Braudel, Fernand. *Civilization and Capitalism: 15th-18th Century.* 3 vols. Trans. by Siân Reynolds of *Le Temps du Monde.* [Paris: Librairie Armand Colin, 1979]. New York: Harper & Row, 1984.

Bredvold, Louis I. *The Intellectual Milieu of John Dryden: Studies in Some Aspects of Seventeenth-Century Thought.* Ann Arbor: University of Michigan Press, 1934.

Brettell, Caroline B. "Introduction: Travel Literature, Ethnography, and Ethnohistory." *Ethnohistory* 33:2 (1986): 127-38.

Bristol, Michael D. *Carnival and Theater: Plebeian Culture and the Structure of Authority in Renaissance England.* New York: Routledge, 1985.

Brockbank, Philip. "*The Tempest*: Conventions of Art and Empire." In *Later Shakespeare.* Ed. J. R. Brown and B. Harris. London: Edward Arnold, 1966. 183-201.

Brody, Jules. *Lectures de Montaigne.* Lexington, KY: French Forum, 1982.

Brotherston, Gordon. *Image of the New World: The American continent portrayed in native texts.* Trans. Gordon Brotherston and Ed Dorn. London: Thames and Hudson, 1979.

Brown, Paul. "'This thing of darkness I acknowledge mine': *The Tempest* and the discourse of colonialism." In *Political Shakespeare.* Ed. Jonathan Dollimore and Alan Sinfield. Ithaca: Cornell University Press, 1985. 48-71.

Bullough, Geoffrey. *Narrative and Dramatic Sources of Shakespeare.* Vol. 8: *Romances.* London: Routledge & Kegan Paul, 1975.

Burckhardt, Jakob. *The Civilization of the Renaissance in Italy.* Trans. S. G. C. Middlemore. 4th ed., rev. London: Phaidon Press, 1951.

Burnyeat, Miles, ed. *The Skeptical Tradition.* Berkeley: University of California Press, 1983.

Butzer, Karl W. "From Columbus to Acosta: Science, Geography, and the New World." *Annals of the Association of American Geographers* 82:3 (1992): 543-65.

Cain, Thomas. *Praise in* The Faerie Queene. Lincoln: University of Nebraska Press, 1978.

Campbell, Mary B. "The Illustrated Travel Book and the Birth of Ethnography: Part I of De Bry's *America.*" In *The Work of Dissimilitude: Essays from the Sixth Citadel Conference on Medieval and Renaissance Literature.* Ed. David G. Allen and Robert A. White. Newark: University of Delaware Press, 1992. 177-95.

———. *The Witness and the Other World: Exotic European Travel Writing, 400-1600.* Ithaca: Cornell University Press, 1988.

Carew, Jan. *Fulcrums of Change: Origins of Racism in America and Other Essays.* Trenton, NJ: Africa World Press, 1988.

Carrasco, Davíd. *Quetzalcoatl and the Irony of Empire: Myths and Prophecies in the Aztec Tradition.* Chicago: University of Chicago Press, 1982.

Cave, Terence. *The Cornucopian Text: Problems of Writing in the French Renaissance.* Oxford: Clarendon Press, 1979.

Cawley, Robert Ralston. "Shakspere's Use of the Voyagers in *The Tempest.*" *PMLA* 41 (1926): 688-726.

———. *The Voyagers and Elizabethan Drama.* Boston: Modern Language Association of America, 1938.

———. *Unpathed Waters: Studies in the Influence of the Voyagers on Elizabethan Literature.* Princeton: Princeton University Press, 1940.

Certeau, Michel de. "Montaigne's 'Of Cannibals': The Savage 'I'." In *Heterologies: Discourse on the Other.* Trans. Brian Massumi. Minneapolis: University of Minnesota Press, 1986. 67-79.

———. *The Writing of History.* Trans. by Tom Conley of *L'écriture de l'histoire.* [Paris: Editions Gallimard, 1975]. New York: Columbia University Press, 1988.

Cheney, Donald. *Spenser's Image of Nature: Wild Man and Shepherd in* The Faerie Queene. New Haven: Yale University Press, 1966.

Chiappelli, Fredi, Michael J. B. Allen, and Robert L. Benson, eds. *First Images of America: The Impact of the New World on the Old.* 2 vols. Berkeley: University of California Press, 1976.

Chinard, Gilbert. *L'Exotisme Américain dans la Littérature Française au XVIe Siècle.* Paris: Librairie Hachette, 1911.

Clendinnen, Inga. *Ambivalent Conquests: Maya and Spaniard in Yucatan, 1517-1570.* Cambridge: Cambridge University Press, 1987.

———. "Cortés, Signs, and the Conquest of Mexico." In *The Transmission of Culture in Early Modern Europe.* Philadelphia: University of Pennsylvania Press, 1990. 87-130.

———. "'Fierce and Unnatural Cruelty': Cortés and the Conquest of Mexico." *Representations* 33 (Winter 1991): 65-100.

Clifford, James. "On Ethnographic Authority." *Representations* 1:2 (Spring 1983): 118-46.

Clifford, James, and George E. Marcus, eds. *Writing Culture: The Poetics and Politics of Ethnography.* Berkeley: University of California Press, 1986.

Cole, Richard G. "Sixteenth-Century Travel Books as a Source of European Attitudes Toward Non-White and Non-Western Culture." *Proceedings of the American Philosophical Society* 116 (February 1972): 59-67.

Colie, Rosalie L. *Paradoxia Epidemica: The Renaissance Tradition of Paradox.* Princeton: Princeton University Press, 1966.

Colin, Susi. "Holzfäller und Kannibalen: Brasilianische Indianer auf frühen Karten." In *America: Das frühe Bild der Neuen Welt.* Ed. Hans Wolff. Munich: Prestel-Verlag, 1992. 175-81.

Compagnon, Antoine. "A Long Short Story: Montaigne's Brevity." Trans. Carla Freccero. *Yale French Studies* 64 (1983): 24-50.

———. *Nous, Michel de Montaigne.* Paris: Éditions du Seuil, 1980.

Conley, Tom. "Montaigne and the Indies: Cartographies of the New World in the *Essais,* 1580-88." *Hispanic Issues* 4: *1492-1992: Re/Discovering Colonial Writing* (1989): 225-62.

Cooper, Helen. *Pastoral: Mediaeval into Renaissance.* Ipswich: D. S. Brewer, 1977.

Corfield, Cosmo. "Why Does Prospero Abjure His 'Rough Magic'?" *Shakespeare Quarterly* 36:1 (Spring 1985): 31-48.

Cullen, Patrick. *Spenser, Marvell, and Renaissance Pastoral.* Cambridge: Harvard University Press, 1970.

D'Amico, Robert. *Historicism and Knowledge.* New York: Routledge, 1989.

Danby, John F. *Shakespeare's Doctrine of Nature: A Study of* King Lear. London: Faber and Faber, 1961.

Davis, Jack. "Civilizing the Europeans." *Idaho: The University* 9:2 (Spring 1992): 4-11.

Dawson, Anthony B. *Watching Shakespeare: A Playgoer's Guide.* New York: St. Martin's Press, 1988.

Defaux, Gérard. "Readings of Montaigne." Trans. John A. Gallucci. *Yale French Studies* 64 (1983): 73-92.

De Man, Paul. "Montaigne and Transcendence." Trans. by Richard Howard of "Montaigne et la transcendance" (*Critique* 79 [December 1953]: 1011-22). In *Paul de Man: Critical Writings, 1953-1978*. Ed. Lindsay Waters. Minneapolis: University of Minnesota Press, 1989. 3-11.

Demure, Catherine. "Montaigne: The Paradox and the Miracle—Structure and Meaning in 'The Apology for Raymond Sebond' (*Essais* II:12)." Trans. Dianne Sears. *Yale French Studies* 64 (1983): 188-208.

Derrida, Jacques. *Of Grammatology*. [Paris, 1967]. Trans. Gayatri Chakravorty Spivak. Baltimore: Johns Hopkins University Press, 1976.

Dessen, Alan C. "Conceptual Casting in the Age of Shakespeare: Evidence from *Mucedorus*." *Shakespeare Quarterly* 43:1 (Spring 1992): 67-70.

Dickason, Olive. *The Myth of the Savage in the New World*. Edmonton: University of Alberta Press, 1984.

Dobson, Michael. "'Remember / First to Possess his Books': The Appropriation of *The Tempest*, 1700-1800." *Shakespeare Survey* 43 (1991): 99-108.

Dollimore, Jonathan. *Radical Tragedy: Religion, Ideology and Power in the Drama of Shakespeare and his Contemporaries*. Chicago: University of Chicago Press, 1984.

Dollimore, Jonathan, and Alan Sinfield, eds. *Political Shakespeare: New essays in cultural materialism*. Ithaca: Cornell University Press, 1985.

Drakakis, John, ed. *Alternative Shakespeares*. London: Methuen, 1985.

Dudley, Edward, and Maximillian E. Novak, eds. *The Wild Man Within: An Image in Western Thought from the Renaissance to Romanticism*. Pittsburgh: University of Pittsburgh Press, 1972.

Duval, Edwin M. "Lessons of the New World: Design and Meaning in Montaigne's 'Des Cannibales' (I:31) and 'Des coches' (III:6)." *Yale French Studies* 64 (1983): 95-112.

———. "Montaigne's Conversions: Compositional Strategies in the *Essais*." *French Forum* 7 (1982): 5-22.

Eagleton, Terry. "Ideology and Scholarship." In *Historical Studies and Literary Criticism*. Ed. Jerome J. McGann. Madison: University of Wisconsin Press, 1985. 114-25.

———. *William Shakespeare*. Oxford: Blackwell, 1986.

Edmonson, Munro S., ed. *Sixteenth-Century Mexico: The Work of Sahagún*. Albuquerque: University of New Mexico Press, 1974.

Edwards, Philip. *Shakespeare: A Writer's Progress*. Oxford: Oxford University Press, 1987.

Eliade, Mircea. *Myths, Dreams, and Mysteries: The Encounter between Contemporary Faiths and Archaic Realities*. Trans. Philip Mairet. New York: Harper and Row, 1960.

———. *The Myth of the Eternal Return*. Trans. Willard R. Trask. New York: 1954.

———. "The Yearning for Paradise in Primitive Tradition." *Daedalus* 88 (1959): 255-67.

Elliott, John Huxtable. "Discovery of America and the Discovery of Man." *Proceedings of the British Academy* 58 (1972): 101-25.

———. "The Mental World of Hernán Cortés." *Transactions of the Royal Historical Society, Fifth Series* 17 (1967): 41-58.

———. *The Old World and the New, 1492-1650.* Cambridge: Cambridge University Press, 1970.

Elton, W. R. *Shakespeare's World: Renaissance Intellectual Contexts, A Selective, Annotated Guide, 1966-1971.* New York: Garland, 1979.

Empson, William. *Some Versions of Pastoral.* (London, 1935). Norfolk, CT: New Directions, 1960.

Fairchild, Hoxie Neale. *The Noble Savage: A Study in Romantic Naturalism.* New York: Columbia University Press, 1928.

Febvre, Lucien. *The Problem of Unbelief in the Sixteenth Century: The Religion of Rabelais.* Trans. by Beatrice Gottlieb of *Le Problème de l'incroyance au XVIe siècle: la religion de Rabelais.* (Paris, 1942). Cambridge: Harvard University Press, 1982.

Fell, Barry. *America B.C.: Ancient Settlers in the New World.* 2d ed. New York: Pocket Books, 1989.

Fiedler, Leslie A. *The Stranger in Shakespeare.* New York: Stein and Day, 1972.

Fish, Stanley. *Is There a Text in This Class? The Authority of Interpretive Communities.* Cambridge: Harvard University Press, 1980.

Fitz, L. T. "The Vocabulary of the Environment in *The Tempest.*" *Shakespeare Quarterly* 25 (1975): 42-47.

Flagstad, Karen. "'Making this Place Paradise': Prospero and the Problem of Caliban in *The Tempest.*" *Shakespeare Studies* 18 (1986): 205-33.

Foucault, Michel. *The Archaeology of Knowledge.* Trans. by A. M. Sheridan Smith of *L'archéologie du savoir.* [Paris, 1969]. New York: Pantheon Books, 1972.

———. *The Order of Things: An Archaeology of the Human Sciences.* Trans. by Alan Sheridan of *Les Mots et les choses: une archéologie des sciences humaines.* [Paris, 1966]. New York: Vintage Books, 1973.

Fox-Genovese, Elizabeth. "Literary Criticism and the Politics of the New Historicism." In *The New Historicism.* Ed. H. Aram Veeser. New York: Routledge, 1989. 213-24.

Frame, Donald M. *Montaigne: A Biography.* New York: Harcourt, Brace, 1965.

———. *Montaigne's Discovery of Man: The Humanization of a Humanist.* New York: Columbia University Press, 1955.

———. *Montaigne's Essais: A Study.* Englewood Cliffs, NJ: Prentice-Hall, 1969.

Franklin, Wayne. *Discoverers, Explorers, Settlers: The Diligent Writers of Early America.* Chicago: University of Chicago Press, 1979.

Frey, Charles. "*The Tempest* and the New World." *Shakespeare Quarterly* 30:4 (Winter 1979): 29-41.

Friede, Juan, and Benjamin Keen, eds. *Bartolomé de Las Casas: Toward an Understanding of the Man and His Work.* DeKalb: Northern Illinois University Press, 1971.

Friedman, John Block. *The Monstrous Races in Medieval Art and Thought.* Cambridge: Harvard University Press, 1981.

Friedrich, Hugo. *Montaigne.* [Berne, 1949]. Trans. Robert Rovini. Paris: Gallimard, 1968.

Frye, Northrop. *Northrop Frye on Shakespeare.* Ed. Robert Sandler. New Haven: Yale University Press, 1986.

Galeano, Eduardo H. *Genesis* (Part I of *A Memory of Fire*). Trans. Cedric Belfrage. New York: Pantheon Books, 1985.

Gagnon, François. "Le thème médiéval de l'homme sauvage dans le premières représentations des Indiens d'Amérique." In *Aspects de la marginalité au Moyen Age*. Ed. Guy H. Allard, et al. Montreal: Les Éditions de l'Aurore, 1975.

Geertz, Clifford. *The Interpretation of Cultures.* New York: Basic Books, 1973.

———. *Local Knowledge: Further Essays in Interpretive Anthropology.* New York: Basic Books, 1983.

———. *Works and Lives: The Anthropologist as Author.* Stanford: Stanford University Press, 1988.

Gerbi, Antonello. "The Earliest Accounts on the New World." In *First Images of America.* Ed. Fredi Chiappelli. Vol 1. Berkeley: University of California Press, 1976. 37-43.

———. *Nature in the New World: From Christopher Columbus to Gonzalo Fernandez de Oviedo.* [Milan, 1975]. Trans. Jeremy Moyle. Pittsburgh: University of Pittsburgh Press, 1986.

Giamatti, A. Bartlett. *The Earthly Paradise and the Renaissance Epic.* Princeton: Princeton University Press, 1966.

———. "Primitivism and the Process of Civility in Spenser's *Faerie Queene.*" In *First Images of America.* Ed. Fredi Chiappelli. Vol. 1. Berkeley: University of California Press, 1976. 71-82.

Gibson, Charles. *Spain in America.* New York: Harper & Row, 1966.

———, ed. *The Black Legend: Anti-Spanish Attitudes in the Old World and the New.* New York: Knopf, 1971.

———, ed. *The Spanish Tradition in America.* New York: Harper & Row, 1968.

Gide, André. "Montaigne." Trans. Dorothy Bussy. In *The Living Thoughts of Montaigne.* London: Cassell, 1939. 1-23.

Gillies, John. "Shakespeare's Virginian Masque." *ELH* 53 (1986): 673-707.

Ginzburg, Carlo. *The Cheese and the Worms: The Cosmos of a Sixteenth-Century Miller.* Trans. by John and Anne Tedeschi of *Il formaggio e i vermi: Il cosmo de un mugnaio del '500.* [Giulio Einaudi Editore, 1976]. Harmondsworth: Penguin, 1982.

Goldberg, Jonathan. *Endlesse Worke: Spenser and the Structures of Discourse.* Baltimore: Johns Hopkins University Press, 1981.

———. "The Politics of Renaissance Literature: A Review Essay." *ELH* 49 (1982): 514-42.

Goldsmith, R. H. "The Wild Man on the English Stage." *Modern Language Review* 53 (1958): 481-91.

Graff, Gerald. "Co-optation." In *The New Historicism.* Ed. H. Aram Veeser. New York: Routledge, 1989. 168-81.

Grafton, Anthony, with April Shelford and Nancy Siraisi. *New Worlds, Ancient Texts: The Power of Tradition and the Shock of Discovery.* Cambridge: Harvard University Press, 1992.

Gramsci, Antonio. *Selections from Prison Notebooks.* Trans. and ed. Quintin Hoare and Geoffrey Nowell Smith. London: Lawrence and Wishart, 1971.

Greenblatt, Stephen. "Culture." In *Critical Terms for Literary Study*. Ed. Frank Lentricchia and Thomas McLaughlin. Chicago: University of Chicago Press, 1990. 225-32.

———. Introduction. "New World Encounters." In *New World Encounters*. Ed. Stephen Greenblatt. Berkeley: University of California Press, 1993. vii-xviii.

———. Introduction. "The Forms of Power and the Power of Forms in the Renaissance." *Genre* 15:1 and 15:2 (1982): 3-6.

———. "Learning to Curse: Aspects of Linguistic Colonialism in the Sixteenth Century." In *First Images of America*. Ed. Fredi Chiappelli. Vol. 2. Berkeley: University of California Press, 1976. 561-80.

———. *Learning to Curse: Essays in Early Modern Culture*. New York: Routledge, 1990.

———. *Marvelous Possessions: The Wonder of the New World*. Chicago: University of Chicago Press, 1991.

———. *Renaissance Self-Fashioning from More to Shakespeare*. Chicago: University of Chicago Press, 1980.

———. *Shakespearean Negotiations: The Circulation of Social Energy in Renaissance England*. Berkeley: University of California Press, 1988.

Greenblatt, Stephen, and Giles Gunn, eds. *Redrawing the Boundaries: The Transformation of English and American Literary Studies*. New York: Modern Language Association of America, 1992.

Griffiths, Trevor R. "'This Island's mine': Caliban and Colonialism." *Yearbook of English Studies 13: Colonial and Imperial Themes*. Ed. G. K. Hunter and C. J. Rawson. London: Modern Humanities Research Association, 1983. 159-80.

Grisel, Etienne. "The Beginnings of International Law and General Public Law Doctrine: Francisco de Vitoria's *De Indiis prior*." In *First Images of America*. Ed. Fredi Chiappelli. Vol. 1. Berkeley: University of California Press, 1976. 305-26.

Guttman, Selma. *The Foreign Sources of Shakespeare's Works: An Annotated Bibliography of the Commentary Written on this Subject between 1904 and 1940*. New York: King's Crown Press, 1947.

.Hamlin, William M. "Attributions of Divinity in Renaissance Ethnography and Romance; Or, Making Religion of Wonder." *The Journal of Medieval and Renaissance Studies* 24:3 (1994): 415-47.

———. "Imagined Apotheoses: Drake, Harriot, and Ralegh in the Americas." *Journal of the History of Ideas* (forthcoming).

———. "Men of Inde: Renaissance Ethnography and *The Tempest*." *Shakespeare Studies* 22 (1994): 15-44.

Hanke, Lewis. *All Mankind Is One: A Study of the Disputation Between Bartolomé de Las Casas and Juan Ginés de Sepúlveda in 1550 on the Intellectual and Religious Capacity of the American Indians*. DeKalb: Northern Illinois University Press, 1974.

———. *Aristotle and the American Indians: A Study in Race Prejudice in the Modern World*. London: Hollis and Carter, 1959.

————. The First Social Experiments in America: A Study in the Development of Spanish Indian Policy in the Sixteenth Century. Cambridge: Harvard University Press, 1935; rpt. Gloucester: Peter Smith, 1964.

————. "Pope Paul III and the American Indians." Harvard Theological Review 30 (1937): 65-102.

————. The Spanish Struggle for Justice in the Conquest of America. Philadelphia: University of Pennsylvania Press, 1949.

Hankins, J. E. "Caliban the Bestial Man." PMLA 62:3 (September 1947): 793-801.

Hanna, Warren L. Lost Harbor: The Controversy over Drake's California Anchorage. Berkeley: University of California Press, 1979.

Hart, Jonathan. "Images of the Native in Renaissance Encounter Narratives." Unpublished essay presented at the Pacific Northwest Renaissance Conference (University of British Columbia, Vancouver, B.C., March 1993).

Hawkes, Terence. Shakespeare's Talking Animals: Language and Drama in Society. Totowa, NJ: Rowman and Littlefield, 1974.

————. That Shakespeherian Rag: Essays on a Critical Process. London: Methuen, 1986.

Haydn, Hiram. The Counter-Renaissance. New York: Scribner's, 1950.

Heffner, Ray. "Spenser's View of Ireland: Some Observations." Modern Language Quarterly 3:4 (1942): 507-15.

Heinemann, Margot. "Demystifying the Mystery of State: King Lear and the World Upside Down." Shakespeare Survey 44 (1992): 75-83.

Heizer, Robert F. Francis Drake and the California Indians, 1579. Berkeley: University of California Press, 1947.

Helgerson, Richard. Forms of Nationhood: The Elizabethan Writing of England. Chicago: University of Chicago Press, 1992.

————. "The Land Speaks: Cartography, Chorography, and Subversion in Renaissance England." Representations 16 (Fall 1986): 51-85.

Helms, Mary W. Ulysses' Sail: An Ethnographic Odyssey of Power, Knowledge, and Geographical Distance. Princeton: Princeton University Press, 1988.

Hodgen, Margaret T. Early Anthropology in the Sixteenth and Seventeenth Centuries. Philadelphia: University of Pennsylvania Press, 1964.

————. "Montaigne and Shakespeare Again." Huntington Library Quarterly XVI (1952): 23-42.

Hoffman, Nancy Jo. Spenser's Pastorals: The Shepheardes Calender and "Colin Clout". Baltimore: Johns Hopkins University Press, 1977.

Hoffmann, Bernard G. From Cabot to Cartier. Toronto: University of Toronto Press, 1961.

Honour, Hugh. The European Vision of America. Cleveland: Cleveland Museum of Art, 1975.

————. The New Golden Land: European Images of America from the Discoveries to the Present Time. New York: Random House, 1975.

Howard, Jean E. "The New Historicism in Renaissance Studies." English Literary Renaissance 16 (1986): 13-43.

Huddleston, Lee Eldridge. *Origins of the American Indians: European Concepts, 1492-1729.* Austin: University of Texas Press, 1967.

Hulme, Peter. *Colonial Encounters: Europe and the Native Caribbean, 1492-1797.* London: Methuen, 1986.

———. "Hurricanes in the Caribbees: The Constitution of the Discourse of English Colonialism." In *1642: Literature and Power in the Seventeenth Century.* Ed. Francis Barker, et al. Colchester: University of Essex, 1981. 55-83.

Hunt, Lynn, ed. *The New Cultural History.* Berkeley: University of California Press, 1989.

Hunter, G. K. "Elizabethans and Foreigners." *Shakespeare Survey* 17 (1964): 37-52.

Jaenen, Cornelius J. *Friend and Foe: Aspect of French-Amerindian Cultural Contact in the Sixteenth and Seventeenth Centuries.* New York: Columbia University Press, 1976.

James, D. G. *The Dream of Prospero.* Oxford: Oxford University Press, 1967.

James, H. L. *Acoma: People of the White Rock.* West Chester, Pennsylvania: Schiffer, 1988.

Jameson, Fredric. *The Political Unconscious: Narrative as a Socially Symbolic Act.* Ithaca: Cornell University Press, 1981.

Jennings, Francis. *The Invasion of America: Indians, Colonialism, and the Cant of Conquest.* Chapel Hill: University of North Carolina Press, 1975.

Jones, Howard Mumford. *O Strange New World. American Culture: The Formative Years.* New York: Viking Press, 1964.

Jones, W. R. "The Image of Barbarians in Medieval Europe." *Comparative Studies in Society and History* 13:4 (October 1971): 376-401.

Jorgensen, Paul. "Shakespeare's Brave New World." In *First Images of America.* Ed. Fredi Chiappelli. Vol. 1. Berkeley: University of California Press, 1976. 83-89.

Julien, C. A. *Les Débuts de l'Expansion et de la Colonisation Française.* Paris, 1947.

Kavanagh, James H. "Ideology." In *Critical Terms for Literary Study.* Ed. Frank Lentricchia and Thomas McLaughlin. Chicago: University of Chicago Press, 1990. 306-20.

Keen, Benjamin. *The Aztec Image in Western Thought.* New Brunswick: Rutgers University Press, 1971.

Kelley, Donald R. "'Second Nature': The Idea of Custom in European Law, Society, and Culture." In *The Transmission of Culture in Early Modern Europe.* Philadelphia: University of Pennsylvania Press, 1990. 131-72.

Kermode, Frank, ed. *English Pastoral Poetry from the Beginnings to Marvell.* London: George G. Harrap, 1952.

———. Introduction. The Arden Shakespeare Edition of *The Tempest.* Ed. Frank Kermode. London: Methuen, 1954. xi-xciii.

Kerrigan, William, and Gordon Braden. *The Idea of the Renaissance.* Baltimore: Johns Hopkins University Press, 1989.

Klor de Alva, J. Jorge. "Sahagún and the Birth of Modern Ethnography: Representing, Confessing, and Inscribing the Native Other." In Klor de Alva, et al., *The Work of Bernardino de Sahagún: Pioneer Ethnographer of Sixteenth-Century Aztec Mexico.* Austin:

University of Texas Press for the Institute for Mesoamerican Studies at the State University of New York at Albany, 1988. 31-52.

Klor de Alva, J. Jorge, H. B. Nicholson, and Eloise Quiñones Keber, eds. *The Work of Bernardino de Sahagún: Pioneer Ethnographer of Sixteenth-Century Aztec Mexico*. Austin: University of Texas Press for the Institute for Mesoamerican Studies at the State University of New York at Albany, 1988.

Knapp, Jeffrey. "Elizabethan Tobacco." *Representations* 21 (1988): 26-66.

———. *An Empire Nowhere: England, America, and Literature from* Utopia *to* The Tempest. Berkeley: University of California Press, 1992.

———. "Error as a Means of Empire in *The Faerie Queene* 1." *ELH* 54:4 (Winter 1987): 801-34.

Knight, G. Wilson. "Caliban as a Red Man." In *Shakespeare's Styles: Essays in Honour of Kenneth Muir*. Ed. Philip Edwards, Inga-Stina Ewbank, and G. K. Hunter. Cambridge: Cambridge University Press, 1980. 205-20.

———. "'Great Creating Nature': An Essay on *The Winter's Tale*." In *Shakespeare: Modern Essays in Criticism*. Rev. ed. Ed. Leonard F. Dean. London: Oxford University Press, 1967. 423-55.

Knowles, Jr., A. Sidney. "Spenser's Natural Man." In *Renaissance Papers 1958, 1959, 1960*. Ed. G. W. Williams and P. G. Phialas. Durham, NC: Southeastern Renaissance Conference, 1961. 3-11.

Kott, Jan. *Shakespeare Our Contemporary*. Trans. Boleslaw Taborski. New York: Norton, 1964.

———. "*The Tempest*, or, Repetition." Trans. Daniela Miedzyrzecka. *Mosaic* 10:3 (1977): 9-36.

Krailsheimer, A. J., ed. *The Continental Renaissance, 1500-1600*. Harmondsworth: Penguin, 1971.

Krupat, Arnold. *Ethnocriticism: Ethnography, History, Literature*. Berkeley and Los Angeles: University of California Press, 1992.

Kupperman, Karen Ordahl. *Settling with the Indians: The Meeting of English and Indian Cultures in America, 1580-1640*. Totowa, NJ: Rowman and Littlefield, 1975.

LaCapra, Dominick. "On the Line: Between History and Criticism." *Profession* 89 (1989): 4-9.

Lamming, George. "A Monster, a Child, a Slave." [1960]. In *The Pleasures of Exile*. London: Allison and Busby, 1984. 95-117.

Laslett, Peter. *The World We Have Lost, Further Explored*. 3d ed. New York: Scribner's, 1984.

Lebel, Roland. *Histoire de la Littérature Coloniale en France*. Paris: Librairie Larose, 1931.

Lee, Sidney. "The American Indian in Elizabethan England." In *Elizabethan and Other Essays*. Ed. F. S. Boas. London: Oxford University Press, 1929. 263-301.

Leininger, Lorie Jerrell. "Cracking the Code of *The Tempest*." *Bucknell Review* 25 (1980): 121-31.

———. "The Miranda Trap: Sexism and Racism in Shakespeare's *Tempest*." In *The Woman's Part: Feminist Criticism of Shakespeare*. Ed. Carolyn Ruth Swift Lenz, Gayle Greene, and Carol Thomas Neely. Urbana: University of Illinois Press, 1980. 285-94.

Leonard, Irving A. *Books of the Brave: Being an Account of Books and of Men in the Spanish Conquest and Settlement of the Sixteenth-Century New World.* Cambridge: Harvard University Press, 1949; rpt. New York: Gordian Press, 1964.

Lestringant, Frank. "The Philosopher's Breviary: Jean de Léry in the Enlightenment." Trans. Katharine Streip. *Representations* 33 (Winter 1991): 200-11.

Lévi-Strauss, Claude. *Tristes Tropiques.* [Paris, 1955]. Trans. John and Doreen Weightman. New York: Atheneum, 1975.

Levin, Harry. *The Myth of the Golden Age in the Renaissance.* Bloomington: Indiana University Press, 1969.

Lewis, C. S. *The Allegory of Love: A Study in Medieval Tradition.* London: Oxford University Press, 1938.

———. *English Literature in the Sixteenth Century.* Oxford: Oxford University Press, 1954.

Lockhart, James, and Enrique Orte. *Letters and People of the Spanish Indies: The Sixteenth Century.* Cambridge: Cambridge University Press, 1976.

Lovejoy, Arthur O. *Essays in the History of Ideas.* Baltimore: Johns Hopkins University Press, 1948.

Lovejoy, Arthur O., Gilbert Chinard, George Boas, and Ronald S. Crane, eds. *Primitivism and Related Ideas in Antiquity.* Vol. 1 of *A Documentary History of Primitivism and Related Ideas.* Baltimore: Johns Hopkins University Press, 1935.

Mack, Maynard. *King Lear in Our Time.* Berkeley: University of California Press, 1965.

McCann, Franklin Thresher. *English Discovery of America to 1585.* New York: King's Crown Press, 1952.

McDonald, Russ. "Reading *The Tempest.*" *Shakespeare Survey* 43 (1991): 15-28.

McGann, Jerome J., ed. *Historical Studies and Literary Criticism.* Madison: University of Wisconsin Press, 1985.

McGrane, Bernard. *Beyond Anthropology: Society and the Other.* New York: Columbia University Press, 1989.

MacNutt, Francis Augustus. *Bartholomew de Las Casas: His Life, His Apostolate, and His Writings.* New York: Putnam's, 1909.

McPeek, James A. S. "The Genesis of Caliban." *Philological Quarterly* 25 (1946): 378-91.

Mallette, Richard. *Spenser, Milton, and Renaissance Pastoral.* Lewisburg, PA: Bucknell University Press, 1981.

Maltby, William S. *The Black Legend in England: The Development of Anti-Spanish Sentiment, 1558-1660.* Durham, NC: Duke University Press, 1971.

Mannoni, Dominique Octave. *Prospero and Caliban: The Psychology of Colonization.* Trans. by Pamela Powesland of *Psychologie de la Colonisation.* [Paris, 1950]. New York: Praeger, 1956; rpt. Ann Arbor: University of Michigan Press, 1990.

Marienstras, Richard. *New Perspectives on the Shakespearean World.* Trans. by Janet Lloyd of *Le Proche et Le Lointain.* [Paris, 1981]. Cambridge: Cambridge University Press, 1985.

Mason, Philip. *Prospero's Magic: Some Thoughts on Class and Race.* London: Oxford University Press, 1962.

Marx, Leo. *The Machine in the Garden. Technology and the Pastoral Ideal in America.* London: Oxford University Press, 1964.

Meek, Ronald. *Social Science and the Ignoble Savage.* Cambridge: Cambridge University Press, 1976.

Minge, Ward Alan. *Acoma: Pueblo in the Sky.* Albuquerque: University of New Mexico Press, 1976.

Montrose, Louis A. "'Eliza, Queen of Shepheardes' and the Pastoral of Power." *English Literary Renaissance* 10 (1980): 153-82.

———. "The Elizabethan Subject and the Spenserian Text." In *Literary Theory/Renaissance Texts.* Ed. Patricia Parker and David Quint. Baltimore: Johns Hopkins University Press, 1986. 303-40.

———. "Of Gentlemen and Shepherds: The Politics of Elizabethan Pastoral Form." *ELH* 50 (1983): 415-59.

———. "Gifts and Reasons: The Contexts of Peele's *Araygnement of Paris.*" *ELH* 47:3 (Fall 1980): 433-61.

———. "Professing the Renaissance: The Poetics and Politics of Culture." In *The New Historicism.* Ed. H. Aram Veeser. New York: Routledge, 1989. 15-36.

———. "Renaissance Literary Studies and the Subject of History." *English Literary Renaissance* 16:1 (1986): 5-12.

Morison, Samuel Eliot. *Admiral of the Ocean Sea: A Life of Christopher Columbus.* Boston: Little, Brown, 1942.

———. *Christopher Columbus, Mariner.* Boston: Little, Brown, 1955.

———. *The European Discovery of America: The Northern Voyages, A.D. 500-1600.* New York: Oxford University Press, 1971.

———. *The European Discovery of America: The Southern Voyages, A.D. 1492-1616.* New York: Oxford University Press, 1974.

Mullaney, Steven. "Brothers and Others, or the Art of Alienation." In *Cannibals, Witches, and Divorce: Estranging the Renaissance.* Ed. Marjorie Garber. Baltimore: Johns Hopkins University Press, 1987. 67-89.

———. "Strange Things, Gross Terms, Curious Customs: The Rehearsal of Cultures in the Late Renaissance." *Representations* 3 (1983): 40-67. Rpt. in *Representing the English Renaissance.* Ed. Stephen Greenblatt. Berkeley: University of California Press, 1988. 65-92.

Nash, Gary B. "The Image of the Indian in the Southern Colonial Mind." In *The Wild Man Within: An Image in Western Thought from the Renaissance to Romanticism.* Ed. Edward Dudley and Maximillian E. Novak. Pittsburgh: University of Pittsburgh Press, 1972. 55-86.

Nash, Roderick. *Wilderness and the American Mind.* Rev. ed. New Haven: Yale University Press, 1973.

Obeyesekere, Gananath. *The Apotheosis of Captain Cook: European Mythmaking in the Pacific.* Princeton: Princeton University Press, 1992.

O'Connell, Michael. *Mirror and Veil: The Historical Dimension of Spenser's* Faerie Queene. Chapel Hill: University of North Carolina Press, 1977.

O'Gorman, Edmundo. *The Invention of America: An Inquiry into the Historical Nature of the New World and the Meaning of its History*. Bloomington: Indiana University Press, 1961.

Olschki, Leonardo. "What Columbus Saw on Landing in the West Indies." *Proceedings of the American Philosophical Society* 84:5 (July 1941): 633-59.

Ong, Walter J. "Spenser's *View* and the Tradition of the 'Wild' Irish." *Modern Language Quarterly* 3:4 (1942): 561-71.

Orgel, Stephen. Introduction. The Oxford Shakespeare Edition of *The Tempest*. Ed. Stephen Orgel. Oxford: Clarendon Press, 1987. 1-87.

———. "Shakespeare and the Cannibals." In *Cannibals, Witches, and Divorce: Estranging the Renaissance*. Ed. Marjorie Garber. Baltimore: Johns Hopkins University Press, 1987. 40-66.

———. "Prospero's Wife." *Representations* 8 (Fall 1984): 1-13.

Orkin, Martin. "Othello and the 'plain face' of Racism." *Shakespeare Quarterly* 38:2 (1987): 166-88.

Ornstein, Robert. *The Moral Vision of Jacobean Tragedy*. Madison: University of Wisconsin Press, 1960.

Orwell, George. *A Collection of Essays by George Orwell*. San Diego: Harcourt, Brace, Jovanovich, 1946.

Pagden, Anthony. "*Ius et Factum*: Text and Experience in the Writings of Bartolomé de Las Casas." *Representations* 33 (Winter 1991): 147-62.

———. *The Fall of Natural Man: The American Indian and the Origins of Comparative Ethnology*. Cambridge: Cambridge University Press, 1986.

———. "The Savage Critic: Some European Images of the Primitive." In *Yearbook of English Studies 13: Colonial and Imperial Themes*. Ed. G. K. Hunter and C. J. Rawson. London: Modern Humanities Research Association, 1983. 32-45.

Parks, G. B. *Richard Hakluyt and the English Voyages*. New York: American Geographical Society, 1928.

Parry, J. H. *The Age of Reconnaissance: Discovery, Exploration, and Settlement, 1450-1650*. New York: Praeger, 1969.

Patterson, Annabel. *Pastoral and Ideology: Virgil to Valery*. Berkeley: University of California Press, 1987.

———. *Shakespeare and the Popular Voice*. Oxford: Blackwell, 1989.

Paz, Octavio. *The Labyrinth of Solitude*. [1961, 1968]. Trans. Lysander Kemp. New York: Grove Press, 1985.

———. "The Power of Ancient Mexican Art." Trans. Anthony Stanton. *The New York Review of Books* 37:19 (6 December 1990): 18-21.

Pearce, Roy Harvey. "Primitivistic Ideas in *The Faerie Queene*." *Journal of English and Germanic Philology* 44 (1945): 139-51.

———. *The Savages of America: A Study of the Indian and the Idea of Civilization*. Baltimore: Johns Hopkins University Press, 1953. Rev. ed., 1965 (retitled *Savagism and Civilization: A Study of the Indian and the American Mind*).

Pechter, Edward. "The New Historicism and its Discontents: Politicizing Renaissance Drama." *PMLA* 102:3 (May 1987): 292-303.

Peckham, Howard, and Charles Gibson, eds. *Attitudes of the Colonial Powers Toward the American Indian.* Salt Lake City: University of Utah Press, 1969.

Penelhum, Terence. "Skepticism and Fideism." In *The Skeptical Tradition.* Ed. Miles Burnyeat. Berkeley: University of California Press, 1983. 287-316.

Penrose, Boies. *Travel and Discovery in the Renaissance, 1420-1620.* New York: Atheneum, 1962.

Pinciss, G. M. "The Savage Man in Spenser, Shakespeare, and Renaissance English Drama." *The Elizabethan Theatre VIII.* Ed. G. R. Hibbard. Port Credit: P. D. Meany, 1982. 69-89.

Pohl, F. J. *Amerigo Vespucci: Pilot Major.* New York: Columbia University Press, 1944.

Popkin, Richard H. *The History of Scepticism from Erasmus to Spinoza.* Berkeley: University of California Press, 1979.

———. "Skepticism." In *The Encyclopedia of Philosophy.* Ed. Paul Edwards. Vol. 7. New York: Macmillan & Free Press, 1967. 449-60.

Porter, Harry Culverwell. *The Inconstant Savage: England and the North American Indian, 1500-1660.* London: Duckworth, 1979.

Portinaro, Pierluigi, and Franco Knirsch. *The Cartography of North America, 1500-1800.* New York: Crescent Books, 1987.

Pratt, Mary Louise. "Arts of the Contact Zone." *Profession 91* (1991): 33-40.

———. "Fieldwork in Common Places." In *Writing Culture: The Poetics and Politics of Ethnography.* Ed. James Clifford and George E. Marcus. Berkeley: University of California Press, 1986. 27-50.

Prosser, Eleanor. "Shakespeare, Montaigne, and *the Rarer Action." Shakespeare Studies* 1 (1965): 261-64.

Quinn, David Beers. *The Elizabethans and the Irish.* Folger Monographs on Tudor and Stuart Civilization. Ithaca: Cornell University Press, 1966.

———. *England and the Discovery of America, 1481-1620.* New York: Knopf, 1974.

———. "New Geographical Horizons: Literature." In *First Images of America.* Ed. Fredi Chiappelli. Vol. 2. Berkeley: University of California Press, 1976. 635-58.

Rabasa, José. "Utopian Ethnology in Las Casas's *Apologética." Hispanic Issues 4: 1492-1992: Re/Discovering Colonial Writing* (1989): 263-89.

Read, David. "Hunger of Gold: Guyon, Mammon's Cave, and the New World Treasure." *English Literary Renaissance* 20:2 (Spring 1990): 209-32.

———. "Ralegh's *Discoverie of Guiana* and the Elizabethan Model of Empire." In *The Work of Dissimilitude: Essays from the Sixth Citadel Conference on Medieval and Renaissance Literature.* Ed. David G. Allen and Robert A. White. Newark: University of Delaware Press, 1992. 166-76.

Rees, Joan. "Hogs, Gulls, and Englishmen: Drayton and the Virginian Voyages." In *Yearbook of English Studies 13: Colonial and Imperial Themes.* Ed. G. K. Hunter and C. J. Rawson. London: Modern Humanities Research Association, 1983. 20-31.

Regosin, Richard L. "The Boundaries of Interpretation: Self, Text, Contexts in Montaigne's *Essays.*" In *Renaissance Rereadings: Intertext and Context.* Ed. Maryanne Cline Horowitz, Anne J. Cruz, and Wendy A. Furman. Urbana: University of Illinois Press, 1988. 18-32.

――――. *The Matter of My Book: Montaigne's Essais as the Book of the Self.* Berkeley: University of California Press, 1977.

Reiss, Timothy J. "Montaigne and the Subject of Polity." In *Literary Theory/Renaissance Texts.* Ed. Patricia Parker and David Quint. Baltimore: Johns Hopkins University Press, 1986. 115-49.

Rendall, Steven. *Distinguo: Reading Montaigne Differently.* Oxford: Clarendon Press, 1992.

Retamar, Roberto Fernández. *Caliban and Other Essays.* Trans. Edward Baker. Minneapolis: University of Minnesota Press, 1989.

Ribner, Irving. "The Gods Are Just: A Reading of *King Lear.*" *Tulane Drama Review* 2:3 (May 1958): 34-54.

Robe, Stanley L. "Wild Men and Spain's Brave New World." In *The Wild Man Within: An Image in Western Thought from the Renaissance to Romanticism.* Ed. Edward Dudley and Maximilian E. Novak. Pittsburgh: University of Pittsburgh Press, 1972. 39-54.

Root, Deborah. "The Imperial Signifier: Todorov and the Conquest of Mexico." *Cultural Critique* 9 (Spring 1988): 197-219.

Rowe, John Howland. "Ethnography and Ethnology in the Sixteenth Century." *The Kroeber Anthropological Society Papers* 30 (1964): 1-19.

――――. "The Renaissance Foundations of Anthropology." *American Anthropologist* 67 (February 1965): 1-20.

Rowse, Alfred Leslie. *The Elizabethans and America.* New York: Harper and Brothers, 1959.

Ryan, Michael T. "Assimilating New Worlds in the Sixteenth and Seventeenth Centuries." *Comparative Studies in Society and History* 23:4 (October 1981): 519-38.

Said, Edward. *Orientalism.* [London, 1978]. New York: Vintage Books, 1979.

Sale, Roger. *Reading Spenser: An Introduction to* The Faerie Queene. New York: Random House, 1968.

Salingar, L. G. "The Social Setting." In *The Age of Shakespeare.* (Vol. 2 of *The New Pelican Guide to English Literature*). Ed. Boris Ford. London: Penguin, 1982.

Sauer, Carl Ortwin. *The Early Spanish Main.* Berkeley and Los Angeles: University of California Press, 1966.

Sayce, Richard A. *The Essays of Montaigne: A Critical Exploration.* London: Weidenfeld and Nicolson, 1972.

Scaglione, Aldo. "A Note on Montaigne's 'Des Cannibales' and the Humanist Tradition." In *First Images of America.* Ed. Fredi Chiappelli. Vol. 1. Berkeley: University of California Press, 1976. 63-70.

Schiffman, Zachary S. "Montaigne and the Rise of Skepticism in Early Modern Europe: A Reappraisal." *Journal of the History of Ideas* 45 (1984): 499-516.

————— *On the Threshold of Modernity: Relativism in the French Renaissance.* Baltimore: Johns Hopkins University Press, 1991.

Screech, Michael Andrew. Introduction. Penguin Classics Edition of Michel de Montaigne's *An Apology for Raymond Sebond.* Trans. Michael Andrew Screech. Harmondsworth: Penguin, 1987.

—————. *Montaigne and Melancholy: The Wisdom of the Essays.* London: Duckworth, 1983.

Sharp, Sister Corona. "Caliban: The Primitive Man's Evolution." *Shakespeare Studies* 14 (1981): 267-83.

Sheehan, Bernard W. *Savagism and Civility: Indians and Englishmen in Colonial Virginia.* Cambridge: Cambridge University Press, 1980.

Shire, Helena. *A Preface to Spenser.* London: Longman, 1978.

Shweder, Richard A. "On Savages and Other Children." *American Anthropologist* 84 (1982): 354-66.

Simpson, David. "Literary Criticism and the Return to 'History.'" *Critical Inquiry* 14:4 (Summer 1988): 721-47.

Sinfield, Alan. "Against Appropriation." *Essays in Criticism* 31 (July 1981): 181-95.

Skura, Meredith Anne. "Discourse and the Individual: The Case of Colonialism in *The Tempest.*" *Shakespeare Quarterly* 40:1 (Spring 1989): 42-69.

Smith, Hallett. *Shakespeare's Romances: A Study of Some Ways of the Imagination.* San Marino: The Huntington Library, 1972.

Smith, James. "The Tempest." [1954]. In *Shakespearian and Other Essays.* Ed. E. M. Wilson. Cambridge: Cambridge University Press, 1974. 159-261.

Spencer, Theodore. *Shakespeare and the Nature of Man.* 2d ed., rev. Cambridge: Harvard University Press, 1949.

Starobinski, Jean. *Montaigne in Motion.* Trans. by Arthur Goldhammer of *Montaigne en mouvement.* [Paris: Editions Gallimard, 1982]. Chicago: University of Chicago Press, 1985.

Sturtevant, William C. "First Visual Images of Native America." In *First Images of America.* Ed. Fredi Chiappelli. Vol. 2. Berkeley: University of California Press, 1976. 417-54.

Tayler, Edward William. *Nature and Art in Renaissance Literature.* New York: Columbia University Press, 1964.

Taylor, G. C. "Montaigne—Shakespeare and the Deadly Parallel." *Philological Quarterly* 22 (1943): 330-37.

—————. *Shakespeare's Debt to Montaigne.* Cambridge: Cambridge University Press, 1925.

Todorov, Tzvetan. "L'Etre et l'Autre: Montaigne." Trans. Pierre Saint-Amand. *Yale French Studies* 64 (1983): 113-44.

—————. *The Conquest of America: The Question of the Other.* Trans. by Richard Howard of *La Conquête de L'Amérique.* [Paris, 1982]. New York: Harper and Row, 1984.

Tonkin, Humphrey. *Spenser's Courteous Pastoral: Book Six of* The Faerie Queene. Oxford: Clarendon Press, 1972.

Vaughan, Alden T. "Shakespeare's Indian: The Americanization of Caliban." *Shakespeare Quarterly* 39:2 (Summer 1988): 137-53.

Vaughan, Alden T. and Virginia Mason Vaughan. *Shakespeare's Caliban: A Cultural History.* Cambridge: Cambridge University Press, 1991.

Vaughan, Virginia Mason. "'Something Rich and Strange': Caliban's Theatrical Metamorphoses." *Shakespeare Quarterly* 36:4 (Winter 1985): 390-405.

Veeser, H. Aram, ed. *The New Historicism.* New York: Routledge, 1989.

Villey, Pierre. *Les Sources et L'Évolution des Essais de Montaigne.* 2 vols. Paris: Librairie Hachette, 1908.

Wachtel, Nathan. *The Vision of the Vanquished: The Spanish Conquest of Peru through Indian Eyes, 1530-1570.* Trans. by Ben and Siân Reynolds of *La vision des vaincus: Les Indiens du Pérou devant la conquête espagnol, 1530-1570.* [Paris: Editions Gallimard, 1971]. New York: Barnes and Noble, 1977.

Wagner, Roy. *The Invention of Culture.* Rev. ed. Chicago: University of Chicago Press, 1981.

Walker, D. P. *The Ancient Theology: Studies in Christian Platonism from the Fifteenth to the Eighteenth Century.* Ithaca: Cornell University Press, 1972.

———. "The Faith of a Skeptic." *The New York Review of Books* (14 February 1985): 37-38.

Wall, Jr., John N. "'Fruitfullest Virginia': Edmund Spenser, Roanoke Island, and the Bower of Bliss." *Renaissance Papers* (1984): 1-17.

Weinberg, Bernard. "Montaigne's Readings for 'Des Cannibales'." In *Renaissance and Other Studies in Honor of William Leon Wiley.* Ed. George Bernard Daniel, Jr. University of North Carolina Studies in the Romance Languages and Literatures, Number 72. Chapel Hill: University of North Carolina Press, 1968. 261-79.

Whatley, Janet. "Food and the Limits of Civility: The Testimony of Jean de Léry." *Sixteenth Century Journal* 15:4 (Winter 1984): 387-400.

White, Hayden. "The Forms of Wildness: Archaeology of an Idea." In *The Wild Man Within: An Image in Western Thought from the Renaissance to Romanticism.* Ed. Edward Dudley and Maximilian E. Novak. Pittsburgh: University of Pittsburgh Press, 1972. 3-38.

———. "New Historicism: A Comment." In *The New Historicism.* Ed. H. Aram Veeser. New York: Routledge, 1989. 293-302.

———. *Tropics of Discourse: Essays in Cultural Criticism.* Baltimore: Johns Hopkins University Press, 1978.

Whitney, Lois. "Spenser's Use of the Literature of Travel in *The Faerie Queene.*" *Modern Philology* 19 (1921): 143-62.

Williams, Raymond. *The Country and the City.* New York: Oxford University Press, 1973.

———. *Marxism and Literature.* Oxford: Oxford University Press, 1977.

———. *Problems in Materialism and Culture: Selected Essays.* London: New Left, 1980.

Willis, Deborah. "Shakespeare's *Tempest* and the Discourse of Colonialism." *Studies in English Literature, 1500-1900* 29:2 (Spring 1989): 277-89.

Wright, Louis B. *Religion and Empire: The Alliance between Piety and Commerce in English Expansion, 1558-1625.* Chapel Hill: University of North Carolina Press, 1943.

Young, David. "Where the Bee Sucks: A Triangular Study of *Doctor Faustus*, *The Alchemist*, and *The Tempest*." In *Shakespeare's Romances Reconsidered*. Ed. Carol McGinnis Kay and Henry E. Jacobs. Lincoln: University of Nebraska Press, 1978. 149-66.

Zamora, Margarita. "Christopher Columbus's 'Letter to the Sovereigns': Announcing the Discovery." In *New World Encounters*. Ed. Stephen Greenblatt. Berkeley: University of California Press, 1993. 1-11.

Zavala, Silvio. "Sir Thomas More in New Spain: A Utopian Adventure of the Renaissance." In *Essential Articles for the Study of Sir Thomas More*. Ed. Richard S. Sylvester and G. P. Marc'hadour. Hamden, CT: Archon Books, 1977. 302-11.

Zeeveld, W. Gordon. *The Temper of Shakespeare's Thought*. New Haven: Yale University Press, 1974.

Reference Works

Cotgrave, Randle. *A Dictionarie of the French and English Tongues*. [London, 1611]. Amsterdam: Theatrum Orbis Terrarum, 1971.

Edwards, Paul, ed. *The Encyclopedia of Philosophy*. 8 vols. New York and London: Macmillan & Free Press, 1967.

Encyclopédie, ou Dictionnaire Raisonné des Sciences, des Arts et des Métiers. [Paris and Neufchâtel, 1751-65]. 5 vols. New York: Readex Microprint, 1969.

Hamilton, A. C., ed. *The Spenser Encyclopedia*. Toronto and Buffalo: University of Toronto Press, 1990.

Johnson, Samuel. *A Dictionary of the English Language*. [London, 1755]. New York: Arno Press, 1979.

The Oxford English Dictionary. 2d ed. Prepared by J. A. Simpson and E. S. C. Weiner. Oxford: Clarendon Press, 1989.

Pollard, A. W., and G. R. Redgrave, comps. *A Short-Title Catalogue of Books Printed in England, Scotland, & Ireland, and of English Books Printed Abroad, 1475-1640*. Rev. Katharine F. Pantzer, W. A. Jackson, and F. S. Ferguson. 2d ed., rev. and enlarged. 3 vols. London: The Bibliographical Society, 1976-1991.

Spevack, Marvin. *The Harvard Concordance to Shakespeare*. Cambridge: Harvard University Press, 1973.

Tilley, Morris Palmer. *A Dictionary of the Proverbs in England in the Sixteenth and Seventeenth Centuries: A Collection of the Proverbs Found in English Literature and the Dictionaries of the Period*. Ann Arbor: University of Michigan Press, 1950.

Index